East Asia's Haunted Present

EAST ASIA'S HAUNTED PRESENT

Historical Memories and the Resurgence of Nationalism

Edited by

Tsuyoshi Hasegawa and Kazuhiko Togo

PSI Reports

PRAEGER SECURITY INTERNATIONAL
Westport, Connecticut · London

Library of Congress Cataloging-in-Publication Data

East Asia's haunted present : historical memories and the resurgence of nationalism /
   edited by Tsuyoshi Hasegawa and Kazuhiko Togo.
      p. cm.
   Includes bibliographical references and index.
   ISBN: 978–0–313–35612–4 (alk. paper)
1. East Asia—Foreign relations—Japan. 2. Japan—Foreign relations—East Asia. 3. Nationalism—East
Asia. 4. World War, 1939–1945—East Asia—Historiography. 5. Japan—Foreign relations—1945– I.
Hasegawa, Tsuyoshi, 1941– II. Togo, Kazuhiko, 1945–
DS518.45.E37 2008
327.5205—dc22   2008008984

British Library Cataloguing in Publication Data is available.

Library of Congress Catalog Card Number: 2008008984
ISBN: 978–0–313–35612–4

First published in 2008

Praeger Security International, 88 Post Road West, Westport, CT 06881
An imprint of Greenwood Publishing Group, Inc.
www.praeger.com

Printed in the United States of America

The paper used in this book complies with the
Permanent Paper Standard issued by the National
Information Standards Organization (Z39.48–1984).

10 9 8 7 6 5 4 3 2 1

We dedicate this book to those who were killed, wounded, and suffered in the wars and colonial occupations in Asia

Contents

Acknowledgments

We are profoundly grateful to all participants of the Conference, "Historical Memories and Resurgence of Nationalism: Paths to Reconciliation," held in May 2007, at Santa Barbara. In addition to the authors included in this volume, we extend our appreciation to the following participants: Michael Berry, Charles Burress, Parris Chang, Leif Easley, Peter Digeser, Sabine Frühstück, Haruhiko Fukui, Cynthia Kaplan, Ji Xiaobin, Luke Roberts, Gi-Wook Shin, Ryoichi Hamamoto, Andrew Horvat, Masahiro Kohara, Ellis Krauss, Fumio Matsuo, Paul Midford, Mike Mochizuki, Dan Sneider, Ming Wan, John Woolley, and Jai Hoon Yang.

We would like to thank the U.S.-Japan Foundation and its president George Packard for generously providing the funding for the conference and publication of the conference papers. Its program officer, David Janes, has given us constant support and encouragement. Melvin Oliver, Dean of Social Sciences at the University of California at Santa Barbara provided us with additional financial assistance for the conference, and David Marshall, Dean of Humanities and Fine Arts at the University of California at Santa Barbara, made it possible for Ambassador Togo to spend two quarters as a visiting professors at the University of California at Santa Barbara. This project has been a genuine collaboration between the UC Santa Barbara's Center for Cold War Studies and the Department of Political Science. We are thankful for John Woolley, Chair of the Department of Political Science, for his wise counsel and enthusiastic support for the project. Susan Shirk and Elisa Lurkis of the University of California Institute on Global Conflict and Cooperation (IGCC) extended their help for the conceptualization of the project and for crafting a grant proposal. IGCC also provided funding for the presentation of our findings in Washington D.C.

Brandon Seto, who served as the conference coordinator, performed thankless tasks for all logistics and finances for the conference. Tom Bennett and Justin Dodds of the Interdisciplinary Humanities Center at UC Santa Barbara helped us navigate through the complicated maze of financial affairs. George Fujii helped us to copyedit many chapters of the original manuscript.

We are also grateful to Robert Hutchinson of Praeger, whose enthusiasm for the book inspired us to complete the manuscript. We also thank Haylee Schwenk of Bea-conPMG for her thorough copyediting of the manuscript.

As we were editing this book, we learned that Professor Shinkichi Eto, who was our mentor at the University of Tokyo at Komaba, had passed away. He would have appreciated the value of this book.

Finally, we thank our wives, Tomoko Togo and Deborah Steinhoff, for their support and understanding.

Kazuhiko Togo and Tsuyoshi Hasegawa

Introduction

Kazuhiko Togo and Tsuyoshi Hasegawa

A specter is haunting East Asia, a specter of the memories of the past, resurrected by the resurgence of nationalism that is gaining momentum in Japan, China, and South Korea, and snatching away hope for forging a new international framework based on regional cooperation.

Since the 1970s, East Asia has achieved unique economic prosperity, establishing itself as a center of one of the most vibrant economic regions of the world economy. Although the once-confident model of economic growth led by Japan as the head of a flock of flying geese, followed by the rest of Asian nations, was shattered by the recession of the late 1990s, East Asia nonetheless continues to be a vital economic region in the global economy, particularly with the emergence of China as an important economic player.

In the political and security areas, the end of the Cold War blessed East Asia with an unprecedented opportunity that it had not experienced since the end of the nineteenth century. Fundamental conflicts that divided the great powers—Russo-Japanese rivalry from the end of the nineteenth century until the Russo-Japanese War, the ascendancy of a militarized, aggressive Japan, and various Cold War rivalries, first between communist powers (the Soviet Union and the People's Republic of China [PRC]) and the "Free World," and later multiple rivalries between the Soviet Union and the U.S. -led anti-Soviet alliances, between the Soviet Union and the PRC, and the strategic triangle that grew out of these multiple conflicts—all disappeared. Starting with the Opium War in the mid-nineteenth century, East Asia saw catastrophic wars, civil wars, and foreign interventions, experiencing the Sino-Japanese War (1894–95), the Russo-Japanese War (1904–5), Allied Intervention into Siberia and the Far East (1918–22), the Japanese invasion of Manchuria (1931), the Second Sino-Japanese War (1937–45), the Pacific War (1941–45), and the Korean War (1950–53). The Vietnam War, although not fought in East Asia, had serious consequences in East Asia as well.

These wars, civil wars, and interventions left deep scars in the peoples in East Asia. Although the issue of historical memory sporadically flared up during the Cold War, the conflicts were largely contained without causing major disruptions in Japan's relations with either China or South Korea. With the end of the Cold War the situation has drastically changed. Three factors are important to understanding the background for the sudden emergence of historical memories as the major contentious issues that divide the three major countries in East Asia.

First, the end of the Cold War meant the disappearance of strategic interests that united these countries against a common foe. With the collapse of communism in the Soviet Union and Eastern Europe, the communist ideology was no longer sufficient to hold China together. Nationalism has replaced communist ideology for ascertaining the legitimacy of the Chinese Communist Party's rule. Likewise, anti-communism once anchored South Korean identity, but as communism collapsed elsewhere, and as South Korea gained confidence with its economic prosperity and the establishment of democracy, anticommunism gradually gave way to nationalism. In Japan, the ideological divide that once separated the ruling Liberal Democratic Party and the permanent opposition party, the Socialist Party, disappeared in 1993 with the collapse of the 1955 political system that defined most of the postwar period in Japan. Together with the end of this once-bedrock political stability, the collapse of the bubble economy and the continuous economic recession severely shook Japan's confidence. Amid this confusion and erosion of traditional values, a strong right-wing revisionist movement has emerged, calling for a new interpretation of history restoring the positive aspects of modern Japanese history, with some justifying Japan's past aggressions and colonialism. Each country is struggling to seek a new national identity in the post–Cold War reality, and nationalism seems to provide an answer in the quest for the self-identity of each nation.

The second factor is the new reality of economic development in East Asia. Unlike the previous decades from the 1960s to the end of the 1980s, during which Japan overshadowed the other economies in the region, South Korea and China have emerged as independent economic powers since the 1990s. In recent years, China in particular has begun to challenge Japanese supremacy. Whereas in previous decades cooperation with Japan was a *sine qua non* precondition for economic development for China and South Korea, both latecomers can now stand on their own. The resurgence of nationalism was thus a reflection of the economic reality of East Asia. Nationalism in China and South Korea is an expression of their growing confidence in their own economic power. In contrast, nationalism in Japan can be interpreted as a psychological reaction to compensate for the loss of its economic supremacy and resentment for the latecomers that have attained their current economic status thanks to Japan's generous help, but that are now challenging this supremacy.

Third, the resurgence of nationalism in East Asia can also be a reflection of social changes within each country. Economic growth in China and South Korea has engendered the growing voice of the middle class, and nationalism is in a way an expression of the empowerment of this class. In addition, the revolution in information technology has altered the nature of political movement in both countries, where the government in power can no longer control the popular movements. Nationalism in Japan in turn reflects Japan's search for new values after the erosion of the old social structures based on lifelong employment and the secure welfare system. In Japan as well, the government has to navigate the treacherous path between international and domestic pressures.

Nationalism in East Asia is on a collision course. The conflicts that emerged over the issues of Yasukuni Shrine visits, textbooks, comfort women, and the territorial disputes over the contested islands have become serious causes for fueling nationalism in China and South Korea. In other words, the specter of the memories of the past is haunting the present, aborting as stillborn any hope of reconciliation of these East Asian neighbors and blocking them from seizing the historic moment to develop a regional community bound by their common security and economic interests.

This situation has caused great concern among scholars and policy-makers. Can the conflicting views of historical memories be reconciled in such a way to satisfy the needs for national aspirations that are emerging in response to the new economic and social reality of each country? If divergences of views are inevitable and impossible to reconcile, how can we forge a new international system that will foster cooperation while leaving aside these divergences?

Tsuyoshi Hasegawa and Kazuhiko Togo, both deeply concerned with the dangers that these contentious historical memory issues pose to the future of cooperation between Japan and its important neighbors in East Asia, decided to hold a conference. After nearly one year of preparation, the Center for Cold War Studies at the University of California at Santa Barbara (UCSB), in cooperation with the UCSB Department of Political Science, held a conference, "Historical Memories and Resurgence of Nationalism in East Asia: Paths to Reconciliation" from May 23 to 25, 2007. A special workshop was held one week later on the special case dealing with Taiwan. After the conference, participants to this conference agreed that the revised papers should be published. This book represents the collegial efforts of participants of this conference.

The conference organizers were careful in selecting the conference participants. We were interested in specialists who share our general goals that reconciliation by overcoming divergent historical interpretations is necessary to forge a new cooperative international system. We did not expect that all participants would agree on all issues, but we attempted to select scholars and specialists who believe that any attempts to resolve these contentious issues or to reduce tensions arising from these contentions must seek measures with sensitivity to the roots of nationalism in each country. This meant, specifically, we intentionally excluded two extremes. We excluded the left-wing scholars and advocacy groups who believe that everything that happened in modern Japanese history is a series of unmitigated transgressions against Japan's neighbors and that historical reconciliation can be achieved only by the wholesale rejection of Japan's modern history. We also intentionally excluded the right-wing nationalists in Japan who seek to revise the interpretation of modern Japanese history in such a way as to justify Japanese colonialism and aggressions. We consider their views to be one of the sources of conflict over historical memories with China and South Korea, and a key impediment to resolving these differences.

Thus, we make it clear from the beginning that all-inclusiveness is not the path we have chosen. We firmly believe that ultimate reconciliation will not be achieved by the complete rejection of Japan's past as an unmitigated disaster or by defending Japanese colonialism, aggressions, and the Pacific War as completely justifiable actions. We can resolve the contentious issues of historical memories or at least reduce the tensions arising from these conflicts by somber realism, a willingness to understand others, and a firm conviction that the need to establish a regional community based on cooperation takes precedent over differences in historical memories. As the readers can see, the contributors have disagreements on a number of issues, but on these general principles, we firmly agree.

LEARNING FROM PAST PROJECTS

The conference held in May 2007 began with three presentations, which introduced previous projects aiming toward ultimate reconciliation. The first concerned a project on "Memory, Reconciliation, and Security in the Asia-Pacific Regions: Implications for U.S.-Japan Relations" that was organized by the Social Science Research Council and funded by the Japan Foundation Center for Global Partnership. The project co-conveners were Charles Burress of the *San Francisco Chronicle* and Mike Mochizuki of George Washington University, and a preliminary workshop was held January 31–February 1, 2003 at George Washington University to sharpen the research agenda and review paper proposals. After this initial meeting, Yoshihisa Komori, one of the invited participants, labeled the workshop as an "anti-Japan seminar" in a front-page article and in subsequent articles in the *Sankei Shinbun*. The articles, which, according to Mochizuki and Burress, contained several misrepresentation and factual errors, also accused the Japanese Foreign Ministry of not exercising sufficient oversight over the publicly funded Japan Foundation. Komori's articles provoked a serious political controversy that threatened the existence of the Japan Foundation itself and triggered Diet interpellations about the project. Eventually, Burress and Mochizuki were able to publish in the *Sankei Shinbun* a rebuttal that refuted Komori's charges. But the controversy delayed by three years the second workshop of this project and preparations for an edited volume. This experience provided a powerful cautionary tale about the extent to which historical memory is a politically sensitive issue in Japanese domestic politics.

Gi-Wook Shin and Daniel Sneider made the second presentation on "the Divided Memories and Reconciliation Project" currently under way at the Shorenstein Asia-Pacific Research Center at Stanford University. The first part of this project is a comparative examination of high-school history textbooks in Japan, China,

South Korea, Taiwan, and the United States, focusing on the period from the beginning of the Sino-Japanese war in 1931 until the San Francisco Peace Treaty of 1951. This will be followed by a second comparative study of popular cinema dealing with historical subjects from roughly the same period. Designed in parallel with these two comparative studies is a comprehensive survey of elite opinion-makers.

Researchers have translated in full all writing and graphic materials in the textbooks. How do the textbook versions of history compare to contemporary scholarship on the same period and events? How do the textbooks compare to one other, both in accuracy and in presentation? How do these distinct versions of history relate to current widely held views in those countries on historical events? These are key issues examined in this project. Participants of the May conference received a positive impression about the approach and mechanism employed to bring about in an objective light high-school textbooks based on those common criteria, although they have not had the time to consult the published results. Given the complexity of the historical memory issue, choosing Taiwan and the United States in addition to Japan, China, and South Korea received positive comments. The explanation of this project was a nice introduction to the two presentations on textbooks by Hiroshi Mitani and Mikyoung Kim. The Stanford textbook project is well underway, and the first part of this project has been published.[1]

Ryoichi Hamamoto, a visiting lecturer from the *Yomiuri Shinbun* and the Graduate School of Journalism at the University of California at Berkeley, made the third presentation on a past project aiming at reconciliation. Hamamoto explained in detail how Tsuneo Watanabe, editor-in-chief of the *Yomiuri Shinbun,* took the initiative of embarking on a two-year research regarding "responsibility for war (*senso sekinin*)." Watanabe was strongly motivated by the fact that Japanese themselves never drew their own conclusions and identified those who were responsible for the events that took place between 1931 and 1945. The Yomiuri project examined the structure of the Imperial Armed Forces and the relationship among the Imperial Armed Forces, the government, and the Emperor. It analyzed how the Japanese leadership perceived the world affairs at that time. The International Military Tribunal for the Far East (IMTFE) was critically examined. The book singled out 15 individuals, whom the *Yomiuri Shinbun* concluded were responsible for the war.

The outcome of the research was published in 2006, first in Japanese in two volumes in July and October, and then in English in December. Together with the *Yomiuri Shinbun,* James Auer coedited the English version, entitled, *Who Was Responsible? From Marco Polo Bridge to Pearl Harbor.* Individual circumstances and the extent of respective responsibility are debatable. But the overall efforts to come up with concrete names for war responsibility by the Japanese themselves 60 years after World War II are commendable.[2]

PART I: OVERVIEW OF JAPAN'S HISTORICAL MEMORY

Three chapters in this section by Thomas Berger, Gilbert Rozman, and Kazuhiko Togo give a broad perspective on the Japanese historical memory issue.[3] In Chapter 1,

Thomas Berger, political scientist at Boston University, develops his analysis through a theoretical and comparative framework. The first half of his chapter is a presentation of three broad categories to explain how the past shapes the politics of the present: the experiential model ("history makes historical consciousness"), the instrumental model ("politics determines historical consciousness"), and the cultural model ("discourse shapes historical consciousness"). Berger takes an eclectic approach, positing that, in the real world, experiential, instrumental, and cultural forces are all present, shaping the official narrative and the politics of history, although he asserts that, based on the evidence he has collected, he favors a modified cultural position.

With this theoretical framework he analyzes how history was dealt with in Europe, notably in Germany, Austria, and France, and argues that although some major steps were taken toward reconciliation, the reality is far more complex than usually asserted. He then compares the European case with the Asian situation and maintains that far more than what is usually believed has been done in Asia. He emphasizes pragmatism on the part of Asian leaders, accompanied by a readiness to reciprocate, and backed up by a deeply rooted process of societal discourse. He argues: "Dealing with tensions over history is an ongoing enterprise, but one that with wisdom and determination is manageable—in Europe as in Asia."

In Chapter 2, Gilbert Rozman of Princeton University, a specialist in East Asian affairs, describes Japan's inability to face the memory of victimized nations in Asia, notably China and Korea. He first goes back to Japan's normalization with South Korea and China during the Cold War era, and shows how the leadership of South Korea and China had economic and strategic imperatives to improve relations with Japan by suppressing resentment toward Japan deeply felt in their societies as a whole.

From the late 1980s and after the end of the Cold War, Rozman asserts that there were numerous missed opportunities for the Japanese leadership to confront the historical memory issues head-on and overcome these issues once and for all. From the latter part of the 1990s there was a rise of Japanese nationalism, which served to alienate Japan from its Asian neighbors. The Six-Party Talks dealing with the North Korean nuclear issue, one of the last such opportunities, for instance, brought about an unprecedented opportunity for developing Northeast Asian regionalism, but the Japanese government, by fixating on the abduction issue, failed to use this mechanism to improve Japan's relations with its neighbors. Rozman's conclusion is starkly pessimistic: "There is no basis of optimism that narrow, emotional thinking about Japan's past actions in Asia and indifference toward reassuring the nations that had been victimized advancing in the right direction of reconciliation." Things will get worse before they get better, he concludes.

In Chapter 3, Kazuhiko Togo first goes back to 1945 and describes the spiritual vacuum that emerged because of the unprecedented total defeat and the internal contradictions that emerged since then between those who totally denounced modern Japanese history as a negative legacy and those who maintained, to varying degrees, that some aspects of Japan's modern history contained facts of which the

Japanese should rightfully feel proud. He argues that although the divergence between the two extreme schools was wide, there were continuing efforts to find a synthesis between them.

Togo then examines five specific historical memory issues: comfort women, the Nanjing Massacre, forced labor, POWs, and Unit 731. All these issues still provoke anger from the victims in other countries. Although Togo strongly believes that there is a general feeling of remorse and apology for prewar atrocities, the Japanese people have been unable to reconcile this feeling with their other need to feel pride in Japan's accomplishments since the Meiji Restoration. This disconnect makes it impossible for the Japanese to produce a synthesis. Togo argues, however, that in almost all issues there are hopeful signs toward a synthesis, although the degree of such hopeful signs varies in each case.

With regard to the five issues that address more general aspects of war and its memory—textbooks, apology, responsibility for the war, the Yasukuni Shrine, and the International Military Tribunal for the Far East (IMTFE)—the textbook and apology issues seem to have made certain progress toward synthesis. What Togo proposed on war responsibility and the Yasukuni issue has not gained political support inside Japan. Opinions are starkly divided on the IMTFE issue. Togo concludes that there is a need to make further serious efforts on these issues to seek a synthesis on conflicting views. Thus, Togo, like Berger, is guardedly optimistic, but more from a normative position than an analytical position.

PART II: SPECIFIC ISSUES: TEXTBOOKS, YASUKUNI, AND COMFORT WOMEN

Part II of this book is devoted to the discussion of specific contentious issues. Analyzing history textbooks is a useful measure of how history is remembered, and why history is remembered in a certain manner in that country. An attempt to reach an understanding of how history is remembered in other countries may lead eventually to a better understanding of how reconciliation could be achieved. We have already mentioned above that the Walter H. Shorenstein Asia-Pacific Research Center at Stanford University has embarked on a worthwhile project in that direction. In Chapter 4, Hiroshi Mitani, historian at the University of Tokyo, first gives an overview of the textbook controversy in Japan, outlines international collaborative efforts to write joint regional textbooks, and introduces four specific books published in Japanese in collaboration with East Asian scholars. His examples show that gradually but steadily East Asian scholars are beginning to share historical facts. In the end, we may not be able to reach a consensus about how to interpret these events, since, as we borrow Berger's approach, each country has different experiences, political needs, and cultural traditions. Nevertheless, the process of gaining a better understanding of the reasons behind these differences is a valuable step. In particular, the joint publication in Japanese and Chinese of *Contentious Issues in Sino-Japanese Relations* is a fascinating example little known to English-speaking readers. Mitani also calls for the eventual formation of a regional history that transcends national history.

In Chapter 5, Mikyoung Kim, a South Korean sociologist who now teaches in Japan, begins her chapter by distinguishing ontological historical facts from perceptual historical memory, which fuels the "memory war" in the region. While discerning historical facts from myths as contested in the realm of history textbooks in China, Japan and Korea, she links the different manifestations of collective memory to the rapidly shifting sociopolitical milieu of the regional landscape. She analyzes each case from an equidistant standpoint. For Japan, the ideological pendulum swing between the left and the right has been reflected on the changes of Japanese texts, and that is an extension of the unsettled war memories and their meanings for the country. She continues with China, showing that Chinese memories remain mixed and ambivalent about Japan, and the texts contain some narratives about the Japanese actions against China that can be misconstrued. The case of Korea sheds a light on stringent moral measurement applied to the wounds inflicted by its powerful neighbors, exemplified by the Japanese colonialism. At work is the framework of its own self-projection as a virtuous victim and resister. Her chapter itself could be considered as a significant effort toward reconciliation.

Chapter 6 by Akihiko Tanaka, a political scientist at the University of Tokyo, examines the Yasukuni Shrine issue. This was the single biggest issue during Prime Minister Junichiro Koizumi's tenure from 2001 to 2006 that alienated Japan from China and South Korea. Tanaka gives key background details about the Yasukuni Shrine and examines why this issue became so intertwined in Japan and its neighbors both by delineating four categories of conflicting constitutive symbols hidden in the Yasukuni issue and by discussing how these symbols have been used by different actors at different times. Tanaka concludes that while Koizumi did not lose by visiting Yasukuni, he did not win, either. Likewise, by simplistically equating Yasukuni visits with the revival of Japanese militarism, the Chinese also inadvertently contributed to the alienation of Japanese public opinion from sympathy with the Chinese view. The ultimate question of how to mourn those who were killed in the war to the satisfaction of all concerned remains unresolved.

Kazuhiko Togo examines in Chapter 7 the comfort women issue. During Prime Minster Shinzo Abe's tenure, this became the most widely discussed issue. This issue is no longer confined to the debate between Japan and its immediate neighbors, but also, with the passing of the July 30, 2007 House Resolution, the United States has become an important player in the debate.

More than any other subjects, the debate on comfort women is politically sensitive in the United States because this issue is now seen in the light of human rights and gender equality. Therefore, a moral and political evaluation of this issue is essential for any writer who writes on the subject. Togo presents three schools of thought in Japan: first, those who consider the system primarily as one through which institutional rape was committed and perpetuated; second, those who consider it as a system of military brothels; and, third, those who do not go into definitions but acknowledge the pains inflicted on comfort women, apologize, and show readiness for compensation. Togo makes it clear that he supports the third approach, which is the cornerstone of the 1993 Kono Statement of apology.

We might add that, in addition to the chapters included in this volume, Sabine Frühstück presented a paper analyzing how museums on Japanese Self-Defense Forces bases commemorate the war and the war dead. For service members of the SDF, it is neither Yasukuni nor Yushukan, its history museum, but the base museums of the unit to which they belong that creates ersatz histories. Her analysis of the strategies employed by individual units to break with the past (the discontinuity required for public consumption) while simultaneously building a military tradition (the continuity required for unit cohesion) was a valuable attempt to discover an area about which very little is currently known. Her findings are incorporated into the book she published in 2007.[4]

PART III: REGIONAL PERSPECTIVES

Three chapters examine the historical memory issue from the perspective of China and South Korea. In Chapter 8, Jin Linbo, Director and Research Professor, Department of Asia-Pacific Studies, China Institute of International Studies in Beijing, examines Japan's treatment of historical issues from the Chinese perspective, especially with respect to three contentious issues: textbook, Yasukuni visits, and Taiwan. As the underlying motive of these events, he sees Japan's desire to become a normal country, an idea he accepts. But he makes a clear distinction between Japan's realist position and nationalist revisionism. Jin strongly cautions that the revival of Japanese nationalism has negatively affected Japan's relations with its Asian neighbors, and he argues that the blurring distinction between realists and nationalists stems from the failure of the Japanese to confront their past squarely. He perceptively acknowledges many negative elements of nationalism witnessed in China, but precisely because of this, he is pessimistic that "the interactions between the two nationalisms would make the way to reconciliation in East Asia even harder and longer."

While Jin examines the historical memory debate in Japan from the Chinese perspective, Zhu Jianrong, as a Chinese scholar now teaching in Japan, turns his attention in Chapter 9 to the role Japan has played in Chinese nationalism and how the historical memory issue has become an intractable problem in Sino-Japanese relations. According to Zhu, there are three important reasons for the recent rise in Chinese nationalism: (1) the fall of communist ideology and the rise of "patriotism education"; (2) rapid economic growth, and the resultant emergence of a new middle class, which clamors for a Chinese place in the sun among other major nations; and (3) the Chinese government's one-sided treatment of Japan, which overemphasizes Japan's invasion while neglecting postwar Japan's pacifism. He, however, gives a stern warning about Japan's lack of efforts to "soften the severe anti-Japanese feelings that exist in the Chinese public's psychology." He argues that conciliatory signals sent by Hu Jintao in hopes of achieving a mutually beneficial compromise, reconfirmed by Wen Jiabao's speech at the Diet of Japan in April 2007, should not be missed by Japanese authority and opinion leaders.

In Chapter 10, Cheol Hee Park, a leading specialist on Japanese politics in South Korea, gives the South Korean perspective. Park analyzes how nationalism in

South Korea was formed as a reaction to two external threats: Japan's colonial rule and communist expansion. During the Cold War, deep-seated South Korean anger toward Japan was suppressed for the country's strategic and economic needs. The end of the Cold War brought about a new situation. As South Korea established relations with the Soviet Union/Russia and China, new possibilities opened up. South Korea turned itself into a democratic society, and accomplished economic growth. In these new circumstances, South Koreans began to explore the possibility of unification with North Korea. Park argues that South Korea's strengthened external and internal position changed it from a proactive Japan basher to a reactive responder to Japanese provocations. He argues that Japan took several provocative actions against Korea and China and states that rising nationalism causing Japan to retreat from its Asia-friendly policy runs the risk of uniting South Korea and China, resulting in a clear strategic failure for Japanese foreign policy.

Another important issue that the conference organizers felt important to include was the issue of Taiwan. As explained above, given the sensitive nature of cross-strait relations, we held a separate session on historical memory in Taiwan. Parris Chang, Professor Emeritus of Political Science at Pennsylvania State University and President of the Taiwan Institute for Political Economic and Strategic Studies in Taipei, was invited to present a paper, which was commented on by Ming Wan of the Department of Public and International Affairs at George Mason University. Taiwan's historical memory in relation to Japan and to mainland China is a complicated one. Although Taiwan became a Japanese colony, the Taiwanese perceived Japanese colonialism in somewhat different terms than did the Koreans toward Japanese colonial rule in Korea. Although the Japanese regime did its best to suppress, subvert, and disrupt extremist Taiwanese political movements, the Japanese colonial power helped to modernize Taiwan in the areas of economic development, health care, and education, all of which served as the foundations for subsequent Taiwanese economic development. Nationalist rule in Taiwan further complicated the historical memory issue, making it essentially distinct from mainland Chinese historical memory. The conference organizers strongly feel that this complicated issue, though difficult to disentangle from the current political importance of the Taiwan issue, should be included in the discussion of historical memory. Unfortunately, Chang's paper was withdrawn from this volume because Chang was appointed as the representative of the Republic of China (Taiwan) to Bahrain in the fall 2007, and it became increasingly difficult for Chang to express his opinions without associating himself with the Taiwan government.

PART IV: TWO BYSTANDERS

The unique feature of this collective volume is the inclusion of two chapters dealing with two important bystanders often ignored in discussions on the historical memory debate in East Asia: the United States and Russia. In Chapter 11, David Straub, a former State Department official now associated with the Walter H. Shorenstein Asia-Pacific Research Center at Stanford University, argues that in the postwar era the U.S. government "did not ignore historical issues involving Japan but treated them as distinctly secondary in importance to perceived strategic interests." He confirms the widely shared view that the United States has consciously avoided expressing sympathy with any one side in any history-related dispute where Asian countries' views differed from one another. Such an intervention would most likely result in unfavorable consequences for the United States with one of the disputing partners accusing the United States of being unfair and one-sided. But Straub frankly admits that "American officials, like most knowledgeable American citizens, tend not to sympathize with Japanese conservatives' positions on several of the disputes" and therefore sends a clear cautionary message to self-righteous and seemingly unrepentant nationalists that their views would not likely be acceptable to the United States.

Straub also touches on a potentially divisive issue that separate Japanese public opinion from its American counterpart: the atomic bombings on Hiroshima and Nagasaki. He introduces the hitherto little-known episode of Ambassador Walter Mondale's abortive visit to Hiroshima, which was cancelled due to the repercussions such a visit would have had back in the United States. The recent episode in July 2007 in which the Defense Minister, Fumio Kyuma, was forced to resign because of a storm of protests against his statement that justified the U.S. atomic bombings on Hiroshima and Nagasaki, illustrates the deep perception gap that separates the Japanese from the Americans on this issue.

The plea for achieving historic reconciliation made by the mutual visits of the prime minister of Japan to the USS Arizona Museum at Pearl Harbor and the American president's visit to Hiroshima is the main theme of the paper presented at the May conference by Fumio Matsuo, former correspondent of *Kyodo Tsushin*. Matsuo further expounded on how the leaders of five North East Asian countries should "hold mutual wreath-laying ceremonies to remove the respective thorns of the past, to reconfirm reconciliation, and to cooperate toward the creation of a new age." Although Matsuo's paper received some support, many at the conference felt such a proposal was an unrealistic dream at present. Time and further efforts for mutual understanding are necessary before such a ritual could become an effective form of reconciliation for countries in the region.

In Chapter 12, Tsuyoshi Hasegawa broadens the discussion on historical memory by including Russo-Japanese relations. Together with Hiroshima and Nagasaki, Japan's historical memory as victim is fixated on the Soviet attack on Japan on August 9, 1945. Many Japanese remember the Soviet invasion of Manchuria, Korea, Sakhalin, and the Kurils as actions committed in violation of the existing Japan-Soviet Neutrality Pact (betrayal), entailing killing and rapes of civilians and internment of soldiers (atrocities) and culminating in the unlawful territorial occupation of four islands in the Kurils north of Hokkaido (territorial expansion).

The first half of Hasegawa's chapter deals with the history of territorial disputes between Japan and Russia and their contemporary implications. While acknowledging legitimacy in the Japanese territorial claim, Hasegawa argues that Japan should look at the territorial dispute in a wider historical scope. The Soviet Union entered the Pacific War as an ally of the United States, China, and other allied powers and therefore the Soviet-Japanese War should be understood in the longer historical context of Russo/Soviet-Japanese relations. Although the Japanese have legitimate grievances against the Soviet Union over the treatment of Japanese prisoners of war and territorial expansion, Hasegawa argues that this sense of justifiable victimhood must be attuned to understand the pains the Japanese had inflicted on the Chinese and the Koreans by Japan's colonialism and aggressions.

The second part of Hasegawa's chapter goes back to the historical rivalry between Japan and Russia in Manchuria and Korea, as well as the Sino-Soviet conflict during the Cold War to broaden the scope of analysis of Japanese imperialism in a wider scale of imperialist activities from the middle of the nineteenth century. Russia was one of the most rapacious imperialist powers in Northeast Asia, and, therefore, both the Chinese and the South Koreans have reasons for not wishing to bring Russia into the current debate on historical memory. But Hasegawa argues that Japanese aggression and colonialism in China and Korea were unique in themselves, and, hence, the Chinese and the Koreans have legitimate reasons to single out Japan as the most aggressive power that inflicted more pain on them than any other imperialist power.

What follows in this volume are our collective efforts to understand the roots of divergent historical memories in East Asia. We have a number of disagreements on specific issues, but we are in complete agreement on one point: whatever differences we might have and will have in the future over history, we must move ahead to create a regional community bound by common interests.

NAMES AND TERMS

For Japanese words, we have adhered to the Hepburn transliteration system, with slight modifications. For instance, we write *shinbun* instead of *shimbun*. Macrons are not used for Japanese words either in the text or in endnotes. Thus, "Showa Emperor" instead of "Shōwa Emperor." Japanese names in the text and endnotes, as well as the authors of chapters are given with given (first) names first followed by family names. Therefore, Yasuhiro Nakasone, instead of Nakasone Yasuhiro, and Junichiro Koizumi rather than Koizumi Junichiro. Citations from Japanese books and articles, however, retain the original order, family names first followed by given names. Thus, "Fukuzawa Yukichi (not Yukichi Fukuzawa), *Gakumon no susume*." But English books and articles, written by Japanese authors, will follow the usual English-language pattern, first names first followed by family names. Thus, "Kiichi Fujiwara (not Fujiwara Kiichi), 'Remembering the War—Japanese Style,' *Far Eastern Economic Review*."

As for Korean and Chinese names, we follow the system of giving family names first, followed by given names. Thus, we use "Jin Linbo" and "Park Chun-hee" The only exceptions are "Mikyoung Kim" and "Cheol Hee Park" (two authors), Singman Rhee, and Korean authors in English books and articles. In these cases, given names come first, followed by family names.

NOTES

1. Gi-wook Shin and Daniel C. Sneider, eds., *Cross Currents: Regionalism and Nationalism in Northeast Asia* (Stanford, CA: The Walter H. Shorenstein Asia-Pacific Research Center, Stanford University, 2007).

2. Yomiuri Shinbun Senso Sekinin Kensho Iinkai, *Kensho: Senso sekinin,* 2 vols. (Tokyo: Chuokoron shinsha, 2006); James Auer, ed., *Who Was Responsible? From Marco Polo Bridge to Pearl Harbor* (Tokyo: Yomiuri Shinbun, 2006).

3. Rozman's and Togo's papers were originally presented as keynote speeches in a televised open public forum on May 23, 2007. The televised video is available: UCTV 4420, "Historical Memories & Resurgence of Nationalism in East Asia: Paths to Reconciliation."

4. Sabine Frühstück, *Uneasy Warriors: Gender, Memory and Popular Culture in the Japanese Army* (Berkeley and Los Angeles: University of California Press, 2007).

Part I

An Overview

1

Dealing with Difficult Pasts: Japan's "History Problem" from a Theoretical and Comparative Perspective

Thomas U. Berger

When it comes to dealing with the past, Japan is widely viewed as being incorrigible. Over the past 25 years, Japan has been castigated time and again for its failure to acknowledge its history of aggression and oppression prior to 1945. Yet, time and again Japanese leaders have asserted that they have the right, as a sovereign nation, to define their history as they believe it to be. How Japanese textbooks deal with historical atrocities, or how the Japanese prime minister chooses to commemorate the nation's war dead, are issues that other countries have no right to meddle with. While such an unapologetic stance can be viewed as the exercise of Japan's sovereign right as a nation, it comes at a price, and it is commonly argued that Japan's obstinate unwillingness to admit its past wrongdoings is at the root of many of Asia's ills, including simmering disputes over territorial issues, an exaggerated sensitivity to every gyration in Japanese defense policy, and the relative inability of East Asia to construct a strong framework of regional institutions.[1]

Japan is often compared unfavorably in this regard to Germany. Whereas Japan has been unwilling to confront the past, Germany has been steadfast in confronting its dark history, offering apologies and paying compensation to the victims of Nazi atrocities. Whereas Japanese leaders have either tried to legitimate Japan's history of aggression or else offered apologies that are so vague and watered down that they almost come off as excuses, their German counterparts have gone out of their way to condemn the crimes of the Nazi regime and have made denying the Holocaust a crime. And while conservative Japanese leaders continue visit the controversial Yasu-kuni Shrine in Tokyo, Germany is filled with monuments that commemorate the victims of German aggression, not the perpetrators. As a result, it is argued, the peace and stability that eludes Asia today has become a solid reality in Europe (at least the Western portions of it).[2] In short, Germany has been a model penitent, a country that can serve as an example to the rest of the world of how a principled acknowl-edgement of responsibility for past atrocities can have beneficial results. Japan, in this view, is the opposite—a moral dunce, whose obstinate denial of guilt has damaged both its own interests and those of the region.

While these views may be stereotypical, there are good reasons why they have become so widespread. Japan's leaders have indeed been resistant to acknowledging Japanese wrongdoing prior to 1945, while Germany has been relatively open to doing so. And these differences in how the German and Japanese states deal with the past undoubtedly have had significant implications for the development of international relations in Europe and Asia.

At the same time, however, a closer examination of these two cases quickly reveals many glaring inconsistencies in this narrative of Germany as the model penitent and Japan as the moral dunce. Japan has been far more willing to apologize for its past misdeeds than is commonly acknowledged, while Germany was slower in coming to terms with its past than is usually recognized. The German decision to adopt a contrite stance was motivated by more than a strong sense of moral responsibility; throughout the process of Germany's wrestling with its past, cool calculations of national interest played a central role. Moreover, if one expands the range of comparison beyond Germany—to Austria, France, or the United States, one finds that, time and again, considerations of economic gain and strategic security have weighed heavily on the decision of states to adopt a penitent or impenitent approach to history. By the same token, Japan's resistance to taking responsibility for past wrongdoings was far from irrational. While a good case can be made that it has become increasingly dysfunctional over time, it can also be argued that there are many pitfalls and potential dangers if Japan were to try to emulate a "German" approach to history. Finally, it must be pointed out that the history issue is far from dead in the European case. Even in the case of Germany, it has reemerged to trouble the Federal Republic's relations with its Eastern neighbors, especially Poland. Changes in national interest and the vagaries of domestic and international politics have thrown the floodgates of history wide open once more in central Europe, and currently Germany faces some very "Japanese" style problems regarding history.

This chapter demonstrates not that the history issue is simply a by-product of other, more fundamental issues and that efforts at reconciliation are useless. Although factors such as economic interest or the balance of power powerfully influ-ence debates over history, once a particular historical narrative becomes established as the basis of the official narrative of the state, it takes on a dynamic of its own and becomes difficult to change. The official narrative (or more accurately, complex of historical narratives) is tied to various national policies, including defense and national security policies, and, thus, becomes tied to concrete definitions of interest. These narratives and policies then interact with the historical narratives and associated patterns of behavior that are established in other countries. They themselves become social facts, part of the basic reality with which policy-makers, as they seek to pursue their own and the national interest, have to contend. At times, these narratives are more or less harmonious; at other times, however, they can cause considerable interstate friction as well as domestic political controversy. It is precisely this complex interrelationship of thought and behavior among an array of actors, both domestic and international, that makes the history issue so vexing and potentially volatile. It is also why it is vital that Japan—as well as other countries—develop a better understanding of the dynamics involved in the history issue in order to develop better, more realistic policies.

This chapter begins by briefly laying out some common ways of understanding the history issue in a general theoretical sense, with an aim to help define more clearly the dynamics underlying the history issue, both in Asia and in general. The chapter then outlines the way the history issue evolved in Europe and Asia. Here, it will first briefly describe how historical legacies were resolved in Europe, with a special emphasis on France, Germany, and Austria, before contrasting developments there with the way the issues of historical justice were dealt with in Asia. The chapter then explores how and why the history issue reemerged in the Asian context, beginning in the 1980s, before touching briefly on the ways that it is reemerging in Europe today. Needless to say, these issues can be dealt with here only in a very broad and cursory fashion. Nonetheless, such a broad-stroke analysis may prove useful in understanding the complex dynamics that are at work in the Japanese case. In conclusion, some consideration is given to the policy implications of this analysis.

WHEN HISTORY BECOMES AN ISSUE—THEORETICAL APPROACHES

The question of when history becomes a political issue, and the necessarily related question of what determines the kind of historical narratives that states choose to adopt (what will be called here the "official narrative"), is one that has attracted little attention among political scientists and analysts of international and domestic politics.[3] In recent years, however, the question has emerged with increasing force and frequency, both in domestic politics (appearing often under the rubrics of "transitional justice"[4] and "identity politics") and in international relations (as can be seen in the controversies over not only Japan and Germany's pre-1945 past, but also the Arab-Israeli dispute, the tensions over the Turkish massacre of the Armenians, and the Soviet Union's historic role in central Europe). As a result, a number of different models for explaining how the past shapes the politics of the present are on offer. There are three broad categories of arguments: experiential models ("history makes historical consciousness"); instrumental models ("politics determines historical consciousness"); and cultural models ("discourse shapes historical consciousness"). It is a modified version of this last position that is advocated in this chapter.

Each of these can be viewed as "ideal types" in the Weberian sense, useful for heuristic purposes but not existing in reality. Real-world dynamics are determined by a complex mix of factors that defy capture by any single theoretical model. Nonetheless, in practice different versions of these three schools of thought shape how people, scholars and non-scholars alike, talk about the past as an issue, and each has significant practical implications for the kinds of policies or remedies that they suggest.

Experiential explanations of official narratives and the politicization of history are based on the straightforward proposition that historical experiences are the driving force behind the formation of historical narrative. The way in which the past has been experienced by the population of a given society determines the general parameters of the historical narrative that the society is likely to establish or is able to establish. The central dilemma, of course, is that experiences of the past are likely to vary considerably even within a given society. Fortunately, experiences can be communicated through various means—be they cultural ones, such as films or books, or political ones such as truth commissions and official inquiries—that allow differences in historical experience to be overcome and enable the creation of common historical narratives.[5]

The process of communication allows for a certain degree of manipulation and even suppression of the past for political or other purposes. Likewise, psychological variables, such as traumatic suppression of memory and generational shift, can distort or influence the way in which the past is remembered, both by individuals and by society as a whole. Yet, experiential models tend to insist that there is an underlying core of root experiences.[6] These experiences can have a profound impact and can give rise to complex and powerful emotions such as anger, hatred, sympathy, guilt, pride, and even love. When the memory of the original event is suppressed or denied, the effect can be traumatic on an individual level, creating a wide range of negative effects, including feelings of helplessness, rage, and pain. On a societal level, the suppression of memory can have similarly negative results, preventing societal healing and preserving animosities and tensions between groups or nations.[7] Once the factors that block the expression of traumatic memory are weakened, they often erupt in unpredictable and disruptive fashion.[8]

From this perspective, states can adopt a number of different official narratives as suits their needs. The more pluralistic and open a society, however, the more constrained the ability of the state to manipulate the past. When versions of history clash on important points, conflict can emerge, both domestically and internationally. Experientialists argue that in such situations differences over the past can only be resolved by developing fuller, more sophisticated and nuanced versions of history that communicate to the different parties their respective versions of history and allow them to understand the perspective of the other side. In this sense, experientialists tend to be wedded to some version of the Positivist conception of history, summarized by Leopold von Ranke's famous proposition that the purpose of history is to uncover the past as it actually was.

An almost diametrically opposed view of the sources of the official narrative and the politics of history is offered by those who see historical memory as a tool for pursuing concrete interests. History, from this perspective, is not so much about the past as it is about the present and the future. Various groups—governments, political parties, organizations purporting to represent ethnic, social, or gender groups, publishing houses, veterans' organizations, and so forth—seek to shape the official narrative of the state in order to pursue a variety of different objectives, including monetary gain, political office, security, or affirmation of their identity as groups.[9]

Instrumentalists tend to reject the experientialists' preoccupation with the past as both naïve and irrelevant to the politics of history. The experience of individuals is fleeting and uncertain, and the expression of those experiences in forms accessible to others such as books, novels, and exhibitions, not to mention government-issued textbooks or statements by politicians, are almost infinitely malleable. There is no such thing as an "authentic" voice, even though the feelings and emotions that can be evoked through references to the past are very real. The public and even the elite resemble nothing so much as Leonard Shelby, the hapless protagonist of the film "Memento," who is trying to track down his wife's murderers while suffering from a condition that makes him unable to form memories of everything that has happened to him since his wife's death. As a result, he constantly falls preys to people who use his condition to pursue their own agendas.

Instrumentalists argue that conflicts over the past are the product of the clash of concrete interests. Countries or groups adopt antagonistic versions of history when they calculate it is in their interests; they adopt more conciliatory ones when they believe it to be politic for them to do so. Efforts to resolve conflicts by changing the perspectives of others on the past are bound to fail as long as the root causes of the conflict are not addressed.

A third perspective on the origins of official narratives and the politics of history emphasizes the way in which experience and perception are culturally embedded.[10] People, culturalists argue, view the world through culturally defined lenses. The way one group views an event depends crucially on the ways in which that event is defined by the group, which in turn depends on the way in which that group understands the world, both past and present. That understanding, which has normative (the way the world should be) as well as cognitive (the way the world is) dimensions, is rooted in the ways in which groups teach their members to think about the world.

Cultural theorists often disagree with one another about the dynamics of culture. Classical anthropological theory, à la Meade, Gorer, and Ruth Benedict, as well as some symbolic interactionists such as Clifford Geertz, tended to see culture as relatively static and holistic. Cultures change only very slowly and different cultural elements tend to reinforce one another. Post-modernists argue that, on the contrary, culture is fluid and self-contradictory, an ongoing discourse that has become increasingly cacophonous and empty of meaning over time.[11] All culturalists, however, argue that both experience and interest are culturally bound, that the way the present is experienced depends on how it is defined by the group, and that notions of interest are similarly determined by what the group believes its interests to be.[12]

Culturalists tend to argue that the official narrative of the state is ultimately dependent on culturally determined understandings of how the past should be portrayed. They emerge out of a broader societal discourse on the past that is largely immune to either evidence as produced by professional historians and others seeking to uncover the past, or to how political leaders and other elites may want the past to be understood. Different understandings of the past are likely to be conflictual if they are seen to threaten the interests of groups as they are culturally determined. It is perfectly possible that a history of past conflicts is largely insignificant politically, until broader cultural changes suddenly make them significant. For example, the rediscovery of a Serb identity in the former Yugoslavia in the late 1980s led to a rekindling of ancient animosities toward Bosnia, to the point where ordinary Serbs began to refer to the Muslim Bosnians and Kosovars as "Turks" and the defeat of Prince Lazar at the Field of Crows in 1389 became a rallying cry for the Serb nation. Likewise, the kind of emotional responses that are called forth by a particular understanding of events is likely to be culturally bound. Hence Ruth Benedict's famous argument that Germans felt guilt over their atrocities while the Japanese did not because the two societies had very different understandings of the kind of responsibility that individuals and groups hold for their past actions. In the case of Germany, with its Christian, strongly Protestant traditions, individuals and groups are responsible to a higher, transcendent authority for their actions. When those actions are reprehensible, they should feel guilt and pay penance. In the case of Japan, with its very different Buddhist-Shinto religious traditions, there is no equivalent concept of guilt, only feelings of shame that are rooted in how one is viewed by the broader community.[13]

The practical ramifications of the culturalist view of the politics of history naturally depend very much on the particular cultural context of each specific case. If a culture is closed and immalleable, there will be little opportunity to reshape the understandings of history that society holds and conflicts over the past are likely to prove intractable. If, on the other hand, there is a good deal of fragmentation and fluidity in collectively held views of history, it is possible to reshape historical understandings through a sustained effort to re-socialize the way the population thinks about the past.

As pointed out earlier, all three of these positions are ideal types and in the real world experiential, instrumentalist, and culturalist forces are all present, shaping the official narrative and the politics of history. The extent to which these different factors are decisive probably varies and requires a careful examination of the evidence. To undertake such an investigation, however, goes beyond what is possible in the context of this chapter. The position that I adopt here is in favor of a modified culturalist position. Experiential factors, while important, are of limited utility in understanding the debate over the past more than 60 years after the end of World War II. Instead, calculations of interest loom large in the history debate, but those calculations of interest are unfolding against the backdrop of existing historical understandings that have taken root in postwar Europe and Asia. As a result, efforts to change the historical narrative, especially in democratic and pluralistic societies such as Japan, constantly face resistance and are difficult to achieve. To understand better why efforts to change the past are proving so difficult in the Asian context, and why they remain more fragile than is commonly believed even in the European context, is the object of the rest of this chapter.

THE RESOLUTION OF THE HISTORY ISSUE IN POST-1945 EUROPE

The destruction wreaked by World War II was enormous—over 50 million people were killed between 1939 and 1945, over half of them civilians. Another 12 million or more people were killed by Nazi Germany as a result of deliberate state policy aimed at eliminating undesirable groups, including approximately six million Jews. Millions more died as the result of planned and unplanned expulsions of populations as borders were redrawn in postwar Europe and various groups whose loyalty was viewed as questionable were forced to leave their homes. Many of the continent's cities had been reduced to rubble, and in the 1945 to 1947 period most of Europe's population suffered enormous deprivations.[14]

In the aftermath of these events, a natural demand for justice and retribution rose up across the continent. Many actors could be, and were, held responsibility for the catastrophe of the war and the horrors that had occurred; yet the way in which European societies responded to those demands varied enormously. In the end, a kind of stability was achieved, even though in almost every instance the results that were achieved were rough and imperfect.

Germany

Contrary to the conventional view, after 1945 Germans as a whole were not smitten with a sense of overriding guilt when confronted with the evidence of what they had done. The war crimes tribunals, while initially welcomed by many Germans, became increasingly unpopular as their limitations became clear. The purges and efforts at reeducating the German population by the Allied powers were even less successful, and by the late 1940s a powerful political backlash emerged that led to a far-reaching, if less than complete reversal of the purges.[15] Overwhelmingly, the German population focused on their own problems and privations—a reflection of the traumatic experiences that they had gone through. As a result, a powerful sense of victimization, rather than guilt, colored much of the German popular discourse well into the 1960s.[16]

At the same time, instrumental considerations of various sorts played an important role in forcing the German state to adopt a penitent official narrative regarding the past. Of crucial importance in the German case was the international context in which German debates over the past unfolded. While American pressures for a reckoning with the past diminished with the onset of the Cold War, Germany remained under continued pressure from two other important groups—the world Jewish community and Germany's Western European neighbors. Both groups felt that they had been victimized by German actions and were able to successfully press the German government to go beyond the terms of the eventual peace settlement and institute ongoing programs of compensation. By the end of the Cold War, Germany had paid something on the order of $70 billion to individual claimants.[17] The Federal Republic, bound to its European neighbors by NATO and the institutions of what eventually became the European Union, and sensitive (probably oversensitive) to the influence of the Jewish lobby in American public opinion, felt in no position to ignore these demands.[18] Notably, the largest group of victims of Nazi aggression, the populations of Eastern Europe, received relatively little compensation until the Cold War ended. The willingness of the different actors to accept German efforts to reconcile was critical to the overall success of the program, so that by the late 1950s Germany had been able to rehabilitate itself as a good citizen of the Western community—albeit at a price in terms of both money and national pride.

The tortured German confrontation with the past that has become such a familiar trope in the current discourse really only began in the 1960s, when German Social Democratic leaders tapped into the frustrations of a new generation of students and radicals to launch an attack on the policies of their conservative Christian Democratic rivals. Spurred by the shifting tides of the Cold War and the emergence of detente, Chancellor Willy Brandt made reconciliation with Germany's Eastern neighbors the centerpiece of his foreign policy of *Ostpolitik*. Calling on the German people to "wager more on democracy," Brandt and his successors made an active confrontation with Germany's Nazi past a top domestic and international policy priority.[19]

These efforts were fiercely contested in ways that would seem familiar to an observer of the current Japanese debate over history and relations to China. Conservatives opposed these efforts and instead advocated the propagation of a "healthy patriotism," one that affirmed the positive aspects of Germany's past and could motivate the German people to defend their country if needed. A symbolic high point of the conservative campaign came in 1985, around the same time that Yasuhiro Nakasone made his controversial visit to Yasukuni, when Chancellor Helmut Kohl invited President Ronald Reagan to visit the German military cemetery at Bitburg.[20] In the end, however, the *Ostpolitik* and a more active engagement with the Nazi past proved popular, leading the Christian Democrats under Kohl to accept the broad outlines of Brandt's policies. Although the conservatives enjoyed the upper hand in the mid-1980s, they were not able to overcome the powerful dynamics both inside their society and in the international system to dramatically change Germany's official historical narrative. Instead, just a few weeks after the trip to Bitburg, a dramatic consolidation of the German discourse took place when Federal President Friedrich von Weizäcker—a conservative politician—made a much celebrated speech commemorating the 40th anniversary of the German defeat in World War II in which he argued that it had been a day of liberation for Germany as well as the rest of Europe and that Germans should be proud of their willingness to confront critically the dark chapters in their history.[21]

In short, it took nearly 40 years before Germany adopted the resolutely penitent stance regarding its past that it is usually credited with, and at every step of the way, calculations of interest played an important role alongside the powerful moral arguments that were being made by the German elite. As we shall see, even then, history remained a controversial issue in Germany, one that would come to haunt German policy-making again two decades later.

Austria

In other European countries the process of dealing with the past took a very differ-ent course. In Austria, which in many ways was as implicated in the crimes of the Third Reich as the Federal Republic was, the path to facing up to the past took much longer. Having been defined in the 1943 Moscow declaration by the leaders of the Allied powers as the "first victim of Nazism,"[22] during the Cold War Austria never came under the same pressures that Germany did to apologize and offer compensa-tion for wartime atrocities. Indeed, Austria seemed to make it its mission to "astonish the world" with its lack of guilt. With Austria regarded as a neutral country between East and West, its Western neighbors and the world Jewish community (despite the best efforts of Nahum Goldman and the World Jewish Congress) had relatively little ability to apply pressure on the Austrian government. The Austrian government refused to pay compensation to the victims of Nazism, and it resolutely avoided any admission of responsibility for the horrors of the Hitler era.[23]

In addition, unlike Germany, where the far right was marginalized in the political debate, both the Austrian Socialists and the conservative Austrian People's Party vied for the support of the organization that represented the former members of the Nazi party and the Waffen SS. As a result, in 1971 when Bruno Kreisky—who was Jewish —became the first Social Democratic Chancellor of the Austrian Republic, his cabinet had more former Nazis in it than had been in the original national unity cabinet that was established in 1938 after Austria's annexation by Germany. While Austria was heavily criticized for its impenitence, it was able to shake off such concerns for decades.[24] Even the storm of controversy that exploded over revelations of President Kurt Waldheim's possible involvement as an intelligence officer in brutal German counterinsurgency operations in the Balkans was incapable of penetrating Austria's resolutely impenitent stance. Waldheim, who was standing for reelection at the time when the unsavory details of his past were revealed, handily won reelection in 1987, with over 53% of the popular vote.[25]

Austria only really began to change its position on the past in 1991, over concern of the damage the Waldheim affair had done to Austria's image. In a series of speeches the Socialist-led government of Franz Vranitzky admitted "co-responsibilty" for the Holocaust and began to seriously tackle the long-neglected task of compensating the victims of Austrian Nazism. Full official acknowledgement by all the major par-ties, both on the left and right of the political spectrum, came only in 2000, after the country had joined the European Union and the Social Democrats were forced out of power by a coalition of the right and the far-right led by Jörg Haider. Alarmed that a man with Haider's resolutely revisionist views on the past should be part of the ruling government, and concerned that the far-right's Freedom Party's success in Austria could encourage other far-right wing parties such as the Front National in France and the Vlams Blok in Belgium, the European Union mounted a boycott of Austria inside EU institutions, while the Social Democrats launched a fierce cam-paign of criticism inside of Austria. Faced with powerful internal as well as external pressure, for the first time the Austrian government acknowledged that Austria had not simply been a victim of Nazism, but also bore moral and ethical responsibility for the crimes of the Third Reich.[26]

France

In France as well the past has been a highly explosive subject, because of the degree to which much of the French political class and many ordinary French people collaborated with the Nazi occupation and were implicated in the extermination of the Jews (with the help of the French Vichy government the Nazis rounded up over 60,000 French Jews, the large majority of whom were killed). As with Germany and Austria, after an initial attempt to come to terms with the past, there was a *de facto* moratorium, supported by both the left and the right, on issues of historical justice. All of France, with the exception of a few collaborators, were defined as valiant supporters of the French resistance, which successfully liberated their country from the yoke of German oppression (with perhaps a little bit of help from the Allies).

The French confrontation with the past began in the 1970s, spurred by a sharp critique of the conservative French governments of the time period launched by French intellectuals. The emergence of a populist far-right political formation, the Front National under the leadership of Jean Marie Le Pen in the 1980s and into the 1990s, rallied both left-wing and conservative French political elites in favor of a more penitent French stance on the past, culminating in President Jacques Chirac's 1995 apology for France's involvement in the crimes of the Nazi past.[27]

Europe's Historical Memory

In all three cases—Austria, France, and Germany—there was an initial period of intense preoccupation with the issue of pursuing those who were responsible for misconduct under the previous regime, followed by a consensus that the nation had to put the past behind it and get on with the tasks of reconstruction and facing new challenges. Thereafter, in all three cases there was a similar movement toward acknowledgement of moral responsibility for the crimes of the Nazi era. This movement is closely linked both to the development of an international normative regime regarding historical justice issues that legitimate demands for dealing with past atrocities and to the thickening of international institutions as a result of increased interdependence between the countries. The magnitude of the atrocities—as a simplistic form of experientialism would have it—is not enough. Countries that are deeply implicated in the crimes of the past can remain oblivious to them for decades—as can be seen in the case of Austria. Countries that, objectively speaking, were more tenuously responsible for crimes of a lesser magnitude (although still atrocious)—such as France—can become embroiled in deep soul-searching relatively early. In all three cases, domestic political factors played a decisive role. Not until key political actors—the SPD in Germany, the SPÖ in Austria, and left intellectuals in France—strongly came out in favor of opening the question of history, did real debates get under way. Not until the major political actors at both the left and the right ends of the political spectrum, often for openly instrumental reasons, accepted that there were things in their nation's history that were regrettable, did the official historical narrative move decisively in the direction of contrition.

THE (NON-)RESOLUTION OF THE HISTORY ISSUE IN ASIA

The Pacific War and the Sino-Japanese war in Asia were enormously destructive events, inflicting vast suffering on huge numbers of people. While more people were killed in the European theater between 1939 and 1945 than were killed in Asia between 1937 and 1945 (approximately 50 million versus 20 million), and the Japanese militarists had not embarked on a genocidal policy designed to wipe out an entire population group based on its purported racial characteristics, the war in Asia left behind a similar legacy of pain and anger.[28]

As in Germany, the Allied powers, especially the United States, were not content with winning a military victory over Japan and dismantling the Empire; they wished to win a moral victory as well. To this end, the American occupation authorities sought to implant a new historical narrative, one emphasizing Japanese responsibility for the war and for wartime atrocities. The key instrument in this enterprise was war crimes trials, capped by the International Military Tribunal for the Far East.

Almost from the start, however, the war crimes tribunals—as in Germany—proved a deeply flawed undertaking. Although there was widespread anger in Japan directed at the wartime leadership, the obvious flaws in the proceedings led to popular disenchantment with the process within a short time. Many of the crimes with which the defendants were charged had not been established formally at the time they were committed. Some of the charges—the wanton slaughter of civilians in areas under Imperial control—could just as easily have been leveled against the Allied powers—notably the Soviets—as against the Japanese. Perhaps most importantly, the choice of both crimes and defendants reflected very much the interests and preoccupations of the victorious powers, leading to an impression of "victor's justice." Many crimes of which the Allied powers could be viewed as guilty were conspicuously absent from the list of charges—including unrestricted submarine warfare, the indiscriminate aerial bombings of civilian targets, and (notably for the purposes of the present discussion) the colonial subjugation of peoples in violation of their right to self-determination.[29]

Equally damaging was the decision not to try the Japanese Emperor, Hirohito, even though as head of state all major decisions had to be approved by him and in a number of critical instances he had used that power to decisively shape policy. Although public opinion of the Allied countries strongly favored putting the emperor on trial, the head of the U.S. occupation in Japan, General Douglas MacArthur, opposed, arguing that to do so would destabilize the country and stiffen Japanese resistance.[30]

Despite these and other difficulties, the trials marked a sharp rupture with the Imperial period. While many—probably most—Japanese were skeptical about the tribunals, they embraced the opportunity that the trials and the occupation afforded them to break with the political traditions of the pre-1945 order. Many Japanese felt doubly victimized. First, they felt victimized by the Allied powers who had waged the war with a savage ferocity against Japanese soldiers and civilians alike and who had used the most terrible instruments of destruction, the atomic bomb, to achieve victory. Second, the Japanese people—much like the Austrians and the Germans—felt that they had been victimized by their own government and its military leaders, who had foolishly embroiled them in a war with an overwhelmingly more powerful adversary (the ratio of U.S. to Japanese GDP in 1941 was on the order of 10:1) and who then stubbornly refused to sue for peace despite an increasingly hopeless military situation and mounting casualties. By the end of the war over three million Japanese had died in the war, most major cities lay in ruins, and the country was faced with the very real prospect of mass starvation and total economic collapse.

As a result, postwar Japan turned sharply away from the policies of the prewar period. In the realm of defense and foreign policy, the postwar Japanese state chose to turn its back on the maintenance of a powerful military establishment, choosing instead to rely on its new security relationship with the United States. With regards to foreign economic policy, Japan continued to be constrained by its lack of natural resources to look to trade to maintain the level of prosperity that its people had come to expect. However, whereas in the prewar period it had sought to secure access to vital raw materials through the construction of a vast colonial sphere of influence, in the postwar period it chose to rely on the international trading order centered on the United States and the West.

What Japan did not do was to adopt an official policy of penitence regarding the past. In this respect, Japan was closer to Austria and France than it was to Germany (although, as we have seen, the degree of German penance in the 1940s, 1950s and into the 1960s should not be exaggerated). Under the terms of the Treaty of San Francisco, Japanese overseas assets (valued at approximately $25 billion in 1945), were seized by the countries in which they were located. The Japanese government paid an additional $1 billion to the countries that it had occupied between 1941 and 1945 (Burma, Indonesia, the Philippines, and Vietnam). The Western powers, led by the United States, agreed to forgo demanding further reparations, although the Japanese government paid the relatively paltry sum of approximately $16 million to the Red Cross to help compensate former Allied prisoners of war. In subsequent diplomatic negotiations between Japan and other Asian countries, the Japanese government steadfastly resisted pressures to pay further indemnities for its actions, offering instead to provide generous sums of overseas development assistance.[31] Claims made by various victim groups, such as the hundreds of thousands of Korean and Chinese forced laborers who had been brought to Japan to work, often under hellish conditions, were rebuffed. Similarly, the plight of the estimated 50,000 to 200,000 women who had coerced to serve as prostitutes to the Japanese armed forces (the so-called "comfort women") was ignored both by the Japanese and their own governments.[32]

In short, after 1945 Japan created a post-Imperial identity for itself that conveniently absolved it of any moral or legal responsibility for its past actions. While from a contemporary standpoint one might well be critical of the way in which Japan sought closure on the Empire, it is also important to recognize that it was by and large successful for nearly 30 years. To understand why Japan chose and was able to achieve closure on these terms, and why that closure ultimately proved unsustainable, requires a closer examination of the domestic and international political background against which the Japanese debate over the Empire unfolded.

THE POLITICAL PARAMETERS OF CLOSURE

On a domestic political level, the issue of the Japanese Empire was part of a larger controversy over who should be held responsible for the war (*senso sekinin*). On the one side of the debate stood the Japanese conservatives, the majority of whom had been deeply implicated in the Imperial enterprise (although a few, such as Tanzan Ishibashi, had been outspoken critics). For obvious reasons, the conservatives wished to avoid pursuing an issue that could damage their own legitimacy. Consequently, they favored an interpretation of the war as an unfortunate and ultimately ill-considered response to the challenges of Western Imperialism and the provocative policies of the United States and the Nationalist government in China. Japan, according to this point of view, had been compelled to build an empire because it lived in a world dominated by powerful, Western empires intent on expanding their influence. Conservatives tended to accept the old Imperial world view at face value, focusing on the concrete benefits that Japan had brought to its colonized peoples through the introduction of primary education, the building of modern infrastructure such as railways, and the creation of modern industrial enterprises.[33]

This is not to say that Japanese conservatives were wholehearted defenders of the war time regime. Many postwar leaders on the right and right of center, such as Ichiro Hatoyama and Shigeru Yoshida, were deeply critical of Japan's war time leadership and especially of the Japanese military leaders, who they felt had acted in an irrationally aggressive manner that ultimately visited disaster upon the nation.[34] Nonetheless, they rejected the notion that the Japanese Empire had been a morally bankrupt enterprise and the version of history that had been established by the Tokyo War Crimes Tribunal (although they could not do so officially because of the Treaty of San Francisco and the alliance relationship with the United States).

On the other side of the debate stood the Japanese political left, who shared a far more critical view of the Japanese Empire and its role in Asia. Unlike the conservatives, leftists tended to openly talk about Japanese wartime atrocities, and argued that as a result Japan bore a heavy burden of moral responsibility to the nations it had once victimized. The left's criticism of the state, however, was tempered by both tactical and ideological considerations. On a tactical level, many on the left were concerned with mobilizing the Japanese population in opposition to the Mutual Security Treaty system with the United States. To that end, the left found it more useful to focus on the atrocities that had been committed against Japan, and in particular the atomic bombings of Hirsohima and Nagasaki, as opposed to the atrocities that Japan may have committed against the peoples of Asia. Aggrievement, it seems, was a better motivator of the masses than guilt. In so doing, the left inadvertently contributed to the general Japanese preoccupation with their own suffering and helped foster what some have described as Japan's "Cult of Victimization."[35]

In the end, the Japanese conservatives, aided by their close ties to the United States and buoyed by an increasingly vibrant economy, won out in the domestic political battles of the 1940s and 1950s. While unable to challenge directly the verdict of the IMTFE, they were able to shape the official historical narrative propagated by the Japanese state through the schools, government-sponsored cultural institutions such as museums, policies dealing with such historically laden issues such as compensation and restitution for past wrongs, and officially sanctioned commemorative practices in ways that were consonant, or at least not opposed, to their understanding of Japanese colonial history. In this, however, they found themselves constantly challenged by the left, which was able to maintain a dissident historical narrative through its influence on the teachers union, the press, and Japanese intellectual life in general.

In addition to these domestic political factors, three international factors played an important role. First, the exigencies of the Cold War led the major powers in the region to subordinate the history issue to larger strategic considerations. While many in the United States were critical of the revisionist views espoused by the Japanese conservatives, Japan was too valuable an ally in the fight against communism to alienate it over what was perceived as being basically secondary issues. Similar calculations played a role in the stance of the People's Republic of China. During the Maoist era, China's leader identified the Japanese people as victims of Western imperialism in order to mobilize them against the U.S.-Japanese alliance. After China's rapprochement with the West in the 1970s its needs for Japanese assistance in rebuilding its moribund economy was too great to allow questions of historical grievances to come up.[36]

Second, the strongly authoritarian character of most Asian governments during the 1950s, 1960s, and 1970s enabled their respective governments to squelch popular pressures that might have made for the emergence of the history issue. In 1965, for example, the dictatorial Park Chung-hee government was able to ignore student organized street riots in Seoul in opposition to the normalization of diplomatic relations with Korea's erstwhile colonial master. Criticism of the United States and other Western (former Imperial) powers were generally suppressed, or at least contained, by anticommunists for similar reasons in South Korea, the Philippines, and elsewhere in the region.

Third, and finally, the institutional structure of the Cold War in Asia provided little incentive for history problems to come to the fore. Unlike Western Europe's extensive and complex network of regional institutions, a system of only loose and highly compartmentalized bilateral relations between the United States and its Asian allies characterized the East Asian situation. There was no East Asian economic community, nor was there a multilateral security alliance even remotely comparable to the North Atlantic Treaty Organization. After the collapse of its Empire, Japan had turned away—politically, economically, and psychologically—from Asia and looked to the West. South Korea was overwhelmingly oriented toward the United States.

The nations of Southeast Asia represented a partial exception in that they formed the Association of South East Asian States in 1967. ASEAN, however, was designed to overcome tensions between its members over postcolonial boundaries and embraced the strict principle of noninterference in internal affairs of other member states, and thus enforced a *de facto* moratorium on historical differences. As a result, Asian leaders, unlike their counterparts in Europe, had little incentive to face up to the thorny political problems posed by feelings of historical injustice.

GLOBALIZATION AND THE RENEWED SALIENCE OF HISTORY

The parameters of Asia's closure of the history issue began to unravel in the 1980s and 1990s. As with Austria, changes in the international system as well as the domestic politics of countries in the region played a key role in putting the question of Japanese responsibility for pre-1945 atrocities back on the domestic as well as international political agenda.

Internationally, the factors that had helped allow Japan to achieve closure on Imperial issue began to erode from the early 1980s on. Democratization in Korea and Taiwan, and relative political liberalization in China, allowed new voices to be heard on the subject of those countries' relations to Japan. Frequently these were voices critical of their government's willingness to drop historical justice issues pertaining to the Empire. In Korea, the willingness of the military governments to suppress or ignore the claims of the victims of Japanese colonialism was seen as a reflection of their insensitivity and corrupt character. Pressing issues of historical justice vis-à-vis Japan was thus seen as a necessary and logical outgrowth of the democratization project. In China, following a time-honored tradition dating back to the emergence of modern Chinese nationalism in 1919, those critical of the regime felt safer criticizing the regime's policies on the basis of its putative lack of concern for national pride and honor rather than attacking the regime directly.[37]

In addition, increased intraregional trade and efforts at institution building gave the former colonized countries increased leverage against Japan. Groups representing victims of Japanese wartime and colonial policies—such as Korean comfort women and former forced laborers and prisoners of war—were able to press their claims in Japanese and American courts (albeit with limited success). More importantly, they were able to gain a greater audience for their grievances through the international media, and gain a hearing for their views in important political venues, including the U.S. Congress. In addition, the Japanese business community relatively early on became concerned that anti-Japanese sentiment could damage Japanese business interests, and it began to lobby the Japanese government actively to show greater sensitivity to the issue.[38]

As a result of these international developments, both of which were part of the more general phenomenon of globalization, international controversy over Japan's responsibility for the pre-1945 period began to reemerge in the early 1980s. The first sign of the increased salience of history came with an unexpected burst of acrimony over proposed changes to Japanese school textbooks that would have diluted or

justified Japanese responsibility for the war in China.[39] In 1985 even greater controversy was stimulated by Prime Minister Yasuhiro Nakasone's visit to the Yasukuni
Shrine in Tokyo, the first official such visit made since the names of 14 Japanese leaders condemned as Class-A war criminals by the IMFTE had been enshrined in the
Shrine in 1978. Although Nakasone visited the shrine, the intensity of the anger it
generated, especially in China, caused him to hold off on any further trips.[40]

With the end of the Cold War, external pressures on the Japanese government to
confront the legacy of the past intensified, leading to a sustained diplomatic campaign in which Japanese leaders, beginning with Prime Minister Toshiki Kaifu in
1991, apologized for the past and tried to push forward the cause of reconciliation
with Japan's Asian neighbors.[41] Letters of apology and compensation were offered
to women who could be shown to have been pressed into service as comfort women,
and there was a general increased level of public interest in the question of Japanese
war crimes and the necessity for apologizing for them. These efforts, however, met
constant resistance from Japanese conservatives, who actively criticized these efforts
as "self-flagellating" (*jigyaku*) exercises that eroded Japanese national pride and
self-confidence.[42] Although in instrumental terms adopting a more penitent official
historical narrative had come to make sense for Japan, a relatively impenitent view
of the past had become too deeply rooted in Japan's political culture to be easily overcome. The factionalized nature of Japanese policy-making—which makes it difficult
to achieve progress on any controversial political issue—further makes it difficult for
Japanese political leaders to make a clean break on this issue, more difficult than it
was for their European counterparts.

On the level of domestic politics, the end of the Cold War triggered a far-reaching
reorganization of Japan's political landscape. The Liberal Democratic Party (LDP)'s
monopoly on the control of government was broken in 1993 with the emergence
of a non-LDP coalition led by Prime Minister Morihiro Hosokawa. Although thereafter the LDP was able to reemerge as the dominant political party and regain control
of the prime minister's office, the LDP has only been able to rule in coalition with
other parties, first together with their former Socialist rivals and then with the
Komeito. In addition, the power of the Japanese bureaucracy in setting Japan's political agenda was decisively shaken during the 1990s, leading to the emergence of
populist politicians such as Prime Ministers Junichiro Koizumi and Shinzo Abe.

These developments had complex and contradictory impacts on Japan's official
historical narrative. On the one hand, they allowed new voices to have a greater
impact on the formulation of the official historical narrative. During the Hosokawa
government, and then later when they were in coalition with the LDP, the Japanese
socialists in particular made the adoption of a conciliatory stance on history an important policy objective.[43] On the other hand, they enabled Japanese political leaders to
engage more openly on the history issue when they chose to, moving beyond the
narrow, legalistic approach that had been favored by the bureaucrats in the Ministry
of Foreign Affairs in the past. One reflection of this change was the creation of the
Asian Women's Fund in 1993, established to identify and compensate the surviving
comfort women. Even more dramatic was the summit between Prime Minister Keizo

Obuchi and South Korean President Kim Dae-jung in 1998, when apologies for Japan's colonial domination of Korea were both offered and accepted by the two sides, ushering a relatively brief, but significant period of improved relations between the two countries.[44]

On the other hand, Japan's changed domestic political environment also created an incentive for Japanese leaders to cater to nationalist sentiment, as Prime Minister Koizumi did between 2001 and 2006 by making repeated trips to Yasukuni despite increasingly vehement Chinese and South Korean objections. As a result of his visits, during the Koizumi period much of the tentative progress that had been made on the history issue in the previous decade was undone. Increasingly, tensions associated with the history issue spilled over into other issues, such as long-standing territorial disputes between Japan and China over the Senkaku/Diaoyutai islands and the boundaries of each nation's exclusive economic zone in the East China sea, and between Korea and Japan over the Takeshima/Dokdo island in the Sea of Japan (or Eastern Sea, as the Koreans preferred to call it). In 2005 and 2006, the dispute over history reached unprecedented proportions, with fierce anti-Japanese riots breaking out in many parts of China[45] and with increased willingness on the part of all three countries to use their armed forces to underscore their contending claims to the disputed islands.

Eventually, tensions over history were brought under control before the situation worsened any further. The Chinese leadership intervened to quell anti-Japanese agitation while Prime Minister Koizumi publicly reaffirmed Japan's recognition of responsibility for and repugnance over its aggressive behavior prior to 1945. A military confrontation was averted over Takeshima/Dokdo. And Koizumi's successor, Abe, promised not to make any further official visits to Yasukuni (leaving open the possibility that he might continue to make private, unofficial visits) and restoring high-level meetings between China's and Japan's senior political leaders.[46] Although a more serious crisis was averted, the fear that tensions could be reignited remained widespread. Unfavorable comparisons between Asia and Europe with regard to their ability to manage the history issue and the nationalist passion with which it was associated were made by numerous commentators. Yet, ironically, at the same time history—and with it the history issue—continued to develop in the European context as well.

THE REEMERGENCE OF HISTORY IN EUROPE

In recent years, history has reemerged as a problem for Europe. This was most dramatically and surprisingly the case in Germany. After the unification of Germany, debates over history reemerged with a vengeance as a result of change in German domestic politics and foreign policy. Domestically, efforts to reintegrate Eastern Germany, and to fend off the potential for a right-wing nationalist revival, has led to a new effort to define national symbols, including ones that stress German suffering (e.g., the Neue Wache in Berlin commemorating those killed trying to flee communist dictatorship in the East). In addition, a more activist German foreign and national security policy pushed the Federal Republic to redefine the moral lessons from World War II from "never again war" to "never again Auschwitz," with Germany playing an expanded role in humanitarian interventions in the Balkans and beyond.[47] Together, these two developments have fed the reemergence of a sense of German victimization that, while not denying Germany's past misdeeds, demands recognition for the millions of Germans who died as a result of the war and its aftermath, particularly in Eastern Europe.[48]

This new German sense of victimization has provoked a political backlash in Germany's Eastern neighbors, especially Poland, and to a lesser extent the Czech Republic. In ways reminiscent of recent problems between Japan and South Korea, nationalist politicians on both sides have fueled a cycle of mutual recrimination over past injustices. In particular, the proposed German construction of a monument commemorating the victims of ethnic expulsion (including German victims) has sparked a fierce war of words, despite German efforts to water down these proposals, and led to Polish demands for increased compensation for the damage done in World War II, and to Polish and Czech efforts to block German proposals inside the context of regional institutions.[49] Differences between Germany and Poland over history were particularly visible at the EU summit in Brussels in the spring of 2007, when the Polish side demanded increased voting rights inside of EU institutions to compensate it for the loss of population it suffered as a result of German depredations during World War II.[50] Other issues, such as the construction of a gas pipeline in the Baltic directly linking Germany and Russia (and thus bypassing Poland, Belarus and the Baltic states), have stirred long-dormant animosities. The Polish foreign minister, for instance, compared the Russian-German proposal with the Molotov-Ribbentrop pact that divided Poland into Soviet- and Nazi-controlled zones in 1939.[51] In short, although German Chancellor Angela Merkel has succeeded in defusing some of these tensions, history seems to have roared back with a vengeance on the German political agenda.

Elsewhere in Europe, new or long submerged disputes over the past have also reemerged with unexpected force and vigor. Of particular importance have been the tensions that have emerged between Russia and its former satellites over symbolic issues such as the Statue of the Unknown Soldier erected in Talinn, Estonia, in honor of Soviet soldiers who died in Estonia during World War II. For Russia, the statue is a tribute to the enormous sacrifices Russia made to defeat Nazi Germany; to most Estonians it marks the imposition of Soviet tyranny and the depredations of the Red Army (many Estonians refer to it as the "tomb of the unknown rapist"). These symbolic issues have been reinforced by disputes over more conventional issues, while in turn exacerbating those disputes—such as energy provisions to Eastern Europe, EU support for democratization, and the proposed construction of a rudimentary missile defense shield for Western Europe.

Similarly disruptive has been the eruption of the long-simmering dispute between Turkey and Western nations over the slaughter of Armenians inside of Turkey during World War I. Members of the Armenian diaspora, empowered by the growing international regime on historical justice, have successfully lobbied legislatures—notably in France and the United States—to define the massacres as a "genocide," thus placing Turkey in the same camp morally with respect to the past as Germany, Austria, and Japan. Nationalists in Turkey have responded with outrage at these accusations, triggering a fierce international crisis that is still unfolding at the time of this writing (Fall, 2007).

CONCLUSIONS

What the recent developments in Europe suggest is that the difficulties that Asians had over the past is hardly unique to that region—a conclusion that would be doubt-lessly reinforced if we were to widen the scope of our analysis and include other intractable problems in which emotional disputes over history appear to play a large role, such as the Arab-Israeli struggle over Palestine or the Indian-Pakistani rivalry regarding Kashmir. Indeed, it would appear that all around the world there has been an upsurge in these types of diplomatic controversies. At the same time, the European and Japanese cases also suggest that the history problem is neither merely the product of other, more mundane forces such as the balance of power or the pursuit of economic self-interest, nor is it an unmanageable phenomenon created by unbridled nationalist passions.

The battles between Japan and South Korea over the past have demonstrably been in neither country's interest, delaying the normalization of relations for over a decade in the 1950s and 1960s, and preventing these two countries who share many common interests from establishing more stable relations more recently. Sino-Japanese disputes have been similarly counterproductive and undesirable from the point of view of both governments. Likewise, the recent German and Polish fracas over the expulsions of ethnic Germans and the Nazi past in general has served largely to isolate Poland diplomatically within the European Union, and to slow down and complicate the process of European integration. While countries do not go to war because of disagreements over the past, diplomatic relations clearly can be disrupted, and issues that otherwise should be manageable—such as the Takeshima/Dokdo or Senkaku/Diayutai islands—can turn into crises, potentially militarized ones.

At the same time, over and again we have seen that political leaders have been able to contain nationalist pressures regarding historical issues, and to create more stable environments within which relations between their countries can be restructured. The paradigmatic example of this can be seen in the case of France and Germany, in which nearly a century of deeply rooted animosity was set aside to allow the two countries to come closer to one another. The same holds true even for German-Polish relations today. Despite the recent acrimony, public opinion data shows an overall positive attitude toward Germany inside of Poland, with a marked decline in the perception of threat and a continued readiness to work with Germany despite differences over historical and other issues.[52] In a different way, Austria has been able to change its stance on history, and inside of Austria today there is a far-reaching transformation of Austrian attitudes toward its past that is likely to prevent the reoccurrence of a crisis like the one it experienced in 2000.

In the case of Asia, history has proven on the whole more difficult to deal with. Structural factors made the issue a less pressing one in the Asian context than in the European, and by the time that countries began to deal with them—in the 1980s—nationalist-driven discourses regarding the past had become embedded in the domestic political systems of China, Japan, and South Korea in ways that made it very difficult for these countries to find common ground. Nonetheless, in Asia as well it has been possible for political leaders to contain these passions—as China and Japan did in 2006—and even to achieve significant progress in improving relations between their countries, as Kim Dae-jung and Keizo Obuchi managed to do in 1998. In the future, Asian leaders, if they chose to do so, can build on these earlier successes.

When they do so, however, they would be well advised to draw certain lessons regarding the dynamics of historical disputes that can be drawn from the cases briefly elaborated on here. First, leaders need to view disputes over history in a pragmatic fashion, as very real issues with dangerously disruptive potential, but responsive nonetheless to more mundane forces such as material interest. This means that dealing with the history problem can be very costly politically, but so too can be the decision not to deal with it. Political leaders need to assess the costs versus the benefits before they commit themselves to addressing the issue. Popular sentiment probably made it impossible for any of the countries discussed here—Austria, France, Germany, or Japan—to adopt a fully penitent stance in the 1950s. To the extent that it had to, Germany adopted a partially penitent stance, Japan only a superficially penitent one, and Austria and France resolutely impenitent stances.

Second, when leaders choose to open a diplomatic dialogue over history, it helps greatly if there is general readiness to reciprocate. There must be some assurance that apologies will be accepted before leaders will risk giving them. This has been a problem that has bedeviled Sino-Japanese relations, since it is feared that Chinese leaders are not in a position to accept a Japanese apology because of deficits in their own moral legitimacy. The reverse may be true as well—countries should be wary of demanding apologies if they clearly are not forthcoming, as may prove to be the case with Turkey and the Armenian genocide today.

Third, policies that are made on the level of the national leadership need to be followed through on other policy levels. It is not enough for leaders to meet on the functional equivalent of the White House lawn and shake hands. If a more deeply rooted process of reconciliation, or at least harmonization of views over history is to take place, such top-level symbolic gestures need to be backed up by policies such as adopting new commemorative practices and changes in portrayal of history in officially approved textbooks or museums. If the broader societal discourse on the past is not shifted, any reconciliation on the international level will always be subject to the vagaries of domestic politics.

Fourth, and finally, this history of the history problem underlines that the ways in which states and societies view their history, and the political implications of how they do so, are part of an ongoing process. Changes in political leadership, shifts in societal generations, or a country's domestic or international situation can all lead to subtle or not so subtle changes in the official historical narrative and how it serves the national interest. German reunification and a new German international security role unexpectedly revived history as an issue in Europe. Democratization in South Korea and a relative liberalization of discourse in China helped do the same in Asia. Political leaders can never assume that simply because equilibrium has been achieved at one point, it will continue to hold in the future. Dealing with tensions over history is an ongoing enterprise, but one that with wisdom and determination is manageable—in Asia as in Europe.

NOTES

1. On the negative impact of the history on regionalism, see Gilbert Rozman, *Northeast Asia's Stunted Regionalism: Bilateral Distrust in the Shadow of Globalization* (Cambridge and New York: Cambridge University Press, 2004); Edward Lincoln, *East Asian Economic Regionalism* (Washington, DC: Brookings, 2004); and Keichi Tsunekawa, "Dependent Nationalism in Contemporary Japan and Its Implications for the Regional Order in the Asia Pacific," (Perth: Asia Research Centre, Murdoch University, 2006), available at http://wwwarc .murdoch.edu.au/wp/wp133.pdf). On how it negatively affects Chinese threat perceptions, see Thomas Christensen, "China, The U.S.-Japan Alliance and the Security Dilemma in East Asia" *International Security* 23, no. 4 (Spring 1999): 49–80.

2. Nicholas Kristof, "The Problem of Memory," *Foreign Affairs* 77, no. 5 (November/ December 1988).

3. For notable exceptions, see Elazar Barkan, *The Guilt of Nations: Restitution and Negotiating Historical Injustices* (Baltimore: Johns Hopkins University Press, 2001); Jan Werner Mueller, ed. *Memory and Power in Post-War Europe: Studies in the Presence of the Past* (New York and Cambridge: Cambridge University Press, 2002); John Torpey, ed., *The Politics of the Past* (Lanham, MD: Rowman and Littlefield, 2003); Richard Ned Lebow, *The Politics of Memory in Postwar Europe* (Durham, NC: Duke University Press, 2006); and Jeffrey Olick, *The Politics of Regret: On Collective Memory and Historical Responsibility* (London and New York: Routledge, 2007).

4. See Ruti G. Teitel, *Transitional Justice* (New York and London: Oxford University Press, 2000).

5. See Martha Minow, "The Hope for Healing: What Can Truth Commissions Do?" in *Truth versus Justice: The Morality of Truth Commissions,* ed. Robert I. Rotberg and Dennis Thompson (Princeton, NJ: Princeton University Press, 2000), especially pp. 248–52.

6. See James V. Wertsch, *Voices of Collective Remembering* (New York: Cambridge Universiy Press, 2002).

7. See Martha Minow, "Breaking Cycles of Hatred," in *Breaking the Cycles of Hatred: Memory, Law and Repair,* ed. Nancy L. Rosenblum (Princeton, NJ: Princeton University Press, 2002); and Jenny Edkins, *Trauma and the Memory of Politics* (Cambridge: Cambridge University Press, 2003).

8. See Edkins, *Trauma and the Memory of Politics;* Tina Rosenberg, *The Haunted Land: Facing Europe's Ghosts after Communism* (New York: Random House, 1995), especially p. 27; and Alexander Wilde, "Irruptions of Memory: Expressive Politics in Chile's Transition to Democracy," in *Genocide, Collective Violence and Popular Memory: The Politics of Remembrance in the Twentieth Century,* ed. David E. Lorey and William H. Beezley (Wilmington, DE: Scholarly Resources, 2002).

9. A classic example of this is Eric Hobsbawm and Terrence Ranger, eds., *The Invention of Tradition* (Cambridge: Cambridge University Press, 1983). This perspective has become commonplace in the analysis of nationalism, including of Japan and Germany,. See for instance Carol Gluck, *Japan's Modern Myths* (Princeton, NJ: Princeton University Press, 1987); and John Breuilly. *Nationalism and the State* (Chicago: University of Chicago Press, 1994).

10. The culturalist position as described here is quite close to what Jeffrey Olick, a leading contemporary sociologist working on the politics of memory, calls a functionalist approach to the study of collective memory. See Jeffrey Olick, "From Usable Pasts to the Return of the Repressed," *The Hedgehog Review* 9, no. 2 (2007):19–31, especially pp. 20–21. Olick, however, eschews the word culture and prefers to focus on how identity and the moral purposes with which it is associated generate the need for a particular kind of history.

11. For a succinct summary of the difference, see Yosef Lapid, "Culture's Ship: Returns and Departures in International Relations Theory," in *The Return of Culture and Identity in IR Theory,* ed. Yosef Lapid and Friedrich Kratochwil. (Boulder: Lynne Rienner, 1996), especially pp. 6–9.

12. See Harry Eckstein, "A Culturalist Theory of Political Change," in *Regarding Politics: Essays on Political Theory, Stability and Change* (Berkeley and Los Angeles: University of California Press, 1992); Victoria E. Bonnell and Lynn Hunt, eds., *Beyond the Cultural Turn* (Berkeley and Los Angeles: University of California Press, 1999).

13. Ruth Benedict, *The Chrysanthemum and the Sword: Patterns of Japanese Culture* (Boston: Houghton Mifflin, 1946); and Victor Koschman, *Authority and the Individual in Japan: Citizen Protest in Historical Perspective* (Tokyo: University of Tokyo Press, 1978).

14. See Rudolph Rummel, *Democide: Nazi Genocide and Mass Murder* (New Brunswick, NJ: Transaction Press, 1992) and *Statistics of Democide: Genocide and Mass Murder since 1900* (Münster: Lit Verlag, 1999).

15. See Norbert Frei, *Adenauer's Germany and the Nazi Past: the Politics of Amnesty and Integration,* trans. Joel Golb (New York: Columbia University Press, 2002), published originally as *Vergangenheitspolitik* (Munich: C. H. Beck, 1997).

16. For an insightful review of the debates over history and historical responsibility in West Germany during the early postwar years, see Jeffrey Olick, *In the House of the Hangman: The Agonies of German Defeat, 1943–1949* (Chicago: University of Chicago Press, 2005). For a discussion of the German sense of victimization, from the early postwar years to the present, see Bill Niven, ed., *Germans as Victims* (New York: Palgrave Macmillan, 2006).

17. For a detailed discussion of German reparations, see Constantine Goschler, *Schuld und Schulden: die Politik der Wiedergutmachung für NS-verfolgte seit 1945* (Göttingen: Wallstein, 2005).

18. See Goschler, *Schuld und Schulden*; Susanna Scharfstetter, "The Diplomacy of Wiedergutmachung: Memory, the Cold War and West European Victims of Nazism, 1956–1964," *Holocaust and Genocide Studies* 17, no. 3 (2003): 459–79; and Susanna Scharfstetter, "Die einfachen Leute werden für die Gerechtigkeit sorgen! Die deutsch-britischen Verhandlungen über ein Abkommen zur Entschädigung von Opfern nationalsozialistischer Verfolgung, 1956–1965." *Zeitenblicke* 3, no. 2 (2004): 1–13, available at http://zeitenblicke.historicum.net/2004/02/schrafstetter/index.html

19. David Art, *The Politics of the Nazi Past* (Cambridge and New York: Cambridge University Press, 2006), pp. 57–58.

20. For an overview and extensive collection of documents and commentaries pertaining to the visit, see Ilya Levkov, ed., *Bitburg and Beyond: Encounters in American, German and Jewish History* (New York: Shapolsky Publishers, 1987).

21. For the text of this Richard von Weizäcker, "Der 8.Mai 1945: 40 Jahre danach," in Weizäcker, *Von Deustchalnd aus: Reden des Bundespräsidenten* (Munich: Deutscher Taschenbuch Verlag, 1987), English translation in *Bitburg and Beyond,* ed. Levkov, pp. 262–73. For a discussion of its impact on the German public discourse on the past, see Art, *The Politics of the Nazi Past,* pp. 73–74.

22. See Hella Pick, *Guilty Victims: Austria from the Holocaust to Haidar* (London: I.B. Tauris, 2000), pp. 17–23.

23. In 1962, after nine years of negotiations, the Austrian government finally agreed to pay a token sum of $22 million to Jewish survivors of the Holocaust. See Bruce Pauley, "Austria" in *The World Reacts to the Holocaust,* ed. David S.Wyman (Baltimore, MD: Johns Hopkins University Press, 1996), pp. 496–97.

24. On Austria's reaction to criticisms of Kreisky, see Art, *Politics of the Nazi Past,* pp. 114–15, and Pick, *Guilty Victims,* pp. 105–9.

25. Art, *The Politics of the Nazi Past,* pp. 111–30.

26. "EU Issues Unprecedented Warning against New Austrian Government," *Europe* 393 (February 2000): 24.; Michael Merling, Cas Mudde, and Ulrich Sedelmeier, "The Right and the Righteous? European Norms, Domestic Politics and the Sanctions against Austria?" *Journal of Common Market Studies* 39, no. 1 (2001): 59–77. Austria had begun to move in this direction earlier, with important speeches by President Franz Vranitzky in 1991 and 1993 in which he acknowledged that Austria bore coresponsibility.

27. See Henry Rousso, *The Vichy Syndrome: History and Memory in France since 1944* (Cambridge: Harvard University Press, 1991); and Eric Conan, Henry Rousso, and Nathan Bracher, trans., *Vichy: An Ever-Present Past* (Hanover, NH: Dartmouth Press, 1998).

28. See Rudolf Rummel, *China's Bloody Century* (New Brunswick, NJ: Transaction Books, 1991), Table 5a. Rummel estimates that the total number of those killed as a matter of deliberate Japanese policy—that is worked to death in slave labor camps, killed in counterinsurgency operations, and so forth—to be 5,964,000. See his Web site, http://www.hawaii.edu/powerkills/SOD.CHAP3.HTM (accessed May 16, 2006).

29. See Yoshida Yutaka, *Showa Tenno no shusenshi* (Tokyo: Iwanami Shoten, 1992).

30. For sharply critical assessments of the trials, see Richard Minear, *Victor's Justice: The Tokyo War Crimes Tribunal* (Princeton, NJ: Princeton University Press, 1971) and Arnold C. Brackman, *The Other Nuremberg: The Untold Story of the Tokyo War Crimes Trials* (New York: Morrow, 1987).

31. *Asahi Shinbun,* November 13, 1993; and Kiyomizu Masayoshi, "Sengo hosho no kokusaihikaku," *Sekai* (February 1994).

32. On forced laborers, see Willam Underwood, "Chinese Forced Labor, the Japanese Government and the Prospects for Redress," *Japan Focus,* available at http://japanfocus.org/products/details/1693 (accessed November 18, 2005); and Underwood, "Mitsubishi, Historical Revisionism and Japanese Corporate Resistance to Chinese Forced Labor Redress," *Japan Focus* (February 6, 2006), available at http://japanfocus.org/products/details/1823 (accessed March 21, 2005). On the comfort women, see Yoshimi Yoshiaki, *Comfort Women: Sexual Slavery in the Japanese Military* transl. Suzanne O'Brien (New York: Columbia University Press, 2000). For a different interpretation of the comfort women issue, see Togo Kazuhiko's chapter in this volume.

33. For a positive assessment of the impact of Japan's Empire on East Asian economic development, see Atuhl Kohli, *State-Directed Development: Political Power and Industrialization with Global Periphery* (Cambridge and New York: Cambridge University Press, 2004).

34. John W. Dower, *Empire and Aftermath: Yoshida Shigeru and the Japanese Experience, 1876–1954* (Cambridge, Mass.: Council on East Asian Studies, Harvard University, 1979).

35. James J. Orr, *The Victim as Hero: Ideologies of Peace and National Identity in Postwar Japan* (Honolulu: University of Hawa'i Press, 2001).

36. Yinan He, "National Mythmaking and the Problems of History in Sino-Japanese Relations," paper presented at the workshop on "Memory of War," at the Center for International Affairs, Massachusetts Institute of Technology, January 24–25, 2003.

37. See He, "National Mythmaking"; James Reilly, "China's History Activists and the War of Resistance against Japan," *Asian Survey* 44, no. 2 (2004): 276–94; and Peter Hays Gries, *China's New Nationalism: Pride, Politics and Diplomacy* (Berkeley and Los Angeles: University of California Press, 2004).

38. See Ichiro Ozawa, *Blueprint for a New Japan: The Rethinking of a Nation* (Tokyo: Kodansha International, 1994), pp. 128–29; and *Gekkan Keidanren,* April 1992, cited in Yoshida Yutaka, *Nihonjin no sensōkan* (Tokyo: Iwanami Shoten, 1995).

39. *Asahi Shinbun,* July 26, 1982. See also *Shukan Asahi,* August 13, 1982, p. 20.

40. Daiki Shibuchi, "The Yasukuni Shrine Dispute and the Politics of Identity in Japan: Why All the Fuss?" *Asian Survey* 45, no. 2 (2005), cited in Daqing Yang, "The Malleable and the Contested," in *Perilous Memories: The Asia Pacific War[s]* ed. Takashi Fujitani, et.al. (Durham, NC: Duke University Press, 2001) pp. 62–63. See also Akihiko Tanaka's chapter in this volume.

41. William Lee Howell, "The Inheritance of War: Japan's Domestic Political Politics and the Domestic Political Ambitions," in *Remembering and Forgetting: The Legacy of War and Peace in East Asia,* ed. Gerrit W. Gong (Washington, DC: Center for Strategic and International Studies, 1996), pp. 82–101.

42. John W. Dower, "An Aptitude for Being Unloved: War and Memory in Japan," in *Crimes of War: Guilt and Denial in the Twentieth Century* ed. Omer Bartov, Atina Grossman, and Mary Nolan (New York: The New Press, 2002). On compensation for forced labor, see William Underwood, "Chinese Forced Labor," p. 2. A convenient online list attached to Wikipedia that keeps track of Japanese official apologies is to be found at http://www.reference.com/browse/wiki/List_of_war_apology_statements_issued_by_Japan (accessed March 15, 2008). Also very useful is the more scholarly "Memory and Reconciliation in the Asia-Pacific" Web site maintained by the Sigur Center for Asian Studies at George Washington University, at http://www.gwu.edu/~memory/. See also Kazuhiko Togo's Chapters 3 and 7 in this volume.

43. See Asano Atsushi, *Renritsu seiken: Nihon no seiji* (Tokyo: Bungeishunju, 1999), Part II, chapter 3.

44. See *Asahi Shinbun* and *Yomiuri Shinbun,* October 8, 1998, p. 1. For more on the background of the visit, Yoshibumi Wakayama, *The Postwar Conservative View of Asia* (Tokyo: LTCB International Library Foundation, 1998), pp. 256–59.

45. *Asahi* satellite edition, April 9, 10, 11, 17, 18, and 21, 2005, p. 1.

46. Thomas Berger, "Overcoming a Difficult Past: The History Problem and Institution Building in North East Asia," *Institution Building in North East Asia* ed. Martina Timmerman and Jitsuo Tsuchiyama (Tokyo: United Nations University Press, forthcoming 2008).

47. Thomas U. Berger "A Perfectly Normal Abnormality: German Foreign Policy after Kosovo and Afghanistan," *Japanese Journal of Political Science* 3, no. 2 (2002): 173–93.

48. See Bill Niven, ed., *Germans as Victims* (New York: Palgrave Macmillan, 2006).

49. "Polen erwarten von Deutschland Reparationszahlungen," *Der Spiegel,* September 22, 2004, http://www.spiegel.de/politik/ausland/0,1518,319231,00.html (accessed Spetember 22, 2004).

50. "Schwierige Verhandlungen in Brüssel," *Frankfurter Allgemeine Zeitung,* June 23, 2007, pp. 1 and 2.

51. "Poland Compares German-Russian Pipeline to Nazi-Soviet Pact," *EUobservor* May 2, 2006, at http://euobservor.com/9/21486/ (accessed October 3, 2006).

52. Mateusz Falkowski, Meinungen der Polen über die deutsch-polnischen Beziehungen nach dem Regierungswechsel in beidern Länder November 2005, available at http://www.isp.org.pl/files/20442810390940702001134394938.pdf (accessed April 20, 2007).

2

East Asian Historical Issues in a Contemporary Light

Gilbert Rozman

For someone steeped in the Confucian worldview, chronicling the past has special meaning. It serves the principle of "rectification of names," a vital consideration for an orderly society and proper governance. In this way, it builds a foundation for legitimacy, moral authority, and national (or civilizational) identity. This occurs at multiple levels: for family and kinship ties through regular maintenance of a genealogy; for community and local area ties through the occasional preparation of a gazetteer or company history; and, above all, for nation or state through the formulaic compilation of official histories. Remembering the past and didactically constructing its meaning for the benefit of future harmony and support are critical responsibilities within the East Asian cultural sphere. If official Confucianism is a distant memory, its legacy in thinking about "face," respect, and linkages between a nation's past and present may be becoming more visible now that East Asian states newly confront each other at the same time as they free themselves from the tight confines of international relations established over 150 years through the dominance of Western states.[1]

The history of the Japanese state over the half century from 1895 to 1945 occupies an important place in the transition from the traditional Confucian order of hierarchy and harmony to the modern international system premised on the equality of states. Entering the final decade of the nineteenth century, China clung to its

Confucian world order reinforced by the tributary system that recognized it as the central kingdom. Korea persevered in its identification as a Confucian state, claiming to surpass others in upholding this tradition as it was being eroded elsewhere. On the surface, only Japan seemed to be jettisoning this heritage, captivated by the idea of "leaving Asia" as it imbibed the harsh lessons of ruthless competition among nation-states driven by *realpolitik* with scant regard to moralistic claims. Yet, Japanese officials and scholars were conscious of their responsibility to history to explain the conduct of their country in a manner that would invoke pride and instill confidence in future generations. Writing history would be the final battleground in the struggle to remake history. Japan's time in the spotlight would be judged not only by its neighbors increasingly inclined to combine the Confucian historiographic legacy with newfound nationalism, but by the Japanese people, too, in search of a moral anchor to keep them from straying in uncertain times.

The discourse of Japanese imperialism borrowed heavily from the accepted language of international law of the time and of enlightened tutelage in a world still under the spell of the "civilizing mission" of conquerors at a time of modernization first by a small number of states. In its annexation of Korea in 1910 Japan took pains to present its actions as "legal" as well as "just." This set a precedent for further depredations in Asia, each rationalized as for the well-being of the subjugated nations and as accomplished with pure motives and proportionate use of force. Defeat was not accompanied by much assessment of how this discourse had distorted the truth and how the exploited nations had perceived—or would likely continue to perceive—their invaders.[2] Writings on healing the wounds of Japan's transgressions failed to prepare the Japanese people for future trust.

After its unconditional surrender on August 15, 1945, Japan faced the glare of historical judgment along with its principal victims. The matter would not be settled in one quick stroke, especially because of two factors: the dominance of the United States as the occupier of Japan and the patron in nursing it back into the international system, and the spread of communism to China and North Korea. Along with it there was the initial dominance of a Marxist-Leninist formula for explaining history to Japanese intellectuals, a worldview that simplified explanations of historical progress or transgressions. Three tests would eventually loom for moralistic judgments about Japan's role in Asia during its half-century dominance: (1) normalization of relations with its victim states; (2) commemoration of the landmarks of that era after the Cold War had ended and linkages among nations in the region were well established; and (3) resolution of differences in the process of establishing a framework for regional security and regionalism to institutionalize economic integration. The path to normalization began in South Korea, turned to China, and still awaits a breakthrough with North Korea. The remembrances that mattered came as acknowledgements of major events, including in 1995 the 50th anniversary of the end of the war. Finally, the search for regionalism and a new security framework, which was intensified in the North Korean nuclear crisis, would test the principal actors further. As Japan pursued the objectives of regaining a military role and constitutional revision in an uncertain environment, its principal victims would be inclined to confuse normal realist goals of a great power with revisionist thinking of an unrepentant aggressor, and some Japanese nationalists would be tempted to insert their revisionist agenda in the guise of restoring a realist state.

NORMALIZATION WITH SOUTH KOREA AND CHINA IN THE COLD WAR ERA

If, instead of the San Francisco Peace Treaty in 1951, the interlude of a defeated power without sovereignty had ended for Japan with a comprehensive settlement with Asian as well as Western targets of its aggression, there is little doubt that admissions of guilt and resolution of territorial issues would have been more thorough. Had Tokyo over the next decade diversified its foreign policy and moved with some sense of urgency to settle these matters with the governments in Beijing, Seoul, or Pyongyang, the results also would likely have been significantly different. Instead, delay gave leaders time to strengthen Japan's international standing as the principal Asian ally of the United States. It emboldened conservative politicians as they solidified their grip on power and saw the progressive camp lose credibility with its idealistic quest for pacifism and neutrality. And it gave the state the clout through a decade of double-digit economic growth to make use of the "economic card" in enticing the lesser victim states of Southeast Asia to normalize relations in a manner that minimized the need to apologize or expose the details of the injustices to which they had been subjected. Supported by the U.S. determination to keep communism from spreading to the remaining maritime periphery of Asia, eventually focusing on South Vietnam as the critical barrier to prevent the "dominos" from falling, Japan became the gateway to "free Asia" and then the substitute for a chastened U.S. government that was retreating after the miscalculations that mired it in the Vietnam War.

In 1965 circumstances were ideal for normalizing diplomatic relations with South Korea on terms favorable to Japan. Eager to diminish the burden of its responsibilities, Washington pressed both Seoul and Tokyo to put an end to more than a decade of fierce haggling over the terms of an agreement. Nervous about Pyongyang's rapid expansion of its military industrial complex, Seoul was desperate to jump-start its languid economy. In power was Park Chung-hee, whose abrogation of the democratic provisions of the state left the legitimacy of his military dictatorship in grave doubt. Having collaborated as an officer in the Japanese army, Park was sympathetic with the goal of covering up past misdeeds. Hiding portions of the normalization agreement from the public and appealing to anticommunism as its compelling justification, Park gave Japan's conservatives what they most wanted: a first step toward reentry into Northeast Asia with minimal need to apologize, resolve a territorial dispute, or stir up debate at home about the past.[3] This set a precedent for using the strength of an economic power to overcome the weakness of a state unpopular with its neighbors and recognized as owing a great debt for its behavior.

Normalization of diplomatic relations with China in 1972 occurred in similarly favorable circumstances. For a decade Mao Zedong had steered Chinese foreign policy in an ideological direction with dangerous consequences. After Leonid Brezhnev sent troops to Czechoslovakia in 1968 to extinguish the "Prague Spring" and China attacked a disputed island held by the Soviet Union on the Amur River in 1969, concern rose that the next move could be a preemptive strike on China's nuclear weapons facilities in Xinjiang province. Having, at the peak of the Cultural Revolution, let foreign policy deteriorate to the point that only Albania was left as a friend, Mao and his more pragmatic Premier Zhou Enlai were ready to respond to Richard Nixon's overtures for a breakthrough in the "Strategic Triangle," elevating China into a recognized status not only as one of the three greatest powers but also as the one whose moves caused tectonic shifts in the global system. This entirely realist turn opened the way to Japan to try its hand at realism too.

Ideological to an extreme in his domestic policies, China's charismatic leader had no opposition to striking a realist deal with Japan's leadership that concentrated on joint opposition to the common enemy, the Soviet Union, and Japan's abandonment of official support for the rival state on Taiwan, the Republic of China. After the United States had made a similar deal, Japan had no choice but to follow, as its Liberal Democratic Party (LDP) leaders took much satisfaction from again being spared claims to reparations and excused from making more than the most unspecific, superficial apology for the past.[4] With a desperate Taiwan having as the supposed representative of China made a similar arrangement early in the 1950s and South Korea and the People's Republic of China now in tow, Japanese leaders could look ahead to a deal someday with North Korea as finalizing the restoration of diplomatic ties in the region. Success with China could be the turning point in putting a lid on the history issue without conceding much and leaving it to later leaders to recast events as desired.

Negotiations over a peace treaty with China in 1977–78 completed this phase of normalization. Unlike the stumbling block of four islands disputed with the Soviet Union in 1955–56 that resulted in diplomatic relations but no prospect that a peace treaty would follow, the Senkaku/Diaoyutai islands were handled with more flexibility. Deng Xiaoping decided to go ahead while leaving them in Japan's hands, declaring that this matter could be set aside for the next generation. Before that, a fragile Chinese leadership in the midst of the succession crisis after Mao's death had again put priority on anti-Soviet objectives, demanding that Japan accept language little disguised in its rebuke to Soviet hegemonism. Deng and his colleagues finished the process with newly aroused interest in economic modernization that placed priority on Japanese investment and Official Development Assistance (ODA). By the beginning of the 1980s China seemed to be in precisely the position of South Korea in the 1960s, ready for a long period of economic dependence where a government anxious about its legitimacy and lacking foreign policy options would be careful not to revisit agreements that had allowed Japan to overcome its past aggression. While some emotional outbursts could not be excluded, national interests centered on economics and security favored Japan's strategy of waiting as war memories faded with the older generation, and seizing additional opportunities as they arose, reflecting its enormous economic advantage.[5]

In 1983–84 this strategy seemed to be working well. Prime Minister Yasuhiro Nakasone transformed what were formal but distant ties through personal meetings with Chun Doo-hwan in Seoul and Tokyo and Hu Yaobang in Beijing and Tokyo. The logic for Chun was much as it had been for Park, an urgent need for an infusion of assistance and capital in part to raise his legitimacy after the suppression of democratic activity. For Hu economic objectives were important too, but he was also prepared to develop exchanges and build trust in the younger generation. In new circumstances, each of these leaders aroused opposition. Chun would not long be able to restrain the advancing social forces calling for democracy, who found his fuller political reconciliation with Japan one move that could be exploited in the battle for public opinion. Hu was more vulnerable, serving at the discretion of Deng Xiaoping as well as other party elders and suspect not only for being too soft on Japan but also for various liberal transgressions. If Nakasone and other LDP conservative leaders prematurely concluded that they had reached a breakthrough in normalization and now had the economic clout and political influence to approach the history issue in a bolder manner, symbolized by Nakasone's visit to the Yasukuni Shrine in 1985, they underestimated the backlash building among the public in China and South Korea. Student demonstrations with a decidedly critical outlook on Japan set in motion a process that toppled Hu, and much more wide-ranging demonstrations in which Japan was not at all in the forefront forced Chun to step down, bringing to power governments beholden to the electorate and, thus, unlikely to cut a favorable deal with Japan without much greater attention to the public's historical sensitivities.[6]

The normalization process was, on the surface, a great success for those Japanese who wanted to preserve freedom of action to revisit the legacy issues of wartime defeat. In the mid-1980s Japanese leaders and politicians were emboldened by the country's strong position in Northeast and Southeast Asia. Domestic opposition was marginalized by the way the Cold War was ending, and conservative forces in the LDP were gaining ground that could free them to proceed with a long-stymied agenda. Yet, few recognized that developments in Asia would reveal that behind the facade of normalization troubling cracks were opening. Instead of anticipating the problems ahead and taking advantage of the most favorable environment of bubble economy prosperity and U.S. alliance security, the leaders of Japan squandered their chance to face its problems from a position of strength. If they retreated somewhat in confronting critics abroad and at home, this only postponed taking action on their agenda until Japan's indispensability had grown or, as in fact happened, a growing sense of threat allowed leaders more leeway to boost national pride.

China and South Korea remained in an abnormal state through the mid-1980s. Public opinion was suppressed. Recent rejection of past orthodoxy about national identity had not yet yielded to clarity about a more internationalized identity with a different lens for what deserves recognition as the nation's essence. One-sided foreign policy focused on coping with an enemy was only slowly shifting to greater flexibility in great power relations. Instead of anticipating how these states might look anew at them, Japanese saw prospects ahead that would give their state no less leverage in dealing with history as one bilateral issue of many.[7] Others supposedly needed Japan more than it needed them; it would soon be free from pressure to reinterpret the past and pursue nationalism as desired. Such reasoning could be clearly seen in the response to the Soviet Union at a time when its transformation loomed as the most important matter facing the global community.[8] Missed opportunities amidst emboldened ambitions were a sign of what lay ahead.[9] Behind the facade of normalized relations lurked levels of distrust at a high level in the neighbors of Japan and disguised plans incubating among many in Japan's political elite.

ANNIVERSARY REMEMBRANCES AFTER THE COLD WAR

With the end of the Cold War opportunities increased to reach new understandings about historical issues. Each of the three civilian, democratically elected presidents of South Korea took office with the intention of upgrading relations with Japan, including reaching at least a tacit agreement on how to keep emotions related to history in check. Deng Xiaoping and those to whom he delegated power, including Jiang Zemin, spent the first half of 1992 urging Japan to set a date for sending the Emperor to China for the first time. Jiang Zemin may have unleashed more negative feelings toward Japan, but in 1999 he was part of the leadership consensus behind "smile diplomacy" to keep emotions under control. When Hu Jintao took office as party secretary he okayed the publication of a few unprecedented articles calling for "new thinking" toward Japan, as reports spread that he put priority on improving relations.[10] Even North Korea was involved in 1990 when it gave Japan's leaders reason to believe that rapid normalization of relations would bring a deal on history consistent with what Japan had approved previously, and again in the response to Junichiro Koizumi's September 2002 visit where a tentative understanding on history was reported. Of course, China's interest rose at the beginning of the 1990s when it was isolated by international sanctions after the Tiananmen massacre, South Korea's when it was subject to IMF restrictions after the Asian financial crisis, and North Korea's at times of great international pressure when there was no direct route to normalization of ties with the United States.[11] Yet, even if enthusiasm for a breakthrough with Japan (including history) was inconsistently expressed, numerous chances emerged to seek long-term solutions. Repeatedly searching for breakthroughs, the Japanese neglected to take historical reconciliation seriously, waiting instead for historical amnesia by others.

Many in Japan embraced the goal of putting history behind them, but that does not mean their notions of becoming a "normal country" and "reentering Asia" realistically responded to the rapidly changing realities in the region. In 1992 false expectations about the Emperor's trip to China made it seem that the history question could be removed from Sino-Japanese relations regardless of how limited the apology he offered or what doubts lingered in the Chinese public's minds. In 1998 exuberant claims about the significance of the historical reconciliation reached with Kim Dae-jung again spread the word that the issue had been completely settled regardless of what Japanese leaders said about the past in the future.[12] Even in the more unsettled talks with North Korea, commentaries on the September 2002 Joint Communiqué with Kim Jong-il took as a given indications that a deal would be struck inclusive of resolving the history issue, allowing all attention to turn to the abductions issue over the following years without weighing its importance relative to North Korean claims about losses during the 35 years of Japan's occupation. Instead of defining "normal" in a manner that meant reaching a fuller understanding about the past with Japan's victims, it became identified with more aggressively objecting to their views and insisting that there was no longer anything to discuss. Japanese came to perceive talk about the past as the "history card" insincerely manipulated by political leaders abroad rather than the unsettled sentiments of the public abroad from resolutions of important issues left incomplete.

Earlier conditions of one-sided dependence on Japan were receding rapidly. Thus, the strategy of buying silence or counting on U.S. ties to create a favorable environment for silence no longer had prospects of success. The urgent search for additional outside support in the face of a serious threat no longer drove countries to Japan's door. China's national identity had shifted from an isolated, embattled state obsessed with keeping its socialist system to a successful market economy confident of its future in a multipolar global system, albeit still sensitive about criticisms of its socialist political system and inclined to boost patriotism through recollections of historical struggles. South Korean national identity also was greatly transformed. It enjoyed the legitimacy of democratic elections and economic achievement and was turning to great power leverage rather than dependency, as well as reunification, in defining its national goals. Public opinion, newly expressed on the Internet as well as in demonstrations, could no longer be bypassed in efforts to find shortcuts for overcoming differences over history. The fact that Japan's past strategies were of no further use, except with North Korea, warranted rethinking what might work, but the temptation existed just to blame other nations for manipulating memories without taking seriously the challenge of understanding what had changed.

Easy answers satisfied some Japanese observers. Unpopular leaders supposedly pressed the history button to rally a populist outcry, as when Chinese demonstrators took to the streets of Shanghai and other cities in April 2005 at a time of spreading protests in other parts of the state by various disadvantaged groups.[13] The assumption spread that the leadership wanted to divert their attention. Likewise, when Roh Moo-hyun lashed out against Japan starting from March 2005, some Japanese attributed it to his low popularity ratings at home. Demagoguery to deceive the masses rather than statesmanship in leading one's nation became a staple of media explanations of why the history issue kept reappearing abroad. In 2007 many in Japan continued to propagate the notion of Roh and other Koreans as "anti-Japanese" (hannichi) and of an anti-Japanese lobby now reaching across to the United States.[14] Ad hoc interpretations of how values and misperceptions figure into bilateral relations substituted for systematic analysis of how culture influences foreign relations.

Eventually, a hopeful approach to value changes gained popularity against the background of George W. Bush's stress on democratization transforming the world. It was an updated version of modernization theory that emphasized the spread of middle-class values bringing Asia together. If Japan could not escape the accusations of nearby countries over its revival of the history issue, it could change the subject to

concentrate on the failure of China to democratize and the potential serious consequences for regional stability. The gap would keep widening between the aspirations
of a middle-class society in coastal China and across much of Asia, and the autocratic
governance to which leaders often clung. To keep the pressure on China, Foreign
Minister Taro Aso called for an arc of freedom and prosperity along its borders. While
there was much merit in arguments that recognized the spread of middle-class values,
it was hard to avoid accusations of hypocrisy when Prime Minister Shinzo Abe in
early 2007 appeared to deny government responsibility for what others estimate to
have been 200,000 "comfort women" serving as sex slaves to Japanese soldiers in the
war while making the abductions of perhaps 15 to 25 Japanese citizens by North
Korea in the years around 1980 central to his foreign policy. When in July 2007 first
the U.S. House of Representatives passed the Honda resolution critical of Japan's handling of sex slaves, and then Japan's Upper House elections brought a stunning defeat
to the LDP and Abe's emphasis on nationalism as the defining theme in politics, the
values issue no longer seemed to offer the same political boost.[15] .

Anniversaries of memorable historical events occurred with great frequency, first
embraced as a chance to improve ties and then left to fester as a missed opportunity.
Often they appeared in plans for improving relations, capitalizing on commemorations to boost mutual understanding of how much had been achieved in the inter-
vening years or how well they could acknowledge that the past would not be
repeated. Yet, increasingly these chronological markers were viewed with dread rather
than with anticipation. Many passed without the anticipated joint understanding,
such as 1995 and 2005, the 50th and 60th anniversaries of the end of the war. The
confidence that led leaders to plan for commemorative events was receding; they
increasingly just hoped to get past the milestone without another serious setback to
bilateral relations.

In China the apparent vacuum in national identity of the 1980s turned into a
rising consensus by the mid-1990s that still held for many in 2007. It equated
communism with maintaining unity, expanding international influence, and developing the economy to the benefit of the people's livelihood as well as the state's
capacity.[16] It was only natural that the Chinese Communist Party would recall, on
the 50th anniversary of the end of the war with Japan, the conflict that brought it
to the fore as the champion of national unity and the harshest critic of imperialist
repression in the years of struggle against that country. In such circumstances, Japan
could have reinforced an image disassociating its pre-1945 militarist behavior from
its postwar democratic and peaceful orientation. Cultivating an image of a new
nation that disavows its past, even joining Chinese in repudiating some of the
excesses, specifically and with great fanfare, Japan had a good opportunity to make
a fresh start. China's patriotic education movement would have revived memories
of the past, but they would have seemed distant and largely irrelevant to recent
times.[17] Instead, Japanese officials made two serious mistakes for reducing the role
of history in bilateral ties. First, through contradictory messages and inflammatory
statements, they did more to make the past appear relevant than did Chinese leaders.
Second, they one-sidedly laid the blame on the Chinese government for deliberately

arousing a disinterested public against Japan by playing the "history card" to gain an advantage in current relations. Although there was truth to this accusation, it was a self-serving distraction; without any such campaign Japanese conduct would almost certainly have had the same consequences. Indeed, the South Korean people, with less historical justification or evidence of government manipulation (after all the political opposition on the left and the right kept criticizing the leadership for its weakness in responding to Japanese provocations), were also vehement in denouncing the way Japan was handling historical questions.

South Korean reactions were a kind of barometer for measuring the impact of changes in Japan on victims' sensitivities. After Kim Young-sam in 1993–94 showed that he was more forthcoming in improving ties with Japan than any other leader since 1945, his hopes were dashed and for roughly two years a wave of anti-Japanese clamor spread. Instead of the anniversary in 1995 becoming a time of healing, it brought mass arousal to a new peak. Even more committed to improving bilateral ties in all respects was Kim Dae-jung, whose sincerity was eagerly welcomed at the historic summit in October 1998. Yet, in 2001 at a time when speculation was rife that the Emperor might visit Seoul for the opening ceremony of the World Cup in 2002, new middle-school textbooks in Japan rekindled Korean anger over historical matters. A similar scenario played out in 2005 after Roh Moo-hyun had spent two years striving to put bilateral ties on a positive track, agreeing to twice-a-year shuttle summit diplomacy and overlooking the annual Yasukuni Shrine visits of Koizumi. Yet, his restraint drew little appreciation, and the decision by Shimane prefecture to establish an annual "Takeshima Day" proved to be the last straw before Roh lashed out against Japan's handling of history.[18] Three successive Korean leaders and even Hu Jintao in 2002 had come to power with signals about upgrading the ties between their country and Japan only to be thwarted by provocative moves.

NORMALIZATION WITH NORTH KOREA AS A GATEWAY TO REGIONALISM

After the failure of the Koizumi visit to Pyongyang in September 2002, Abe rode the abductions issue to popularity and selection as the next prime minister in September 2006. Over this four year period in the shadow of Koizumi's defiant annual visits to the Yasukuni Shrine and George W. Bush's demonization of North Korea and its leader Kim Jong-il (already labeled part of the "axis of evil" in January 2002), the Japanese recast the struggle over values in Northeast Asia in a new light. Having long been seen as pragmatists or "economic animals," they were assumed not to put much weight on human rights. Sympathetic to arguments about Asian values during the 1990s, many Japanese distanced themselves from U.S. "fundamentalism" that had failed to take into account the greater role of the state in Asian development and the need for a gradual transition toward democratization. On Burma in 1988, China in 1989, and East Timor in 1999—to note just some regional examples—Japan's leaders and media showed concern for injustices, but they also cast doubt about U.S. "overreactions" that were likely to be ineffective in comparison to Japan's less punitive responses.[19] All of this changed when the spot-light shifted to North Korea at the same time as the history issue confounded ties with China.

For four years Japan's worldview solidified around how to deal with a changing Asia. It rested on four pillars: (1) abductions of innocent Japanese going about their daily lives are matters of the highest priority, bringing values to the forefront in foreign affairs; (2) in the competition with a rising China, Japan is correct to play the "democratic values" card; (3) in response to other countries violating Japanese sovereignty or inculcating anti-Japanese sentiments, Japan must assertively stand its own ground and retaliate; and (4) it is time for the revival of moral education with the goal of patriotic belief in a "beautiful Japan." The vilification of North Korea, especially from 2004, served this worldview well.

In 2007 this combination of values assertiveness reached an impasse. The turning point may have been as early as October 2006 when all four pillars were shaken. Just when Japan's leaders were confident that their strategy was working, events under-mined it. Starting his tenure with high popularity, Abe left ambiguous whether he would visit the Yasukuni Shrine and, thus, was welcomed in Beijing as the first stop in his travels as prime minister and then proceeded to Seoul, where he also could claim success. At little cost to his nationalist agenda, he seemed to have put relations with Japan's two leading critics back on track. This supposed high point in overcom-ing the history issue, however, was instead the swan song in imagining that the strat-egy of recent years was effective.

As Abe was traveling, North Korea tested a nuclear weapon. China and South Korea expressed anger, and it appeared that they were drawing closer to the United States and Japan in their readiness to exert pressure on the North. Japan led the way in introducing a resolution calling for sanctions in the UN Security Council, as the public took pride in this principled leadership stance as well as in the diplo-matic success that came when a somewhat less punitive resolution was passed unani-mously. Yet, as the focus in the crisis unmistakably became the nuclear threat, events in the world and the region did not support the leaders' attempts to give credence to their newly coalescing worldview.

In the first months of 2007, it proved difficult to keep the spotlight on abducted Japanese who were suspected of being held even if possibly all had died after decades of forced residence in North Korea. Through this lens the Japanese media had over-shadowed the history issue, portraying the Japanese nation as innocent victims rather than as depraved perpetrators of crimes against humanity. Showing little interest in any transgressions that might have been committed against the Korean people during 35 years of colonial rule, and even claiming that Japan's rule deserves to be seen as benevolent and accepted by the Korean people (two years before becoming foreign minister, Aso spoke on the eve of Roh Moo-hyun's first summit with Koizumi of the Korean people voluntarily forsaking their Korean names for Japanese names), the media wrote with great frequency and emotionalism about the abduction issue. Leaders pressed their counterparts in the Six-Party Talks to make resolution of this issue to Japan's satisfaction a precondition for rewarding the North no matter what concessions it made on its nuclear weapons program. Yet, this approach stumbled before the new urgency to deal with the nuclear danger once a weapon had already been tested. In addition, an uproar arose when Abe seemed to indicate an intention to rescind the 1993 Kono statement that acknowledged the role of the Japanese government in abducting girls and women in Korea and many other states to serve as sexual slaves for the Japanese troops. For the victim nations of Japan's wartime policies this issue trumped the abduction issue, and in the United States the prolonged 2007 House of Representatives debate over the "comfort women" brought the history issue to the foreground even in U.S.-Japanese relations.

Intensified cooperation between China and the United States after North Korea's nuclear test cast new doubt on Japan's strategy of pressuring China while stressing democratic values as the foundation of regional cooperation. Already Abe's visit to China in October had removed the onus on Chinese leaders for refusing to hold summit meetings due to the Yasukuni visits. Rather than appearing unreasonably stubborn in holding bilateral ties hostage to the history issue, China could portray itself as pragmatically committed to a stable relationship by compromising without demanding that Abe promise not to make a visit there as prime minister. Moreover, in the Six-Party Talks China resumed its role as moderator under the new circumstances of four countries working closely together to test North Korea's willingness, in stages with strong incentives, to denuclearize. Only Japan did not pledge to provide some of the one million tons of heavy fuel oil in two stages over the year 2007 as reward for first closing the Yongbyon nuclear reactor under inspection by the IAEA and then disabling it. Attention shifted from China's narrow focus on history in refusing to meet Japan's prime minister to Japan's narrow focus on abductions in isolating itself from the negotiating consensus in Northeast Asia. China had cleverly put the burden on Japan as right-wingers reacted in frustration to Wen Jiabao's visit in April 2007 with accusations that Japan was being tricked by China's "smile diplomacy."[20]

After the Shenyang incident of 2002, when Chinese police removed North Korean refugees seeking asylum in the Japanese consulate with disputed acquiescence by Japan's diplomats, a mood spread across Japan of assertively defending national sovereignty from territorial claims to supposed entitlements in regional and international organizations. By 2005 the Koizumi cabinet had grown more cautious about regionalism, fearing that China in ASEAN+3 or elsewhere would gain the leading role and marginalize Japan's status. The antidote was more inclusive and functionally limited regionalism, such as the East Asian Summit with Australia, New Zealand, and India included. It also meant stronger support for U.S. inclusion in regional entities. Koizumi also pressed for Japan to become a permanent member of the Security Council, befitting its hefty contribution to the UN budget and its economic prowess. In these conditions, Japan was not inclined to approach its neighbors strategically in order to quiet emotions over history, but instead it allowed territorial disputes to fester. During this time Shimane prefecture declared a "Takeshima Day" in defiance of Korea's existing control and nationalist sentiments over Dokdo, and the Ministry of Economy, Trade, and Industry reacted to China's drilling for gas in the East China Sea near the disputed economic zone boundary as an infringement on sovereignty. In the heat of the nuclear crisis when coordination in handling North Korea's bellicose conduct, which was likely to make Japan the primary target, should have brought maximal efforts to draw the region closer together, Japan's leaders were divisively inciting the two countries with the most leverage against North Korea in their handling of matters symbolic of historical misconduct.

During the 1980s, Japanese national identity became intertwined with *Nihonjin-ron* literature that exaggerated what makes this country exceptional and cast doubt on global forces that would internationalize the Japanese people, for instance through tolerance for a more heterogeneous society. Still predominant was strong identification with the West, and the struggle against the threat of Soviet communism or a single international community. The Japanese took pride in their country's superior record of democratization and political stability, postwar economic growth and equality, developmental assistance to poorer states and the success of some economically, support for the United Nations and its peace-enhancing principles, and internationalization of their society without great loss of valued attributes of harmony and cohesion. The failed policies in Asia that led to defeat as well as rejection in 1945 had been increasingly eclipsed by a positive postwar identity. Yet, the lingering division between the ascendant political right and the tenacious political left and the failure to fill the vacuum left by avoiding discussion of the lessons from the era of colonialism left a fragile postwar national identity that proved vulnerable in the 1990s.

After the collapse of the bubble economy and the dashing of hopes for leadership in the post–Cold War era, the Japanese struggled with issues of national identity. Attempting to fill the void were politicians and media who turned the history issue on its head, insisting that a "beautiful" Japan required patriotism based on a more positive evaluation of the war experience. As Abe rode emotions over the North Korean abductions issue to power, he brought with him an agenda to rewrite textbook remarks that criticized Japan's past conduct, deal more assertively with the sensitivities of neighboring countries, and change the verdict in important respects on how the period 1930–45 is evaluated in Japan. Yet, in 2007, Sino-U.S. cooperation on North Korea and China's eagerness for better relations with Japan left Japanese advocates of this revisionist agenda on the defensive. For some it was time to challenge the United States as well to keep this agenda alive, but the case for a more isolated Japan in the Six-Party Talks and beyond would be difficult to make. If nationalism for a time seemed to stand in the way of regionalism,[21] the pendulum was swinging back in 2007, as the November Singapore ASEAN+3 meeting renewed the call for establishing an East Asian Community and Prime Minister Yasuo Fukuda made a warm visit to China.

CONCLUSION

Franziska Seraphim depicts the 1990s as a "radically changed and changing environment in which war memories seemed up for grabs." Instead of 1995 serving to place a marker on the end of an era after a string of unprecedented apologies by

Japan's leaders, she concludes that the 50th anniversary process left "enormous damage done by the preceding political controversies."[22] War memories had acquired a very different meaning in Japan from those held by victim states now entering an era of competition for political leadership in a multipolar Asia. Tsuyoshi Hasegawa notes that "the memory of the Pacific War still remains a divisive contemporary issue among Asian nations." He calls it "hotly contested terrain,"[23] focusing more on how the war ended than on what is even more controversial: why it was fought and what is the appropriate way to reach consensus in various nations on how to characterize its excesses and its meaning for regional history. The victimizer and the victims were artificially separated through much of the Cold War era, but now they face each other without intermediaries and with much less inclination on either side of the divide to put aside the issue of history. Kazuhiko Togo observes that, despite various apologies by Japanese leaders, the Japanese nation still has not resolved who bears responsibility for those excesses. Japan even faces questions about what identity— one that links past and present—is best applied to their own nation, and he warns that future generations will be left with this task if the current generation does not address them.[24]

A growing literature on Japan's "rise" from the 1990s as a multidimensional great power struggled with the challenge of putting nationalist ideology in this context. For some this was a side show of minor significance against the larger drama of a state at last recognizing its "realist" imperative in an uncertain world, in the process becoming more responsible in addressing international threats and potential threats.[25] Others, however, paid close attention to "revisionist" tendencies as driving forces for the decisions being made about possible strategic partners in the midst of books suggesting that Americans had a distorted image of Japan's war and patriotism and appreciating that what is truly in the national interest depends on a revised view of history as well as a more assertive foreign policy.[26] Given the burst of nationalist writings blaming others for anti-Japanese sentiments and the popularity of such views among politicians,[27] one may wonder how much of what are called "realist" responses are actually driven by "revisionist thinking." New books are appearing that glorify all of Japanese history from the Meiji era to the Koizumi period as one continuous stream of just motives in response to evil enemies.[28]

In 2006 almost five times as many Japanese males did not feel friendly toward China as felt friendly, more than two Japanese over age 50 did not feel friendly toward South Korea for every one who did, and more than 20 times as many Japanese females felt unfriendly toward Russia as those who felt friendly.[29] These are but some of the most striking examples of antagonism in the overall record of distrust of neighboring states that shows little sign of lessening. In turn, Japanese in the Koizumi period, with those over age 60 in the lead, showed growing support of the need for more upbringing focused on patriotic feelings.[30]

Kenneth Pyle argues that "Feudal Japan was an 'honor-ridden society'," and he observes that the "Heisei generation" is now insistent about asserting its own identity in international society in order to "rise in the international hierarchy of prestige and to establish its national dignity."[31] Yet, he treats this as a means of regaining the country's voice when, in fact, it was on a path to raise its influence in the early Heisei years and still was making strategic choices that flexibly explored its options until Koizumi took office and damaged relations with the states that are Japan's closest neighbors.

Given both the dangers in the Islamic world that could threaten the world's supply of oil and spur more terrorist acts such as the September 11, 2001 bombings in the United States and the destabilizing impact of nuclear weapons development in North Korea, it may be difficult to understand Japan's preoccupation with overturning historical verdicts. One explanation is that it became easier to do so, given the open-ended commitment of the Bush administration in its eagerness for support from Japanese leaders. Another is that the Japanese were so unprepared for the sudden rise of insecurity in their environment that many fell back on extreme thinking rooted in unqualified reassurance about merits in their own country, past and present. A third is that network linkages and respect for Asian neighbors had been left so underdeveloped or superficial in previous decades amidst preoccupation with views of Japan in the West, that it proved quite easy to step back and pursue a different approach toward Asia. A fourth factor is that democratic politics and education have fallen so short in facing challenging foreign policy issues that few Japanese insisted on weighing the strategic options of a crisis situation rather than embracing simplistic reasoning. Whatever the explanation, there is no basis for optimism that narrow, emotional thinking about Japan's past actions in Asia and its indifference toward reassuring the nations that had been victimized are advancing in the direction of reconciliation.

The environment was less favorable for revisionism from the summer of 2007. The first phase of the Six-Party Talks ended satisfactorily with further talks anticipated. U.S. policy in East Asia had become more pragmatic, as the United States and China collaborated on the North Korean issue. China remained committed to improved ties with Japan. With South Korea preparing for a presidential election, Japanese could find hope that another leader would give priority to improving relations. As Abe's popularity fell sharply over domestic issues other than nationalism, he lacked public support to move aggressively on a controversial agenda even if the fundamental differences over history that had intensified since the 1990s had not been addressed. The path forward remained far from clear when Yasuo Fukuda replaced Abe. Yet, in November 2007 after visiting Washington to try to fortify the alliance against new uncertainties, Fukuda went to Singapore for the ASEAN+3 and East Asian Summit gatherings, showing renewed interest in regionalism. He supported a joint declaration of ASEAN+3 setting a schedule for a second stage of cooperation in forging an East Asian Community, and then agreed with the leaders of China and South Korea on upgrading triangular cooperation even to the point of scheduling three-way summits apart from the ASEAN context. With its new pragmatism Japan seemed to be moving away from nationalistic posturing, even with the possibility that this would extend to the abductions issue with North Korea.

The unrealized agenda of the stage of normalization continues to haunt efforts aimed at mutual understanding. As years of commemoration passed one by one, prospects for celebration are fading amidst expanding dread that they will only exacerbate current animosities. The quest for regionalism and a regional security mechanism that can help to stabilize East Asia stumbles before not only the legacy of history but also new efforts to reinterpret history in ways that are offensive to Japan's neighbors. Yet, the electorate's resounding repudiation of the LDP in the Upper House elections of July 2007 changed the tone of discussion. Fukuda showed his support for closer relations with China in a visit there on December 28–30, 2007. Two months later at the inauguration of Lee Myung-bak as president of South Korea the two leaders pledged to renew shuttle summitry twice a year and move beyond the history issue. Although the fundamentals of party politics and international relations had not changed, Japan had a favorable climate to prevent the history issue from reigniting.

With Fukuda's calming influence and Sino-U.S. cooperation—above all in the Six-Party Talks—serving to maintain stability, a new crisis over history seemed unlikely to arise. Yet, the explosive potential of revisionist nationalism in Japan remains. It may take a crisis of a new kind to serve as a wake-up call, arousing the political center in Japan to look anew at neighboring countries and the weight of history in the context of ongoing challenges. One possibility is that the revisionists in Japan will go so far as to provoke a reaction in the United States, turning the battle over history into a test of this alliance. In 2007 there were signs that this was beginning, as discussions intensified over the U.S. role in the comfort women issue and even in the way the war ended in August 1945. Another possibility is that realist alarm over North Korean weapons of mass destruction or Japan's isolation in the Six-Party Talks will intensify, crowding out revisionist efforts to take charge of this issue. A crisis atmosphere may bring a sobering shift toward realism, but it could also produce the opposite result as loss of trust in the U.S. could lead to a more independent foreign policy and to even less restraint in interpretations of history. It remains to be seen if Koizumi and Abe will stand out as an aberration as later leaders revive the cooperative approach to Asia common in the 1990s, or if their precedents will become the basis for more assertive leadership toward history and, at the same time, toward neighbors in Asia.

NOTES

1. Gilbert Rozman, "Can Confucianism Survive in an Age of Universalism and Globalization?" *Pacific Affairs* 75, no. 1 (Spring 2002): 11–37.

2. Alexis Dudden, *Japan's Colonization of Korea: Discourse and Power* (Honolulu: University of Hawaii Press, 2005).

3. Kimiya Tadashi, "1960 nendai Kankoku ni okeru reisen gaiko no san ruikei: Nikkan kokkyo seijoka, Betonamu happei, ASPAC," in *Shijo, kokka, kokusai taisei*, ed. Okonogi Masao and Moon Chung-in (Tokyo: Keio daigaku shuppankai, 2001), pp. 96–105.

4. Go Ito, *Alliance in Anxiety: Détente and the Sino-American-Japanese Triangle* (New York: Routledge, 2003).

5. Gilbert Rozman, "Japan's Images of China in the 1990s: Are They Ready for China's 'Smile Diplomacy' or Bush's 'Strong Diplomacy'?" *Japanese Journal of Political Science* 2, no. 1 (May 2001): 97–125.

6. Gilbert Rozman, "China's Changing Images of Japan 1989–2001: The Struggle to Balance Partnership and Rivalry," *International Relations of the Asia-Pacific* 2, no.1 (Winter 2002):95–129; Gilbert Rozman, "South Korean Strategic Thought toward Japan," in *Korean Strategic Thought toward Asia* ed. Gilbert Rozman, In-Taek Hyun, and Shin-wha Lee (New York: Palgrave, 2008).

7. Victor Cha, *Alignment Despite Antagonism: The US-Korea-Japan Security Triangle* (Stanford: Stanford University Press, 1999).

8. Gilbert Rozman, *Japan's Response to the Gorbachev Era, 1985–1991: A Rising Superpower Views a Declining One* (Princeton University Press, 1992).

9. Gilbert Rozman, Kazuhiko Togo, and Joseph P. Ferguson, eds., *Japanese Strategic Thought toward Asia* (New York: Palgrave, 2007).

10. Danielle F.S. Cohen, *Retracing the Triangle: China's Strategic Perceptions of Japan in the Post-Cold War Era,* Maryland Series in Contemporary Asian Studies, No. 2-2005 (Baltimore: University of Maryland, School of Law: 2005).

11. Gilbert Rozman, "Japan's North Korean Initiative and U.S.-Japanese Relations," *Orbis* 47, no. 3 (Summer 2003): 527–39.

12. Sang-woo Rhee and Tae-hyo Kim, eds., *Korea-Japan Security Relations: Prescriptive Studies* (Seoul: New Age Research Institute, 2000).

13. Ming Wan, *Sino-Japanese Relations: Interaction, Logic, and Transformation* (Stanford: Stanford University Press, 2006).

14. Kuroda Katsuhiro, "Shijo saiaku no hannichi daitoryo Roh Moo-hyun," *WILL* (May 2007):104–12; "Hannichi robi o hikiiru Kankokukei josei no seijiryoku no gensen," *Foresight* (May 2007):91.

15. Tanaka Akihiko, "Iu wa yasuku okonau wa kataki 'kachikan gaiko,'" *Foresight* (July 2007):27.

16. Gilbert Rozman, "China's Quest for Great Power Identity," *Orbis* 43, no. 3 (Summer 1999): 383–402.

17. Peter Hays Gries, *China's New Nationalism: Pride, Politics, and Diplomacy* (Berkeley: University of California Press, 2004).

18. Gilbert Rozman, "South Korean Strategic Thought toward Japan,"chapter 8 in *South Korean Strategic Thought toward Asia.*

19. Gilbert Rozman, "Japan's Quest for Great Power Identity," *Orbis* 46, no. 1 (Winter 2002):73–91.

20. Okada Hidehiro, "Nihonjin yo, Chugoku no bisho gaiko ni damasareru na," *WILL* (June 2007):38–43.

21. Gi-wook Shin and Daniel C. Sneider, eds., *Cross Currents: Regionalism and Nationalism in Northeast Asia* (Stanford: The Walter H. Shorenstein Asia-Pacific Research Center, Stanford University, 2007).

22. Franziska Seraphim, *War Memory and Social Politics in Japan, 1945–2005,* East Asian Monographs 278 (Cambridge, MA: Harvard, 2006), pp. 280, 301.

23. Tsuyoshi Hasegawa, "Introduction," in *The End of the Pacific War: Reappraisals* ed. Tsuyoshi Hasegawa (Stanford: Stanford University Press, 2007), p. 2.

24. Togo Kazuhiko, "Kokumin no te de senso sokatsu o—samonakuba sekinin o sedai o koe hikitsugareru," in Bungei shunju, *Nihon no ronten 2007* (Tokyo: Bungei shunju, 2006), pp. 236–39.

25. Michael J. Green: *Japan's Reluctant Realism: Foreign Policy Challenges in an Era of Uncertain Power* (New York: Palgrave, 2001).

26. Tato Takahama, *Amerika no rekishi kyokasho ga oshieru Nihon no senso* (Tokyo: Asukomu, 2003); Tahara Soichiro, ed., *Aikokushin, kokueki to wa nanika?* (Tokyo: Asukomu, 2004).

27. Mizutani Naoko, *"Hannichi" kaibo: Yuganda Chugoku no "aikoku"* (Tokyo: Bungei shunju, 2005); Torii Tami, *"Hannichi" de ikinobiru Chugoku* (Tokyo: Soshisha, 2004); Okazaki Hisahiko, *Naze Nihonjin wa Kankokujin ga kirai nanoka?* (Tokyo: WAC bunko, 2006).

28. Watanabe Shoichi, *Nihon kingendaishi* (Tokyo: Kairyusha, 2004).

29. "Gaiko ni kansuru yoron chosa," *Gekkan yoron chosa* (May 2006):24, 28, 32.

30. "Shakai ishiki ni kansuru yoron chosa," *Gekkan yoron chosa* (October 2006):53–54.

31. Kenneth B. Pyle, *Japan Rising: The Resurgence of Japanese Power and Purpose* (New York: Public Affairs, 2007), pp. 63, 373–74.

3

Japan's Historical Memory: Overcoming Polarization toward Synthesis

Kazuhiko Togo

Even over 60 years since the end of the Second World War, memories of it still linger heavily in Japan. It affects important parts of Japanese domestic policy as well as relations with important neighbors such as China and South Korea. Views inside Japan are polarized on all issues related to the memory of war. Why is this polarization happening? What concrete issues still need to be addressed? Is Japan overcoming this internal split or is it drifting toward further polarization? Is the rupture with China and Korea being mended, or is the rift getting worse? These are the issues that I would like to examine in this chapter.

WHY IS HISTORICAL MEMORY HAUNTING JAPAN?

In order to understand the polarization that is happening now in Japan, we need to go back to the nature of World War II and its total defeat in 1945. Japan had fought fiercely against the United States and the Allies until its capitulation. Kamikaze pilots sacrificed their lives. Japan began the war with the slogan "Beat the Americans and the British who are the devil and the beast" and ended it with "One hundred million are ready to die." Yet, when the occupation began, there was no resistance against it. The U.S. occupation forces were generally warmly received. If one considers the bitterness with which the war was fought, Japan's adaptation to the new era was astonishingly smooth and swift. How could it happen?

For the first time in its history, Japan was defeated and occupied by foreign troops. This defeat aroused a huge shock and created a spiritual vacuum among the Japanese people. It was not just a simple military defeat. Japan lost all the territories it had accumulated from the Meiji Restoration until 1945. It also meant the loss of deep-seated values in which the Japanese people believed.

Many people felt that there was something wrong in the way all of Japan was mobilized and fully absorbed to fight that total war. The totalitarian mechanism had created a top-down system of oppression and engendered an inhuman, inefficient, irresponsible, and sometimes cruel system. After the defeat, many people were relieved by the disappearance of that totalitarian oppression. They saw new breathing space to begin a new life. In academic circles and through the media, intellectuals and opinion leaders immediately began a process of soul-searching, questioning why Japan lost the war, and their views greatly influenced public opinion.[1] A reappraisal of democratic thinking, which had achieved the establishment of the Meiji Constitution and the Taisho democracy, underpinned this new trend. The questioning eventually developed from "Where did we go wrong to lose the war?" to "What did we do wrong vis-à-vis those whom we fought, in particular, the people of Asia?"

The occupation lasted from 1945 to 1952. The occupation forces, largely led by the United States, arrived with the intention of creating an entirely new Japan, an example of peaceful democracy, which would never harm U.S. interests in the Asia Pacific region. Demilitarization, democratization, and decentralization became the major policy directions.

The occupation had several distinct characteristics. First, Japan's basic governmental structures were preserved and U.S. occupation policy was carried out through the existing Japanese government. Imperial tradition was preserved to maintain order and continuity from the past. The new Constitution established new values of peace and democracy, but retained the emperor as the symbol of the nation.

Second, the Cold War affected not only the international situation but also the political situation inside Japan. U.S. leaders expected Japan, as a pacified democracy in the Far East, to play a vanguard role in the fight for democracy and against communism in Asia. A new economic policy, initiated from around 1948, emphasized a quick and powerful recovery, and it slowed down dissolution of the *zaibatsu,* which had created the economic might of prewar Japan. Finally, the Yoshida Doctrine placed economic reconstruction as the first and foremost national priority and laid the foundations for Japan's alliance with the United States, both of which matched well with the new direction under the Cold War.

Third, prewar leaders purged from public functions were gradually allowed to return to power and they began to join the reconstruction of the country. The most symbolic example was Mamoru Shigemitsu. Shigemitsu was sentenced to seven years of imprisonment as a Class-A war criminal, but after Japan regained its independence, he became Japan's first foreign minister, who attended the UN Plenary Session in 1956.

In these ways, Japan adapted to its defeat, the occupation, and the rise of the Cold War. A remarkable degree of continuity was preserved from the prewar period in terms of the postwar political structure, governmental personnel, and economic structures. But this continuity blurred the distinction between the prewar and the postwar periods, eventually leading to a shift from questioning "Where did we go wrong to lose the war?" to "Was everything Japan did before the war wrong?" The seeds for future polarization on historical memory were thus well implanted from the early postwar years.

But while the seeds for a sharp split in the future were already planted then, the occupation period brought two distinctive conclusions on prewar Japan that Japan accepted as a nation. Although opinion leaders, intellectuals, and politicians have subsequently seriously questioned these two conclusions, they have never been repudiated by subsequent administrations and will remain the principle of the government policy for the foreseeable future.

The first conclusion is that Japan accepts the 1948 judgments of the International Military Tribunal for the Far East (IMTFE). Altogether 25 Class-A war criminals were found guilty, mostly for crimes against peace for having waged and conspired in the war of aggression, and for conventional war crimes, namely responsibility for allowing or failing to prevent atrocities. Those found guilty of conventional military crimes were primarily charged as Class-B and Class-C war criminals by seven Allied powers, and 984 soldiers received the death sentence.[2] The Japanese government accepted these judgments under Article 11 of the 1951 San Francisco Peace Treaty.

Second, after the conclusion of the San Francisco Peace Treaty, Japan concluded international treaties and agreements to resolve the consequences of war with many other countries, including key countries such as China and South Korea. Through these international agreements, Japan reestablished diplomatic relations, paid reparations, atoned for atrocities committed against prisoners of war, and formally settled all other issues related to World War II. The United States and the Republic of China (and later the People's Republic of China) exempted Japan from reparations. Two issues remained unresolved, however: first, Japan and Russia were unable to settle their territorial dispute and could not conclude a peace treaty; and, second, Japan and North Korea still have not established diplomatic relations. But all other issues related to World War II have been legally settled in accordance with the treaties concluded between Japan and the respective countries.

No one in the Japanese government or among serious opinion leaders is trying to legally renounce the IMTFE judgment or any part of the legal framework that allowed Japan to participate in international society. But because the spiritual vacuum created by the defeat was so deep, the transition from the prewar to the postwar period was so drastic, and the seeds for division implanted from this period were so fundamental, inevitably contradictions and polarization emerged.

Since Japan faced an unprecedented total defeat, many asked, "Where did we go wrong to lose the war?" But from there, to generalize broadly, there emerged a sharp split between those who believed that Japan's modernizing past was an unmitigated march toward militarism, colonialism, and aggression and those who argued that not everything Japan did should be judged negatively, and that some actions were justifiable. On the question of Japan's relations with its Asian neighbors, the former believed that Japan's actions were unjustifiable acts of aggression and colonialism against its Asian neighbors, while extremists in the latter group argued that Japanese actions were dictated by its circumstances, and hence, completely justifiable under the circumstances. In this chapter, I define the first group as "apologizers" and the second group as "nationalists."

Throughout the Cold War and especially during Japan's economic expansion from the 1960s to the 1980s, some government officials and conservative Liberal Democratic Party (LDP) politicians supported the nationalists' position but there was a strong current in public opinion and in the opposition parties supporting the apologizers' cause. Internationally, China and Korea were in the process of reestablishing diplomatic and economic relations with Japan, and neither country was inclined to raise contentious historical issues against Japan. The Japanese people were very busy improving their standard of living and basically thought that the history issue should not be a high priority on the political agenda. Some nationalist intellectuals and opinion leaders emerged who tried to justify prewar Japanese activities, but their influence was not far-reaching. Successive powerful LDP prime ministers such as Nobusuke Kishi, Hayato Ikeda, Eisaku Sato, Kakuei Tanaka, Takeo Fukuda, Masayoshi Ohira, and Yasuhiro Nakasone, despite their individual differences, all successfully managed the balance between the apologizers and the nationalists.[3]

When the Cold War ended, coinciding with the temporary eclipse of the once-omnipotent LDP reign, the ideas of the apologizers briefly shaped government policy. Landmark events such as the 1992 Emperor's visit to China in 1992, Yohei Kono's 1993 statement on comfort women, and Tomiichi Murayama's 1995 statement apologizing for Japanese aggression and colonization were hallmarks of this period. Many Japanese naively expected that clear apologies would result in reconciliation with China and Korea. LDP leaders during that period, such as Kiichi Miyazawa, Kono, Koichi Kato, and Toshiki Kaifu, all apologized for past Japanese conduct as they sought reconciliation with Japan's important neighbors. The shift of power to the socialists, represented by Prime Minister Murayama, inherently an apologizer, strengthened this trend and culminated in the landmark 1995 Murayama Statement. When the LDP regained power in 1996, both Hashimoto and Obuchi understood the sensitivity of the history issue in dealing with China and Korea, while paying due attention to a rising tide of nationalism in Japan.[4]

When Junichiro Koizumi became prime minister in 2001, he began to make annual visits to the Yasukuni Shrine for the next six years. His visits to Yasukuni antagonized China and Korea deeply, while invigorating nationalist opinion leaders and politicians in Japan. Japan suddenly plunged into a recession after its bubble economy burst, which shook Japanese confidence. Political pressure for a more assertive Japan accompanied this economic decline, as did a successful strengthening of ties with the United States. Lurking behind this assertiveness were fears of rising Chinese economic, political, and military power and anger toward China due to its incessant preaching to "learn from history." All these factors contributed toward louder nationalist historical discourse.

In what direction is Japan headed? With Prime Minister Shinzo Abe out of office less than one year, it is very hard to predict the future direction. Abe assumed his post with a history of supporting and of support from nationalist politicians and opinion leaders. But his actual policy was more restrained than one might expect. On the Yasukuni visit issue, he adopted a "No Confirmation No Denial" policy. Even what has been interpreted as his denial of Japanese military's involvement in recruiting comfort women could be understood to be the result of a series of unfortunate misstatements.[5] Yasuo Fukuda, who replaced Abe, has a long record of being less nationalist and more apologist in his foreign policy orientation toward Asia,[6] but the extent to which his thinking will influence the future course of Japanese foreign policy is still unclear.

Obscured by the overall trend toward nationalist views are strenuous and constant efforts since the end of World War II to better anchor Japan in the international structure, while appeasing conflicting domestic political forces. In accordance with Hegelian dialectics, my arguments use the apologizers' views as the thesis and nationalists' views as the antithesis, with the emergence of a patriotic/international view as a synthesis. I then provide evidence for the case that the government, politicians, and opinion leaders should grasp and consolidate this synthesis.

The debate on historical memory involves wide-ranging issues, and the nature of each issue is complex. It is therefore necessary to identify some of the important issues, describe the main contentious points, and examine whether or not a general consensus has emerged. I argue that there are five micro issues, all related to concrete and specific wartime issues: they are the comfort women issue, the Nanjing massacre, forced labor, POWs, and Unit 731. I also argue that there are five macro issues that address overall aspects of the war and its memory in general, which are closely interconnected with each other but can still be analyzed separately. These are textbooks, apology, war responsibility, the Yasukuni Shrine, and the IMTFE (International Military Tribunal for the Far East). I will analyze these ten issues, one by one, in the order that I have mentioned above.

FIVE ISSUES RELATED TO CONCRETE AND SPECIFIC WARTIME ISSUES

Comfort Women

In Japan, there are groups of opinion leaders, scholars, politicians, lawyers, and gender activists who maintain that the comfort women system was basically a system of mass rape, and that the prewar Japanese military must be held responsible for this organized rape. Among others, Yoshiaki Yoshimi is the leading scholar of this school. Some denounced the Japanese government at the human rights commission in Geneva in 1992.[7] A Socialist member of the Diet has been working to enact a law to pin down the Japanese government's legal responsibility.[8] Many Japanese gender activists under the Violence Against Women in War Network Japan (VAWW-NET Japan) organized the Women's International War Crimes Tribunal on Japan's Military Sexual Slavery from December 8–12, 2000, in Tokyo. Those activists have also played an important role in assisting former comfort women in Asia to file lawsuits in Japanese courts.[9]

But there are people who have very different views on comfort women. They maintain that comfort women stations were military brothels. Brothels were then a socially accepted practice in East Asia and other parts of the world. Stations were built to avoid rape, venereal disease, and leaks of confidential information. Primarily it was civilian traders who owned and operated comfort stations. No documents exist proving that officials recruited women from Korea, then a part of Japan, through coerced recruitment (*kyosei renko*). In some instances, Korean women were taken to the comfort station by deception, but military police generally acted to prevent such acts, although admittedly not in all cases could they prevent them. In the occupied areas, in contrast to Korea, there were cases of rape and some women were forced to stay with the military. But these were considered criminal acts, and many perpetrators were court-marshaled by the military authority or punished in postwar tribunals. The Dutch case was an exceptional instance of proven local military involvement.

Ikuhiko Hata is probably the most diligent scholar who represents this school.[10] Tsuneyasu Daishido, a former Japanese colonial officer in Korea now aged 90, writes that in all cases that he knew of there was no physical coercion in comfort women recruiting in Korea.[11] Conservative opinion leaders regularly expound their views in print, and a notable example is in the August 2007 special edition of *Will*, which has a special feature on the comfort women issue.[12] The Liberal Democratic Party's Committee of Parliamentarians to Think about Japan's Future and Historical Education is also reconsidering the comfort women issue.[13]

From 1989 toward the early 1990s this became a hotly debated issue between Japan and South Korea. The two governments had intense talks on this issue when Prime Minister Kiichi Miyazawa visited Seoul in January 1992. Following Miyazawa's visit to South Korea, Chief Cabinet Secretary Yohei Kono made a statement on August 4, 1993, establishing the Japanese government's position. Kono clearly apologized but the Kono Statement was also an attempt to synthesize the gap between apologizers and nationalists. Kono acknowledged that "the then Japanese military was, directly or indirectly, involved in the establishment and management of the comfort stations and transfer of comfort women". He further admitted that in many cases comfort women were recruited by private contractors against their own will, through coaxing and coercion. Kono then expressed "sincere apologies and remorse to all those who suffered immeasurable pain and incurable physical and psychological wounds."[14]

Following the Kono Statement, the Asian Women's Fund was established in July 1995 under Prime Minister Murayama. Each comfort woman was to receive a letter of apology signed by the prime minister in power, accompanied by compensation of two million yen. Compensation from the fund was extended to women from Korea, Taiwan, the Philippines, Indonesia, and the Netherlands, and it concluded its work in March 2007. Prime Minster Abe in his trip to Washington on April 26–27, 2007 expressed his "deep-hearted sympathies for the extreme hardships and expressed his apologies to have put them in that sort of circumstances."[15]

On April 27, 2007, the Supreme Court rejected two cases demanding an apology and compensation from Chinese comfort women based on a judgment that postwar international agreements already renounced both state and private claims. With this precedent, Japanese courts will likely reject any future comfort women cases.

Prime Minister Abe's alleged March 1 statement that coercion did not exist in relation to comfort women and a June 16 *Washington Post* full-page advertisement signed by Japanese politicians and opinion leaders that gave the same impression, angered many U.S. Congressmen. On July 30, the U.S. House of Representatives passed by a unanimous voice vote a resolution presented by 167 cosponsors asking Japan to offer an unequivocal official apology on the comfort women issue.

The Japanese government and politicians so far seem to have acted with restraint. To say the least, Abe's March 1 statement was inadvertent and the June 16 *Washington Post* advertisement produced the opposite of its desired result. But I argue that not fully appreciating the weight of the Kono Statement in the complex conditions of Japanese politics and asking for further "unequivocality" is a demand that goes too far.

Instead, what concerns me more than the House Resolution is that all the good work done by the Asian Women's Fund is now completely terminated.[17] I hinted in an essay that I contributed in *Asahi Shinbun* that the April 27 Supreme Court decision may give the Japanese government a unique opportunity, now that it is not in a position to be legally compelled to act by internal courts, to reconsider this issue on a moral basis and not to discontinue the Asian Women's Fund's activities.[18] This is my proposal to seek a further synthesis. Apart from several positive responses from center to left intellectuals, politically my voice does not seem to have any impact. Even under the new cabinet led by Yasuo Fukuda, the comfort women issue may just be handled quietly with a confirmatory statement of the Kono Statement, as necessary.

Nanjing Massacre

The Nanjing massacre was first brought to the Japanese public's attention at the IMTFE. The Tribunal revealed that more than 200,000 soldiers, civilians, women, and children were massacred from December 1937 to March 1938. The Chinese government later began stating that the number of victims was 300,000 and this is the figure currently displayed at the Nanjing Massacre Museum in Nanjing. Many Japanese scholars, who belong to the apologizers' camp, confirm that atrocities were committed and the overwhelming majority of textbooks in junior high and high school reflect this, although some disagreement exists about the precise figures.[19]

Countering Chinese claims and the arguments of the apologizers, some Japanese historians and opinion leaders, particularly from the mid-1980s, began arguing that there was basically no Nanjing Massacre. Some execution of guerillas (soldiers wearing civilian clothes) took place, but nothing proves that this was done outside the framework of international law. There is no record, credibly shown to be from that period, that any mass murder took place. Masaaki Tanaka, Kanji Katsuoka, and Shoichi Watanabe are known to have this position.[20] The Committee of Parliamentarians to Think about Japan's Future and Historical Education concluded in June 2007 that "Massacre in Nanjing was denied even by the League of Nations, because in 1938 China asked the League of Nations to take concrete actions against Japan for 20,000 massacres and several thousand rapes in Nanjing, but that the request was not accepted."[21]

The number of victims in Nanjing is still very much a controversial issue. But after the sharp rise of public interest in the textbook controversy in 1982 regarding the Nanjing massacre, the Japanese army veterans association, *Kaikosha*, decided to conduct their own research in 1984. Completed in 1985 and published in the March edition of their monthly magazine, *Kaiko*, the results of their research were quite unexpected,[22] confirming that "unlawful actions (*fuhokoi*)" were committed and giving an estimate of 13,000, adding 3,000 as a minimum estimate. In announcing this conclusion in their monthly magazine they made the following statement:

> We apologize deeply to the people of China. We say again. Naturally 13,000, and even our minimum figure of 3,000, is an astonishingly huge number. We began our work of checking the military history, knowing that we were not completely clean. But with this huge number, we simply have no words. Whatever the severity of war or special circumstances of war psychology, we just lose words faced with this mass illegal killing. As those who are related to the prewar military, we simply apologize deeply to the people of China. It was truly a regrettable act of barbarity.[23]

For both the apologizers and the deniers of the Nanjing massacre, to get to the real picture is an important task and the polarized debate continues. But I believe that the *Kaikosha* statement represents best what many people who are seriously interested in history feel about what happened in Nanjing precisely 70 years ago. Scholars may continue arguing which numbers are closest to reality. But in terms of the Japanese facing their own history and reconciling with Asia, the position expressed by *Kaikosha* that, even if the number of victims is less than the one the Chinese believed to be so, the unlawful killing itself is truly regrettable and merits apology is very important. Whether such a view can command a consensus as a synthetic approach including nationalists' opinion leaders is unknown at this point.

Forced Labor

Korean and Chinese workers were moved to Japan and were ordered to work in Japanese companies. The transfer of Korean workers to Japanese companies was done in three stages, from September 1939 as voluntary recruitment (*boshu*), from February 1942 as administrative placement (*assen*), and from September 1944 on government order (*choyo*). The estimated number of those who came to Japan varies, but several studies show the number to be 147,000 in the first stage, 300,000 in the second stage, and 220,000 in the third stage.[24] In all stages, the numbers of Koreans who were mobilized under this program were less than those Koreans who moved to Japan outside this mobilization program. As for the Chinese, based on a Cabinet decision in 1942, about 40,000 workers were sent to 35 companies in 135 sites such as mines and construction sites and 6,830 apparently died under severe conditions.[25]

Those who are critical of this mobilization program argue that all Koreans who came to Japan under this scheme were put under forced labor. It was naturally so for those Chinese who were deported from Japanese occupied areas. From the 1990s forced laborers both from Korea and China who had to endure hardship in Japanese companies brought cases against them in Japanese courts. Lawyers and social activists in Japan helped their court cases. Some companies voluntarily accepted their responsibility and paid compensation and reached agreements with the plaintiffs, but the majority did not consent to the plaintiffs' claims, and the lawsuits continued into the 2000s.

Regarding the Korean cases, scholars and opinion leaders emerged who argued that the mobilization program in its first and second stage could not be possibly considered forced labor. They further argued that the third-stage mobilization was an inevitable program to implement the last stage of war. Korea was then a part of Japan, the Koreans were fighting with the Japanese against the Allies and the Japanese people as a whole by this time had already been subjected to work under their own government order.[26]

On April 27, 2007, together with the two comfort women cases as mentioned above, the Supreme Court made a landmark decision concerning three Chinese forced labor cases. The Supreme Court rejected all Chinese plaintiffs' claims based on the postwar Japanese international agreements that renounced both state and private claims.[27] As with the comfort women cases, these verdicts serve as a precedent for all future cases.

At the same time, while rejecting the plaintiffs' claims, the court acknowledged that forced labor did occur and "the mental and physical pain incurred was extremely serious, whereas the company gained profits from the forced labor, so the company concerned and other entities involved in this matter must make efforts to help the victims."[28]

The plaintiffs expressed deep disappointment and stated that the Japanese judiciary made an incorrect decision, failing to fulfill its responsibility. The Chinese Foreign Ministry issued a statement that the interpretation given by the Supreme Court was illegal and invalid because the Chinese government did not relinquish individuals' compensation rights and it urged the Japanese government to take appropriate measures.

The forced labor issue now clearly stands at a crossroads. One way of looking at it is that Japan and its neighboring countries are now hopelessly deadlocked. But another way of looking at it is that, although companies where Korean and Chinese workers worked no longer need fear being prosecuted according to domestic law, the pain incurred by workers has been acknowledged by the Japanese Supreme Court. Now freed from the fear of legal prosecution, companies may be in a better position to acknowledge voluntarily the pain that they caused and compensate for it accordingly.

But so far, no such action has taken place. As stated in relation to the comfort women, this is the position I argued in my essay in *Asahi Shinbun*. Like the comfort women issue, my proposal is not attracting political interest so far. Under the new cabinet led by Yasuo Fukuda, the forced labor issue may only be handled quietly, possibly with some words of general apology.

POWs

The San Francisco Peace Treaty prescribed that Japan should indemnify the sufferings caused to prisoners of war.[29] In 1955 through the International Committee of the Red Cross, Japan paid 4.5 million pounds to those Allied countries whose POWs suffered in captivity in Japan's prisons and camps. In 1956, the Japanese government paid an additional $10 million to the Netherlands. But the wounded feelings of those POWs were not healed and former Dutch POWs in 1994 and British POWs in 1995 filed lawsuits in Japanese courts.[30]

None of these court cases were won by the POW plaintiffs, and as stated above, after the April 27, 2007 Supreme Court decision, any possibility of winning in the Japanese legal system has apparently disappeared. But while not acknowledging any legal obligation beyond those in the postwar treaties, in an attempt to heal the wounds of those who suffered, the Government of Japan established from 1995 to 2004 the Peace and Friendship Exchange Program. Based on this Program, 784 former POWs from Britain, 425 from the Netherlands, and 56 from Australia were invited to Japan. During their stay in Japan, Japanese hosts, each in his own way tried to express their feeling of apology and show that postwar Japan has moved into a totally different direction than what they experienced as POWs.[31] These steps may have made some contribution to healing the wounds of those who suffered. The British and Dutch programs continued after 2004. Particularly after the April 27 Supreme Court decision, when all cases filed by POWs also lost grounds for victory, continuation of such a program may further contribute toward reconciliation.

Unit 731

The history of Unit 731 is by now covered by abundant documentation both in Japanese and English. In 1933, a small military unit was established in Manchuria within the Kwantung Army to study biological warfare. In 1939, it developed into a powerful unit called "Unit 731" in Pingfang, and human biological warfare experiments started. By the time the war ended this unit had used about 3,000 Chinese prisoners, called "logs," as objects of these experiments. Facing Japan's defeat, the unit destroyed everything possible in Pingfang, and those who worked there returned to Japan with only their memories. The U.S. military authority was to receive all information concerning their knowledge on biological warfare on the condition that they would not be prosecuted. Japanese survivors from the unit began speaking about it in the 1950s, and in 1982, a detailed account of the unit was published as *The Devil's Gluttony*. It became a best-seller in Japan.

Human rights advocates and those who consider this crime impermissible argue that it is simply shameful that, although the basic facts are so well known, the Japanese government has never responded.[32] After the deal was made not to prosecute the individuals in this operation, it may not be possible to indict them or disclose their names officially, but, at least, the Japanese government should recognize that the crime was committed and apologize for it. But some argue that, due to the nature of the deal which Japan had with the United States, it is impossible to disclose all of the information, and the best way the Japanese government can proceed is to keep silent and have this issue quietly disappear into history. No synthesis has been found on this issue yet.

FIVE ISSUES THAT ADDRESS OVERALL ASPECTS OF WAR AND ITS MEMORY

Textbooks

Private companies commissioning historians as authors produce Japanese junior-high-school textbooks, which then go through a screening system established by the government. Recent practice is to approve eight textbooks with variations in content and all junior high schools then have the right to choose one of them. The content of the textbooks and the way history is taught have also been the result of delicate balancing between the teachers union, which has advocated strong apologies, and the government, which has tried to limit excessive self-criticisms of Japan's past.

In 1982 when the textbook controversy erupted under Prime Minister Zenko Suzuki in relation to China and South Korea, the Japanese government acknowledged that the feeling of neighboring countries should be one factor for the screening committee to consider, and this clause began to have certain influence on the content of adopted textbooks.

But the great hero of the textbook controversy in acknowledging Japan's war guilt was Saburo Ienaga, who sued the Japanese government, claiming that the screening system is illegal and nothing but censorship, and that key issues such as the Nanjing massacre, aggression toward China, and comfort women have to be described with much greater clarity. The lawsuit lasted for 32 years from 1965 until 1997, until finally at the Supreme Court Ienaga won many points on his claims, although he lost on the issue of censorship. After Ienaga's victory, textbooks with more critical descriptions of controversial subjects, including the comfort women issue, began to be published.

While Ienaga was gaining his limited but important victory, nationalist scholars and historians began raising their voices. In late 1996, they established an association to produce a new textbook, *Tsukurukai*. Kanji Nishio, Nobukatsu Fujioka, Chubei Takubo, Yoshinori Kobayashi, Susumu Nishibe, Hidetsugu Yagi, and other well-known nationalist historians joined the project, and their textbook, approved by the government, was published in 2001 and 2005 by Fusosha. The Chinese government and the South Korean government each time strongly protested that this textbook whitewashed the history of Japanese aggressions and colonialism. Huge media attention was given to the Fusosha textbook, but, in reality, the adoption rate by junior high schools was extremely low.

Inside Japan, the views held by the apologizers and the nationalists are poles apart. As analyzed in the first section of this chapter, nationalists' views have been publicized more widely in recent years. Since it is not likely that Fusosha would stop publishing its textbook, Chinese and South Korean official criticism would continue. However, as Hiroshi Mitani's chapter in this volume shows, a more synthetic approach has emerged between Japan and China and South Korea. Slow, belated, but important endeavors began between the Japanese government and the Chinese and South Korean governments attempting to understand each other better through candid exchanges of views on history.

With South Korea, the two governments established a committee of scholars to study jointly the two countries' history. The first round of this joint committee operated for two years, from 2002 to 2004. Views on history did not converge but, at least, the two sides came to understand the other country's views better. The second round of the committee, now with a subcommittee on textbook analysis, has started its work in April 2007.[33] A similar joint history group was established with China after Prime Minister Abe's 2006 visit to China. It began its work in December 2006 and is expected to conclude its first round of work in 2008.[34]

If the process of mutual understanding is slow and uncertain, there may be a possibility to narrow gradually the differences, first to understand that the other side has a fundamentally different view on history and, with time, gradually to find ways to reach a common perspective.

Apology

In the years following the end of World War II, many Japanese intellectuals and opinion leaders began seriously thinking about Japanese aggressions from the early 1930s. They argued that Japan had "legal, political and moral responsibility from the point of view of international relations" for the aggressions.[35] They also discussed the nature of the Korean annexation. Strong views were expressed that the IMTFE's indictment of Japanese aggression was made by outsiders, but that Japan itself completely failed to pursue its own legal responsibility.[36] Katsuichiro Kamei, Isao Nakanishi, and Saburo Ienaga are, among others, scholars who acknowledge Japan's guilt in waging wars of aggression from the early 1930s. There are scholars, for instance, Yoshimi Takeuchi, who argue that the war against the United States was a war among imperialists, but they are unanimous about the war with China as a war of aggression.[37] The teachers union generally shares these views, and its negative opinion of Japan's militaristic past are reflected in opposition to showing the national flag and singing the national anthem in schools. At the grassroots level, 1,109 soldiers detained in two prisons in China came back to Japan in the first half of the 1950s. They began confessing atrocities they had committed in China. They established an organization in 1957 and have continued to speak publicly about their past so that these atrocities will not be repeated.[38]

But there were some who presented a different perspective. Most of the accused in the IMTFE argued that they had fought a war of self-defense against Euro-American imperialist powers, whose purpose included the liberation of Asia. Fusao Hayashi supported this view in 1963, as did, strongly, the scholars who gathered at Tsukuru-kai in the 1990s. From their perspective, Japan conducted the war in accordance with the then-existing norms of international law and order. As for the crimes against conventional military law, officers and soldiers were punished in the three classes of war tribunals (A, B, and C). There were cases where judgments were wrongly given, but Japan accepted them. As for the crime against peace that became the basis of the indictment at the IMTFE, although it was a retroactive crime based on victors' justice, Japan also accepted it. There is therefore no need for further apologies.

But the position taken by the Japanese government was different from the two competing schools mentioned above. The government did not pursue any additional legal responsibility after the judgments were rendered at the war criminals tribunals, but it went through a moral reevaluation of the war and its history from the Meiji Restoration. Japanese leaders have expressed numerous apologies to Chinese and South Korean leaders, and Prime Minister Murayama in 1995 gave the clearest statement of apology, as a cabinet decision, stating "deep remorse" and "heartfelt apology" for "the tremendous damage and suffering" that Japan caused by its aggression and colonialism. This statement formed the basis of the Japanese government's reconciliation policy from that date. Prime Minster Koizumi in 2005 at the Bandung Asia-African heads of state conference confirmed this statement practically word for word with further emphasis on Japan's impeccable record of peace in the last 60 years. Prime Minister Abe confirmed the Murayama statement also.

In relation to China, the 1992 Imperial visit and the "deep sorrow" that the Emperor expressed marked an important page of reconciliation from the Japanese perspective. In relation to Korea, President Kim Dae-jung visited Japan in 1998, resulting in a landmark communiqué in which Prime Minister Keizo Obuchi expressed "deep remorse and heartfelt apology" and Kim Dae-jung in turn recognized the need to "overcome their unfortunate history."

Nationalist politicians and opinion leaders severely attacked the Murayama Statement. But if the Japanese government and Japan as a whole are to pursue the basic line advanced by this statement, it will become the basis of Japan's synthetic reconciliation policy.

Responsibility for the War [*Senso Sekinin*]

If the Murayama statement expressed "deep remorse and heartfelt apology" for the "tremendous damage and suffering," then who was responsible for that? This question has remained unanswered to this day. Can Japan really overcome its past without addressing this unanswered question?

The questioning itself stands on a fragile basis.

For the intellectuals of the apologizers' school, for whom the Murayama statement may logically be a half-way achievement, they nonetheless welcome the possibility of pushing his apology position one step farther and seeking where the responsibility for the war lay.

But for nationalist scholars and opinion leaders, the question of the responsibility for the war is a nonissue. They severely attack the Murayama statement, arguing that Japan fought a war accepted by then-existing international law. Not only unlawful activities under military law but also the dubious crimes against peace had already been punished; therefore, why should Japan apologize once more, and all the more, why should Japan give further thought to "war responsibility"?

Despite a growing trend toward nationalist discourse, many center-to-left opinion leaders have recently raised the question of "responsibility for the war." They point out that Japan itself has never faced this issue on its own, and argued that the Japanese people themselves must address the issue of war responsibility. Top leaders of the two major newspapers, *Yomiuri* and *Asahi,* each arguably representing right-center and left-center, respectively, debated the necessity of analyzing the issue of war responsibility and attracted huge media attention in January 2006.[39] *Yomiuri Shinbun* made a two-year research project on the question of war responsibility and published the outcome in both Japanese and English, naming the names of those it deemed responsible for leading Japan down a mistaken path.[40] *Asahi Shinbun* also published recently the result of their research.[41] I also argued in my writing on Yasukuni that the key issue that must be resolved on the issue of historical memory is to face the issue of war responsibility and draw Japan's own conclusion.[42]

Even within the Japanese government, there has emerged an interesting phenomenon hardly noticed by the media and public opinion. Pro forma, things have not changed. The long-standing government position has been not to get involved in this matter, a policy formally confirmed by Prime Minister Abe. On October 2, 2006, in answering a Diet question on the responsibility for the war of Class-A war criminals, Abe stated that "there are various views on the issue of war responsibility, and it is not appropriate for the government to make a judgment."[43] On October 6, the Cabinet responded to a formal question by other Diet members on this issue with the same message.[44]

But at the parliamentary debate that took place practically over the same period, the government made statements that went beyond its previously noncommittal position. On October 5, Abe stated before the budget committee of the Lower House that "As the result of the war, many Japanese have lost their lives and members of their families. It left grave consequences upon the Asian people. I think that the leaders of the period including my grandfather [Nobusuke Kishi, who was the Minister of Commerce and Industry of the Tojo Cabinet,] were responsible."[45] On the following day before the same committee, Abe reconfirmed that "Japanese leaders had naturally grave responsibility for the war of the Showa period."[46]

What does all this mean? It is hard to draw any definite conclusions. The issue has not died down. There may be some more impetus among scholars and opinion leaders to continue this debate, but there are no signs that Prime Minister Yasuo Fukuda may take it up.

Yasukuni Shrine

It is fresh in our memory that six successive visits by Prime Minister Koizumi to the Yasukuni Shrine halted summit meetings for five years between Japan and China. China's objection is simple and almost exclusively based on its protest of the enshrinement of Class-A war criminals at Yasukuni:[47] Class-A war criminals are the leaders who led Japan into the war of aggression against China, causing tremendous damage and suffering to the Chinese. Since mourning war dead at Yasukuni has the inevitable consequence of mourning Class-A war criminals, China cannot accept it. On the part of those who agree or sympathize with China's criticism, the solution so far discussed is either to de-enshrine Class-A war criminals from Yasukuni, or to build a nonreligious memorial to mourn the war dead.

From supporters of Yasukuni, these proposals are clearly nonstarters. Class-A war criminals were punished in accordance with the IMTFE judgment. But the Japanese people have not treated them, beyond accepting judgment by the IMTFE, as criminals in accordance with their domestic law. The enshrinement was done based on a generally shared feeling that even with an incorrect policy, they worked for their country. Furthermore, the Japanese do not have a cultural tradition of prosecuting a person after his or her death. Shinto theology also dictates that once enshrined, it is impossible to separate one's spirit from the holistic whole of the universe of spirits. As for the neutral memorial, one is free to construct such a place, but it would never replace Yasukuni, where soldiers swore before death: "When we die, let us meet at Yasukuni."

In my effort to find a synthetic approach, I proposed in my writing on Yasukuni that we should introduce a period of moratorium.[48] As stated above, I strongly argued that Japan should come to its own conclusions on "war responsibility." We can then judge the appropriateness of enshrining 14 Class-A war criminals, not based on the IMTFE decision, but based on our own evaluation. I also proposed that we should de-ideologize the Yasukuni Shrine and the Yasukuni war museum (Yushukan), and further that we should resolve the current constitutional impasse around Article 20 during this moratorium period. Article 20, which strictly separates the state and religion, obliges Yasukuni mourners not to perform a state function. Many scholars and some court judgment considered it unconstitutional for a prime minister to mourn the war dead in his official capacity for this reason.

Prime Minister Abe adopted a policy of "No confirmation no denial," that is to say, to avoid making it clear whether he intends to visit the shrine or not, and whether he actually went or not. It succeeded in extinguishing the fire from China and Korea, while not arousing excessive anger among nationalist politicians and opinion leaders. One may argue that an undeclared period of moratorium emerged during Abe's tenure as prime minister.

One might conclude that the passionate debate on the Yasukuni issue in the last years under Koizumi substantially calmed down during Abe's period in office. In fact, in July 2007, I strongly argued that more efforts should be made to resolve the Yasukuni issue during this moratorium period.[49] But under a careful observation, one might observe several developments during Abe's term. In August 2006, Foreign Minister Taro Aso proposed the idea of "nationalizing" Yasukuni. In December 2006 Makoto Koga, president of the Japan War-Bereaved Association (*Nippon Izokukai*), stated that Yasukuni needs to be studied regarding the appropriateness of enshrining Class-A war criminals, and the Association started its study meeting in May 2007.[50] Above all, successive memos written by former grand chamberlains of the Showa Emperor, Tomohiko Tomita, Kuraji Ogura, and Ryogo Urabe all indicated that the Showa Emperor stopped visiting Yasukuni since 1978 to show his displeasure against the enshrinement of the Class-A war criminals. These memos are provoking serious discussions about the Yasukuni issue among some scholars, historians, and opinion leaders.[51]

What does all this mean? It is hard to draw any definitive conclusions. Yasuo Fukuda, Abe's successor, is known for his sympathy toward a neutral nonreligious place for mourning. At a press conference on September 15, 2007, he expressed his intention not to visit Yasukuni and confirmed his support for a neutral nonreligious memorial but said that "it has to be supported by the people and that choice of timing is very important."[52] Nothing substantial may happen in terms of Yasukuni reform during Fukuda's tenure, but his quiet views as expressed above may be seeds for further discourse sometime in the future.

International Military Tribunal for the Far East (IMTFE)

On all issues so far discussed (apology, war responsibility, Yasukuni, and even textbooks), in terms of a general understanding of prewar history, the IMTFE plays an essential role.

As stated in the first part of this chapter, by accepting the San Francisco Peace Treaty, the Japanese government also accepted the judgment given by all tribunals for Class-A, B, and C war criminals and is not in a position to reverse the verdicts that it accepted. As far as I know, no serious politicians, government officials, or opinion leaders seek the abrogation of the IMTFE's judgment or the San Francisco Peace Treaty.

And yet, the IMTFE does not cease to be the central issue for the debate on Japan's historical memory. The key issue is the validity of the IMTFE's indictment of "crimes against peace" and its judgment that the war criminals had waged and conspired in a war of aggression. War has always been an accepted action allowed for sovereign states as a continuation of diplomacy and international politics. The difficult question here is how does one define "aggression" and what kind of "war of aggression" should be considered criminal?

Some Japanese scholars and intellectuals concurred, accepted, and supported the notion of a "crime against peace." Despite its retroactivity, they found a way to justify the IMTFE judgment. Well-known postwar international lawyers Kisaburo Yokota, Michitaka Kaino, and Shigemitsu Dando accepted the IMTFE's verdict, and Yasuyuki Onuma inherited this position to date.[53] Apologizers, however, consider that the IMTFE did not pay sufficient attention to Asian sufferings.[54]

But this view has been challenged by the nationalists, who have increasingly and loudly come to voice the total rejection of the judgment of "crime against peace."

Practically all nationalist scholars are united on the points that the IMTFE's judgment was victor's justice, that the IMTFE applied international law retroactively, and that, without punishing the victors' crime, it was unfair justice. Defense lawyers at the IMTFE continued to speak out for their causes after the trial. Many of the scholars who participated in the international symposium on the IMTFE in 1983 shared the nationalists' view.[55] Professors Keiichiro Kobori and Shoichi Watanabe have been particularly vocal in recent years.[56]

The views of these opposing camps are poles apart. Now that we are approaching the 70th anniversary of the IMTFE in 2008, the polarization seems to be even wider. Nationalist opinions are heard more loudly, and their leaders are probably more confident that their causes are gaining popularity, but no concrete proposal has been made to harmonize in any way their views with postwar reality.

IS RECONCILIATION NOT A MUTUAL ENDEAVOR?

China's, Korea's, and the United States' historical memory issues, as discussed in this chapter, are primarily Japanese issues. Japan is primarily responsible for over-coming the challenge that these issues pose. But ultimate reconciliation with each neighboring country can only be done as a two-way process. Apology is, in principle, a one-way action done by the perpetrator's side, whereas reconciliation can be achieved only through two-way actions. The positions on history taken by China and South Korea in many ways are still very distant from the position Japan is now taking. Ultimate reconciliation is a long way ahead. Still, in concluding, I can point to two recent examples that give hope for the future.

In the case of China, Prime Minister Wen Jiabao, during his official visit to Japan in April 2007, made a landmark speech at the Parliament on April 12, 2007. He stated in his speech: "Since the establishment of diplomatic relations the Japanese government and Japanese leaders expressed many times their position on history, officially acknowledged aggression, and expressed deep remorse and apology toward victim countries. The Chinese government and people positively appreciate this position." It was the first instance of official acknowledgement and appreciation by the Chinese government of repeated Japanese apologies.[57]

In the case of South Korea, at the grassroots level many positive developments are taking place. One such development is the Korean cultural boom in Japan called *Kanryu* and the stunning popularity of the Korean actor Pe Yong Jun (called in Japan *Yong-sama*). In relation to historical memory, books written by Professor Park Yuha have caught the attention of many researchers and opinion leaders by her efforts to present both positive and negative aspects of the postwar Japanese society with respect to its attitude toward Korea, as well as to cast an objective light on Korean mentality and behavior toward Japan.[58]

Last but not least is the question of the United States. Issues thus far raised were issues connected primarily with China and Korea. But, as seen in the analysis of the IMTFE, the United States inevitably plays crucial part in Japan's historical memory. This analysis inevitably extends to the issue of how Japan fought the war and ended it, with Soviet intervention and U.S. atomic bombings. I am firmly convinced that whatever debate Japan might have on these issues, these exchanges have to be conducted in a way to strengthen the alliance. Above all, we must avoid politicizing the debate. This is an issue that academics and historians might cautiously take up and continue calm and mutually informative debate for many decades to come until such time as the maturity of the debate engenders mutually acceptable understanding and political action.

CONCLUSION

The issues on historical memory dealing with comfort women, the Nanjing Massacre, forced labor, POWs, and Unit 731 have been the subjects of intense debate in Japan. All these issues still meet with anger and dissatisfaction from the victims and their countries. Although I believe strongly that there is a general feeling of remorse and apology in Japan for prewar atrocities, this feeling has not found meeting ground with the other urge to protect pride and honor in Japan and, thus, is unable to produce a synthesis. But as I have discussed above, in all issues there are hopeful signs for a synthesis, although the degree of such hopeful signs varies with each issue.

With regard to the five issues that address overall aspects of war and its memory—textbooks, apology, responsibility for the war, Yasukuni, and the IMTFE—the textbook and apology issues seem to have made certain progress toward synthesis. What I proposed on war responsibility and Yasukuni has not gained political support. Opinions are starkly divided on the IMTFE issue. There is a need to make further serious efforts on these issues to seek a synthesis on conflicting views.

With the nationalist views becoming increasingly vociferous and influential, how Fukuda, considered to lean toward the apologizers' position, would manage all these issues of historical memory is yet unknown at this point. It is my strong hope that synthetic patriotic/internationalist views would gain further strength. For this objective, such centrist and international scholars as Takashi Inoguchi, Makoto Iokibe, Shinichi Kitaoka, and Akihiko Tanaka, who continue the good tradition of Masataka Kosaka, Masamichi Inoki, Shinkichi Eto, and Seizaburo Sato, should gather strength to express and support synthetic views to guide the basic direction of the debate on historical memory in Japan.

NOTES

1. Masao Maruyama is the most famous scholar to have analyzed this system of pressure from above. See his work, *Gendai seiji no shiso to kodo,* 2 vols (Tokyo: Miraisha, 1964). See also Koguma Eiji, *Minshu to aikoku* (Tokyo: Shinyosha, 2002), pp. 29–66.

2. Togo Kazuhiko, *Japan's Foreign Policy 1945–2003* (Leiden: Brill, 2005), p. 44

3. Among those who are quoted, Kishi and Nakasone may be known as nationalist prime ministers. But Kishi laid the foundation of Japanese policy toward Southeast Asia based on economic cooperation and friendly relations. Nakasone wanted to conclude the postwar era

by officially visiting Yasukuni but suspended it when he felt that it created genuine difficulty in the Chinese leadership.

4. See Togo Kazuhiko, "Japan's Strategic Thinking Second Half of the 1990's, " in *Japanese Strategic Thought toward Asia,* ed. Gilbert Rozman, Kazuhiko Togo, and Joseph P. Ferguson (New York, Palgrave, 2007) pp. 79–108.

5. See Chapter 7 in this volume.

6. Typical examples are his statements that he would not go to Yasukuni (*Asahi Shinbun,* September 15, 2007) and that he is interested in the establishment of secular war memorial in the long run (*Asahi Shinbun,* September 16, 2007).

7. Totsuka Etsuro, *Asahi Shinbun,* March 29, 2007. For more detailed discussion on comfort women, see Chapter 7 in this volume.

8. Motooka Shoji, a socialist parliamentarian, *Asahi Shinbun,* March 28, 2007. The same kind of law was supported and contemplated by a group of human rights advocates and lawyers as early as 1999. *Asahi Shinbun,* August 1,1999.

9. AWW-NET Japan,*Q&A Josei kokusai senpan hotei* (Tokyo: Akashi, 2002), p. 9. From 1991 onward, 3 cases from Korea, 4 cases from China, 1 from Taiwan, 1 from the Philippines, and 1 from the Netherlands have been filed. http://www1.jca.apc.org/vaww-net-japan/slavery/courtcase.html (accessed April 4, 2007).

10. Hata Ikuhiko, *Ianfuto senjono sei* (Tokyo: Shinchosha, 1999); "Maboroshi no jugun ianfu o netsuzoshita Kono danwa wa konaose" *Shokun* May 2007, pp. 138–51.

11. Daishido Tsuneyasu, *Ianfu kyoseirenko wa nakatta* (Tokyo: Tentensha, 1999); "Abesori, Konodanwa no torikeshi ketsudan o," *Seiron,* May 2007, pp. 105–37.

12. Sakurai Yoshiko, Komori Yoshihisa, Nishioka Tsutomu, Watanabe Shoichi, Kobayashi Yoshinori, Kamisaka Fuyuko (*Will,* August 2007), Yagi Hidekatsuin (*Sankei Shinbun,* February 10, 2005), and Fujioka Nobukatsu (*Seiron,* May 2007, pp.128–37; *Sankei Shinbun,* February 2, 2004) are also well-known opinion leaders.

13. It was established in February 1997 (Daishido, 1999, p. 95) and currently headed by Nariaki Nakayama.

14. Yoshiaki Yoshimi published a book and stated that it is not confirmed that such a slave chasing operation was conducted to collect comfort women in Korea and Taiwan. Yoshimi Yoshiaki,*Jugun ianfu,* (Tokyo: Iwanami shoten, 1995); Yoshimi Yoshiaki and Kawada Fumiko, *Jugun ianfu o meguru 30 no uso to shinjitsu* (Tokyo: Otsuki shoten, 1997), p. 24.

15. *The New York Times,* April 28, 2007.

16. I argued in "Jugun ianfu ketsugi wa 'nihongyokusai' no josoka?" *Gekkan Gendai* (September, 2007, pp. 48–55) that while Abe's statement in March was inadvertent and the June advertisement created a completely opposite result from what was intended, the Congressional Resolution would not help change the Japanese government's position and that Japan should take a new approach, based on their own moral thinking and taking into account the situation after April 27, 2007.

17. The Asian Women's Fund compiled their activities in a Web site: www.awf.or.jp.

18. Togo Kazuhiko, "Sengohosho hanketsu, wakai eno shintenki ga otozureta," *Asahi Shinbun,* May 17, 2007.

19. See Kasahara Tokushi and Yoshida Yutaka, ed. *Gendai rekishigaku to Nankin jiken* (Tokyo: Kashiwa shobo, 2006). See also Kasahara Tokushi, *Nankin daigyakusatsu hiteiron 13 no uso* (Tokyo: Kashiwa shobo, 1999). These scholars and activists have been holding sympo-siums for one year starting in March 2007 in nine countries to discuss the Nanjing massacre ("Nankin jiken giron sainen," *Asahi Shinbun,* August 23, 2007.)

20. Takemoto Tadao & Ohara Yasuo, *The Alleged Nanking Massacre* (Tokyo: Meiseisha, 2000).

21. *Asahi Shinbun,* August 23, 2007.

22. "Shogen niyoru Nankin Senshi" *Kaiko,* March 1985, pp. 9–18.

23. Ibid., p. 18; Aoki Hiroshi, *Nihon, Chugoku, Chosen, kingendaishi,* (Tokyo, Gento-sha, 2003), p. 231.

24. Kyosei renko. http://ryutukenkyukai.hp.infoseek.co.jp/kyoseirenko1.html (accessed April 27, 2007).

25. *Mainichi Shinbun,* April 27, 2007.

26. Kyosei renko, http://ryutukenkyukai.hp.infoseek.co.jp/kyoseirenko1.html (accessed April 27, 2007).

27. The international agreement referred to in relation to China was the 1972 Joint Communiqué between the People's Republic of China and Japan.

28. *Yomiuri Shinbun,* April 27, 2007.

29. Article 16 of the San Francisco Peace Treaty.

30. Togo, *Japan's Foreign Policy 1945–2003,* pp. 202, 279.

31. Cabinet Office in Charge of External Affairs, *Heiwa yuko koryu keikaku, junenkan no katsudo hokoku,* April 12, 2005. In the case of the British, this figure includes POWs and private sector detainees (p. 17). In the case of the Dutch, this figure includes mainly former POWs (p. 18). In the case of the Australians, this figure includes scholars or war museums and history education–related people (p. 16).

32. Saburo Ienaga, who fought against the Japanese government on the textbook issue for 32 years, maintains that Auschwitz, Hiroshima, and the 731 form the trio of "intentional extreme atrocities" during World War II. Ienaga Saburo, *Senso sekinin* (Tokyo: Iwanami Bunko, 2002), p. 86. Morishima Seiichi, *The Devil's Gluttony* (Tokyo: Kobunsha, 1982).

33. *Asahi Shinbun,* April 25, 2007.

34. *Asahi Shinbun,* December 30, 2006.

35. Ienaga, *Senso sekinin,* p. 51.

36. Ibid., pp. 409–11.

37. Ibid., pp. 133–35.

38. Chugoku kikoku renmei. http://www.ne.jp/asahi/tyuukiren/web-site/other/gaiyou.htm (accessed April 28, 2007).

39. *Aera,* February edition 2006.

40. Yomiuri Shinbun Senso Sekinin Kensho Iinnkai, *Kensho—Senso sekinin,* 2 vols (Tokyo: Yomiuri Shinbunsha, 2006); Yomiuri Shinbun and James Auer, *Who Was Responsible? From Marco Polo Bridge to Pearl Harbor* (Tokyo: Yomiuri Shinbunsha, 2006).

41. Asahi Shinbun Shuzaihan, *Rekishi to mukiau,* Vol. 1 *Senso sekinin to tsuito,* (Tokyo: Asahi Shinbunsha, 2006); *Rekishi to mukiau,* Vol.2 *Kako no kokufuku to aikokushin* (Tokyo: Asahi Shinbunsha, 2007).

42. Kazuhiko Togo, "A Moratorium on Yasukuni Visit," *Far Eastern Economic Review,* June 2006, pp. 5–15; "Yasukuni Saihen Shian" *Gekkan Gendi,* September 2006, pp. 42–51.

43. *Yomiuri Shinbun,* October 3, 2006; *Mainichi Shinbun,* October 13, 2006.

44. The question was raised by Mizuho Fukushima (Socialist Party, Lower House) and Masayoshi Kano (Democratic Party, Upper House), *Yomiuri Shiunbun,* October 7, 2006.

45. *Mainichi Shinbun,* October 6, 2006.

46. *Yomiuri Shinbun,* October 7, 2006.

47. For more details on the Yasukuni issue, see Akihiko Tanaka's Chapter 6 in this volume.

48. Togo Kazuhiko, "A Moratorium on Yasukuni Visit," pp. 5–15; "Yasukuni Saihen Shian," pp. 42–51.

49. Togo Kazuhiko, "Yasukuni mondai no shikoteishi o ueru" *Gekkan Gendai,* July 2007, pp. 58–67.

50. *Asahi Shinbun,* December 23, 2006, May 9, 2007.

51. Kazutoshi Hando, Ikuhiko Hata, Masayasu Hosaka argue for de-enshrinement of Class-A war criminals from the major part of Yasukuni and transfer the spirits to Chinreisha, where the spirits of war dead of all the past wars are enshrined. See "Showatenno no 'ikari' o ikani shizumerubekika," *Gekkan Gendai,* July 2007, pp. 44–57.

52. *Sankei Shinbun,* September 16, 2007.

53. Ienaga, *Senso sekinin* (2002), pp. 394–99.

54. Ibid, p. 400

55. Sato Kazuo,*Sekaiga sabaku Tokyo Saiban* (Tokyo: Meiseisha, 2005).

56. Kobori Keiichiro, *Tokyo Saiban Nihon-no benmei: Kyakka miteishutsu bengogawa shiryo* (Tokyo: Kodansha, 1995); Watanabe Shoichi, *Tokyosaiban o saibansuru* (Tokyo: Chichishup-pan, 2007).

57. Kokubun Ryosei, "Chugoku no taisei henkaku: Nihon no sokumen shien kagini," *Asahi Shinbun,* April 21, 2007.

58. Park Yuha, *Han-nichi nashonarizumu o koete* (Tokyo: Kawade, 2005); *Wakaino tameni* (Tokyo: Heibonsha, 2006).

Part II

Contentious Issues

4

The History Textbook Issue in Japan and East Asia: Institutional Framework, Controversies, and International Efforts for Common Histories

Hiroshi Mitani

An examination of the history textbooks issue in East Asia leads one to raise several fundamental questions. First, why should we have to treat textbooks as a major issue? We may agree that we have to discuss the memories of Japanese aggressions during the first half of the twentieth century, if we are to reach reconciliation between Japan and its neighboring peoples. It is not self-evident, however, that history textbooks for high-school students should play a major role in solving this problem. After all, those who are engaged in the controversy over modern history are not children, but adults.

Second, is it adequate to examine only Japanese textbooks? East Asian people have the right to check whether or not Japanese textbooks describe the Japanese invasion as it really happened in history. However, it is not self-evident that either Korean or Chinese history textbooks treat history impartially. Today, for example, we observe clashes of nationalist memories between the Koreans and the Chinese concerning their territorial claims to Goguryeo and Bohai. If we are to have peaceful relations in East Asia in the future, it is not adequate to examine only nationalist inclinations among the Japanese.

Keeping these points in mind, I would like to discuss the current situation of history textbooks in Japan, touching on the following four topics. First, I will outline the Japanese institutions concerned with textbooks. Second, I will introduce the controversy over history textbooks in Japan. Third, I will examine efforts to produce common history textbooks in East Asia, and, finally, I will discuss a project to create an East Asian modern history for Japanese adults.

I am a historian, and my particular knowledge about this topic comes from various personal experiences. I am a coauthor of two history textbooks. The first is a junior-high-school textbook from Shimizushoin, and the second is a senior-high-school textbook produced by Yamakawa Publishers. I am also participating in a nongovernmental project in cooperation with scholars from Korea and China to produce a regional history of modern East Asia. The views expressed below are based primarily on my own experiences and research.[1]

THE PROCESS OF JAPANESE TEXTBOOK ADOPTION

First, I would like to present a brief sketch of Japanese institutions involved with textbook selection. Three issues are particularly pertinent. (1) Elementary and middle schools are legally required to choose from officially approved textbooks. (2) The Ministry of Education, Culture, Sports, Science and Technology (hereafter the Ministry of Education) approves the textbooks, which are produced by private publishers. (3) Two systems exist for selecting a particular textbook for school use. Private schools and senior public high schools choose their own textbooks from a list of approved textbooks, while local school boards (about 590 in number) choose textbooks for public elementary and junior high schools. Thus, while the official approval process is centralized in the Ministry of Education, the selection process is decentralized.

According to *The Outline of Textbook Institutions* published by the Ministry of Education, the procedure for official approval is as follows.[2] After preparing a draft of a textbook written by professors and teachers commissioned by a publisher, the publisher presents it to the Ministry of Education for official approval. The ministry appoints a review board, consisting of professional historians and experienced educators nominated by the Ministry of Education, to judge the quality of the draft. In its deliberations the review board consults an elaborate report on the draft textbook written by ministry investigators. If the board judges the textbook to be of good quality, it gives official approval. Usually, the board points out various defects in the draft and, through the ministry investigators, demands revisions of certain portions of the draft. Subsequently, if the list of revisions presented by the publisher is deemed acceptable, then the board gives final approval to the textbook. If the publisher does not agree with the demands for revision, it can present a detailed opinion asking for reconsideration.

Recently, the Ministry of Education has limited itself to observing carefully the official procedures and has made judgments according to published criteria. During the 1960s, however, it imposed nationalist interpretations on publishers. However, the ministry changed its attitude after the famous Ienaga textbook lawsuits resulted in a verdict against the ministry's decision, although the court recognized the ministry's right to officially approve textbooks. In 1975, the Tokyo Higher Court, presided over by Eiji Azegami, severely criticized the ministry, declaring that its rejection of Saburo Ienaga's textbook "was illegal, because the rejection had no basis in the ministry's own criteria and it deviated from the limits of administrative judgments, amounting to an abuse of ministry power."[3] Since this decision, the ministry changed the criteria to a clearer procedure and began to observe it faithfully. Furthermore, after Korean and Chinese protests in 1982, the ministry added to its selection criteria a demand that any texts must embody a spirit of cooperation with neighboring peoples. Today, most demands for revision are made based on factual and typographical errors. The ministry makes severe demands for revision in contents only when it finds extremist descriptions presented by rightists or leftists.

The procedure for adopting specific textbooks for classroom use is too complex to explain here. This complexity is a legacy of bitter controversies in the postwar period over the textbook issue. I would like to limit myself here to pointing out that this system represents an example of Japanese democracy in action today. Unlike the qualifying procedure, the adoption is done by nearly 600 local educational boards, not by the Ministry of Education. The 2001 controversy proved this fact dramatically, and brought the process of textbook adoption to widespread public attention for the first time.

THE RECENT DEBATE OVER HISTORY TEXTBOOKS

In 2001, the Japanese witnessed a bitter dispute over history textbooks.[4] Public eyes were first attracted to the adoption process by local educational boards, because there was debate over whether or not the *Atarashii Kyokasho* (*The New Textbook*) written by the Japanese Society for History Textbook Reform (*Atarashii Rekishi Kyokasho o Tsukurukai*—hereafter Tsukurukai) and approved by the ministry was proper. This debate ended in August when it was revealed that the adoption rate of the textbook did not even reach 0.04 percent. Most Japanese historians and history teachers felt relieved by this number, because they had been worried by the seeming popularity of the assertions made by the Tsukurukai. Certainly, bookstores in Japan displayed many books that supported the Tsukurukai, and ordinary people in Japan seemed to be supporting the Tsukurukai as well.

This debate pitted Tsukurukai against traditional left wing scholars. Tsukurukai criticized postwar Japanese history education as "masochistic" and said that this education deprived the Japanese of national pride.[5] It especially denounced: "Existing textbooks had adopted the historical interpretation propagated by the former enemies, and thus treated the Japanese as criminals who are destined to beg pardon from generation to generation forever."[6] Tsukurukai's *Atarashii Kyokasho* accordingly whitewashed the dark side of modern Japanese history. It excluded any discussion of comfort women and moved the description of the "Nanjing Incident" from the section covering the Japan-China War to the pages dealing with the International

Military Tribunal for the Far East (Tokyo War Crimes Trials) after World War II. The textbook cast doubts about the reality of the Nanjing Massacre and also raised criticisms about the partiality of the Tokyo Trials. On the other hand, Tsukurukai announced that its goal was to create a textbook telling "the Japanese side of stories" that would enable younger generations to learn about great activities of their ancestors and to have self-confidence and responsibility as Japanese. The textbook also devoted several pages to describing the Japanese people as victims of Western aggression. For example, its 2001 version provided an inset that stressed the threat and arrogance of Matthew C. Perry, the first American envoy to Japan in 1853, who, according to the text, provoked Japan to war and handed over two white flags in order for Japanese to express the will to surrender after a battle.[7] This was an erroneous interpretation based on material from unreliable hearsay. This error clearly shows that Tsukurukai wished to present modern Japan as a victim of Western imperialism, while minimizing Japanese aggression against its neighbors.

The majority of Japanese historians, in cooperation with "progressive" media in postwar Japan such as the *Asahi Shinbun* and the publisher Iwanami, criticized *Atarashii Kyokasho*.[8] They pointed out many factual errors left in the textbook even after the supposedly rigorous examination by the Ministry of Education. They also maintained that the Japanese should teach younger generations about the offenses committed by the Japanese during their invasions and colonization of neighboring peoples. Their counterattack might have influenced the decisions of local school boards. Local school board members may have wanted to avoid the bitter debate that would arise if they chose to adopt *Atarashii Kyokasho*. Of course, their decision must also have been based on their judgment of its reliability as an accurate textbook.

On the surface, the dispute looked to be a part of the traditional conflict between the rightists and the leftists in postwar Japan. The scholars who wrote in *Asahi Shinbun* were limited to the leftists. Most were Marxists and leftist liberals, who were united in purpose during the lawsuits of Saburo Ienaga concerning history textbooks.[10] They not only criticized Tsukurukai but also denounced the Ministry of Education for having given its official approval to such a tendentious textbook filled with many factual errors. They had a long tradition of criticizing the government, because the Ministry of Education had advocated and forced the rightists' view of history during the 1960s and 1970s.

This debate over history textbooks in 2001, however, had important new dimensions. As Professor Eiji Oguma pointed out, Tsukurukai was a grassroots movement.[11] In the past, the Japanese rightists who had engaged in the history textbook issue had little roots in civil society. Traditionally, they had sought supporters in the Liberal Democratic Party, the political party in power, and appealed to them that they put pressure on the Ministry of Education. In 2001, however, the leaders who came from nontraditional nationalists movement organized not only nationalists of the old generation but also younger ordinary people who, living in the gloomy depression of the 1990s, had been searching to define their identities as honorable citizens. They welcomed slogans that appealed to the recovery of national pride and denounced postwar indulgence in private affairs. The appeal of Tsukurukai to remove the description of comfort women found enthusiastic support among these people.

On the other hand, new people also appeared on the other side of the debate. In July 2001, Professor Makoto Iokibe, a historian of Japanese diplomacy, closely connected with the Ministry of Foreign Affairs, expounded his view in the monthly journal *Ronza*.[12] He criticized *Atarashii Kyokasho*'s "intentionally neglecting the failures of the government that opened the war against the whole world and that induced young men to suicide attacks, and instead the textbook is designed to deceive junior high students into admiring this government." This was the first time a realist's criticism of *Atarashii Kyokasho* appeared in the media. During the 1990s, in East Asia, not only trade but also mutual visits had greatly expanded and flourished. Business people working in international relations became aware that peace and cooperation in East Asia are indispensable. Iokibe's article revealed for the first time the existence of this latent opinion of realists that accepted the need to face up to unpleasant aspects of the Japanese past.

For their part, Tsukurukai and the rightists also underwent changes. As Professor Oguma predicted, Tsukurukai split a few times, because it had assembled within it different groups of people with divergent ideologies. Founding leaders such as Kanji Nishio and Yoshinori Kobayashi left Tsukurukai because their nationalism would not accept the pro-American policy held by other people. Many grassroots supporters transferred their attention to other nationalist issues such as the kidnapping of Japanese citizens by the North Korean government. After the fiasco of the low adoption rate by local school boards of *Atarashii Kyokasho,* the kidnap issue was more attractive for those who had been searching for a cause to express their nationalistic outrage.

Tsukurukai, however, still has some power today, because of drastic political changes. The conservative hardliners in the Koizumi cabinet gained power when the prime minister strengthened his resolve to visit the Yasukuni Shrine as he received repeated objections from Korea and China. Tsukurukai found strong ideological allies in younger leaders of the LDP such as Shinzo Abe, Shoichi Nakagawa, and others. It seems that Tsukurukai strengthened its ties with traditional rightists and the politicians in power, as it lost support from the grassroots. The hardliners in the Abe cabinet did not openly interfere in the textbook issue and on the whole left the Ministry of Education to maintain its formal procedures, although the potential for interference always existed. Some politicians attempted to change the prerogatives of local education boards to select textbooks, but this attempt failed.[13]

Thus, after the 2001 controversy, the terms of the debate have changed. The traditional split between the right and the left, measured by one's attitude toward Marxist ideology, began to play little role in judging the pros and cons of nationalist history. Instead, there emerged a simpler criterion of whether or not one supports East Asian international cooperation. On the one side, the majority of business people, diplomats, and scholars support a version of history that will promote international cooperation for practical, pragmatic reasons. On the other side, people who value ideologically motivated feelings of national pride gather together to back Tsukurukai. The Japanese media began to ask the general public, long silent in this debate, to take sides.

In 2005, textbooks for junior high students were again sent to local educational boards for selection. This time, a passionate dispute over history textbooks did not occur. It was partly because the Ministry of Education demanded that publishers keep silent; not leak or publish drafts, and not discuss details in the media. However, another reason may be that some degree of consensus was formed during the 2001 controversy. Local educational boards again avoided selecting extremist textbook published by Tsukurukai and by the extreme leftists. The adoption rate of the Tsukurukai textbook did not even reach 0.05 percent of schools. On the other hand, all junior high textbooks removed descriptions of the comfort women. Tsukurukai regarded this fact as their victory. It was true that pressure on publishers from the rightists had some influence in this decision. There was another reason for the removal, however. The editorial board of the textbook published by Shimizushoin, of which I was a member, agreed in the first meeting for the revised edition to remove any mention of the comfort women at a point before sex education courses were given to junior high students. The existence of sex education was the main reason why many publishers maintained the description of comfort women in the textbooks for senior high students. This was a compromise. But this decision is widely supported by the Japanese public today.

At present there is little dispute within Japan over history textbooks. Both sides have already secured supporters and it has become an established routine to denounce the other side. There will be little change in this situation in near future, unless the government makes drastic changes in its policy.

THE EFFORTS TO CREATE COMMON TEACHING MATERIALS

The 2001 debate over Japanese history textbooks generated and accelerated various attempts to create common history textbooks for East Asia. Although the major arena of the debate was in Japan, neighboring people showed serious concern about it. In order to cope with the ethnocentric nationalist interpretation of *Atarashii Kyokasho,* historians in South Korea, Japan, and China started various projects to create common teaching materials. As a result, today, we have at least four such books in Japanese.

The leading figures in this field are the historians who organized the Symposia for Creating Common History Textbooks between Japan and Korea. They are Professors Kazuhiko Kimijima and Shigemitsu Kimura at Tokyo Gakugei University and Professor Cheong Je-Cheong at the University of Seoul. They started their workshops in 1997 to produce common history textbooks. After publishing a few interim books,[14] they finally published a complete history dealing with "the exchanges between Japan and Korea" in 2007.[15] This book for senior high students is an excellent achievement that succeeds not only in presenting objective knowledge as far as possible but also in guiding the readers in both countries to think more from the other sides' viewpoint. As for prehistoric and ancient eras, this book treats them as a regional history exempted from the anachronism of projecting the idea of modern sovereign states. Also, its modern history is valuable as the following examples will show. On the most important topic, Japan's invasion and colonial rule of Korea, this book avoids denouncing Japanese activities hastily but to guide the readers to think why the Japanese invaded and committed cruel acts. Moreover, it introduces a few Japanese intellectuals such as Sakuzo Yoshino, a political scientist and historian, Tanzan Ishibashi, a journalist, and Muneyoshi Yanagi, who were sensitive to the hardships of the Korean people. Yanagi adored Korean folk crafts, and opposed to the destruction of the main gate of the Palace Gyeongbokgung. On the other hand, this book introduces many short biographies of Korean intellectuals. Actually, this is a college-level textbook that, for the first time in history, offers the foundations to shared historical memories of Japan and Korea not only among younger generations but also among adults. In this sense, this is truly a pioneering work. We can imagine how difficult it was to produce this book. The editors confess in their postscript that there remained many differences in interpretation, although they held 15 symposia in 10 years. However, they succeeded in overcoming major differences and collisions by their enthusiasm, perseverance, and sincere will to achieve reconciliation between the Japanese and the South Koreans.

In the past, some older historians in South Korea wanted to change the contents of Japanese textbooks by using diplomatic pressure on the Ministry of Education of Japan. However, this group has changed its approach. They held their symposia on an equal basis and began to pursue the modest goal of creating teaching materials instead of textbooks. In spite of their wish to develop a common interpretation, there still remain differences. However, it is a major contribution of this book that it clearly expresses this fact. This book will be sure to offer the starting point for historical discussion and reconciliation between Japan and Korea.

In addition, we have another teaching material entitled *A History for the Future,* produced by historians from three countries: Japan, South Korea, and China.[16] This book focuses on modern history in East Asia, especially on Japanese aggression toward neighboring peoples. It was the publication of *Atarashii Kyokasho* that provoked these historians to undertake this project. Historians from the three countries gathered at Nanjing in early 2002 to start the project. Leading figures in each country were Professor Tokushi Kasahara from Japan, Professor Kim Song-bo from South Korea, and Doctor Bu Ping from China. It is amazing that the book could be published three years after their first meeting, when we consider the enormous difficulties in interpretation and translation among three languages and the differences of historical interpretation among the three countries.

This book could not avoid some shortcomings, however. One such shortcoming is that it concentrates only on the negative aspects of modern Japan. For middle-school students in Korea and China, this is the common knowledge learned from their detailed history textbooks. There may be nothing fresh as far as the description of Japan is concerned. For Japanese students, it is not pleasant to read only about the dark side of Japanese history. Another problem is that the book became a collection of national histories when it describes aspects of modern East Asia other than Japanese aggression. There is an interesting exception in an inset that describes the commonalities and the differences in the use of Chinese ideographs. However, this

book as a whole could not overcome nationalist interpretations and failed in presenting a well-integrated regional history of East Asia. As Professor Kim Song-bo writes
in his introductory essay,[17] the authors have already noticed these problems and will
improve the book in the future.

Finally, I would like to mention the inadequacy of textbooks written for schools.
It is true that I learned much from the above books. For a specialist of nineteenth
century Japanese history,[18] these books offer valuable knowledge about neighboring
societies. However, we have to find more comprehensive and detailed books on East
Asian history if we are to obtain concrete images of neighboring societies. Teachers in
high schools might not be able to rely solely on these books in order to prepare for
their classes. Furthermore, adults, who are directly responsible for the future, have
to obtain reliable detailed knowledge of history in order to deal with disputes among
East Asian countries. Thus, I consider it very important for historians in East Asia to
provide reliable histories for adults. This is why I coedited the book *Contentious Issues
in Sino-Japanese Relations* with Professor Liu Jie and Yang Daqing and published it
both in Japan and China in 2006.[19] We selected some crucial historical events and
issues that lay between Japan and China: the simultaneous development of mutual
dependence and political strain after World War I, the contending interpretations
on Giichi Tanaka's proposal of expansion, the Nanjing massacre, the complicated situations of Japanese puppet governments, history textbooks in both countries, the
memorial service problem in postwar Japan including the Yasukuni Shrine issue,
the lawsuits for reparation by Chinese individuals, among others. Of course, this list
does not cover all issues, and such important issues as the Tokyo trial and national
compensation are left out. However, there are valuable contributions in this book.
We invited authors from both countries and had frank discussions based on original
materials. During the process, the participants who initially had serious reservations
realized the positive benefits of meaningful discussion beyond borders. We engaged
in dispassionate discussions sharing the modest and critical approach to original
materials. However, the symposia also revealed many differences between nationals
from the two countries, especially in the focuses of concern, not to mention their
evaluation. Nevertheless, it was valuable. Our understanding of the other party was
deepened by understanding the reasons behind differences. We came to comprehend
better why the other party presented different interpretations. Publication in Chinese
was especially epoch-making in that it enabled Chinese people to read for the first
time interpretations by Japanese scholars that differ from the Chinese official interpretation. We wish that this book will not only provide reliable historical knowledge
but also give suggestions for the way of history discussion should be conducted
beyond borders.

THE PROJECT TO PUBLISH EAST ASIAN REGIONAL HISTORY

One of the problems that I have noticed during the textbook controversy is the
ignorance of modern history among Japanese adults. They know little about the facts
of our ancestors: not only negative but also positive achievements such as the

introduction of the constitutional monarchy during the nineteenth century without interference or help from the West. This is not because school textbooks do not cover modern history but because traditionally teachers in middle schools have continued the practice for many years to end their classes of Japanese history at around the end of Tokugawa period. Modern history gets short shrift in actual classroom time. We have to publish a good, detailed history to reeducate Japanese adults if we are to create a favorable setting for reconciliation in East Asia.

I am now preparing in cooperation with some historians studying Japan, Korea, and China to publish a series of books on the modern history of East Asia. It will have three volumes: one for the nineteenth century and two for the first half of the twentieth century. We aim to write a regional history beyond a mere collection of national histories in order to encourage the Japanese to understand the circumstances of neighboring peoples during the modern era, especially under Japanese invasions and colonial rule.

Our approach is different from the projects of international teaching materials that I have introduced above. We decided to provide the book mainly for Japanese audiences and thus organized an editorial committee composed primarily of Japanese historians. However, the goal is not to publish a Japan-centered regional history. Rather it is because Japanese authors have the advantage in finding where the lack of memory and prejudices exist among ordinary Japanese people and deciding what topics are needed to explain. The other reason is the fact that we have few resources, and little time and money for running a big international organization. We have chosen a modest approach to publish an East Asian regional history in a short time.

There are four sections of chapters in our series; the first is the history of international relations in East Asia where the Japanese took major roles; the second is brief sketches of neighboring societies; the third examines the activities of countries like Russia, the United States, and Britain; the fourth is an interpretive overview of the East Asian region. During the process of preparation, we not only found the latest understanding of other historians who specialize in different countries but also noticed the differences among us; China specialists sometimes express China-centric views that I, as a specialist of nineteenth century Japan, cannot accept.

We will engage in extensive discussion in order to combine the chapters into a consistent body. However, we will also add some comments to each chapter. This is to show the possibility of different interpretations of history to the readers. There are many topics in history that we can understand in various ways. Because the differences in some historical events continue to provoke international conflicts in East Asia, we decided it was best not to give rigid, monolithic interpretations but rather encourage readers to think about the possibilities of different understandings. Thus, we are going to invite some historians not only from Japan but also from foreign countries as commentators. We expect that this way of description will nurture a more tolerant attitude in history among the readers.

In the future, we would like to publish this series in different languages. The purpose is not to expand a Japan-centric interpretation of East Asian history. On the contrary, we eagerly wish that neighboring people will publish other regional histories of East Asia and translate them into Japanese. These regional histories in East Asia may not ever fully converge. However, by carefully reading other regional histories, we can begin to see why people understand history in different ways. This meta-level insight must offer us a deeper understanding of other people and then will widen the area of shared memories.

CONCLUDING REMARKS

Professor Shinichi Kitaoka, one of the chairs of the Committee for the Cooperative Research of History between Japan and China, recently announced that they will adopt a so-called parallel approach for their research. It seems that the Chinese side also adopted this attitude "to agree to disagree." Politically, it may be wise in the recent international situation. However, it is better for the academics outside the political arena to engage in deeper communications with each other. We can reach deeper understanding of neighboring people and establish peaceful relations among us by asking: "Why does the other party understand the same events in different ways?" And, only through this process can we also improve the history textbooks in East Asia.

NOTES

1. Liu Jie, Mitani Hiroshi, and Yang Daqing, eds., *Kokkyo o koeru rekishi ninshiki: Nitchu taiwa no kokoromi* (Tokyo: University of Tokyo Press, 2006); Mitani Hiroshi, ed., *Rekishi kyokasho mondai* (Tokyo: Nihon tosho senta, 2007).

2. Mitani, *Rekishi kyokasho mondai,* Part 2.

3. Ibid., p. 175.

4. Ibid., part 2.

5. For its leaders' opinions, see Fujioka Nobukatsu, ed., *Atarashii rekishi kyokasho o tsukuru kai ga tou Nihon no vijon* (Tokyo: Fusosha, 2003); Sakamoto Takao, *Rekishi kyoiku o kangaeru* (Kyoto: PHP kenkyujo, 1998); and Nishio Kanji,*Kokumin no rekishi* (Tokyo: Sankei shinbun-nyusu saabisu, 1999).

6. The announcement of the establishment of the Tsukurukai on January 30, 1997. It can be found in the society's Web site. http://www.tsukurukai.com/02_about_us/01_opinion.html.

7. Atarashii Rekishi Kyokasho o Tsukurukai, *Atarashii rekishi kyokasho* (Tokyo: Fusosha, 2001), p. 176.

8. Komori Yoichi, Sakamoto Yoshikazu, and Yasumaru Yoshio, eds., *Rekishi kyokasho: tettei kensho Q & A, naniga mondaika* (Tokyo: Iwanami shoten 2001).

9. Fujioka Nobukatsu severely criticized the attitude of a local educational committee in Tochigi prefecture as a coward. See his interview in Mitani, ed., *Rekishi kyokasho mondai,* p. 130–43.

10. For a survey and related books, see Part 3 of Mitani, ed., *Rekishi kyokasho mondai.*

11. Oguma Eiji and Ueno Yoko, *'Iyashi' no nashonarizumu: kusa no ne hoshu undo no jissho-teki kenkyu* (Tokyo: Keio gijuku daigaku shuppankai, 2003), partially included in Mitani, ed., *Rekishi kyokasho mondai.*

12. Iokibe Makoto, "Tsukuru Kai no 'Atarashii rekishi kyokasho' o yomu: Kokka no sonbo dake de rekishi o kataru mazushisa," *Ronza,* July 2001, pp. 18–26. He was appointed the president of the National Defense Institute in 2006.

13. During Abe's tenure of office, a textbook investigator in the Ministry of Education demanded that publishers change the description of the battle of Okinawa in such a way to whitewash the role of the Japanese Imperial Army in the collective suicides of the Okinawan civilians during the last stage of World War II. When this demand was reported in the media, there was a sudden outburst of protests in Okinawa. The ministry soon demoted the official in charge. When the Fukuda cabinet took over, the ministry withdrew the demand.

14. Rekishi Kyoiku Kenkyukai-Nihon, ed., *Nihon to Kankoku no rekishi kyokasho o yomu shiten: senshi jidai kara gendai made no Nikkan kankei* (Tokyo: Nashinokisha, 2000); Rekishi Kyoiku Kenkyukai-Nihon, ed., *Nihon to Kankoku no rekishi kyotsu kyozai o tsukuru shiten: senshi jidai kara gendai made no Nikkan kankei shi* (Tokyo: Nashinokisha, 2003).

15. Rekishi Kyoiku Kenkyukai-Nihon and Rekishi Kyokasho Kenkyukai-Kankoku, ed., *Nikkan kyotsu rekishi kyozai: Nikkan koryu no rekishi* (Tokyo: Akashi shoten, 2007).

16. Nitchukan Sangoku Kyotsu Rekishi Kyozai Iinkai, *Mirai o hiraku rekishi: Higashi Ajia sangoku no kingendaishi*, 1st ed. (Tokyo: Kobunken 2005).

17. Kim Song-bo, "Higashi ajia no rekishi ninshiki kyoyu no dai ippo: 'Mirai o hiraku rekishi' no shippitsu keika to Kankoku kokunai no hanno," *Sekai,* October 2006, pp. 225–34.

18. Major works are Hiroshi Mitani, *Escape from Impasse: The Decision To Open Japan* (Tokyo, I-House Library, 2006); Mitani Hiroshi, *Meiji ishin o kangaeru* (Tokyo: Yushisha, 2006). The latter includes two essays on historical memories and nationalism written in 2001 and 2005 when the bitter debate on Japanese attitude toward its past was taking place.

19. Liu, Mitani, and Yang, *Kokkyo o koeru rekishi ninshiki.*

5

Myths, Milieu, and Facts: History Textbook Controversies in Northeast Asia

Mikyoung Kim

The past, an entity of lost empirical relevance, is haunting Northeast Asia. The China-Japan-Korea triad has been on an occasional collision course over how each perceives the others regarding the shared past. The triad, bound by dense memory web, cultural affinity, and geographical proximity, has been making confusing historical claims against one another, dampening the spirit of peaceful coexistence in the global era. The region is haunted by the sticky past.

Geographical demarcation is a precarious enterprise, and defining Northeast Asia from a collective-memory perspective cannot escape the challenge. Northeast Asia on the geographical map is larger than the territories occupied by the three countries. The region, in general terms, consists of China, Japan, Korea, Mongolia, Russia, and Taiwan. Regional identity, however, is not coextensive with geography.[1] Demarcation between nationality and identity is malleable. Much of Russia resides in Northeast Asia, but most Asians regard all Russia as a European nation. Japan's identification with the West became stronger after the Russo-Japanese War (1904–5); yet, the resulting confidence led to its belligerence toward Western as well as Asian countries.[2] Mongolia shares substantial ethnic and racial similarities with Korea, China, and Japan; however, its cold relations with China make it less Asian, politically, than European. Mongolia has been politically closer to Russia than China.[3] Taiwan's case differs. Although Taiwan was under Japanese rule starting with the Treaty of Shimo-noseki in 1895, Taiwanese islanders did not feel oppressed during that period and bear little resentment toward Japan. Indeed, the trauma that the Taiwanese remember most acutely is Chiang Kai-shek's massacre of indigenous people in the February 28 Incident in 1947.[4] Today, many of these Mainlanders' descendants remain attached to Chinese culture. North Korea, too, is a geographical part of Northeast Asia but its sociopolitical isolation makes an analysis of its role in the region's mnemonic praxis difficult.

China, Japan, and Korea constitute the core of the Northeast Asian "community." According to Robert Nisbet, "community" encompasses "religion, work, family, and culture; it refers to social bonds characterized by emotional cohesion, depth, con-tinuity, and fullness."[5] No community, however, can be totally unified; indeed, national communities can be mutually repulsive rather than shared, and the constitu-ents of a community are not necessarily content with one another's presence. The community of China, Japan, and Korea are like "neighbors who are stuck with each other." Their relationship is like "a bad marriage charged with intense but coexisting feelings of love and hate." The triad bound by *felt* history engages in intense discourse for which history textbook serves as a medium for mnemonic contention.

HISTORY AND MEMORY IN NORTHEAST ASIA

China, Japan and Korea call the disputes over the past "history problems (*rekishi mondai-lishi wenti-yoksa munjae*)." But is it really a "history" problem? History and memory, often being used interchangeably, are nevertheless two discernable con-cepts. History is an objective past whose *theoretical* ontology is rooted in undisput-able facts.[6] Historians, therefore, try to unearth the truth of the bygone era *as if* truth can be comprehended in a consensual manner. Memory, on the other hand, is mostly a malleable entity being subject to change according to present needs.[7] Our beliefs about the past are dependent on circumstances of the present and differ-ent elements of the past become more or less relevant as these circumstances change. Memory and commemoration, then, are, as Karl Mannheim states, "only possible from an ascertainable intellectual location" and "presuppose a subject harboring def-inite aspirations regarding the future and actively striving to achieve them. Only out of the interest which the subject at present acting has in the pattern of the future, does the observation of the past become possible."[8] Thus, each new generation forges a past compatible with its present situation. Some contemporary scholars would accept presentism in whole; most, in part. Kiichi Fujiwara, for instance, connects the past to the future from today's prism, as he states: "I use the word 'remember,' but actually, when people think of any conflict, they do not remember it as such, but rather reconstitute the past in a way that suits our needs today. We imagine the future in a way that suits our known experiences, so we remember the past, but we are not really interested in objectively studying the past. Rather, we extract useful bits of the past in order to prove in the present that something 'actually' happened before. Thus, we imagine the past and remember the future."[9] Mannheim's statement makes sense to the presentists because it roots understandings of the past in new social realities, denying the existence of an objective benchmark for assessing different versions of the past.[10] Since any version of the past articulates conditions of the present, there is no reason to revere or otherwise rely on it as a source of instruction, benefit, or harm.[11] Then, why does the Northeast Asian mnemonic community present their cases as a "history problem?"

Memory scholarship is a recent introduction to Asia. Memory as a legitimate intellectual genre arose in the West as an effort to systemize post–World War I disillusionment and doubt. "What nobody would have thought possible" in these days "suddenly turned out to be real; what everyone had taken to be reality itself now stood revealed as an illusion."[12] Appalling human potential for self-destruction and the empirical reality at the Nazi camps cornered Europeans to pursue the ontological questions that were never very seriously visited before. Against this backdrop, not many people in Asia are aware of the subtle conceptual differences between memory and history, and use the terms interchangeably. This explanation, however, might be too naive an academic explanation given the politicized nature of the "history problem" within the community. The "history problem" is, in fact, a memory problem that historical facts cannot resolve.

Establishing moral authority over the other carries extra weight in voicing grievances in general. The powerful adjectives in use (e.g., "divided," "contentious," "conflicting," "entangled," "controversial") reveal the charged nature of the history debates. All three in the triad project themselves as the victim, and a victim is the one often commanding the upper hand in moral discourse.[13] Japan, the victim of U.S. atomic bombings, designates itself to be the torchbearer of a world peace movement. Indiscriminate civilian killings in Hiroshima and Nagasaki propelled Japan to be at the forefront of antinuclear activism since the 1950s. This moral crusade, unfortunately, has been in procession without serious self-reflection on the prime causes of its victimization.[14] China and Korea, on the other hand, were on the receiving end of Japan's imperial ambitions. In these complicated claims of victimhood, all three cannot afford to draw on their position from memory, a soft, malleable and manipulative existence. Their logic has to come from history, a hard, unchangeable and absolute ontology. By framing this memory problem as a history problem, each tries to preempt the other in establishing the victim vis-à-vis villain framework. Labeling may not be a simple act of careless semiotics, but rather be (un)conscious exercise of moral superiority. What they present is actually memory, but they claim it to be history because establishment of moral superiority works better within the frame of history than that of memory.

HISTORY TEXTBOOKS AS A MEMORY SITE

History textbooks are a site of "memory war."[15] In the aftermath of the 1982 history textbook controversies, the Japanese government enacted the "Neighboring Country Clause" with a statement that "from the perspective of building friendship and goodwill with neighboring countries, Japan will pay attention to these criticisms and make corrections at the Government's responsibility." In 2001, 20 years after the conciliatory gesture, the Chinese youth took to the streets protesting against Japan's *New History Textbook* (*Atarashii Rekishi Kyokasho*). In 2005, the South Korean Ministry of Foreign Affairs and Trade suggested 51 items in the Japanese history textbooks where it wished the Tokyo government would instruct the publishers for revision. South Korea's commercial market quickly cashed in on public sentiment by introducing a popular computer game called, "Hideyoshi's Aggression and Chosun's Counterattacks."[16] As history issues surfaced as one very contested area of concern in the community, the Chinese and Korean news media began covering the stories on the Yasukuni visits and history textbooks. Then, why do the countries in Northeast Asia intervene into each other's domestic issues such as the contents of history books? Where can we draw the line in respecting other nation's sovereignty?

History education needs to be contextualized within the global expansion of mass education. The increasing availability of compulsory education for the general populace has resulted in bigger government control, as pedagogical contents became more standardized.[17] Establishment of a ministry of education led to the bureaucratization of the educational process. Education, furthermore, is a "system of legitimization" where "schools process individuals," as it gears to instill commonly shared values among the citizenry.[18] Whereas school and family functioned as the primary socialization units, school is now assuming a bigger role in educating the future generations.[19] The youth establishes self-identity in his or her relations to group membership, where knowledge on reified national history plays a crucial role. Emile Durkheim led us to believe that "a man is surer of his faith when he sees how distant a past it goes back and what great things it has inspired."[20] Remembering noble deeds, he said, elevates the community's dignity and moral values. In that regard, national history education is "model of" and "model for" society. The common past is the story of a nation, and history textbooks are how a nation tells its story to the citizens. Overlapping histories make textbooks a site where the nations engage in "memory war."

MYTHS, MILIEU, AND FACTS ABOUT HISTORY TEXTBOOKS

Japan: The Price of Ambivalence

Post–Cold War Japanese history education places emphasis on two main goals: (1) understanding national history from the world's historical trajectory; and (2) educating citizens as members of an international community.[21] The empirical realities have not been in sync with the educational goals: history education, instead, has been the target of domestic ideological contention and international criticisms.

Political bifurcation over history textbooks is nothing new in Japan. The ideological pendulum has been in constant swing between the right and the left. Textbooks approved by the Ministry of Education after the beginning of the screening system in 1947, for instance, were liberal enough to contain narratives on the Manchurian and Nanjing incidents. Such critical self-historicism under the SCAP (Supreme

Command for the Allied Powers) provoked the conservatives who deemed Japan's aggressive wars the only viable option for Japan to secure its own survival. With the pendulum swinging to the right, the Japanese Democratic Party's 1955 proposal ignited the first history textbook controversies. The proposal aimed to augment the supervising and screening authority of the Ministry of Education. It argued that the textbooks up for approval contained subversive elements such as bleak living condition of the working class and rosy depiction of the People's Republic of China and the Soviet Union.[22] In this political atmosphere of "Red Purge," the Ministry disapproved more than 80 percent of the textbooks citing "factual distortions."[23] Tightening of the screening process continued for the following 20 years or so.[24]

Japan swung back to the progressive left with the momentum of the second history textbook controversies in 1982. It started with a Chinese newspaper's allegation that the Ministry of Education pressured the textbook publishers to replace "aggression [toward China]" with "advancement [into China]," and "independence movement [in Korea]" with "riots [by the Koreans]." This allegation, which turned out to be false, was repeatedly picked up by the Korean and Japanese news media fueling the "history" debates. As more and more media outlets copied and embellished each other's accounts, history emerged as an "important diplomatic issue." The Suzuki cabinet proceeded to make accommodative gestures by enacting the "Neighboring Country Clause," as noted above. Then, why did Japan change its historical perception toward the Asian countries in spite of the factual inaccuracies of the alleged claims? I argue that it was a reflection of changing perceptual milieu: Japan was rediscovering Asia.

Japan made a conscious decision to distance itself from Asia at the turn of nineteenth century. Very influential opinion leaders such Yukichi Fukuzawa were at the forefront advocating Japan's de-Asianization policy.[25] In order for Japan to catch up with the advanced West, they argued, it had to shed its backward and feudalistic Asian identity. Asia lapsed into oblivion until the 1982 textbook controversies drove it home. A 1987 survey shows the Japanese self-identity between the West and the East (see Table 5.1). The majority of the respondents, 49 percent, regarded Japan as part of the West, whereas there was almost an even split between Asian and neither/no opinion.

Table 5.2 and Table 5.3 suggest that the postwar Japanese perception of East Asians (i.e., Chinese and Koreans) was negative, while Americans were regarded in a very positive light. The survey results suggest that average people living in the

Table 5.1   If divided in the following categories, which category do you think Japan belongs to? (1987, %)

Part of the nations of Asia	Part of the western first world	Does not belong to either group	I don't know/No answer
27	49	16	8

Source: NHK (October 1987) in Elizabeth Hann Hastings and Philip K. Hastings, eds., *Index to International Public Opinion, 1988–1989* (Westport, CT: Greenwood Press, 1990), pp. 283–84.

Table 5.2 Do you LIKE or DISLIKE the following ethnic groups? (1951)

Ethnic Group	Percentage		Frequency		Total
	Like	Dislike	Like	Dislike	
Korean	5.06	94.94	8	150	158
Chinese	22.92	77.08	22	74	96
American	96.53	3.47	167	6	173

Source: Adapted from Seiichi Izumi, "Tokyo shoshimin no iminzoku ni taisuru taido," in *Shakaiteki kincho no kenkyu,* ed. Nihon Jinbun Kagakukai (Tokyo: Yuhikaku, 1951), p. 431 (Table 4).

Tokyo area were contemptuous of Japan's former victims in East Asia, whereas they felt positive about the former enemy, the United States.

Table 5.4 holds more empirical data showing the Japanese feelings of superiority toward its former victims. While ranking themselves as the most superior race, they also thought very highly of the victor. The Chinese and Koreans were placed at the lowest rank among the different ethnic categories. A longitudinal comparison of the Japanese attitude toward the East Asians from the 1950s until the 1980s is very illuminating: Japan was rediscovering Asia around the 1982 history textbook controversies.

Table 5.3 What do you think of characters of the following ethnic groups? [(1) dishonest, (2) honest, (3) kind, (4) not kind, (5) polite/courteous, (6) rude, (7) friendly, (8) unfriendly, (9) wicked, (10) good-natured, (11) stingy, (12) generous] (1951, %)

	1	2	3	4	5	6	7	8	9	10	11	12
Korean	44	1	1	9	1	15	2	6	16	0	5	1
Chinese	32	7.3	6	5	5	9	8	3	13	2.2	9	2
American	2	7.4	41	0	7	1	25	1	2	1.9	0	10

Source: Adapted from Seiichi Izumi, "Tokyo shoshimin no iminzoku ni taisuru taido," in *Shakaiteki kincho no kenkyu,* ed. Nihon Jinbun Kagakukai (Tokyo: Yuhikaku, 1951), pp. 434–35 (Table 5).

Table 5.4 Among the peoples on this list, who do you think are superior? You may name as many as you like.

Ethnic group	1958	1963	1968
Japanese	57	52	59
Americans	47	46	43
Chinese	9	6	9
Koreans	1	—	—

Source: Research Committee on the Study of Japanese National Character (Nationwide survey), quoted from *Social Attitudes in Japan: Trends and Cross-National Perspectives,* ed. Masamichi Sasaki and Tatsuzo Suzuki (Leiden and Boston, MA: Brill Academic Publishers, 2000), p. 112.

While Asia was reemerging on the Japanese mind map in the 1980s, the Japanese were holding rather complicated perceptions about the war. More than half of the respondents defined the war as an act of aggression, and the absolute majority felt the need to apologize. There was a split in assessing the war. About half of the people saw the inevitability for Japan in attacking other Asian countries: it needed resources in order to fend off aggressive postures of the western imperial powers. And more than half of the respondents believed Japan's war-making had a positive impact on the Asian countries by introducing systems of modernization (see Table 5.5).

However, the Japanese were having a hard time assuming responsibility for the war. Table 5.6 shows that the respondents more or less saw themselves as the victims of the fascist military for having been "duped" to fight the unwinnable war.[26] Some exempted themselves from the sense of responsibility for having fought the wars out of self-defense. Table 5.5 and Table 5.6 suggest similar perceptual continuum where mixed emotions coexist in the Japanese psyche. The Japanese sense of victimization at the hands of military government and the United States can explain the overall ambivalence toward the historical past. The respondents feel regretful about the war, and yet they are also aware of the circumstances of the aggression. At the same time, they feel sorry for what Japan did to China and Korea, and yet they also believe their experiences were not all negative.

Table 5.5   Japan was involved in a number of wars and territorial expansions from the Meiji era until the defeat of WWII in 1945. What do you think of such history? (1982, 1987, %)

Items	Agree	Disagree	The past has nothing to do with me	Don't know/ No answer
Those 50 years in Japanese history from the Sino-Japanese war in 1894 to the Pacific war that ended in 1945 constituted a history of aggression (*shinryaku*) against our Asian neighbors	51.4 ('82) 48 ('87)	21.9 ('82) 25 ('87)	10.4 ('82) 14 ('87)	16.3 ('82) 13 ('87)
Japan's military expansion against other countries was unavoidable because Japan was a poor country with few resources	44.8 ('82) 40 ('87)	38.7 ('82) 42 ('87)	4.2 ('82) 6 ('87)	11.9 ('82) 12 ('87)
As Japanese citizen, we should wholeheartedly reflect on what we did to Korean and Chinese since the Meiji era including severe discrimination/ persecution and odious slaughters.	82.5 ('82) 73.4 ('87)	5.2 ('82) 4.2 ('87)	4.2 ('82) 3.4 ('87)	8.2 ('82) 7.3 ('87)
It should be appreciated that Pacific War expedited/spurred the independence of Asian countries who suffered from Western imperialism.	51.4 ('82) 48 ('87)	21.9 ('82) 25 ('87)	10.4 ('82) 14 ('87)	16.3 ('82) 13 ('87)

Table 5.6   What do you think is the war responsibility of ordinary Japanese people in the Sino-Japanese War and the Pacific War, which lasted 15 years from 1931? (1982, %)

Questionnaire Items	%
Ordinary Japanese citizens were the victims of militarism and its propaganda. Therefore, we should not be responsible.	36.3
Japanese admired and supported militarism. Therefore, we should feel responsible toward Asians.	29.5
Japan had to fight the wars for self-defense and peace in Asia. Therefore, Japanese as the people have nothing to do with the concepts of militarism, victims and aggressors.	17.6
Others	0.5
Do not know/No answer	16.1

Source: NHK (October 1982, N=3,600; Age over 20), quoted from Yoshida Yutaka, *Nihonjin no sensokan*, p. 216, Table 2.

About the specific issue regarding the 1982 textbook controversies, the majority was empathetic with China and Korea. More than half of the respondents saw inaccuracies in the terms of "advancement" and "riots," and were concerned about the Chinese and Korean sentiments. One notable item in this questionnaire is the high percentage of "I don't know/No answer" (see Table 5.7).

When we juxtapose the analyses of Table 5.7 and Table 5.8, however, we get to observe the persistence of ambivalence where contradictory thoughts coexist. Even though the majority was empathetic with the Chinese and Korean sentiments (56%), apologizers and nonapologizers were roughly split in Table 5.8. Roughly the same percentage of respondents thought that Tokyo had done enough (7%) and had not apologized at all (6%), while the rest was split between moderate positive (i.e., have done so to some extent) and moderate negative (i.e., have not done enough). The feelings of regrets did not necessarily bring about seeing the need to make apologies.

Table 5.7   There are some high-school history textbooks that describe Japanese military's "invasion" as an "advance," and the Korean Independence movement in March 1919 (the March First Movement) as a "riot." What do you think about this? Choose the one closest to your opinion from the following. (1982, %)

Questionnaire Item	%
Descriptions such as "advance" and "riot" are historically inaccurate.	27.6
Although I am not sure whether the description is historically incorrect or not, it lacks consideration for China and Korea.	28.5
Descriptions such as "advance" and "riot" are historically accurate.	18.3
I don't know/No answer	21.9

Source: Yomiuri Shinbun (September 1982, N=2,130) in Yoshida Yutaka, *Nihonjin no sensokan*, p, 199, Table 22.

Table 5.8   To what extent do you think the Japanese government has apologized for the damages they caused other Asian countries during World War II? (1995, %)

Questionnaire Item	%
They have apologized enough.	7
They have apologized to some extent.	45
They have not apologized enough.	35
They have not apologized at all.	6
I do not know/No opinion	7

Source: NHK (June 1995, N=1,275) in *Index to International Public Opinion, 1995–1996,* Elizabeth Hann
Hastings and Philip K. Hastings, eds. (Westport, Connecticut: Greenwood Press, 1997), p. 285.

How does memory, as a self-reflexive entity, work at the empty center in the Japanese mind? The psychologist Hayao Kawai has proposed the concept of the "hollow center" as the key to the Japanese mind. Beginning with the Japanese mythology, he claims that the structure of Japanese culture, society, and human relations are characterized by the emptiness at the center.[27] When forces confront one another on either side of this empty center, the emptiness serves as a buffer zone that prevents the confrontation from growing too intense. The avoidance of confrontation at "the empty center" provides a partial explanation of the Japanese ambivalence as a mnemonic praxis. The difficult past is better avoided than directly confronted. While many of the circumstances involved in preparing, prosecuting, and ending the war remain to be unearthed, and interpretations are often ideologically loaded, the Japanese continue to withhold judgment about the war-related past. The "hollow center," being devoid of absolute moralism and religious dogma, allows such ambivalence. As a country with eight million divinities, Japan's multiple identities as aggressor, victim, and survivor of World War II do not have to constitute a perceptual assault. In fact, the acceptance of coexisting contrasts within one entity is a pervasive cultural norm in Japan. As the context dictates the character of a manifested deity, the ebb and flow of time determines the contemporaneous war-related memories in Japan.

The international criticisms of Japanese history textbooks were a wake-up call for the Tokyo government. Japan began paying attention to its former "victims" as a legitimate concern for diplomatic relations. From the 1982 controversies until the 1990s, the Japanese government extended unprecedented number of apologies to China and Korea.[28] Prime Minister Zenko Suzuki (August 24, 1982)[29] and Chief Cabinet Secretary Kiichi Miyazawa (August 26, 1982),[30] for instance, made specific reference to the textbook issues in their apologies. As the "comfort women" issues were emerging as another source of diplomatic contention, more apologies were extended to China and Korea. Prime Minister Miyazawa (January 17, 1992),[31] Chief Cabinet Secretary Koichi Kato (July 6, 1992),[32] Chief Cabinet Secretary Yohei Kono (August 4, 1993),[33] Prime Minister Tomiichi Murayama (August 31, 1994; July 1995),[34] and Prime Minister Ryutaro Hashimoto (June 23, 1996; July 15, 1998) apologized for the pain and suffering endured by the women. Many other apologies on the war in general were made by the Emperor and political leaders.

At issue is the implacable refusal of the Chinese and Koreans to accept sincere declarations of regret, to demand in every gesture of apology a level of incontestable "sincerity"—in short, proof of the unprovable. Regret and apology are two different things. Regret is a sentiment accompanying the realization of wrongdoing; apology, the communicative format through which regret is conveyed. Even today, China and Korea, under the influence of Confucian formalities, remain too aware of the separate realms occupied by sentiment and ritual, and of the telltale signs of inauthentic performance. The theories of Japanese dual consciousness (*tatemae-honne*) fuel the suspicion of performance-only insincerity in the apology rituals.[35] Repeated insults and denials by Japanese politicians confirm suspicions of Japanese indifference and intensify demands for authentic remorse.[36] A deep perceptual dilemma between Japan and its former victims fuels the memory problem.

With the pendulum back to the left, the 1994 textbooks contained descriptions of the difficult past, such as Comfort Women, Unit 731, and the Nanjing Massacre.[37] The conciliatory policy stance provoked hostile reactions from the rightists for being "masochistic" and "biased." This round of clash led to the 1996 making of Tsukurukai, which consists of Liberal Democratic Party members and conservative academics.[38] The Tsukurukai authored and published many books that could reach the general public. The "Research Association of Liberal Historical Perspectives (*Jiyushugi Shikan Kenkyukai*)" was another advocate of conservative views that engaged in active pubic outreach programs such as publishing *Manga History of Japan: What the School Textbooks Do Not Teach* (*Manga: Kyokasho ga oshienai rekishi*) (3 volumes).[39]

The saga continues into the twenty-first century. Upon the Ministry of Education's approval of the *New History Textbook* (*Atarashii Rekishi Kyokasho*) authored by Tsukurukai in April 2001, China and Korea demanded revisions of the text, but to no avail. China Radio International, as an example, reported about the Beijing government and the Chinese people's strong dissatisfaction with the new Japanese history textbook authored by the right-wing academics.[40] The controversies continued until the following year when a Chinese newspaper report linked Japanese corporations to Tsukurukai. The Chinese began boycotting the companies lined up as the sponsors of Tsukurukai, mistakenly thinking the listed individual sponsors were representing their companies. Amid the mass protests led primarily by the youth, Asahi Breweries, Ltd., became the first target of boycott. A 2005 clash was also the result of the Chinese and Korean protests against the *New Japanese History*, which was accused of downplaying the nature of Japan's militarism, including its past aggression toward China and Korea, and the circumstances of World War II. The teachers union denounced the book published by Fusosha, and only 18 out of 11,102 junior high schools adopted the book, taking up only about 0.04 percent of the total market share. Despite Beijing's and Seoul's persistent protests, the market share of "problematic" texts has been consistently dismal (see Table 5.9).[41]

A survey of the Japanese history textbook controversies suggests two persistent patterns. First, Japan's domestic political divide has been fueling the memory debates.

Table 5.9   Market share of junior-high-school history textbooks (1966–2002)

1966	1972	1978	1984	1990	1997	2002
Chukyo 37.5	Chukyo 33.5	Tokyo 26.8	Tokyo 31.3	Tokyo 35.0	Tokyo 41.1	Tokyo 51.3
Tokyo 19.0	Tokyo 18.7	Shoseki 20.0	Shoseki 20.0	Shoseki 16.5	Dainihon 19.3	Dainihon 14.0
Shoseki 14.1	Shoseki 16.3	Chukyo 18.5	Dainihon 14.8	Dainihon 16.3	Kyouiku 17.8	Kyouiku 13.0
Dainihon 8.2	Dainihon 8.9	Dainihon 13.9	Chukyo 14.2	Kyouiku 16.0	Shoseki 12.9	Teikoku 10.9
Gakkou 6.8	Kyouiku 8.5	Kyouiku 10.1	Kyouiku 11.8	Chukyo 8.7	Bunkyo 3.5	Nihon 5.9
Shimizu 6.4	Shimizu 7.6	Gakkou 5.5	Shimizu 5.6	Shimizu 4.3	Shimizu 3.4	Shimizu 2.5
Kyouiku 5.9	Gakkou 4.9	Shimizu 4.7	Gakkou 2.3	Gakkou 1.9	Teikoku 1.9	Bunkyo 2.3
Teikoku 2.1	Teikoku 1.5	Teikoku 0.5	—	Teikoku 1.4	—	**Fusosha 0.0**

Source: Adapted from Naigai Kyoiku (http://book.jiji.com/kyouin), No. 5251, November 20, 2001.

A sequence of attacks and counterattacks has been in motion without reaching a meaningful synthesis. The latest episode comes from the island of Okinawa. The Okinawa prefecture protested the Ministry of Education's instructions to retract the descriptions of the Battle of Okinawa in June 2007. The military was known to have forced the residents to commit mass suicides as the battle was ending in its defeat. The Tomigusuku Municipal Assembly in Okinawa stated that the instructions were to "deny the historical facts, accumulated through studies of the Battle of Okinawa that are based on the numerous testimonies of those who experienced it."[42] Japan as a country is still grappling over what *really* happened during the war. Posing questions on why the nation started the unwinnable war, how it engaged in the military theater, and what the defeat means might be too complex to address in straightforward manner.

Second, most of the international controversies began with erroneous allegations and misunderstandings. Contrary to the pervasive belief in the region, the Japanese Ministry of Education neither authors nor exercises a heavy-handed direct intervention in the text writing and screening processes. With the availability of commercialized textbooks, the process is decentralized where a local board of education enjoys a substantial amount of autonomy in the textbook selection process. In 47 prefectures, 500 Textbook Screening Committees are formed every four years under the auspices of local boards of education. A committee usually consists of about 20 school principals, teachers, experts and ordinary citizens who provide advice and consultations to the board of education. After holding public textbook exhibitions and internal discussions, the Committee selects the textbook to be adopted for the school district.[43] An analysis of 33 junior-high-school history textbooks (1950–2000) shows very little narrative change over time.[44] When compared to Japan, the Chinese and Korean systems of textbook writing, screening, and marketing are much less decentralized. The Ministry of Education in Korea exercises almost sole supervisory authority,[45] while the Chinese system allows, since the 1980s, private companies and individuals to author the texts, which are subject to stringent screening process.[46]

China: Somewhere in the Middle

The Chinese Communist Party censures a wide spectrum of the society. Free dissemination of information is closely monitored, and the field of education is no exception. Debates on the tumultuous internal strife (e.g., Great Leap Forward, Cultural Revolution, Tiananmen Square Incident) have been banned in the public forum, and few people have open access to factual information in this culture of forced silence.[47] History textbook narratives are also selective.

From the 1950s until the 1990s, noticeable changes took place in the three areas: bigger emphasis on economy, science, and culture; more descriptions of the Japanese invasion; and strengthening of nationalistic and patriotic messages. The "Opium Wars" section of the junior-high-school history textbook (1994 edition) uses the terms "[foreign] invasion," "[Chinese] people," and "[Chinese] bravery [at the battlefields]" more than five times each out of the total 600 word counts. The descriptions of humiliations suffered at the hands of foreign powers (e.g., the Opium Wars [1839–42 and 1856–60], Taiping Rebellion [1850–64], and the Boxer Rebellion [1899–1901]) increased accordingly.[48] There are also some narratives that cast Japan in a positive light by describing it as a country of cherry blossoms, home to Mount Fuji, and also a country of advanced science and technology. Shin Kawashima's analysis of *Early Modern and Modern History of China,* however, points out the inaccurate narratives. For instance, the section on the Sino-Japanese War (1894–95) describes post–Meiji Restoration Japan as follows:

> Japan remained home to forces of feudalism with considerable power, and as the domestic markets were not large enough to bring economic benefits to everyone, there were numerous popular uprisings. Japan's rulers quickly decided that Japan's path to continued growth lay in taking over foreign lands, and they put together a "continental strategy" aimed mainly at invading China.[49]

The text notes that Japan became a modern nation through the Meiji Restoration (1868), but it exaggerates social instability amid the rapid changes. With the exception of the Saga uprising staged by the remaining samurai class in 1874, popular rebellions such as Shimabara Uprising (1637–38) and urban riots (around 1767) took place before the Restoration. An exemplary remnant of feudalistic social order, the samurai class, faced a fatal blow with the suppression of the Keian Incident (1651) and the Forty-Seven Ronin incident (1703) before the Restoration. On the "continental strategy," it was the outcome of Japans' strategic choice in pursuing its identity as a "continental country" as opposed to an "oceanic country." Its subsequent invasion into China was a result of the doctrine rather than a cause of the doctrine.[50]

In addition, on the topic of the Twenty-One Demands of 1915, the text narratives can be misconstrued by accentuating the Chinese humiliations suffered due to Japan:

> The European powers no longer had the energy to spend on Asian matters, and Japan took advantage of this opportunity to accelerate its encroachment into China, plotting to take over the entire nation for itself.... Finally, offering support for Yuan Shi-kai's bid to become emperor of China, Japan set as its conditions the Twenty-One Demands, which were tantamount to the very destruction of China as a nation. On May 9, 1915.... Yuan's government accepted these conditions. This is known as the "national shame of May 9."[51]

Even though the narratives are not inaccurate, the implication is that the Japanese manipulated domestic Chinese politics for its own opportunistic advantage in the increasing European power vacuum. The list continues on the narratives on the 1931 Manchurian Incident which states "Japan had a desperate craving for Chinese territory"; on the more open conflicts with Japanese forces in China: "There was nothing surprising about the fact that the Japanese imperialists conducted their war of aggression against China. This conflict was the natural outgrowth of a long-standing policy in Japan, built up over many years, that pursued the annexation of China, the control of all Asia, and finally world supremacy as its goals"; and on the defeat of the Japanese armed forces in China: "China's victory in the war against Japan was the first total victory in a war that the Chinese people had fought against imperialism for more than a hundred years. This gave great courage to and boosted the self-respect of all the peoples of the nation. It also formed a solid foundation of the triumph that the people's revolution would soon see. China's war against Japan was an integral part of the global war against fascism, and the Chinese people, by playing their part in this war made great contributions to this worldwide struggle and helped to boost China's position on the global stage."[52] With "humiliation" as the running theme of the modern and contemporary periods, the overall narrative tone emphasizes the Chinese victimization at the hands of imperial powers. And Japan stands out as the "ungrateful beneficiary" of the Chinese culture.[53]

In this milieu of historical misconstruction, psychological distance between Japan and China is increasing. Figure 5.1 shows that the unfavorable image of the Japanese among the Chinese is growing since the late 1990s, and the gap is getting bigger.

Japanese data indicate a corresponding trend. Figure 5.2 demonstrates the decreasing level of friendliness toward the Chinese among the Japanese. The Chinese perception of Japan became further deteriorated around Prime Minister Koizumi's Yasukuni visits in the early 2000s. A 2001 pubic opinion poll shows that the Chinese regard the history issues more seriously than their Japanese counterparts. Table 5.10 reveals the two groups might be talking past each other on the history problem.

Korea: Far From Being Fault-Free

In portraying Korea's relations with Japan, two main themes are running in the textbooks: victimhood and resistance. The sense of victimhood comes from the

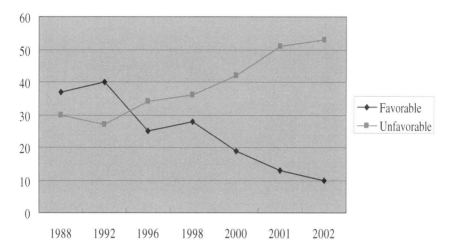

Figure 5.1   Changing Chinese Attitudes toward Japan (1988–2002) *Source:* Shiyan Zhongguo Diaocha Wang: "China-Japan Joint Poll" (http://www.comrc.com.cn/index.asp)

deeply internalized feelings of wounds. Korean history can be literally defined by foreign threat. According to Yoon Tae Rim, the number of raids, incursions, and other offenses against Korea from the seas and by neighboring peoples were no less than 1 to 1.5 times a year during the Koryo (918–1392) and Chosun (1392–1910)

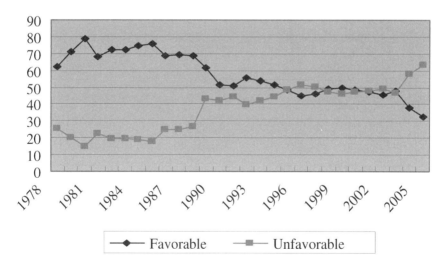

Figure 5.2   Japanese Attitudes toward China (1978–2005) *Source: Public Opinion on Foreign Affairs* (Cabinet of Japan), quoted from Xiaohua Ma, "Yasukuni Controversy: Commemorative Politics and Conflicting Memories in China and Japan," paper in progress, 2007, p. 23.

Table 5.10 How important is the historical perception in Sino-Japan relations? (%)

	Very important	Somewhat Important	Not very important	Not important at all	Others/No answer
China	66	21	10	2	1
Japan	21	46	24	4	5

Source: Abridged and adapted from *Asahi Shinbun*, December 25, 2001.

dynasties. The figure comes only from the official record, implying that the actual amount of aggression could be much higher.[54] Korean's sense of victimhood is neither a contemporary phenomenon nor only related to Japan. The middle-school textbook stated the following:

> We have suffered from many invasions by neighboring countries throughout our long history. However, we have never provoked, exploited, or caused any pain to any of our neighbors. In other words, we have always tried to maintain peaceful international relations and preserve a peace-loving tradition.[55]

The sense of victimhood became stronger around the turn of the nineteenth century when Japan was the primary aggressor. Narratives accentuate the Chosun dynasty's efforts to preserve its sovereign dignity in the whirlwind of imperialism spearheaded by the island country:

> The Chosun government refused Japan's demands for trade because of the inappropriate terms used in the diplomatic documents. The expressions alluded to the superiority of the Japanese Emperor over the Emperor of Chosun. Furthermore, the documents included contents that were out of the conventional diplomatic norms at that time.[56]

> Japan demanded talks [to open up Korea] while dispatching battleships to the Kanghwa Island. The act was meant to impose threats on Korea. Thereupon, the Chosun government refused to meet the Japanese, criticizing their tactics as barbaric and aggressive.[57]

The above narratives juxtapose Korea and Japan: the former as a victim and the latter as an aggressor. Korea's honorable demeanor in facing Japan's naked belligerence can be easily noted. The weak demonstrated moral superiority as opposed to the perpetrator who engaged in unprovoked violence. The text emphasizes how Korea handled the threatening situation in spite of its eventual fall into the hands of imperial Japan. The implicit pedagogical message, therefore, is that Korea was weak in terms of power dynamics, and yet it was superior in moral sense: Korea was an honorable victim.

The theme of resistance is a relatively new introduction. In the aftermath of democratization movements in the 1980s, South Korean textbooks began placing more emphasis on people's power.[58] The middle-school textbook openly acknowledges the need to rewrite history from today's standpoint. It, furthermore, emphasizes the imperatives to shed a new light on the *dark* past, as it declares in the following:

Our history is the record of our people's footsteps. The past events can be re-evaluated from the historian's perspectives [today], and the new meaning of the past gets narrated in the history books. Through this, we get to meet the past, experience the bygone era and learn the accurate meaning of the past. History is today's lamp, and window to the future. Therefore, historical narratives should neither hide the dark past nor exaggerate the non-existent as if it did exist.[59]

Under this new direction, one notable change is the negative assessments of the Park Chung-hee regime. The text states the regime had a "weak will for democratization" drawing "international criticism of the dictatorship."[60] In a similar vein, the text allocates a substantial space on democratization movements of the 1980s and the positive changes taking place in North Korea.

Mnemonic democratization meant giving a bigger voice to the previously silenced.[61] This change was translated into richer narratives on the mass resistance against the Japanese colonialism.[62] But this trend also is criticized. A conservative academic stated that: "Popularization of the Korean history led to demoralization of our achievements. All the modernizing forces like national leaders and capitalists were relegated as the corrupt power...The section on economic growth, for instance, goes in detail about the negative consequences of rapid growth...The history textbooks are not really about our past. It has become a record of resistant movements against *any* status quo."[63]

University textbooks also can be quite distorted for lack of a screening process. The authors tend to instill subjective interpretations of history, and most of them are known to be nationalistic in their tone. Even a popular university textbook, *Our History* (*Uri Yoksa*), by the centrist historian Han Yongu, discusses the colonial period with chapter headings such as "The Plunder of Our Land, Economic Resources, and Industry" and "The Plan by the Japanese Imperialists to Eliminate the Korean Race."[64] The legacy of Japanese colonialism is open to debate, and ideology often gets interjected in the discursive process. The value-laden terms such as "plunder" and "eliminate the Korean race," however, seem to lack objectivity in conveying persuasive argument. Like the case of China, Korea cannot be fault-free in claiming its impartiality in textbook narratives.

The Korean case stands out with two distinctive features. The Korean textbooks devote more space than the Chinese and the Japanese counterparts to the narratives on the threats of western imperialism and Japanese colonialism. Second, its focus on Northeast Asian history is the most substantial (see Table 5.11). The Korean Ministry of Education and Human Resources announced its plan to further expand the sections on modern and contemporary periods in its 2006 policy statement.

MUTUAL PERCEPTIONS: COMPARISON OF PUBLIC OPINION SURVEYS

Despite the claims and counterclaims, the Japanese and the Koreans overlap on the sources of historical shame. According to a survey, Japanese college students are

Table 5.11   A Comparison of the Amount of Narrative in National History Textbooks (%)

| | | National History (A) | History of Northeast Asia (B) | | | | (A)+(B) Total on NEAsia |
			China	Japan	Korea	Others	
China	Antiquity/Middle ages	90.2	—	1.1	0.4	3.5	95.2
	Early Modern	90.6	—	0.6	0	3.8	95.0
	Modern/Contemporary	80.1	—	7.8	0.6	2.1	90.6
	Subtotal	85.4	—	4.2	0.5	2.9	93.0
Japan	Antiquity/Middle ages	86.7	7.8	—	3.5	1.0	99.0
	Early Modern	85.6	0.9	—	1.8	0.1	88.4
	Modern/Contemporary	67.0	6.3	—	3.4	1.2	77.9
	Subtotal	77.5	5.6	—	3.1	1.0	87.2
Korea	Antiquity/Middle ages	94.0	2.0	0.8	—	0.1	96.8
	Early Modern	95.6	0.8	0.7	—	0	97.1
	Modern/Contemporary	90.7	1.6	2.0	—	0	94.3
	Subtotal	93.0	1.6	1.2	—	0	95.8

Source: Adapted from Inoue Tatsuro, "The Amounts of Issue Descriptions among the Textbooks of Northeast Asian Countries," in *Hirashi asjia rekishi kyokasho,* ed. Nakamura Tetsu, p. 240.

most ashamed of Japan's war in Asia at 54.4%, followed by World War II/Pacific War (24.6%), politics/politicians (10.9%), domestic discrimination (Koreans in Japan, 5.7%), war in general (4.7%), Japanese foreign policies (4.5%), and 4.3 % mentioned Hideyoshi's Korean invasion (see Table 5.12). The ghost of World War II is haunting the nation, and Korea is the main theme for their sense of shame. In other words, the Japanese feel guilty about aggression toward the Koreans throughout history ranging from the sixteenth century invasion of the peninsula until today's discrimination against Korean residents in the country.

In the case of Korea, the college students feel shameful about Japanese colonial rule (56%), the IMF crisis (49%), the Korean War (25%), political corruption (25%), construction accidents (21%), and the "Big Power" abuses of Korea (17%). Out of the six items of answer, two are directly related to Japan: colonial rule and "big power" (e.g., Japan and the United States) abuse. It is important to note that the overriding theme in shameful feelings comes from the experience of victimization. It is not necessarily because they are angry with the aggressors, but because they hold their own weakness accountable for the negative experience (see Table 5.13).

The results are very illuminating because they challenge the validity of nationalistic history education. Had the contents of history textbooks been the most influential in forming historical knowledge, why would the Japanese name the events for which their country's official narratives maintain ambivalence. These empirical findings suggest that Japanese students' access to alternative sources of historical knowledge,

Table 5.12   Sources of Japanese Shame

Event	Number	Percentage Mentioning Event
Japan's war in Asia	230	54.4%
World War II / Pacific War	104	24.6%
War in general	20	4.7%
Politics / politicians	46	10.9%
Japanese foreign policies	19	4.5%
AUM Shinrikyo cult	20	4.7%
Teen Crimes	9	2.1%
Hideyoshi's Korean invasions (sixteenth century)	18	4.3%
Domestic discrimination (Koreans in Japan)	24	5.7%

Source: Adapted from Barry Schwartz, Kazuya Fukuoka, and Sachiko Takita-Ishi, "Collective Memory: Why Culture Matters," in *The Blackwell Companion to the Sociology of Culture,* ed. Mark D. Jacobs and Nancy Weiss Hanrahan (Malden, MA and Oxford: Blackwell Publishing, 2005), p. 259.

such as *manga,* anime, magazines, etc., need to be closely examined in forming historical views. *Manga,* a popular medium in Japan, makes up about 40 percent of the total book sales, and the genre covers a broad range of topics including history, war narratives, and political rhetoric.[65]

CONCLUSION: RECONCILIATION IN THE COMMUNITY

World War II was a pivotal moment of Asian memory. The Japanese wartime atrocities are remembered throughout Northeast Asia. Japan had set into motion

Table 5.13   Sources of Korean Shame

Event	Number	Percentage Mentioning Event
Japanese Colonial Rule (1910–45)	246	56
The IMF Emergency Loan	213	49
The Korean War	109	25
The Wrongdoings of the Former Presidents (Chun Doo-hwan and Roh Tae Woo)	106	25
The Collapses of Sung Soo Bridge and Sam Poong Department Store	91	21
"Big Power" Abuses	72	17

Source: Adapted from Barry Schwartz and Mikyoung Kim, "Honor, Dignity, and Collective Memory: Judging the Past in Korea and the United States," in *Culture in Mind: Toward a Sociology of Culture and Cognition,* ed. Karen A. Cerulo (New York and London: Routledge, 2002), p. 213.

two sins, not one. Japan's first offense was psychological. Reactions to the sudden advent of modernization amid expansive Western imperialism varied: Japan absorbed it and soon became a world power; China sank in dignity, wealth, and influence; Korea vanished into what proved to be the beginning of a Japanese Empire. Meiji elites held China, once the object of unbounded reverence, in contempt, and adopted toward the rest of Asia an attitude of absolute superiority.[66] Japan's successful modernization demoted China from the "Center of the World" to a periphery, and Korea, a transmitter of the Chinese culture to Japan, also suffered from the consequential relegation in the rapidly shifting landscape. This was Japan's first blow to China and Korea.

Japan's second offense was physical. Japan chose not to seal itself off from the Western powers but to become one of them by invading China and annexing Korea. It took advantage of the increasing power vacuum of European powers in East Asia by transforming itself as the dominant ruler of Asia. China, after millennia of dominance, lost the most. From the time it entered into the Anglo-Chinese treaty of Nanjing in 1842 until the economic takeoff under Deng Xiaoping's reform policy, China endured "the century of humiliation."[67] Asians still quarrel over World War II because it provides an arena wherein older disagreements can be worked through. When the Chinese talk about the many humiliations they endured at the hands of the Japanese, they go back as far as 2,000 years when Japan was a reverent borrower of China's glorious culture. Koreans express the similar condescension. The Japanese merely mimicked Western aggression by becoming a colonial power itself and prospered under U.S. patronage after its defeat in World War II. Japan is a country without a "moral principle," they claim.[68] What we can see through the so-called "history textbook controversies" are age-old historical grievances awaiting the right momentum to explode.

Against such criticisms, the Japanese argue that the ongoing memory wars are a mere reflection of a rising tide of nationalism in China and Korea. Some assert that the Beijing and Seoul governments cynically maneuver anti-Japan sentiments among the discontented masses as a means of diverting their attention from inside to outside. During the second half of the twentieth century, Japan quickly restored its influence amid phenomenal economic growth under the auspices of a pacifist Constitution. Japan's neighbors, however, remembered the dark years, and only the clearest expressions of regret for war atrocities could have begun to mitigate Asian resentment directed against Japan's role in the war.[69] Here lies a deep perceptual chasm fueling the memory wars between the former aggressor and its victims. History textbooks are tangible evidence of the Japanese lack of sincere remorse in the eyes of China and Korea.

Then, why do we witness more accusations against Japan since the 1980s than before? How can we explain the cycle of protests? Four explanatory threads can be considered: rising nationalism, increasing self-confidence, domestic situations, and rising pluralism. Those who argue for rising nationalism often contribute to intensifying rivalry in the region. Terumasa Nakanishi, a realist with a tint of conspiracy theorizing, for instance, asserts that the 2005 textbook controversies were nothing more than Beijing's brainchild trying to block Japan's entry bid to the UN Security Council.[70] With China and Korea emerging as rivals in a more integrated global market, their voices become bigger accordingly. Similar observations have been made against the Roh Moo-hyun government in Seoul for its nationalistic policy stance such as U.S.-ROK and ROK-DPRK relations.[71]

An alternative analysis provides a more optimistic perspective. The seemingly anti-Japanese sentiments are not necessarily a reflection of nationalism, but rather an expression of increasing self-confidence.[72] While nationalism is a sentiment of superiority by demeaning others, self-confidence comes from within entailing healthy pride grounded on objective achievements. Given the positive association between economic growth and self-confidence, voicing concerns over history is an end result of decreasing transaction cost. In the changed power equation entailing differential cost and benefit for making a challenging action, angering the powerful (i.e., Japan) no longer entails an equal amount of cost as it once did for the relatively powerless (i.e., China and Korea).[73] Disagreements over the history problem are on the natural course of events in order to achieve mutual acceptance.

Some Japanese analysts claim that Beijing is exploiting the people's anti-Japanese feelings amid rising discontent in the society. Beijing faces a wide range of problems (e.g., the widening gap between rich and poor, the developmental gap between coastal regions and interior provinces, discontent on the part of ethnic minorities, the Falun Gong sect, the "floating" population in search of work, environmental degradation, and energy shortages), and mass discontent is reaching a dangerous level. According to the Chinese Ministry of Public Security, there were 74,000 mass incidents—demonstrations, riots, and other acts of civil disobedience—an average of 200 incidents per day in 2004.[74] The current atmosphere within the country is a manifestation of domestic frustration where Japan happens to be a convenient target.

Finally, some theorists link rising pluralism to historical issues. Others suggest that the real reasons behind the Chinese anti-Japanese sentiments lie with political democratization within the country.[75] As China and Korea are on their trajectory toward mature democracy, it is only natural for them to make efforts in correcting the past wrongs as a way to advance human rights. This line of thought projects historical wrongs as an issue of human rights, where the Japanese military violated the rights of Chinese and Koreans during the war.

Much effort has been made to redress the woes over Japanese history textbooks. Joint colloquia among the historians of three countries have produced textbooks containing neutralized pedagogical contents.[76] Such endeavors, however, carry only symbolic significance given the differences in educational systems. As long as the Beijing and Seoul governments decide not to use the collaborated textbooks, the works cease to have significant empirical impact on the students. Furthermore, a series of actions taken by the Japanese government are alarming the region. The 2007 passage of the revised Fundamental Law of Education with an inserted "Patriotism Clause" stirs new worries dampening the cooperative spirit.[77] Despite the mixed signals, traditional hostilities are being weakened by the growing diversity, and openness, of Asian societies in this quickly changing world.

NOTES

I would like to thank Barry Schwartz and Kazuya Fukuoka for their input.

1. Geography is generally congruent with territorial demarcation drawn by national boarders, while regional identity can be reflective of constitutive elements such as cultural heritage, religion, and historical experiences. Jurgen Habermas, *The Structural Transformation of the Public Sphere: An Inquiry into a Category of Bourgeois Society* (Cambridge, MA.: MIT Press, 1989); and Marc Lynch, *State Interests and Public Spheres: the International Politics of Jordan's Identity* (New York: Columbia University Press, 1999).

2. Marius B. Jansen, *The Making of Modern Japan* (Cambridge, MA and London: The Belknap Press of Harvard University Press, 2000), pp. 439–42.

3. Since Mongolia's declaration of independence in 1911, it became a virtual protectorate of Russia. With the help of the Red Army, it became Mongolian People's Republic in 1924 and was a satellite state of the Soviet Union. Caroline Humphrey, "Remembering an 'Enemy': The Bogd Khaan in Twentieth-Century Mongolia," in *Memory, History, and Opposition Under State Socialism,* ed. Rubie S. Watson (Santa Fe, NM: School of American Research Press, 1996), pp. 21–44.

4. See Paul R. Katz, "Governmentality and Its Consequences in Colonial Taiwan: A Case Study of the Ta-pa-ni Incident of 1915," *The Journal of Asian Studies* 64, no.2 (2005): 281–94.

5. Robert A. Nisbet, *The Sociological Tradition,* 7th ed. (New Brunswick and London: Transaction Publishers, 2005), p. 6.

6. See Joan Wallach Scott, *Gender and Politics of History* (New York: Columbia University Press, 1999).

7. On more debates on the relationship between history and memory, see Jacques Le Goff, *History and Memory,* trans. Steven Rendall and Elizabeth Claman (New York: Columbia University Press, 1992); Paul Ricoeur, *History, Memory and Forgetting,* trans. Kathleen Blamey and David Pellauer (Chicago: University of Chicago Press, 2004).

8. Karl Mannheim, "The Problem of Generations," in *Essays on the Sociology of Knowledge,* ed. Paul Kecskemeti (London: Routledge and Kegan Paul, 1952), pp. 276–320.

9. Kiichi Fujiwara, "Remembering the War—Japanese Style," *Far Eastern Economic Review* 157, no. 12 (December 2005): 53.

10. As opposed to presentism, which deems present situation as the sole determinant of what we choose to remember and forget, an alternative school of thought, culturalism, sees the resiliency of memory by emphasizing continuity, tradition, and essentialism: the present is rooted in the past. Culturalists argue that revisions of history and tradition elaborate existing ideas rather than create new ones unconnected to the past: we are what history and tradition make us. For more on the theoretical debates, see Edward Shils, *Tradition* (Chicago: University of Chicago Press, 2006). Also see Thomas Berger's chapter in this volume.

11. For more details on the theoretical approach to memory and history, see Maurice Halbwachs, *Les cadres sociaux de la mémoir* (Paris: Presses Universitaires de France, 1926); Maurice Halbwachs, *Collective Memory* (New York: Harper and Row, 1980 [1950]; Eric Hobsbawm, "Introduction: Inventing Traditions," in *The Invention of Tradition,* ed. Eric Hobsbawm and Terence Ranger (Cambridge, England: Cambridge University Press, 1983), pp. 1–14; John Bodnar, *Remaking America: Public Memory, Commemoration, and Patriotism in the Twentieth Century* (Princeton: Princeton University Press, 1992); John R. Gillis, ed., *Commemorations: The Politics of National Identity* (Princeton: Princeton University Press, 1994); Eviatar Zerubavel, *Time Maps: Collective Memory and the Social Shape of the Past* (Chicago: University of Chicago Press, 2003).

12. Paul Kecskemeti, "Introduction," in Mannheim, p. 2.

13. John K. Downey, "Suffering as Common Ground," in *Constructing Human Rights in the Age of Globalization,* ed. Mahmood Monshipouri, Neil Englehart, Andrew J. Nathan, and Kavita Philip. (Armonk and London: M.E. Sharpe, 2003), pp. 308–27; James J. Orr, *The Victim as Hero: Ideologies of Peace and National Identity in Postwar Japan* (Honolulu: University of Hawai'i Press, 2002).

14. There exists a vocal progressive minority advocating the need for Japan to engage in serious soul-searching. This group includes the teachers union (*Nikkyoso*) and Saburo Ienaga, who initiated a series of lawsuits against the Japanese governments. *The Asahi Shinbun* and Iwanami Publisher, as popular outlets, continue to represent progressive views in the society.

15. Takashi Yoshida, "The Making of the Rape of Nanking: History and Memory" in *Japan, China, and the United States* (Oxford and New York: Oxford University Press, 2006), pp. 129–33.

16. For example, see Gamania Korea, www.gamania.co.kr.

17. Japanese compulsory education started during the Meiji period, while the Korean system began under the U.S. military rule after its liberation from Japan in 1945. In the case of the People's Republic of China, the compulsory education became available with the passage of "People's Republic of China Compulsory Education Law" in 1986. For more information on the global trend, see Francisco O. Ramirez and John W. Meyer, "Comparative Education: The Social Construction of the Modern World System," *Annual Review of Sociology,* 6 (1980):369–99; Francisco O. Ramirez, and John Boli, "Global Patterns of Educational Institutionalization," in *Institutional Structure: Constituting State, Society, and the Individual,* ed. George M. Thomas, John W. Meyer, Francisco O. Ramirez and John Boli (Newbury Park and London: Sage Publications, 1986), pp. 150–72; John W. Meyer, , Francisco O. Ramirez and Yasemin Nuhoglu Soyal, "World Expansion of Mass Education, 1870–1980," *Sociology of Education* 65, no. 1 (1992):128–49.

18. John W. Meyer, "The Effects of Education as an Institution," *American Journal of Sociology* 83, no. 1(1983):56.

19. Steven Brint, *Schools and Societies* (Thousand Oaks: Pine Forge Press, 1998), pp. 136–70.

20. Emile Durkheim, *The Elementary Forms of the Religious Life* (New York: Free Press, 1965 [1915]), p. 311.

21. Shimanuki Manabu, "Nihon," in *Higashi Ajiano rekishi kyokasho wa do kakarete Iruka,* ed. Nakamura Tetsu (Tokyo: Nihon Hyoron-sha, 2004), pp. 13–38.

22. The party later moved on to publish three volumes of pamphlets, which they entitled as *Pathetic Textbooks* (*Ureubeki Kyokasho*).

23. For the "Red Purge" carried out under the auspices of SCAP, see Leonard Schoppa, *Education Reform in Japan* (London: Routledge, 1991), p. 39.

24. The Ministry of Education made a clear statement emphasizing the "political neutrality" of school teachers. See Christopher Hood, *Japanese Education Reform: Nakasone's Legacy* (London and New York: Routledge, 2001), p. 20. In this continuum, the Hatoyama cabinet passed a law abolishing the electoral system of City Board of Education. Masamura Kimimasa, *Zusetsu Sengoshi* (Tokyo: Chikuma Shobo, 1990), pp. 164–65.

25. Kakuzo Okakura, *The Awakening of Japan* (New York: Century, 1904).

26. Carol Gluck, "The Past in the Present," in *Postwar Japan as History,* ed. Andrew Gordon (Berkeley and Los Angeles: University of California Press, 1993), p. 68.

27. Hayao Kawai, *The Japanese Psyche: Major Motifs in the Fairy Tales of Japan* trans. Hayao Kawai and Sachiko Reece (Woodstock, CT: Spring Publications, 1996).

28. Prior to the flurry of apologies made in the 1980s and 1990s, Prime Minister Tanaka extended an apology that was included in the 1972 Joint Communiqué of the Government of Japan and the People's Republic of China: "The Japanese side is keenly conscious of the responsibility for the serious damage that Japan caused in the past to the Chinese people through war, and deeply reproaches itself." For more details, see the Web site of the Ministry of Foreign Affairs of Japan at http://www.mofa.go.jp/region/asia-paci/china/joint72.html.

29. Tahara Soichiro, *Nihon no senso* (Tokyo: Shogakukan, 2000), p. 161.

30. Miyazawa's statement can be found on the Web site of the Ministry of Foreign Affairs of Japan, http://www.mofa.go.jp/policy/postwar/state8208.html.

31. "The World and Japan" Database Project. http://www.ioc.u-tokyo.ac.jp/~worldjpn/documents/texts/exdpm/19920117.S1J.html.

32. Kato's statement can be found on the Web site of the Ministry of Foreign Affairs of Japan, http://www.mofa.go.jp/policy/postwar/state9207.html.

33. Kono's statement can be found on the Web site of the Ministry of Foreign Affairs of Japan, http://www.mofa.go.jp/policy/women/fund/state9308.html.

34. http://www.mofa.go.jp/policy/women/fund/state9507.html.

35. Yoshio Sugimoto, *An Introduction to Japanese Society* (Cambridge: Cambridge University Press, 2002), pp. 28–30.

36. "'Hoeru Daijin' Ooinihoeru," *Sekai,* October 1986. pp. 122–33.

37. Adachi Yoshihiko, "Kodomo seinentachi ga toikakeru mono: otonatachi wa ano senso kara nani o manandanoka?" in *Ajia Taiheiyo Senso kara nani o manabuka?* ed. Rekishi Kyoiku-sha Kyogikai (Tokyo: Aoki Shoten, 1994), pp. 4–24.

38. Tawara Yoshifumi, "Dokyumento: Tsukurukai undo towa nandattaka?" *Sekai,* December 2001, pp. 105–20.

39. Fujioka Nobukatsu/Jiyushugi Shikan Kenkyukai, *Manga: Kyokasho ga oshienai rekishi,* 3 vols. (Tokyo: Fusosha, 1998).

40. China Radio International, http://web12.cri.com.cn/english/2001/Apr/13714.htm.

41. *Cable News Network.* April 14, 2005.

42. *The Japan Times,* May 15, 2007.

43. *Japan Echo,* 34, no. 2 (2007):11.

44. Julian Dierkes, "The Stability of Postwar Japanese History Education amid Global Changes," in *History Education and National Identity in East Asia,* ed. Edward Vickers and Alisa Jones (London and New York: Routledge, 2005), pp. 255–74; Takashi Yoshida, "The Making of the Rape of Nanking," pp. 81–101.

45. Seo Tae-Yol, "Urinara Sahoegwa Gyoyukgwajung Gaebaleui Munjaejumgwa Gaesun-banghyang: Jae 7 cha mit 8 cha Gyoyuk Gwajungeul Jungshimeuiro," a paper presented at the 5th Gyogwaseo Forum (April 6, 2006): Seoul, Korea.

46. The Chinese textbooks after the liberalization are subject to stringent screening processes. Oshiba Ryo, "National History-kara Transnational History-e: Nihon-ni okeru rekishi kyokasho mondai o jirei-toshite," in *Kiokuto shiteno Paru Haba,* ed. Hosoya Chihiro, Irie Akira, and Oshiba Ryo (Tokyo: Mineruva Shobo, 2007), pp. 400–20.

47. Anne F. Thurston, "Community and Isolation: Memory and Forgetting: China in Search of Itself," in *Memory and History in East and Southeast Asia: Issues of Identity in International Relations,* ed. Gerrit W. Gong (Washington, DC: The Center for Strategic & International Studies, 2001), pp. 149–72.

48. Cho Satoshi, Ko Kenshuku, and Ou Koshun, "Chugoku," in Nakamura, *Higashi Ajiano rekishi kyokasho wa do kakarete Iruka*, pp. 39–78.

49. Shin Kawashima, "The History Factor in Sino-Japanese Ties," *Japan Echo* 32, no. 5 (2005):20.

50. Shoji Junichiro, "Ilboneui Daeasia Jungchaekeui Yoksajuk Baegyung," *Gukjaehak Nonchong*, Vol. 8 (Daegu, Korea: Kemyung University) (February 2004), pp. 344–55.

51. Kawashima, "History Factor," p. 20.

52. Ibid., p. 20.

53. Wu Xinbo, "Memory and Perception: The Chinese Thinking of Japan," in Gong, *Memory and History in East and Southeast Asia*, pp. 65–85; En Iji, "Kindaika to Chugoku no rekishi kyokasho mondai," in *Chugoku no rekishi kyokasho mondai* (Tokyo: Nihon Kyoho-sha, 2006), pp. 51–79.

54. Choi Su Byon, "Hakmunjok Sadaewa Jajon," in *Hangukin Hangukbyong* (Seoul, Korea: Ilnyum, 1987), p. 180.

55. Korean Ministry of Education, *Junghakgyo Guksa* (sophomore) (Seoul: Korean Ministry of Education, 1998), pp. 10–11.

56. Guksa Pyonchan Wiwonhoe/Gukjung Doseo Pyonchan Wiwonhoe, *Junghakgyo Guksa* (Seoul: Korean Ministry of Education and Human Resources, 2007), p. 194.

57. Ibid., p. 197.

58. For the Kwangju uprising for the nationwide democratization, see Henry Scott-Stokes and Lee Jae Eui, eds., *The Kwangju Uprising: Eyewitness Press Accounts of Korea's Tiananmen* (Armonk, NY and London: M.E. Sharpe, 2000); Linda A. Lewis, *Laying Claim to the Memory of May: A Look Back at the 1980 Kwangju Uprising* (Honolulu: University of Hawai'i Press and Center for Korean Studies, University of Hawai'i, 2002).

59. Guksa Pyonchan Wiwonhoe/Gukjung Doseo Pyonchan Wiwonhoe, p. 2.

60. Ibid., p. 311; for a critical assessment of the official textbook narratives, see Gyogwaseo Forum, ed., *Gyungjae Gyogwaseo, Mueutsi Munjaeinga?* (Seoul: Duraesidae, 2006).

61. See Anna M. Alonso, "The Effects of Truth: Re-presentations of the Past and the Imagining of Community," *Journal of Historical Sociology* 1, no. 3 (1988):33–57.

62. Park Sopu, "Korea," in Nakamura, *Higashi Ajiano rekishi kyokasho*, pp. 79–92.

63. Interview with a leading conservative academic in Korea on February 16, 2005; also see Gyogwaseo Forum, *Hanguk Hyundaesaeui Huguwa Jinsil* (Seoul: Duraesidae, 2004); Park Hyo Jong, Choi Mun Hyung, Kim Jae Ho, and Lee Ju Young, *Ppaeatkin Uri Yoksa Doechatki: Gyogwaseo Forumyi Haebuhan 'Waegok'eui Jinsang* (Seoul: Giparang, 2006).

64. Donald Baker, "Exacerbated Politics: The Legacy of Political Trauma in South Korea," paper in progress, 2007; see Han Yongu, *Uri Yoksa* (Seoul: Kyongsewon, 2001).

65. See also Kobayashi Yoshinori, *Sensoron*, 3 vols. (Tokyo: Gento-sha, 1998, 2001, 2003).

66. Mayumi Itoh, *Globalization of Japan: Japanese Sakoku Mentality and U.S. Efforts to Open Japan* (New York: St. Martin's Press, 1998).

67. Wu Xinbo, "Memory and Perception: The Chinese Thinking of Japan," in Gong, *Memory and History in East and Southeast Asia*, pp. 65–85.

68. See Mari Yamamoto, *Grassroots Pacifism in Post-War Japan: The Rebirth of a Nation* (New York: RoutledgeCurzon, 2004).

69. Tatsumi Okabe, "Historical Remembering and Forgetting in Sino-Japanese Relations," in Gong, *Memory and History in East and Southeast Asia*, pp. 47–63.

70. Terumasa Nakanishi, "China Plays Its History Cards," *Japan Echo*, 32, no. 4 (2005):18–23.

71. See Kan Kimura, "A Dangerous Current in Roh's South Korea," *Japan Echo*, 31, no. 4 (2004):44–48.

72. Ryosei Kokubun and Liu Jie, "The Danger of China's Disaffected Masses," *Japan Echo*, 31, no. 6 (2004):51–55.

73. See Douglas North, "A Transaction Cost Theory of Politics," *Journal of Theoretical Politics*, 2, no. 4 (2004):335–67.

74. Melinda Liu, "Line of Defense," *Newsweek*, October 24, 2005, pp. 26–30.

75. See Zhu Jianrong, "The Real Reasons for the Anti-Japanese Outburst," *Japan Echo*, 32, no. 4 (2005):14–17.

76. See Ni-Chu-Kan Sangoku Kyotsu Rekishi Kyozai Iinkai,ed., *Mirai o hiraku rekishi: Higashi Ajia sangoku no kingendaishi* (Tokyo: Kobunken, 2005/2006).

77. "Kawaru rekishi kyoiku: Ni-Chu-Kan-Tai saishin jijo," *Asahi Shinbun*. May 28, 2007, p. 13.

6

The Yasukuni Issue and Japan's International Relations

Akihiko Tanaka

To visit or not to visit the Yasukuni Shrine: that is the question that every Japanese prime minister is expected to answer at the outset of his administration. Whether to pay tribute to two million soldiers and a limited number of political leaders enshrined in this Shrine is one of the most controversial symbolic acts of prime ministers in Japan. If the answer is in the affirmative, the prime minister should expect substantial international criticism, especially from China and Korea. If the answer is in the negative, he should expect substantial criticism from the veterans association (*izokukai*) of Japan and other conservative segments of Japanese society. Junichiro Koizumi, as a candidate of the Liberal Democratic Party (LDP) presidential election in April 2001, promised to visit the Yasukuni Shrine on August 15, the date of Japan's defeat in World War II, once he became prime minister. In 2001, accepting the advice that a visit on August 15 could be too provocative to Yasukuni critics, he visited there on August 13. Though changing the dates of his visits, Koizumi kept visiting the shrine once a year. Every time he visited the shrine, Beijing and Seoul raised strong voices of criticism. Koizumi's visit to the Yasukuni Shrine became the central issue of Japan's bilateral relations with China and South Korea. After Koizumi's visit to the Shrine in October 2005, the leaders of both countries went so far as to refuse bilateral summit meetings with Koizumi. Japan-China relations reached the most abnormal stage since

1972, when two countries established formal diplomatic relations. The Japanese-South Korean relationship also sank to the bottom since Prime Minister Yasuhiro Nakasone's visit to South Korea in 1984, the first visit of Japan's prime minister to South Korea. Koizumi made his final visit to the shrine as prime minister on August 15, 2006, the date of visit he promised as a candidate in 2001; Koizumi said that he decided to visit the shrine on this day because no matter how he changed the dates or styles of visit, he was criticized in any case.

Shinzo Abe, successor to Koizumi, declared that he would not say either to visit or not to visit the Shrine, saying either would create unnecessary political and diplomatic turmoil. Accepting his "ambiguous strategy," China and South Korea welcomed Abe when he visited both countries immediately after he became prime minister in September 2006. Yasuo Fukuda, who assumed the prime minister's post after Abe's sudden resignation, declared that he would not visit the Shrine. By saying so, Fukuda would be free from international criticism. It remains to be seen, however, whether he would be free from domestic criticism. It seems possible that this issue may become dormant after a great turmoil during the Koizumi era. The fact that even Abe, the champion of the conservative nationalists, shied away from the issue indicated the degree of political danger that this issue evokes. The result of the House of Councilors election in July 2007 also made the revival of this issue less likely, since the Democratic Party of Japan, the winner of the election, had been critical of Koizumi's visits to the Shrine. However, the fundamental issue surrounding the Yasukuni Shrine has not yet been resolved: how the Japanese as a nation are to properly mourn and pay respects to the soldiers and victims of wars in the modern period. This chapter first describes the history of the Yasukuni Shrine, second examines the evolution of domestic controversy of the Shrine, and, third analyzes how it evolved as a diplomatic issue.[1]

HISTORY OF YASUKUNI

The Yasukuni Shrine was founded by order of the Meiji Emperor in June 1869 under the name of Tokyo Shokonsha (Shrine to Invite Spirits) mainly to mourn the war dead of the Boshin War of 1867, the war between the forces of Tokugawa Shogunate and the anti-Shogunate forces. The Anti-Shogunate forces created the Meiji government under the Meiji Emperor and decided to establish a spiritual site to pay tribute to the 3,500 soldiers who sacrificed their lives in a war that played an important role in bringing about the Meiji Restoration. The Tokyo Shokonsha was renamed Yasukuni Jinja (Shrine to Pacify the Country) in 1879 and was officially sanctioned as a Special Class State Shrine (*bekkaku kanpeisha*). The Yasukuni Shrine was distinct among Shinto shrines in that it enshrines ordinary subjects without particular distinction other than they sacrificed their lives for the Emperor. Most traditional shrines enshrine mythological gods, former emperors, members of imperial families, and other "great figures" in history. Yasukuni, in contrast, was a shrine for ordinary people.

Yasukuni was, in a way, a symbolic representation of nation-building under the Meiji government. Yukichi Fukuzawa lamented in 1874: "Japan, though it has a government, does not have a nation."[2] The Meiji government's introduction of conscription was an attempt to incorporate the Japanese into a nation-state. In the beginning, this measure met strong protests among peasants. By enshrining ordinary soldiers who died for the Meiji Emperor, Yasukuni played an important role in unification of the nation.

However, not all those who died in the war, but only those who fought for the government were deified in the Shrine. In other words, those soldiers who fought on behalf of the Shogunate and followers of Takamori Saigo in the Seinan War that challenged the Meiji government were not enshrined. Because of this character, the number of deities increased as Japan engaged in many wars in the late nineteenth and the twentieth centuries. Table 6.1 shows the number of deities thus enshrined in each war. As these numberd indicate, the overwhelming majority of gods in the shrine were from the Japanese wars in the 1930s and 1940s.

As Japan was defeated in 1945 and occupied by the Allied forces, the fundamental nature of the Yasukuni Shrine changed. In order to eradicate the sources of militarism in Japan, the General Headquarters (GHQ) of the occupation forces ordered the Japanese government to implement the principle of separation of religion and state and therefore to dismantle the system of National Shinto. Article 20 of the Constitution of Japan, which was drafted under the strong influence of the GHQ, stipulates: "(1) Freedom of religion is guaranteed to all. No religious organization shall receive any privileges from the State, nor exercise any political authority. (2) No person shall be compelled to take part in any religious acts, celebration, rite or practice. (3) The State and its organs shall refrain from religious education or any other religious activity." The alternatives that GHQ posed to Yasukuni were (1) to become a secular national memorial facility or (2) to become a private religious body separated from the state. Yasukuni and the Japanese government chose the latter.[3] When Japan restored independence in April 1952, Yasukuni became a private religious corporation under the Religious Corporation Law.

Table 6.1   The Number of Deities Enshrined in the Yasukuni Shrine

Meiji Restoration	7,751
Seinan War (Satsuma Rebellion)	6,971
Sino-Japanese War	13,619
Taiwan Expedition	1,130
Boxer Rebellion	1,256
Russo-Japanese War	88,429
World War I	4,850
Jinan Incident	185
Manchu Incident	17,176
Sino-Japanese War	191,250
Asia-Pacific War (*Daitoa* War)	2,133,915

Source: Tokyo Shinbun, August 10, 2005

Three issues emerged surrounding Yasukuni after 1952: the first was the treatment of the "war criminals," the second, the issue of "re-nationalization" of the shrine, and the third, the constitutional issue of politicians' visits to the shrine. The issue of "war criminals" can be divided into two parts: the Class-A war criminals and the Class-B and C war criminals. The former were judged by the International Military Tribunal for the Far East (Tokyo Military Tribunal) on the charges of "crimes against peace," while the latter were tried at 47 courts in seven countries on the charges of conventional war crimes. Those indicted as Class-B or C criminals numbered 5,644, and 934 of them were sentenced to death.[4] The Japanese public showed a great deal of sympathy to the families of those Class-B and C criminals who were sentenced to death or those who died during the imprisonment immediately after they regained independence in 1952. Some questioned the fairness of the trials and many sympathized with their families who lost fathers and husbands. As the Bereaved Family Support Law, which passed the Diet immediately after the independence in 1952, did not cover those families, nearly bipartisan support was formed in the Diet to revise the law to include the bereaved families of the war criminals. The revision of the law passed the Diet unanimously in 1953. With the revision of the law, the death of the war criminals came to be recognized as a special type of death (*homushi,* literally meaning "death of legal duty") separated from conventional death penalty under the Japanese legal system. The supporters of the bereaved families began to consider the passage of the law as the rehabilitation of those judged as war criminals by military trials of the Allied countries.[5] Yasukuni, however, did not take actions on those "deaths of legal duty."

There were a huge number of war dead who had not been enshrined even in the early 1950s. Despite the fundamental change of legal status, Yasukuni and the government had to cooperate if the war dead were to be enshrined; unless the government provided the data of the war dead, Yasukuni alone was not able to identify who were qualified to be enshrined. The Ministry of Health and Welfare, which took over the management of the prewar military personnel, continued to provide the data of the war dead to Yasukuni. As the process of enshrinement of normal war dead proceeded, the Ministry of Health and Welfare started sounding out the enshrinement of war criminals. Though there was some hesitation in the decision-making body of Yasukuni, it accepted to enshrine Class-B and C war criminals in 1959. Yasukuni proceeded with the enshrinement of some 1,000 Class-B and C war criminals quietly along with other war dead.

Yasukuni was more cautious about the enshrinement of the Class-A war criminals. The Class-A war criminals were the top leaders of Japan judged by the Tokyo Military Tribunal to have committed "crimes against peace." Altogether 28 political, military, and intellectual leaders were indicted; seven of them (General Hideki Tojo, General Seishiro Itagaki, General Kenji Dohihara, General Iwane Matsui, General Heitaro Kimura, Lieutenant General Akira Muto, and Prime Minister Koki Hirota) were sentenced to death; 16 were sentenced to imprisonment for life; one (Shigenori Togo) was sentenced to imprisonment for 20 years; and one (Mamoru Shigemitsu) was sentenced to imprisonment for seven years. Yosuke Matsuoka, the foreign minister who concluded the Japan-Germany-Italy alliance, and Admiral Osami Nagano died during the trials. Shumei Okawa, a militarist ideologue, was discharged for mental derangement. General Yoshijiro Umezu, Ambassador Toshio Shiratori, Foreign Minister Shigenori Togo, General Kuniaki Koiso, and Prime Minister Kiichiro Hiranuma died during imprisonment. Shigemitsu was released on parole in October 1950. Others sentenced to life imprisonment were released on parole and in 1958 eleven countries involved in the Tokyo Military Tribunal agreed to release all remaining Class-A war criminals. The lenience on the surviving Class-A war criminals may have been judged necessary by the United States and other countries involved in the Tokyo Tribunal if only to promote strong ties with the now allied Japan in the Cold War. However, it also encouraged the critics of the Tokyo Tribunal to argue that the sentences were not fair. As Shigemitsu became Foreign Minister and Nobusuke Kishi, one of the suspects of Class-A charges, who was released before indictment, became prime minister, conservative forces in Japan began to argue that all war criminals needed to be rehabilitated.[6]

After all surviving Class-A war criminals were released in 1958, the Ministry of Health and Welfare began to sound out with Yasukuni about the possibility of their enshrinement along with Class-B and C war criminals. Yasukuni under the leadership of Chief Priest Fujimaro Tsukuba did not make any decision. The Ministry of Health and Welfare sent a list of Class-A war criminals who were supposed to be qualified for enshrinement to Yasukuni in February 1966. The list included seven Class-A war criminals sentenced to death and seven others who died during trials and imprisonment. The Council of Worshipers' Representatives (*Sukeisha Sodaikai*), the decision-making body of Yasukuni, decided that they were qualified to be enshrined in January 1969.[7] Whether or not to actually enshrine them was decided to be in the discretion of the Chief Priest. Chief Priest Tsukuba did not enshrine them; after 32 years of service as Chief Priest, he died in March 1978.

Nagayoshi Matsudaira, grandson of Lord Yoshinaga Matsudaira of Fukui and a former Self-Defense Force official, was appointed by the Council of Worshipers' Representatives as Chief Priest in June 1978. One of the strong supporters of Matsudaira was Kazuto Ishida, former Chief Justice of the Supreme Court, who was known for conservative thinking and was a supporter of Yasukuni. When Ishida asked Matsudaira to assume the position of Chief Priest, Matsudaira told Ishida, "Overturning the verdicts of the Tokyo Tribunal is essential to achieve Japan's spiritual renaissance. Therefore, it is necessary to enshrine those who are called Class-A war criminals."[8] Matsudaira enshrined 14 Class-A war criminals in October 1978. The enshrinement was not publicized and it was only in April 1979 that newspapers reported about it. Many Yasukuni supporters welcomed Matsudaira's decision. It was not known then, however, that the Showa Emperor was deeply disturbed by the enshrinement of the Class-A war criminals. In a memo of Tomohiko Tomita, former grand chamberlain of the Imperial Household, dated April 28, 1988, which was made public posthumously by his family only in June 2006, the Showa Emperor indicated that because of the enshrinement of Class-A war criminals, he decided not to visit the shrine any more. The Showa Emperor lamented that Chief Priest Matsudaira did not know his father's strong desire for peace.[9] Matsudaira's father served the Emperor as the first grand chamberlain of the Imperial Household from 1946 to 1948.

The second issue surrounding Yasukuni is the possibility of re-nationalization. The *Nippon Izokukai,* Japan Association of Bereaved Families of the War Dead, together with other organizations, first called for the re-nationalization of the Yasukuni Shrine in 1956. The Liberal Democratic Party (LDP) made its draft proposal for re-nationalization in 1956. Yasukuni itself created a research committee on the ritual system of the Yasukuni Shrine. But supporters of re-nationalization were unable to find a solution that could preserve the essential religiosity that Yasukuni had without violating Article 20 of the Constitution that stipulates the separation of religion and the state. If re-nationalized Yasukuni was to preserve Shinto style rituals, it would violate the Constitution. If re-nationalized Yasukuni did not allow Shinto-style rituals and dismantled Shinto symbols such as the torii (Shinto gate), it would not be Yasukuni any more. On the occasion of the 100-year anniversary of the Yasukuni Shrine, the LDP put the Yasukuni Shrine Bill on the agenda of the Diet for the first time. However, even among the LDP members, there emerged many differences and the bill was not deliberated. The LDP staged re-nationalization bills several times to no avail.

As the re-nationalization debate was getting nowhere, the focus of the Nippon Izo-kukai and other organizations was directed to formalizing official visits by prime ministers and other members of the cabinet. It was customary for prime ministers to visit the shrine from the 1950s to the early 1980s. The Emperor also visited the shrine until 1975. During this period, a number of lawsuits were brought against the government involvement in Shinto-related rituals such as whether a local government could use budget to fund a Shinto ceremony of purifying a building site. Against such a backdrop, Prime Minister Takeo Miki visited the Yasukuni Shrine on August 15, 1975. In response to a question whether his visit was an official one, Miki responded that his visit was his personal one. From this time one, the prime ministers were always asked by reporters if their visits were private or official. Given this distinction, supporters of Yasukuni began their efforts to attain "official visits" of the prime ministers, partly now that re-nationalization became impossible. Official visits of prime ministers became a substitute goal for them. Table 6.2 shows the visits of the Yasukuni Shrine by the Showa Emperor and the prime ministers.

Yasuhiro Nakasone, who became prime minister in 1983, declared that his government was to pursue "complete resettlement of postwar politics" (*sengo seiji no sokessan*). One of the most important symbolic acts that he planned was to make his visit to the Yasukuni Shrine an official one. Nakasone created an advisory council on visits of members of the cabinet to the Yasukuni Shrine in August 1984 and asked the panel to present to him how it is possible for the prime minister to visit the shrine without violating the Constitution. The advisory panel submitted its report on August 9, 1985, which indicated that there was a way to make an official visit without violating the Constitution, if visitors did not follow Shinto-style rituals, although the recommendation was not a unanimous one. Nakasone, regarding the panel's report as justification of an official visit, made a visit to the Yasukuni Shrine on

Table 6.2   Visits of the Showa Emperor and Prime Ministers to the Yasukuni Shrine*

The Emperor Showa	Oct. 16, 1952; Oct. 19, 1954; Apr. 23, 1957; Apr. 23, 1959; Oct. 19, 1965; Oct. 20, 1969; Nov. 21, 1975
Shigeru Yoshida	Oct. 18, 1951; (May 5, 1952); Oct. 17, 1952; Apr. 23, 1953; (Oct. 24, 1953); (Apr. 25, 1954); (Oct. 20, 1954)
Nobusuke Kishi	Apr. 25, 1957; Oct. 21, 1958
Hayato Ikeda	Oct. 10, 1960; Jun. 18, 1961; Nov. 15, 1961; Nov. 4, 1962, Sep . 22, 1963
Eisaku Sato	Apr. 21, 1965; Apr. 21, 1966; Apr. 22, 1967; Apr. 23, 1968; Apr. 22, 1969; Oct. 18, 1969; Apr. 22, 1970; Oct. 17, 1970; Apr. 22, 1971; Oct. 18, 1971, Apr. 22, 1972
Kakuei Tanaka	Jul. 8, 1972; Oct. 17, 1972; Apr. 23. 1973; Oct. 18, 1973; Apr. 23, 1974; Oct. 19, 1974
Takeo Miki	Apr. 22, 1975; Aug. 15, 1975; Oct. 18, 1976
Takeo Fukuda	Apr. 21, 1977; Apr. 21, 1978; Aug. 15, 1978; Oct. 18, 1978
Masayoshi Ohira	Apr. 21, 1979; Oct. 18, 1979; Apr. 21, 1980
Zenko Suzuki	Aug. 15, 1980; Oct. 18, 1980; Apr. 21, 1981; Aug. 15, 1981; Oct. 17, 1981; Apr. 21, 1982; Aug. 15, 1982, Oct. 18, 1982
Yasuhiro Nakasone	Apr. 21, 1983; Aug. 15, 1983; Oct. 18, 1983; Jan. 5, 1984; Apr. 21, 1984; Aug. 15, 1984; Oct. 18, 1984; Jan. 21, 1985; Apr. 22, 1985; Aug. 15, 1985
Ryutaro Hashimoto	Jul. 29, 1996
Junichiro Koizumi	Aug. 13, 2001; Apr. 21, 2002, Jan. 14, 2003; Jan. 1, 2004; Oct. 17, 2005; Aug. 15, 2006

*The visits on the list are the publicly known visits. It is generally believed that Kiichi Miyazawa made a
   secret visit in November 1992.
Source: Dates of Prime Ministers' visits to the Shrine is from Kazuo Ichitani, "Yasukuni jinja sampai
   mondai," in *Kiro ni tatsu Nicchu kankei: kako to no taiwa, mirai e no mosaku,* ed. Iechika Ryoko,
   et. al. (Tokyo: Koyo-shobo, 2007), p. 40; also see the government's response to Representative Kiyomi
   Tsujimoto, February 10, 2006. http://www.kiyomi.gr.jp/kokkai/inquiry/02_a/20060210-591.html.

August 15, 1985. Supporters of Yasukuni applauded Nakasone but this visit was the
beginning of the long period when prime ministers were virtually banned from
visiting the shrine.

YASUKUNI AS AN INTERNATIONAL ISSUE

Nakasone's official visit to the Yasukuni Shrine on August 15, 1985, added an
international dimension to the controversy as the Chinese government openly criticized him. *The People's Daily* (*Renmin Ribao*) carried a report on August 11 from
Tokyo, firing the first salvo of criticism on his visit and the problem of enshrinement

of the Class-A war criminals including Hideki Tojo.[10] A day before Nakasone's visit, the spokesman of the Chinese foreign ministry said, "If Prime Minister Nakasone and other cabinet members of Japan visit Yasukuni Shrine, they will hurt the people of the world and Asian people including Japanese and Chinese people who suffered a great deal from the militarism."[11] However, the Chinese government and media did not immediately raise much criticism after his visit. *The People's Daily* covered this issue on August 15 and 16 but made no reports after then.

It was only in late August that the Chinese leaders conveyed their concerns to Japanese visitors. On August 27 Deng Xiaoping told the Japanese visitors that he had concerns about "the movements of the militarist elements in Japan."[12] On September 3, the day commemorating the 40th anniversary of the victory over Japan, Peng Zhen, Chairman of the Standing Committee of the People's National Congress, warned that the revival of militarism in Japan would do harm to Sino-Japanese friendship. Chen Junsheng, Vice-Chairman of the All China Federation of Trade Unions, said on the same occasion that "Japanese leaders hurt the Chinese people and Southeast Asian peoples who suffered from the aggressive war [of Japan] by making official visits to Yasukuni Shrine where Japan's Class-A war criminals are enshrined."[13] On September 7, Peng Zhen told a delegation of the LDP politicians that there existed in China complaints that the Chinese leaders did not take up issues of Japan's aggression that caused 20 million deaths while they talked much about Sino-Japanese friendship.[14] Some in Japan expected that this issue seemed over when Peng Zhen told another delegation of Japanese Diet members that "if strangled too much by the past issues, we cannot proceed with friendship, it is better to put uncomfortable things behind us."[15]

The issue was by no means over, however. On September 18, students of Peking University made a protest rally on campus and on Tiananmen Square. They started posting wall papers a few days before calling for a demonstration on Tiananmen Square on September 19 to mourn the victims of the war against Japan and to protest the revival of Japanese militarism and Japan's current economic aggression. They also sent telegrams to other universities throughout China. The University authorities denied their involvement in the demonstration and stated that their demonstration did not necessarily represent the entire opinion of Peking University.[16] The Chinese government tried to moderate their movements by sending such figures as Yang Zhenya, Director General of Asian Bureau of the Foreign Ministry, to Peking University on September 17 to no avail. Students gathered together on Tiananmen Square and shouted such slogans as "Down with Nakasone!" "Down with Japanese Militarism!" and "Oppose the visit to Yasukuni Shrine." The police did nothing to stop them. The posters denounced Nakasone's Yasukuni visits in the most violent tone. One of them warned that the visit of Yasukuni that enshrined war criminals' ghosts was to "ridicule the peace, and challenge the Chinese people." Another stated: "The new devils are enshrining the tombs of the old ogres. Yasuhiro pays tributes to the spirit of Hideki Tojo. Raise your eyebrows and see your three foot sword in the snow. Raise 100 million and destroy Ogres." "The land of China was once humiliated," another wall paper lamented and called: "Get rid of militarism! Stinking bugs conspiring to create troubles are destined to be destroyed. You stupid! Nakasone."[17]

On the following day, the spokesman of the Chinese Foreign Ministry made the following statement:

> The government of China expressed its opinion to the government of Japan on the issue of official visits of Japanese cabinet members to Yasukuni Shrine and asked the government of Japan to handle the issue cautiously. Regrettably, the Japanese side, without heeding to our friendly advice, went ahead of the official visit and hurt the people of China. It is an established policy of the government of China to develop neighborly and friendly relations between China and Japan with the government and people of Japan based on the principles decided by the China-Japan Joint Communiqué and the China-Japan Peace and Friendship Treaty. We hope that the leaders of the government of Japan fulfill the promise not to take the road of militarism and to contribute to establishing the Sino-Japanese friendship and peace in the world.[18]

Anti-Japanese protests spread to various parts of China. Students in Xian were reported to have made protests from September 30 to October 2. It was also reported that anti-Japanese demonstrations took place in Chengdu in Sichuan Province. One poster in Yan'an was reported to have pointed out that there had been protests in eight major cities in China.[19] The Chinese government under the leadership of Hu Yaobang, on the one hand, tried to stop these anti-Japanese movements, while, on the other hand, it stepped up its efforts to demand that Japanese leaders stop visiting the Shrine. Wu Xuequan, China's Foreign Minister, asked Shintaro Abe, Japan's Foreign Minister, who visited China in early October, "to understand the feelings of the Chinese people that existed behind the demonstration in Beijing on September 18."[20]

Strong reaction and protests in China on his visit to Yasukuni were unexpected developments for Nakasone. Since he became prime minister, Nakasone attached importance to diplomacy especially with the United States and China. After solidifying his personal relationship with President Ronald Reagan, he made special efforts to cultivate friendship with Hu Yaobang, General Secretary of the Chinese Communist Party, who was regarded as the designated successor to Deng Xiaoping. As Hu Yaobang also welcomed Nakasone's positive attitude toward China, he made various attempts to improve Sino-Japanese relations such as inviting 3,000 Japanese youths to China in 1984. The Japanese government itself called the state of the Japan-China relationship " the best in history." The strong reaction of the Chinese government and the students' protests demonstrated the vulnerability of the relations between Tokyo and Beijing.

The pressing issue for Nakasone then was whether to repeat the official visit to Yasukuni during its autumn festival starting in the middle of October. In addition to Foreign Minister Abe's report of his conversation with his Chinese counterpart, Nakasone received information from various sources, all of which indicated that Nakasone's Yasukuni visit put Hu Yaobang in a difficult political condition in China. On October 18, Chief Cabinet Secretary Kosei Fujinami announced that Prime Minister Nakasone would not visit the Shrine during its autumn festival. Tadashi Itagaki, LDP

Representative for the Lower House, a leading figure of promoting prime ministers' official visits to the shrine, and a son of General Seishiro Itagaki, went to Nakasone's office and criticized him. Nakasone told Itagaki, "China's opposition is not a mere threat. If I continue to visit the shrine, student demonstrations will continue and Hu Yaobang may lose his job. It is not in Japan's national interest to let Japan-China relations deteriorate and to see the pro-Japan government toppled in China. The heroic spirits would not want this. Therefore, I am going to cancel the visit. China's reaction to the enshrinement of Class-A war criminals was strong. The imperial army's conduct, including the Manchurian Incident, were factually excessive."[21]

Nakasone did not visit the Yasukuni Shrine any more. On August 14, 1986, Masaharu Gotoda, Chief Cabinet Secretary, made the following statement:

> Partly due to the fact that Yasukuni Shrine enshrines what is called Class-A war criminals, the official visit to the shrine last year brought about the critical views among the citizens of the neighboring countries who suffered tremendous pains and damages from the conduct of our country in the past. [They criticize] that we visited the shrine to pay respects to the Class-A war criminals responsible for our past conduct. These views may lead to misunderstanding and distrust to Japan's reflections of the past war [that have been] revealed on various occasions and Japan's determination to pursue peace and friendship based on such reflections. That is not in the national interest of Japan, which desires to promote friendship with other countries and does not suit to the ultimate desires of the war dead.[22]

Gotoda, however, did not deny the validity of the report of the advisory panel on the Yasukuni Shrine nor did he renounce the constitutional interpretation of the official visits. He maintained that it was possible for the cabinet members to make official visits to the shrine. What he insisted was that under the international circumstances it was not wise for the Japanese prime ministers to visit the shrine.

The official visit of Nakasone in 1985 and the eventual decision not to visit the shrine gave birth to at least two structural factors that were to affect Japan's relations with neighbors. The first factor was the solidification of the symbolic meaning of the visit of the Yasukuni Shrine. The second factor was the determination of the conservative nationalists to fight against "infringement into internal affairs of Japan."

YASUKUNI VISITS AS SYMBOLIC ACTS

Like any other contentious symbolic acts, visiting the Yasukuni Shrine can symbolize many different things to many people. Sources of conflict over such symbolic acts lie in how to interpret the symbolic meaning of the act. Put differently, contentious symbolic acts are those whose "constitutive rules" in John Searle's sense are not collectively agreed. Searle shows that constitutive rules takes the form of "X counts Y in context C."[23] Many socially accepted symbolic acts have fairly stable constitutive rules. For example, raising a white flag counts as "surrender" in the context of war.

Clapping hands counts as "applause" in the context of musical and other performance. Languages are possible because of innumerable number of stable constitutive rules determining meaning of words and sentences. Conflicts sometimes emerge in these constitutive rules of certain symbols. For example, certain words are sometimes contended to be "offensive" to certain people and, therefore, are banned from use on television. To this type of contention, certain other people may argue that these words mean totally acceptable things in normal circumstances and therefore should be allowed for use on the air.

The visit of Yasukuni has a similar but complex character: it involves the contention among at least four different constitutive rules; (1) to many bereaved families, a prime minister's visit means official appreciation of the responsible person of Japan to their fathers and husbands—"mourning of the dead soldiers"; (2) to those whose religious beliefs are not compatible with the Shintoism, it means the undue and unfair endorsement of the government of Japan in support of a single shrine—"state intervention in religion"; (3) to those who believe that Class-A war criminals were not entitled to be enshrined in Yasukuni, it means the justification of the improper act of Yasukuni or, more strongly, the justification of the Japanese aggression,—"justification of aggression"; (4) to those who supported the enshrinement of Class-A war criminals, it means Japan's official rejection of the view of history imposed on by the Tokyo Military Tribunal—"rejection of the Tokyo Military Tribunal."

The conflict over Yasukuni in domestic politics from the 1950s to the 1980s generally centered on the battle between (1) "mourning of dead soldiers" and (2) "state intervention in religion." But with Matsudaira's enshrinement of Class-A war criminal in 1978, the battle between (3) "justification of aggression" and (4) "rejection of the Tokyo Military Tribunal" came to increase its weight gradually. The Showa Emperor was apparently in support of the third view, though his view was a weaker one only to criticize Yasukuni's improper treatment. The battle between the "justification of aggression" and the "rejection of the Tokyo Military Tribunal" were not known very widely in Japan until China came into this scene. Until China started its criticism against Japan over Yasukuni, many Japanese did not know that the Class-A war criminals were enshrined in Yasukuni. Susumu Nikaido, then vice president of the LDP, told Chinese Ambassador Zhang Shu that he had not known that Tojo and others had been enshrined.[24] However, the involvement of China in this issue made a critical turn in this debate in Japan. First, it propagated in Japan the idea that the interpretation of "justification of aggression" could be very important. Second, by successfully persuading Nakasone to stop visiting the shrine, China gave a significant strength to the "justification of aggression" interpretation. Though Nakasone and Gotoda agreed that "justification of aggression" was not the only valid interpretation of the official visit, it was significant that the Japanese government stopped the contentious symbolic act after China used the "justification of aggression" interpretation. The termination of the prime minister's visit to the shrine was tantamount to accepting this interpretation.

Faced with the victory of the "justification of aggression" interpretation, there emerged another structural factor in Japan: the determination among the conservative nationalists to continue the battle with the interpretation of "rejection of the Tokyo Military Tribunal" and the logic of dispelling Chinese interference into Japan's domestic affairs. In fact, the issue of Chinese interference into Japan's domestic affairs constitute another symbolic conflict: this one over conflicting constitutive rules about China's criticism against Japan. One obvious position that the Chinese government maintains is that the Chinese criticism are genuine revelations of the people of China who suffered from atrocities made by the Japanese militarism. On the other hand, the Japanese conservative nationalists argue that Chinese criticism could be motivated more by political gains that China tried to obtain from Japan. One of the reasons for the latter contention was the Chinese silence over the enshrinement of Class-A war criminals from 1979 to 1985. If enshrinement of Class-A war criminals really hurt the Chinese, why did they not start by criticizing Prime Minister Ohira who visited the Shrine in 1979 or Prime Minister Suzuki and Prime Minister Nakasone who made numerous visits to the shrine before 1985?

Actually, the Chinese media began to pay attention to Yasukuni as early as August 1980. The article carried on August 17, 1980, reviewed the history of the Yasukuni Shrine issue and it pointed out the Class-A war criminals were enshrined. *The People's Daily's* coverage on Yasukuni became increasingly more critical on Yasukuni. In this sense, the Chinese could argue that China observed Japan's movement very carefully and Nakasone's decision to make the visit official exceeded the threshold of Chinese tolerance. The Japanese conservative nationalists could still argue that China said nothing until 1985 knowing the Class-A war criminals were enshrined at least since 1980. In line with this view, the conservative nationalists began attacking Nakasone as backing down to China's interference into domestic affairs. Here, too, there emerged a battle over the symbolic act of stopping the visit; while stopping the visit means a responsible act to protect Japan's national interest for Nakasone, it was a dangerous act, from the nationalists' view, to allow China's interference into Japan's domestic politics.

To the dismay of the conservative nationalists, most of the succeeding prime ministers of Japan have followed Nakasone and stayed away from the Yasukuni Shrine. After the eruption of Chinese criticisms against his visit to the Yasukuni Shrine and the student demonstrations, Nakasone began to distance himself from the revisionist views of Japan's modern history. In the spring of 1986, a draft of a high-school textbook under the review of the Ministry of Education attracted the media and international attention. The textbook was prepared by the National Congress to Protect Japan (*Nihon o Mamoru Kokumin Kaigi*) and had a revisionist orientation. With the criticism from China and Korea mounting, Nakasone ordered the Ministry of Education to make necessary revisions to the draft of the textbook. Masayuki Fujio, Minister of Education, openly voiced his complaints against foreign critics of the textbook.[25] Fujio went ahead to prepare an article to be published by an influential monthly, *Bungei Shunju,* criticizing the Tokyo Military Tribunal and pointing out the responsibility of Korea for Japan's annexation of Korea. After the media reported the draft of Fujio's article, Nakasone summarily dismissed Fujio.

YASUKUNI AFTER NAKASONE

The succeeding prime ministers have not touched on the Yasukuni issue partly because many of them were required to handle many other pressing issues as the world entered into the ending process of the Cold War and Japanese politics also entered into a turbulent era during the 1990s. Some prime ministers not only stayed away from the Yasukuni issue, but also made an attempt to clarify Japan's responsibilities for the war and the colonization. Morihiro Hosokawa, the first non-LDP prime minister since 1955, openly declared that Japan was responsible for the aggression in the 1930s at his press conference immediately after he became prime minister. Tsutomu Hata, prime minister succeeding Hosokawa, also showed a similar view. Tomiichi Murayama, a socialist prime minister who was selected by a surprise coalition between the LDP and the Socialist Party in June 1994, made a historic pronouncement on August 15, 1995, admitting Japan's responsibilities for the war and the colonization and extending formal apologies to the neighboring countries.

With respect to the Yasukuni issue, two prime ministers, Kiichi Miyazawa and Ryutaro Hashimoto, were exceptions for different reasons. Miyazawa, a long-time liberal who finally achieved the position of prime minister in 1991, had a record of accepting foreign criticisms; he was a Chief Cabinet Secretary who accepted Chinese criticism on Japan's high-school textbooks in 1982 and agreed to change the textbook review process of the Ministry of Education; as a prime minister he accepted Korean criticism about the "comfort women," apologized and committed to make necessary investigations in the Japanese government. However, when he ran for the LDP's presidential election in October 1992, Miyazawa told Itagaki that he would visit the Yasukuni Shrine once he became prime minister. In response to Miyazawa's commitment, Itagaki told him that Nippon Izokukai would support him in the presidential election.[26]

Miyazawa was also determined to improve Japan-China relations when he became prime minister. One of the biggest requests from China to him was the Emperor's visit to China. Jiang Zemin, General Secretary of the Chinese Communist Party, extended a clear invitation in April, 1992, when he visited Japan. Many conservative nationalists in the LDP as well as those who criticized China for the 1989 Tiananmen Incident staged a large scale campaign to thwart the Emperor's visit to China. Because of this opposition, Miyazawa did not respond to China about the Emperor's visit until after the LDP's victory in the House of Councilors election in July 1992. Remembering his commitment to Izokukai, Miyazawa might have thought that the Emperor's visit to China would be politically impossible unless he made some action as to Yasukuni. Obviously, however, Miyazawa's visit to Yasukuni on August 15 would be impossible, as it would derail Japan-China relations and destroy the prospect of the Emperor's visit to China. Instead, he revealed his intention, on August 9, 1992, to make a private visit to the Yasukuni shrine at an appropriate occasion without specifying the timing. The Emperor visited China in October 1992. Miyazawa told Itagaki in the spring of 1993, "Mr. Itagaki, I fulfilled my promise to you. I visited Yasukuni Shrine."[27] Miyazawa's visit to the shrine was not confirmed, however. He said nothing about it since then until his death in 2007. Some speculate that his visit took place sometime in November 1992 after the Emperor's visit to China.[28]

Ryutaro Hashimoto's case was different from Miyazawa in the sense that Hashimoto had long been closely associated with the movements to support the Yasukuni Shrine. He served as Chairman of Nippon Izokukai from 1993 to 1995. Before becoming prime minister, he made regular visits to the shrine on its spring and autumn festivals as well as on August 15. When Hashimoto became prime minister in January 1996, Yasukuni supporters naturally expected that he would make the official visit long terminated after 1985. Hashimoto, a mainstream politician in the LDP, however, became cautious once he became prime minister. He seemed to have wanted to avoid a kind of diplomatic turmoil as experienced by Nakasone in 1985. In May, 1996, he said to the press, "I would refrain from visiting the shrine on August 15 and on spring and autumn festivals. However, no one would prevent me from making a private visit on other days."[29] Hashimoto in fact visited the shrine on July 29, his birthday. He explained: "Until I was a second grader in a primary school, I kept seeing soldiers off. Then, most of them told us to come to Kudan [where Yasukuni is located], if they died. They did not come home. I feel I need to fulfill the promise of my childhood." Because his intention was an extremely private one, he chose the most private date, his birthday. He also mentioned about his cousin who took a good care of him. "The cousin departed by saying that he would come back there (Yasukuni), I would like to visit the shrine when the official notice of his death arrived."[30] Hashimoto's visit on July 29 could be interpreted as an attempt to change the context in which a symbolic act is made. In Searle's formula, X counts as Y in context C, by changing C, he tried to redefine the meaning of the visit to Yasukuni (X) from what the Chinese and others regarded as the "justification of the aggressive war" (Y) to a purely private mourning of somebody dear to Hashimoto (Y′). To use the previous categorization above, he tried to reattach the meaning of "mourning of dead soldiers" to the visit by changing the date from August 15 to his birthday and by emphasizing the "private" nature instead of Nakasone's "official" nature.

However, his attempt was bombarded by Chinese criticism nearly as harsh as in the autumn of 1985. China's Foreign Ministry spokesman denounced Hashimoto saying, "We express our deep regret about Prime Minister Hashimoto's visit to the Yasukuni Shrine on the morning of July 29. His visit hurt the Asian people including the Chinese who suffered a great deal from Japan's militarists. Japan should reflect on the history of the aggression from the bottom of its heart and show its willingness to take the road of peaceful development by actual behavior."[31] Chinese media carried programs and articles pointing out "Dark clouds of militarism covering Japan's sky" and "Japan should rectify its reactionary view on history."[32]

From the viewpoint of China, the context in which Hashimoto made a visit to Yasukuni was not a private one. Chinese articles criticizing his visit indicated that the context was the incessant trends of the Japanese right wing to promote Japanese nationalism and to antagonize China. Hashimoto, in the Chinese analysis, was a hawkish politician with full right-wing credentials. He had taken a very tough position in the Taiwan Strait crisis the previous March. He promoted redefinition of the Japanese-U.S. alliance by signing the Japan-U.S. Joint Declaration with President Bill Clinton in April, which appeared to endorse a "China threat" thesis and to justify Japan's remilitarization. Furthermore, about two weeks before Hashimoto's visit to the shrine, a right-wing organization, *Nippon Seinensha*, constructed a lighthouse on Kita-kojima in the Senkaku/Diaoyutai islands. Chinese analyses of Japan aired in the middle of August all indicated that these movements were connected with each other. *The People's Daily* commentary suggested, "it is not an accident that Japan challenged Chinese sovereignty on the Diaoyutai issue; it is an inevitable expression of the trend of Japanese politics to lean to the right and the Japanese desire to display power internationally."[33] Hashimoto's visit to the shrine was "the tip of an iceberg," in the analysis of China's Japan watchers. In a close analysis of the Japanese domestic politics, it is far-fetched to connect Hashimoto's rise to prime minister's position, the Japanese-U.S. joint activities to redefine their alliance, Hashimoto's decision to visit the shrine on his birthday, and the right wingers' attempt to build a light house in the Senkaku/Diaoyutai as an intertwined systemic right-wing attempt. It seems closer to reality to understand all movements having their own independent dynamics. In any case, the context in which China saw in Hashimoto's visit was radically different from Hashimoto's view. In the end, Hashimoto came to believe that it was in the Japan's interest to dispel such Chinese views of Japan and decided that visit to the shrine was not worth continuing. He declared that he would not visit the shrine on October 16, the date the official notice of the death of his beloved cousin arrived. He said, "I, as Prime Minister, should choose action so as not to invite unnecessary suspicions on Japan which might damage Japan's interest."[34]

Hashimoto's attempt to change the context, contrary to his intention, solidify the strength of the Chinese interpretation, the "justification of aggression" interpretation. Furthermore, it added another element in the conflict over the constitutive rule about the meaning of the Yasukuni visit; previously, the context in which the "justification of aggression" interpretation was emphasized tended to be associated with "official visits" on special occasions such as August 15. After the Hashimoto visit, the Chinese insisted that the dates did not matter. As a result of Hashimoto's cancellation of his visit on October 16, the Chinese position in the battle of symbolic acts was strengthened if not completely agreed to by Hashimoto.

The Hashimoto episode also gave another impression on the conservative nationalists and the large number of the Yasukuni supporters not necessarily holding the position of the "rejection of the Tokyo Military Tribunal." Those who subscribe to the "mourning dead soldiers" interpretation began to see the Chinese intention in a more suspicious color. Many Japanese did not see Japan as taking a militarist road in 1996, nor did they believe there was a right-wing conspiracy headed by Hashimoto. Not just the conservative nationalists but the larger public were beginning to revise their views on China's symbolic act of criticizing Japan. They began to suspect that China had other political motivations when it criticized Hashimoto. This suspicion increased a great deal when President Jiang Zemin repeated his lecture on history on various occasions including the imperial reception and meeting with business leaders during his state visit to Japan in late 1998. In 1998, no major political figures in Japan made any symbolic acts that might invite Chinese criticism; Prime Minister Obuchi did not visit the Yasukuni Shrine. From the viewpoint of many Japanese, it was puzzling why the Chinese president was repeatedly raising the issue of history when few Japanese politicians made insensitive statements or acted provocatively. Jiang Zemin's lectures on history had the impact of solidifying the Japanese constitutive rule of the meaning of China's criticism, that is, that China's criticism stemmed largely from political motivations.[35]

KOIZUMI VISITS

It is not clear why, during the LDP presidential election, Junichiro Koizumi made a campaign promise of visiting the Yasukuni Shrine on August 15. Koizumi was not known as a supporter of Yasukuni in any sense. He had challenged the LDP presidential elections two times before, but in neither case had he put the Yasukuni issue on his agenda. On record, he visited the shrine in 1989 and 1997 when he was Health and Welfare Minister. Otherwise, it was not clear how often he visited the shrine. In any case, he had not been regarded as a serious Yasukuni supporter. Based on his previous indifference to Yasukuni, one may be able to explain his campaign pledge simply as a political ploy to increase his support in the presidential election campaign. One factor was Ryutaro Hashimoto, another candidate in the same presidential election in 2001. Until the beginning of the campaign, many media regarded Hashimoto as the strongest candidate. Though he was forced to resign as prime minister in 1997, he was one of the most knowledgeable and experienced politicians in the LDP and was supported by the largest faction. Hashimoto, however, declared that he would not visit the Yasukuni Shrine if he were elected. He mentioned about his previous visit in 1996 saying "it created a big trouble and I stopped visiting there."[36] According to Hiromu Nonaka, a senior politician in the Hashimoto faction and Chief Cabinet Secretary under Prime Ministers Obuchi and Mori:

> Mr. Koizumi said for the first time that he would make an official visit to Yasukuni Shrine after the campaign started. He clearly had in mind the votes that could be cast to Mr. Hashimoto among the local LDP members. Nippon Izokukai and the Military Pension League had long been close to Mr. Hashimoto. By saying that he would visit the shrine, Mr. Koizumi attempted to steal the votes that could have originally gone to Hashimoto.[37]

How critical the Yasukuni issue was in the 2001 LDP presidential election was not evident. As there emerged a sudden popular support to Koizumi in early April, he could have won the election even if he had not made the commitment to visit the shrine.

In addition to the campaign calculation, Koizumi may have genuinely wanted to visit the shrine to dispel the Chinese "justification of aggression" interpretation.

The interpretation he wanted to establish was the "mourning of dead soldiers" interpretation. He had never committed to the "rejection of the Tokyo Military Tribunal" interpretation. In his mind, this was a battle not between the "justification of aggression" interpretation and the "rejection of the Tokyo Military Tribunal" interpretation but between the "justification of aggression" interpretation and the "mourning of dead soldiers" interpretation. Koizumi kept saying that his visit would not justify the aggressive war and that his visit simply reflect his "mind" to mourn the war dead who sacrificed their lives for the nation. He may have been more motivated by his determination to stop China's "interference" into Japan's domestic affairs. As a member of the Hashimoto cabinet in 1996, he may have felt that it was wrong to back down on the matter of "heart" simply because of the criticisms from China.

Before becoming prime minister, Koizumi had been closely united with Koichi Kato and Taku Yamazaki, two politicians who happened to have long acquaintances with China. As August 15 approached, China began its attempt to dissuade Koizumi from visiting the shrine openly. In addition, China asked Kato and Yamazaki to persuade him to stop the visit. In the process, somebody must have suggested that a visit on a date other than August 15 could be less dangerous. Probably heeding this advice, Koizumi visited the shrine on August 13. *Mainichi Shinbun*'s poll indicated 65 percent of the respondents supported Koizumi's visit on August 13. The reasons of support varied: 29 percent of the supporters said that his visit was good for mourning of the war dead; 29 percent said that it was good for Koizumi to show some considerations to China and Korea by shifting the date. On the other hand, of those who did not support Koizumi's visit on August 13, 33 percent said it was not good because he was pressured by China and Korea.[38]

Koizumi was determined to show to the Chinese leaders that his visit was not meant to glorify the Japanese aggression. In his statement released after his visit to the shrine, he stated

> Japan brought about a large damage to many people in the world including our nationals. In a certain period in the past, based on the wrong policies, Japan caused immeasurable damage and pains to our neighboring countries in Asia by colonization and aggression. The damage still remains as incurable wounds in the mind of many people in the region.[39]

When he made a one-day visit to Beijing in October 2001, he went to Marco Polo Bridge, where the Sino-Japanese War had started in 1937, and stated: "I have just observed the display in the museum here with the sense of apology and mourning to the Chinese people who were victimized by the Japanese aggression."[40] Jiang Zemin told Koizumi in their meeting after Koizumi's visit to Marco Polo Bridge that it was not advisable for Mr. Koizumi to visit the shrine. Koizumi made no response to this advice. Probably, Jiang might have misjudged Koizumi's silence. Jiang may have thought Koizumi had finally come to understand the Chinese view. In fact, Koizumi behaved as a strong supporter of Sino-Japanese friendship. When Koizumi was invited to make a speech at the Boao Forum in April 2002, he declared that China was not a "threat" to Japan or to the world. His statement was applauded by Zhu Rongji and other Chinese leaders. However, to the surprise of Jiang, Koizumi visited the Yasukuni Shrine on April 21, 2002.

Koizumi's action has been an attempt to change the context in which the Yasukuni visit is interpreted. He showed to the Japanese and the Chinese that he had a genuine sense of repentance on the aggression and colonization and that he supported China in international arena by saying China was not a threat. Furthermore, this time, he avoided visiting the shrine in August. He may have wondered: How could anyone judge his visit as justifying the war? Contrary to his expectations, President Jiang Zemin was reported to have been angry. He told Takenori Kanzaki, a Komeito Party leader, "I cannot tolerate his visit to the shrine at all."[41] Jiang and other Chinese leaders would not allow Koizumi to change the constitutive rule governing the Yasukuni issue; a visit by the Japanese prime minister on whatever occasion and for whatever reasons always signifies the "justification of aggression" and, hence, hurts the Chinese and the people of Asia.

Based on this determination, when Jiang met with Koizumi on the occasion of the APEC summit meeting in Los Cabos, Mexico, in October 2002, he repeated his warning against Koizumi's visit to Yasukuni three times. Jiang's repeated demand, however, seems to have solidified Koizumi's determination to continue the visit. In his mind, the fact that the Chinese leaders did not understand his explanation and his behavior, i.e., that he would not support or justify the militarism and that he expressed his apology on behalf of the Japanese, was a clear indication that the Chinese criticism was not genuine and politically motivated. He seems to have determined that the best policy to such politically motivated interference was not to back down. Koizumi went to Yasukuni on January 14, 2003.

Hu Jintao, who became China's president in March 2003, initiated a friendly approach to Japan in his early months. Hu and Koizumi met at the G8 summit on the fringe of St. Petersburg. When China's new premier, Wen Jiabao, met with Koizumi on the occasion of the ASEAN+3 summit at Bali, Indonesia, Wen was rather cautious and did not make an explicit opposition to Koizumi's visit to the shrine. After the conference, Koizumi told the press that "both sides understand the situations." Wen was reported to have lost face to Koizumi's statement that could be interpreted as Wen's acquiescence to Koizumi's visit. Anti-Japanese sentiments inside China were growing then. No matter how Koizumi tried to explain that his visit to the shrine had nothing to do with justification of the war, the constitutive rule at least within China that the visit signified the "justification of aggression" had not changed. Every time Koizumi visited the shrine, the case for anti-Japanese action increased its strength. In late October 2003, a large scale anti-Japanese riot took place on the campus of Xibei University in Xian. When Japanese students made an innocent but thoughtless presentation at a university ceremony, this gesture was taken as ridiculing China, igniting anger among fellow Chinese students.

Koizumi's visit to Yasukuni on new year's day certainly did not help reduce anti-Japanese sentiments in China. The Asia Cup soccer tournament held in the summer of 2004 demonstrated anti-Japanese sentiments among Chinese soccer fans; the last game between Japan and China held in Beijing was held in a near emergency situation, where the Japanese supporters were "protected" by the wall of Chinese police officers. The biggest anti-Japanese riots took place in the spring of 2005. Japanese restaurants and supermarkets were damaged by demonstrators in various parts of China. The Japanese General Consulate in Shanghai and the Japanese Embassy in Beijing were surrounded by the Chinese demonstrators and were damaged. To what extent Koizumi's visit to the Yasukuni Shrine caused these anti-Japanese sentiments and riots is yet to be explained. The most dramatic developments of anti-Japanese tendency took place from summer of 2004 to spring of 2005 when Koizumi stayed away from Yasukuni. To be sure, the image that Japan and Koizumi would not listen to Chinese demands may have contributed to the fermentation of anti-Japanese sentiments. Internal politics in China, however, may have had a more direct impact on these developments.

These events did not provide Koizumi with any incentive to give in. Vandalism on the part of some Chinese did not necessitate a change in Koizumi 's position. In any case, he was facing one of the most important issues of domestic politics: the privatization of the postal system. When the House of Councilors rejected the bill for privatization of the postal system, he dissolved the House of Representatives to submit the decision on this issue to the will of the people. He made a charismatic campaign and brought about a landslide victory to his party. He achieved a two-thirds majority in the House of Representatives, which gave him power to override the will of the House of Councilors. With this victory in hand, he declared that he would quit as prime minister when the term of his LDP presidency expired in September 2006. He went to the Yasukuni Shrine after the victory of the general election and showed his determination that he would keep his commitment.

The anti-Japanese riots in April were unexpected events for the Hu Jintao government. If mishandled, anti-Japanese sentiments may turn to the Hu government. Anti-Hu elements in China may use the Japan issue to attack on the government. Hu Jintao and Wen Jiabao seem to have determined that they, too, would not give in to Koizumi and declared as long as Koizumi continued to visit Yasukuni, they would not meet with him on bilateral settings. Until then, it was normal for Japanese and Chinese leaders to have bilateral meetings on such multilateral summits as ASEAN +3 or APEC summits. From 2005 to 2006, no such bilateral meetings took place between the two countries. Soon after, the Roh Moo-hyun government in South Korea followed suit and Japan and South Korea stopped bilateral summit-level meetings.

A month before his resignation, Koizumi visited the Yasukuni Shrine on August 15, 2006. He told the press that previously he listened to advice from many to avoid August 15 because his visit of that day could invite foreign criticism. But, he continued, regardless of the differences of the date of visits, critics, foreign and domestic, would always criticize him. He would not accept the view that he should stop the visit because China opposed it. Altogether 52.5 percent of the respondents to *Yomiuri* poll supported Koizumi; 25 percent of the supporters said that they did not agree to give in to a foreign pressure.

CONCLUSION

Koizumi did not back down. Neither did the Chinese. Sino-Japanese diplomacy, as a result, was in paralysis at least at the top level. The battle was over the constitutive rule about the meaning of the prime ministers' visit to the shrine. Koizumi's position was not the position of the revisionist historians of Japan; he was not intending to glorify the Japanese aggression or justify the conduct of Class-A war criminals. His sentiment was much closer to the sentiments of ordinary bereaved families who want simply to mourn for the dead. However, the history surrounding Yasukuni, as analyzed in this chapter, did not seem to give clear approval to this interpretation.

First, there are those in Japan who openly make an argument to repudiate the validity of the Tokyo Military Tribunal, and some among them go so far as to justify and glorify the role played by the Class-A war criminals. Chief Priest Matsudaira apparently enshrined them as a symbolic act to rectify what he considered to be the wrong interpretation of history of modern Japan. Even if Koizumi insists that his visit does not signify the justification of their argument, the revisionists contend that the prime ministers' visits symbolized their rehabilitation.

Second, from the time that Yasukuni became a private religious corporation, a substantial number of Japanese who do not share Shintoism have opposed the prime ministers' visits to the shrine, especially when conducted "officially." This segment of Japanese population always criticize prime ministers' visit with or without criticisms from China or Korea.

Third, the political process in which the Yasukuni issue was handled by both Japan and China seems to validate the Chinese interpretation of "justification of aggression." When Nakasone visited the shrine, China criticized him because Class-A war criminals were enshrined; and Nakasone declared not to visit the shrine. This process indicates that the Japanese side also agreed with, or at least give tacit acquiescence to, the constitutive rule on which China insisted. When Hashimoto visited the shrine in 1986 for a very private reason, China never accepted this private reason and again criticized him because Class-A war criminals were enshrined; and Hashimoto decided not to visit the shrine any more. Again, the Japanese agreed to the Chinese constitutive rule.

Finally, the constitutive rule on which China insisted, that is, the enshrinement of Class-A war criminals changed the character of Yasukuni, have been shared by substantial number of Japanese. In 2006, it was revealed that none other than the Showa Emperor decided not to visit the shrine after the enshrinement of Class-A war criminals. Furthermore, as this issue attracted attention worldwide thanks to Koizumi's insistence, many international guests including Americans started visiting Yasukuni and discovered the historical accounts that they cannot accept were openly displayed in the museum attached to the shrine. Although the U.S. government made no comments on the Yasukuni issue, if the prime minister's visit to the shrine is to signify the rejection of the Tokyo Military Tribunal and the rehabilitation of the military leaders who started a war on the United States, the U.S. government too may not be easily able to distance itself from the issue.

Koizumi did not lose his battle but he did not win it, either. For the reasons listed above, this is not a symbolic game that a normal Japanese leader could win: Nakasone and Hashimoto understood this; Koizumi, who did not accept this structure, fought until the end of his term; to repeat, he did not lose, but he did not win either. Shinzo Abe, the successor to Koizumi, was regarded by the conservative nationalists as their champion, who could finally help them rectify the wrong interpretation of history by repudiating the verdicts of the Tokyo Military Tribunal. However, Abe seems to have understood this structure of the Yasukuni game. He declared to say nothing about whether to visit or not to visit the shrine. By not visiting the shrine, he prevented Chinese criticism. By not clearly saying that he would not visit the shrine, he tried to keep the support of the conservative nationalists. Abe made a surprise visit to China immediately after he became prime minister; he put the state of Sino-Japanese relations back on track again. He resigned as a result of the LDP's defeat in the House of Councilors' election in July 2007.

Did China win the game of Yasukuni? On the face of it, the interpretation that Japanese prime ministers' visits to the Yasukuni Shrine represents an endorsement of the Class-A war criminals and therefore are undesirable is widely accepted. However, at least among the Japanese public, China paid a fair amount of cost in the involvement of the Yasukuni issue. First, China was not able to demonstrate that its criticism against Japan was always genuine. Many Japanese began to consider Chinese criticism nearly always politically motivated. In the end, Koizumi departed the scene and Abe did not follow Koizumi's pattern. But the fact that the majority of Japanese supported Koizumi indicated the distrust that China created during the process of the Yasukuni controversy.

Second, China's rigid adherence to the constitutive rule of equating the Yasukuni visit to the glorification of militarism tended to give an oversimplified view of Japan to the Chinese public. No matter how much Koizumi insisted that he did not justify the war, the Chinese leaders kept saying that as long as he continues to visit the shrine, they could not believe him. This type of reaction tended to demonize all Japanese who do not agree with the Chinese view, especially on history issues. Out of this demonization of Japanese emerged anti-Japanese riots that the Chinese leaders feel that they cannot easily control. The fact that the Communist Party controlled the anti-Japanese riots indicated that the Communist Party still maintains the power to harness protest movements but depicting foreigners in an overly simplified manner could create danger in the future.

As Yasuo Fukuda, the successor to Abe, made it clear that he would not visit the shrine, the Yasukuni issue does not seem to become an international issue in the near future. That does not necessarily mean the issue of mourning the war dead was over in Japanese politics. In fact, one of the most important contributions of Prime Minister Koizumi in making this issue an international one was to ignite a domestic debate about the proper way that the Japanese people should mourn and pay respects to the war dead and the victims of war, including Japanese and foreign civilians. How to create a system of mourning and paying respects to the war dead and victims without violating constitutional stipulation of separating religion and the state and without inviting international suspicion is an important challenge with which Japan in the twenty-first century still needs to grapple.

NOTES

1. The best, concise analysis of the issue especially in the context of Sino-Japanese relations is Ichitani Kazuo, "Yasukuni jinja sampai mondai" in *Kiro ni tatsu Ni-Chu kankei,* ed. Iechika Ryoko et al. (Tokyo: Koyo-shobo, 2007), pp 37–62.

2. Fukuzawa Yukichi, *Gakumon no susume* (Tokyo: Iwanami shoten, 1978, originally published in 1874), p. 41.

3. Oe Shinobu, *Yasukuni Jinja* (Tokyo: Iwanami shoten, 1984), pp. 36–37.

4. Tanaka Hiromi, *B C-kyu Senpan* (Tokyo: Chikuma-shobo, 2002), p. 14. According to Hiromi Tanaka, the difference between Class-B and Class-C criminals did not mean much, though technically Class B was the category for officers and higher ranking personnel and Class C, that for privates and noncommissioned officers.

5. Article 11 of the San Francisco Peace Treaty stipulates: "Japan accepts the judgments of the International Military Tribunal for the Far East and of other Allied War Crimes Courts both within and outside Japan, and will carry out the sentences imposed thereby upon Japanese nationals imprisoned in Japan. The power to grant clemency, to reduce sentences and to parole with respect to such prisoners may not be exercised except on the decision of the Government or Governments which imposed the sentence in each instance, and on the recommendation of Japan. In the case of persons sentenced by the International Military Tribunal for the Far East, such power may not be exercised except on the decision of a majority of the Governments represented on the Tribunal, and on the recommendation of Japan." Based on the article, the Japanese government requested the relevant governments to agree to release the prisoners. Judgments differed from country to county. The Republic of China and France, for example, agreed to release all prisoners tried by their courts in 1952. The last prisoners were released in 1958. See Tanaka Hiromi, *B C-kyu Senpan,* p. 207–11.

6. For the Tokyo Military Tribunal, see Kojima Noboru, *Tokyo Saiban* (Tokyo: Chuokoron-sha, 1971) and Asahi Shinbun Tokyo Saiban Kishadan, *Tokyo Saiban* (Tokyo: Kodansha, 1983).

7. Mainichi Shinbun "Yasukuni" Shuzaihan, *Yasukuni sengo hishi: A-kyu senpan o goshi shita otoko* (Tokyo: Mainichi shinbunsha, 2007), pp. 142–50.

8. Ibid., p. 64.

9. Ibid., p. 16.

10. *Renmin Ribao,* August 11, 1985.

11. *Nikkan Chugoku Tsushin,* August 16, 1985.

12. *Asahi Shinbun* (Evening), August 27, 1985; *Asahi Shinbun,* August 30, 1985.

13. *Nihon Keizai Shinbun,* September 4, 1985.

14. Ibid., September 8, 1985.

15. Ibid., September 15, 1985.

16. Ibid. (Evening), September 19, 1985.

17. Ibid. (Evening). September 19, 1985.

18. *Renmin Ribao,* September 20, 1985.

19. *Asahi Shinbun,* November 2, 1985.

20. *Asahi Shinbun,* October 11, 1985.

21. Itagaki Tadashi, *Yasukuni koshiki sanpai no sokatsu* (Tokyo: Tentensha, 2000) p. 179. In order to ascertain the plight of his friend Hu Yaobang, Nakasone asked Yoshihiro Inayama,

Chairman of the Japan Federation of Economic Organizations (*Keidanren*) to sound out the situation in China. According to Inayama's report, Gu Mu and Wan Li told him that "paying respects to the war dead in general is a good thing but war criminals who conducted aggression in China were enshrined in Yasukuni. Visiting the shrine, therefore, hurts Chinese people and lowers the global image of Japan. In addition, it would affect China's domestic politics and General Secretary Hu Yaobang himself could not say anything on this. We would all be in a trouble. So, please give our message to Prime Minister Nakasone to stop the visit." Nakasone Yasuhiro, *Tenchi yujo* (Tokyo: Bungei shunju, 1996), p. 463.

22. "The World and Japan" Database Project, http://www.ioc.u-tokyo.ac.jp/~worldjpn/documents/texts/JPCH/19860814.S1J.html.

23. John R. Searle, *The Construction of Social Reality* (London: Penguin, 1995) pp. 27–29.

24. Itagaki, *Yasukuni koshiki sanpai,* p. 182.

25. *Asahi Shinbun,* July 27, 1986.

26. Itagaki, *Yasukuni koshiki sanpai,* p. 275.

27. Ibid.

28. Wakaizumi Hirofumi, *Wakai to nashonarizumu* (Tokyo: Asahi shinbunsha, 2006), p. 316. Wakaizumi points out that one of the concerns of Miyazawa was to prevent a terrorist action by the right wing (*uyoku*). In Wakaizumi's account, Miyazawa and Nakasone both worried about the right wing's activities about the Emperor's visit to China. In March 1992, a right winger attempted to shoot Shin Kanemaru ostensibly for his visit to North Korea in the previous year. Miyazawa might have decided to reveal his intention to make a private visit in order to moderate the right wing.

29. Itagaki, *Yasukuni koshiki sanpai,* p. 281.

30. *Asahi Shinbun,* July 30, 1996.

31. *Nikkan Chugoku Tsushin,* July 31, 1996.

32. Tanaka Akihiko, *Ajia no naka no Nippon* (Tokyo: NTT shuppansha, 2007), pp. 186–88.

33. *Nikkan Chugoku Tsushin*, September 9, 1996.

34. Itagaki, *Yasukuni koshiki sanpai*, p. 287.

35. It is not clear why Jiang Zemin kept repeating his lecture. His act may have been a simple reflection of his unhappiness over the joint statement between Japan and China, which lacked a clear statement of "apology," which existed in the joint statement that Japan had agreed with President Kim Dae-jung a month before Jiang's visit to Japan. According to Masahiko Komura, then Japan's Foreign Minister, Japan agreed to explicitly write down the word "apology" because Kim Dae-jung agreed not to raise the history issue any more once Japan wrote down the word "apology" in the statement. Japan asked the same question to China and China did not make a similar commitment as Kim Dae-jung. In Komura's account, Prime Minister Obuchi agreed to make an oral apology instead of using the word "apology" in a written statement. Funabashi Yoichi, *Za Peninshura Kuwesuchon* (Tokyo: Asahi shinbunsha, 2006) p. 47.

36. *Asahi Shibun* (Evening), April 17, 2001.

37. Nonaka Hiromu, "Kiipason ga kataru shogen 90 nendai, dai 20kai Nonaka Hiromu" *Ronza* (May 2007), p. 251.

38. Ichitani, "Yasukuni jinja sampai mondai," p. 54.

39. "The World and Japan" Database Project, http://www.ioc.u-tokyo.ac.jp/~worldjpn/.

40. Ibid.

41. *Asahi Shinbun,* April 30, 2002.

7

Comfort Women: Deep Polarization in Japan on Facts and on Morality

Kazuhiko Togo

The comfort women system was a highly polemical issue in Japan and, in particular, in Japanese-Korean relations, in the 1990s. In 1993, Yohei Kono, then Chief Cabinet Secretary of the Kiichi Miyazawa government, issued a landmark statement, known as the Kono statement, formulating the Japanese government's view that attempted to synthesize the polarized debate on this issue. Acknowledging the involvement of the military and the tremendous sufferings inflicted on many comfort women, the Kono statement sincerely apologized and accepted the Japanese government's moral responsibility. To compensate the sufferings of comfort women, the Asian Women's Fund was established. The Kono statement, however, did not end this debate. On the contrary, it touched off a heated debate, and many books and articles have been published representing the two polarized views critical of the Kono statement: those who considered the comfort women system a system of institutional rape—the term "rape center" is often used by the advocates of this school—and those who consider it a practice of military brothels that was basically accepted at the time.[1]

This chapter first analyzes the three distinctive positions: the institutional rape school, the military brothels school, and the third school that supports the Kono statement. This is followed by an analysis of four major issues: the role of the military, the process of recruitment, the fundamental nature of the system, and the number and countries of origin of the comfort women. It then tries to describe what the comfort women system was with a view to reach as broad a consensus as possible on this controversial issue.

THE COMFORT WOMEN ISSUE UNDER PRIME MINISTER ABE

Under Prime Minister Junichiro Koizumi, the central issue regarding Japan's historical memories was Yasukuni. Somehow, surprisingly, comfort women became the most explosive historical issue under Prime Minister Shinzo Abe during his tenure. This time it was not so much China, but South Korea, and unexpectedly the United States, that appeared at the forefront of the controversy.

Abe, as early as the spring of 1997, had expressed critical views on the Kono statement, which formulated the Japanese government's position from 1993 onward.[2] Many commentators therefore seriously speculated that Abe might change the government's position on the Kono statement in his newly established cabinet. But the prime minister expressed in the parliamentary debate on October 3, 2006 that his cabinet's policy was "basic continuation of the Kono statement."[3] Abe's statement at the Diet, naturally, was appreciated by those who had supported the Kono statement and created misgivings among those who had criticized it. Yet, Abe had also qualified his parliamentary statement by saying that he had doubts about "whether there was confirmed evidence on coercion in a narrow definition."[4] "Coercion in a narrow definition" means physical abduction by Japanese officials or police in the process of recruitment. Abe apparently tried to explain that "coercion in a wider definition," which meant all other coerced forms of having sexual relations with the Japanese military did exist, and on that basis, he was prepared to support the Kono statement. In early October, Abe's qualification did not raise particular interest or concern and Abe's support of the Kono statement alone was largely publicized. That situation dramatically changed on March 1, 2007, when Abe gave a short press interview, in which he confirmed his position that he had taken in early October, but with an ambiguity which cost him dearly. Without stating his basic policy of adherence to the Kono statement, Abe told reporters: "What was initially defined as enforcement did not exist. I think that it is true that there was no proof for that, and [asked about the revision of Kono statement] we have to think based on the premise that the definition changed." It must be stressed that nothing in Abe's statement at this press conference indicated that he meant to change his policy of following the Kono statement.[5] But this statement was highly ambiguous and it was reported, I believe erroneously, by first the Associated Press and the *New York Times*[6] and other English-language newspapers that Abe denied the fact that comfort women were coerced and that he was contemplating revisions to the Kono statement.

The message that Abe denied coercion against comfort women was catastrophic. The English-language media carrying this report was filled with devastating criticisms against Abe. Congressman Mike Honda (D-California) had already presented a nonbinding resolution, H. RES 121, to the House Subcommittee on Asia, the Pacific, and the Global Environment, asking for Japan's "unequivocal apology" for the exploitation of the comfort women. After March 1, support for this resolution began to increase rapidly.[7]

Abe must have soon realized that his statement created a major unintended confusion, particularly in South Korea and among English-speaking countries including the United States. Beginning with his interview with the NHK (*Nihon Hoso Kyokai*; Japan Broadcasting Corporation) on March 11, the prime minister began emphasizing his sincere apology for those women who suffered and reaffirmed his adherence to the Kono statement, without making any reference to the issue of "narrow" and "wider" coercion.[8] On April 3, Abe expressed in a telephone conversation with President George W. Bush his "heartfelt apology for the comfort women, who were put in a position to endure real pain."[9] During his trip to Washington on April 26–27, Abe confirmed this position and repeated it in his meeting with Congressional leaders. At his joint news conference with the president, the prime minister stated: "I have deep-hearted sympathies—for the people who had to serve as comfort women and were placed in extreme hardships. I express my apologies for the fact that they were placed in that sort of circumstance."[10] Although Honda's House Resolution 121 attracted more attention than Abe's statements reaffirming his endorsement of the Kono statement, the excitement and interest around the Honda Resolution began to calm down after Abe's visit to the United States. Then suddenly the Japanese conservatives made a major *faux-pas*. Conservative Diet members and opinion leaders, who were critical of the Kono statement, and who had been angered by what they considered to be "unfounded criticisms" against the comfort women system, purchased on June 14 in the *Washington Post* a full-page advertisement entitled "Facts," denying that the Second World War comfort women system was a place for sexual slavery.[11] This advertisement created an immediate outcry, or at the very least, consternation, among U.S. policy-makers and Japan specialists. On June 26, the House Foreign Relations Committee adopted H. RES 121 by a vote of 39 to 2. The House subsequently passed this resolution on July 30, now with 167 cosponsors, by a unanimous voice vote. The same resolution had been presented unsuccessfully four times since 2001.[12] Abe's government kept a low profile about the House Resolution, but the opinion leaders who sided with the June 14 *Washington Post* advertisement angrily criticized the House Resolution.

Meanwhile, Abe's popularity declined precipitously with a series of scandals, and the Liberal Democratic Party (LDP) suffered a huge defeat in the July Upper House election. Unable to handle the conflicting political situation and due to poor health, Abe resigned in September. Yasuo Fukuda, who succeeded Abe, favors reconciliation with Japan's Asian neighbors, and is considered to be a supporter of the Kono statement. But the question of whether Fukuda would actively seek measures to repair the damage beyond reaffirming the Kono statement remains to be seen.

THREE BASIC POSITIONS

Under this highly polemical, controversial, sensitive, and emotional atmosphere, it is very hard to conduct a scholarly analysis of the comfort women issue. Objective historical facts appear to differ widely, depending on which position one takes. This applies not only to the international debate but also to the debate inside Japan, where opinions are deeply split and polarized.

In general, there are three fundamental views on this issue in Japan: (1) those who insist that the comfort women system was a system of institutional rape (the institutional rape school), (2) those who argue that the comfort women system was a system of military brothels (the military brothels school) and (3) those who support the Kono statement. Throughout my career in the Japanese Ministry of Foreign Affairs and after I left the ministry, I have stood behind the Kono statement and tried to enhance its cause, wherever possible.[13]

Human Rights Advocates or the Institutional Rape School

There are groups of opinion leaders, scholars, politicians, lawyers, and gender activists, who maintain that the comfort women system was basically a system of mass rape, and that the prewar Japanese military was responsible for this organizational rape. The Japanese government should acknowledge more formally its legal responsibility and pay reparations. Yoshiaki Yoshimi, who has conducted substantial research on the comfort women issue, is the most prominent scholar of this school.[14] There are other such scholars, like Etsuro Totsuka, who denounced the Japanese government at the human rights commission in Geneva in 1992, and who made trips to Korea to help Korean victims speak out. In 2004, Totsuka uncovered a prewar Nagasaki court case in which the judge pronounced a guilty verdict against those who deceived girls and sent them to comfort women stations.[15] Shoji Motooka, former Diet member of the Japan Socialist Party and now a member of the Democratic Party of Japan, has actively pursued the enactment of a law that sees the Japanese government assume legal responsibility for its actions.[16] Koken Tsuchiya, a former president of the Japanese Bar Association, on the op-ed page of the *Asahi Shinbun* recently argued that since the Kono statement does not fulfill Japan's responsibility and serious consideration should be given to passing a bill that would acknowledge the criminality of the military in coercing comfort women during the war against their will.[17]

Efforts by those who denounced the criminality of the comfort women system began to bear concrete results in the international arena. Gay McDougal's report on comfort women, which was submitted to the United Nations on June 22, 1998, was probably one of the clearest denunciations of the comfort women system as an international crime.[18] After many pages detailing general standards for what constitutes rape and sexual slavery, the report has an addendum which states that "Japan and the Japanese Imperial Army made more than 200,000 women sexual slaves in rape centers constructed throughout Asia from 1932 till the end of the war."[19]

The report was followed up by the Women's International War Crimes Tribunal on Japan's Military Sexual Slavery, held in Tokyo from December 8–12, 2000. The final verdict of this tribunal was pronounced in the Hague on December 4, 2001. Ten accused including the Showa Emperor were found guilty and it was determined that the Japanese government has the obligation to pay reparations. An organization called the Violence Against Women in War Network Japan (VAWW-NET Japan), represented by Yayoi Matsui and many women's civil rights activists, played an important role in assisting and organizing this tribunal in Japan.

Japanese activists, who assert the criminality of the comfort women system, have also played an important role in assisting former comfort women in Asia to file lawsuits in Japanese courts. Ten cases were filed.[20] On April 27, 2007, however, the Supreme Court issued a landmark decision that set a precedent for all war-related cases. It rejected five cases from Chinese citizens, including two comfort women cases. The rejection was based exclusively on the legal ground that Clause Five of the 1972 Japan-PRC communiqué, which prescribed that the People's Republic of China "renounces its demand for war reparations from Japan" should be interpreted with the same degree of right and obligation as the San Francisco Peace Treaty where "claims of the Allied Powers and their nationals" (San Francisco Peace Treaty Article 14[b]) are waived.[21] This verdict most likely would be applied as precedent to all other comfort women cases from all countries with which Japan concluded a peace treaty or an equivalent treaty.

Thus, one path to regain honor and compensation through the Japanese judiciary is closed. But the closure of legal avenues may imply that now that the Japanese government is free from legal obligations, it can take measures based on moral considerations.[22] The role that Japanese human-rights and gender activists have played in this process was not for nothing.

For human rights advocates, the position taken by the Japanese government since 1993 based on the Kono statement was not satisfactory. What they see as the greatest fallacy in the Kono statement is that, although Kono acknowledged the involvement of the military and the tremendous sufferings inflicted on many comfort women, and he sincerely apologized for the sufferings that the comfort women had endured, thereby accepting the Japanese government's moral responsibility, he accepted neither the legal culpability nor Japan's obligation to pay reparations as determined by international law.

Military Brothel School

The fundamental point maintained by people belonging to this school is that the comfort women stations were basically military brothels. The brothel advocates usually express deep sympathy to the suffering of women who worked there, but they maintain that these sufferings should be considered as part of the general sufferings of women in that period who were forced to work in brothels. Brothels were a socially accepted practice at that time, and women who were sent to brothels due to poverty or social pressure were not freed until they finished paying their debts. Comfort women working in their military brothels were, in principle, in the same situation. The military brothels school also emphasizes that, particularly in relation to Korea, which was considered a part of Japanese territory, there was no confirmed evidence that proves there was coerced recruitment (*kyosei renko*) by the officials and police. This is the most hotly contested point in the comfort women debate from the early 1990s in

Japan. About the ownership of the military brothels, the military brothels school maintains that primarily it was civilian owners, or private traders, who ran them.

Ikuhiko Hata is the most prolific scholar who takes this position.[23] Tsuneyasu Daishido, a former Japanese colonial officer in Korea aged 90 now, frequently writes, based on his personal experience, that in all cases that he knew of there was no physical coercion in comfort women recruiting in Korea.[24] The May 2007 edition of the monthly magazine *Will* had a special feature on comfort women with Yoshiko Sakurai, Yoshihisa Komori, Tsutomu Nishioka, and Shoichi Watanabe, all well-known scholars and opinion leaders who shared the view that criminalization of Japan over the comfort women issue is unjustified.[25] In August, *Will* published a special edition devoted exclusively to and sharply critical of the U.S. Congressional Resolution with many other opinion leaders.[26] Hidetsugu Yagi and Nobukatsu Fujioka are also well-known proponents of this persuasion.[27]

As for politicians, the LDP formed in February 1997 a Committee of Parliamentarians to Think about Japan's Future and Historical Education, headed by Nariaki Nakayama, to reconsider the comfort women issue.[28] In line with Abe's toned-down rhetoric from the middle of March, the Committee's activities were also kept quiet.[29] On March 9, the like-minded young members of the Democratic Party established a new Committee for Verifying the Truth of the Comfort Women Issue and Nanjing Incident.[30]

As stated earlier in this chapter, on June 14, those politicians and many of the opinion leaders including those mentioned above publicized their views in the *Washington Post* advertisement, which backfired and produced a result entirely opposite from what they had expected, in the form of the Congressional resolution.

The Kono statement is heavily criticized by the advocates of the military brothel school. The first criticism that they raised was that Kono acknowledged "coerced recruitment" when there was no confirmed evidence.[31] The second criticism was that Kono described that "recruitment [in Korea] was conducted *generally* [emphasis added] against their will," which created an impression that recruitment against their will was happening all the time.[32] The military brothel school also angrily denounces the fact that statements based on unconfirmed evidence became an important basis to prove coercion by the Japanese military against comfort women. Both the McDougal Report and Congressman Honda's argument that relied on the Kono statement are often cited as examples of the negative influence of the Kono statement.[33] The military brothel school advocates argue that, had there not been the Kono statement, which exaggerated the military's responsibility for the comfort women system, international reactions to this system would have been more restrained.

The Kono Statement and Its Supporters

The Kono statement, issued on August 4, 1993, constitutes the basic position of the Japanese government to this day. It is accompanied by two other documents: the first was an introductory document that summarizes the process of investigation, and the second was a 30 page collection of records that the government had uncovered in the process of the investigation.[34] Yohei Kono, Chief Cabinet Secretary under Prime Minister Kiichi Miyazawa, made an official statement that had the following four major points.

First, Kono acknowledged the involvement of the military in the comfort women system: "The then Japanese military was, directly and indirectly, involved in the establishment and management of the comfort stations and transfer of comfort women."[35] It represented a major change in the government's position.[36]

Second, as for the recruitment of comfort women, it "was conducted mainly by private recruiters, who acted in response to the request of the military. In many cases they were recruited against their own will, through coaxing[,] coercion, etc., and that at times, administrative/military personnel directly took part in the recruitments." The report placed special emphasis on Korea, where "recruitment, transfer, control, etc., were conducted *generally* [emphasis added] against their will, through coaxing, coercion, etc."[37]

Third, it concluded that comfort women "lived in misery at comfort stations under a coercive atmosphere."

Fourth, he stated that "the Government of Japan...extend[s] its sincere apologies and remorse to all those, irrespective of place of origin, who suffered immeasurable pain and incurable physical and psychological wounds as comfort women."[38]

In order to implement the Kono statement, the Asian Women's Fund was established in July 1995 under Prime Minister Tomiichi Murayama. Each comfort woman was to receive a letter of apology signed by the prime minister in power and an atonement [*tsugunaikin*] of two million yen. The running cost of the secretariat of the fund was financed by the Japanese government, but in order to harmonize the contrition on behalf of Japan as a whole and the government's legal position that all issues related to reparations had already been settled by international agreements, the atonement itself was financed by private contributors. The fund paid atonements to the victims in South Korea, Taiwan, the Philippines, Indonesia, and the Netherlands and concluded its work in March 2007. Altogether 285 women from Taiwan and the Philippines and seven from South Korea received atonement of 2 million yen each, and 79 Dutch women received an equivalent atonement. All these women received a letter of apology from the prime minister in power. In Indonesia, upon request by the government of Indonesia, individual comfort women did not receive an atonement, but 21 homes for the elderly were constructed, with first priority for comfort women. In closing its work, the Fund left a detailed report of its activities on its Web site.[39] The report indicated that particularly in the case of South Korea there was strong pressure by the Korean government and public opinion for each comfort women not to accept the atonement and apology through the Fund. This ultimately brought any activity of the Fund in Korea to a complete standstill.[40]

From the point of view of the Kono statement supporters, the closure of the Asian Women's Fund is a source of concern. When international criticisms about the Japanese government's treatment of the comfort women issue are becoming louder, why should Japan abandon the best measure to prove its contrition? Without the Asian Women's Fund, how can the Japanese government continue to express its apology to those women, who are most likely to continue their claims?

At the same time, in case of South Korea, the comfort women issue carried a particular weight in the process of reconciliation talks, probably because of the position this issue carried in the historical memory both in South Korea and Japan. The historic reconciliation between Japan and South Korea was achieved in October 1998 at the Kim Dae-jung–Keizo Obuchi meeting in Tokyo. In the publicly available record, the comfort women issue was not raised at the summit meeting. But the two leaders must have been fully aware of all discussions that took place between the two governments in 1992–93 and developments that followed after the establishment of the Asian Women's Fund. I therefore argue that, despite serious dissatisfaction remaining in the Korean society, this issue was not considered then as an issue requiring a diplomatic solution.

FOUR ISSUES FOR EXAMINATION

The debate on comfort women is deeply polarized. This chapter attempts to analyze where differences lie among various views and what are objective facts that transcend the differences of interpretations. Through this analysis, it attempts to find, to the extent possible, a common picture of the past. It therefore chooses four major issues, clarification of which should help achieve better understanding of this difficult issue: (1) What was the role of the military in the comfort stations? (2) What was the process of recruitment of comfort women? (3) What were the nature of the comfort stations—a locus for systematic rape or military brothels? (4) How many comfort women were recruited and from which countries?

What Was the Role of the Military in the Comfort Stations?

Advocates for the institutional rape school maintain that evidence of military involvement is overwhelming. As was reported by the *Asahi Shinbun* on January 11, 1992, Yoshiaki Yoshimi discovered an instruction (*Tsucho*) prepared by the Military Affairs Division (*Heimuka*) of the Ministry of War (*Rikugunsho*) dated March 4, 1938 to the expeditionary forces in Northern and Central China (*Hokushi Homengun* and *Chushi Hakengun*). The document instructed that deceptive methods should not be used in the recruitment of comfort women, that each army unit should carefully choose "recruiters" and cooperate closely with local police and authorities.[41] Another document prepared by the Ministry of War in September 1940 stated that the appropriate guidance and control of comfort stations was extremely important for the morale of soldiers.[42] Some memoirs of soldiers describe in concrete terms that they were taught at the Military Academy how to manage and finance comfort stations.[43] Interestingly, military involvement in the comfort stations is not negated at all by the advocates of the military brothels school. The authenticity of Yoshimi's documents is never challenged. In fact, the March 1938 document is used by the advocates of the military brothels school as the number one evidence in the June 14, 2007 *Washington Post* advertisement to show that the military wanted to prevent recruitment by abduction.[44] Daishido introduced an army general's memoirs, in which the general described how his officers discussed the arrival of 150 comfort women led by 15 civilian "owners" and the issue of where to locate the comfort station. Daishido writes: "Just as this example shows, it was a common sense for those who lived in this period that there was military involvement."[45] Hata refers to Yoshimi's analysis of types of comfort stations, and states that he is generally in agreement on the following four categories: (a) direct operation by the military; (b) [civilian operation] controlled by the military for the exclusive use of military personnel; (c) military designated public brothels that civilians could use as well; (d) public brothels where military personnel might go as well. Hata adds that the comfort station in category (a) had a transitional character and disappeared around 1938 but reemerged to serve soldiers stationed at the front in remote areas toward the end of the war.[46]

The Kono statement also underlines military involvement, which in principle does not differ much from the analyses stated above: "The then Japanese military was, directly and indirectly, involved in the establishment and management of the comfort stations and transfer of comfort women." As for the ownership and operation, there is a general knowledge that it was done in principle by civilians. But the military was involved in the establishment, management, and transfer of women. Both the institutional rape school and the military brothels school agree on these points.

It seems possible to make the following three conclusions. First, with some exceptions, where the military operated the comfort stations directly, the majority of comfort stations were run by civilian owners or private traders. Second, the military was, directly and indirectly, involved in the establishment and management of the comfort stations and transfer of comfort women. Third, on the nature of the military's involvement, more analysis is needed to determine whether the primary role of the military authorities was the encouragement or the prevention of rape, as I will discuss below.

What Was the Process of Recruitment of Comfort Women?

About 60 women testified at the Women's International War Crimes Tribunal on Japan's Military Sexual Slavery and gave their account on how recruitment was done. There seems to be a difference between those who were recruited from inside the Japanese Empire, i.e., from Korea and Taiwan and then transported to the front, and those who were recruited directly from the occupied areas.

The majority of those who were transported from the territory of the Japanese Empire at the Women's International War Crimes Tribunal testified that they were recruited through deception. One Korean woman then made a video testimony that "a Japanese police officer grabbed my hair and forcefully took me to the head of the military police."[47] This seems to be the only case at the Tribunal when the recruitment was allegedly made by physical coercion. One testimony by a Taiwanese leaves the process of recruitment vague.[48] But in cases from the occupied areas, there were many cases of women who were raped and then forced to stay with the military.[49]

Surprisingly, the views as revealed in the testimony of comfort women basically were in general agreement with the picture that emerged from the debates that took place in Japan in the 1990s on enforced recruitment (*kyosei renko*). It is essential to note that most of the heated debate on comfort women in the 1990s was conducted in Japan on the issue of the transfer of comfort women from Korea to Japan's occupied areas. What the advocates of the military brothel school insisted was that the Japanese government could not find any evidence in a form of written order, other documents, or other confirmed proofs, to prove that women in Korea were coerced by physical violence by the police, the military, or other government authorities. The Japanese government conducted hearings of former comfort women before it issued the Kono statement. At these hearings, some comfort women stated that they were recruited by coercion by Japanese authorities, but these were testimonies that the Japanese representatives at the hearings were not permitted to verify or question. Hata states that among 19 former comfort women who identified themselves and whose names appeared in the book published in South Korea in 1993, the majority alleged deceptions and only four testified for coerced recruitment. But he argues that none seemed to have a credible case proving that the Japanese military or police authority was really involved.[50]

Daishido is one of the most eloquent advocates of this position. He states that as a former local official in Korea, he had never experienced nor seen such coerced recruitment. He argues that, if such coerced recruitment had taken place, it would have been known by so many in Korea and would have become an object of such national anger that it could not but have been reflected in the negotiations for normalization in 1952–65, whereas this issue was not raised even once from the Korean side during these negotiations. He adds that he cannot guarantee that this never happened, but if this happened, then it was a real exception to the rule. He then suggests that thorough hearings should be conducted among all Koreans who still remember how local administration worked before 1945.[51]

The debate on comfort women between Japan and South Korea began in the 1980s. Daishido and practically every one of the military brothel school argue that several "revelations" in the 1980s and early 1990s in Japan, which ignited political anger in Korea, turned out to be baseless. The first revelation that captured media attention was the 1983 book, *My War Crime: Coerced Recruitment of Koreans,* written by Kiyoharu Yoshida. Yoshida described in an emotional manner how he chased and collected women physically while working as a local government official in Korea. The book apparently created a vivid image and strong impression of coerced recruiting of Korean girls under the Japanese occupation in Korea. Ikuhiko Hata went to the small village in Cheju Island, where the alleged massive coerced recruitment took place, and conducted intensive hearings. Hata discovered that there was no trace of that incident left in the village.[52] Yoshimi later interviewed Yoshida and concluded that his testimony is too weak to prove that coerced recruitment took place in Korea.[53]

The second contention raised by the advocates of the military brothel school was against the *Asahi Shinbun* article that appeared on January 11, 1992, mentioned earlier in this chapter. They argued that although the article's thrust of argument was to prove the military's responsibility, the disclosed documents were issued to prevent wrongdoings against comfort women. Furthermore, an article written by the Asahi reporter stated: "There was coerced recruitment (*kyosei renko*) of mostly Korean girls under the name of the *Teishintai*. It is estimated that their numbers amount to 80,000 to 200,000." The *Teishintai* was a unit for young girls to become engaged in war production work. Organizationally, it was totally separate and different from comfort women, but according to the brothels advocate school, this short explanatory article had a far-reaching impact in Korea because from then onward, the *Teishintai* and comfort stations were perceived as synonymous in Korea.[54]

On the whole, the lack of confirmed evidence on "coerced recruitment" by military or government officials in Korea became generally shared knowledge in Japan. In 1997 Yoshimi himself stated in his introductory book on comfort women that "it is not confirmed that there was such coerced recruitment like slave chasing conducted by Japanese officials or police in Korea and Taiwan. Mobilization of comfort women under the name of *Teishintai* apparently did not exist."[55]

Finally, those who worked for the Kono statement began to confirm the same point. Nobuo Ishihara, Deputy Cabinet Secretary under Kono in 1993, confided in September 1997: "We could not find any proof of 'coerced recruitment', except for the 16 testimonies by Korean women. The Japanese side was not allowed to ask questions and verify the contents of the testimony. But at the strong request of the Korean government, we accepted them for the sake of good will to improve relations between the two countries. If we were to examine legally whether such coercion existed or not, we would not have taken the same approach."[56]

Kono himself in the same year stated at the Committee of Young Parliamentarians to Think about Japan's Future and Historical Education that no government documents could be found that proved that the military gave orders to forcefully recruit women, but that he "considered it important that, among the testimonies by comfort women, there were things that only victims could testify."[57] In an interview for the *Asahi Shinbun* in 1997 he stated that "if asked whether there were documents which stated that the government based on legally sanctioned procedure recruited girls with physical coercion, then there were no such documents. But if we define coercion as being recruited against one's own will, then there were numerous cases of such coercion."[58]

Thus, amid the political turmoil after Abe's statement at the press interview, on March 16, 2007, his cabinet officially responded to the *Shitsumon Shuisho* (formal questioning)[59] by Kiyomi Tsujimoto, a Diet member from the Socialist Party, that "there were no documents which directly describe the 'coerced recruitment' among the materials that the government was able to find."[60] In this sense, if this is the point that Abe stated in early October and tried to restate inadvertently on March 1, the government position has been consistent with the Kono statement.

But after all, what does all this mean? Why is there a heated debate on the sole issue of coerced recruitment? Are there not other issues to be addressed equally seriously? I submit that there are indeed other equally important issues.

First, even if there were no coerced recruitments, or they were exceptional cases, what conclusions should be drawn from the powerful testimonies given by so many Korean women that they were taken to brothels by deception? Here again, there seems to be some convergence of views on facts between the two different schools. Among reliable statements by former military personnel that Hata quotes in his book, six out of nine stated that they were troubled about the fate of women who were deceived and taken to the station. Some stated that they forbade the civilian "owners" from having such women exposed to sexual services.[61]

But after interpreting these facts of deception fundamental differences between the two schools emerge. From the perspective of the advocates of the rape center school, military culpability clearly emerges. Yoshimi argues that, although certain responsibility falls on Korean private brokers, this does not negate the Japanese military's primary responsibility.[62] Even if the military's basic function is to prevent abduction and rape, as is shown in the March 1938 document, if the military police failed to prevent rape of abducted girls, does it not show some fundamental flaws of the system, about which the military bear some responsibility?

In my view, this is the point where the views advanced by the advocates of the military brothel school stand on very shaky ground. But then, the question arises whether it was the general practice to take women to the comfort stations through deception concocted by the brokers or through parental contracts without deception. In the latter case, the advocates of the military brothel school argue that women who were sent by deception were exceptions and that these exceptions should not lead one to conclude that the comfort woman system as a whole was a system of institutional rape.

Yoshimi seems to maintain that, in effect, there were no volunteers, and even in cases where parents sold daughters to private brokers, it was combined with deceptions.[63] Larry Nicksch stated in a Congressional Research Service (CRS) Memorandum that "there is no doubt that from the available evidence that most comfort women were in the system involuntarily if one defines involuntarily to include entering the system in response to deceptive recruitment."[64]

Hata strongly disagrees with this conclusion and maintains that volunteers or those who were sold by parents probably constituted a large portion of recruitment in Korea. He cites the testimony of three Koreans to the U.S. military authorities in March 1945 that "all Korean comfort women that we met in the Pacific front were either volunteers or those who were sold by parents."[65] As we see below, there were so many testimonies by soldiers, who thought that they were dealing with prostitutes, who were at the brothels with their own consent.

But Kono underlined amply the deceptive nature of recruitment and undoubtedly this became one of the reasons why he declared "this [i.e., putting women in comfort women stations] was an act that severely injured the honor and dignity of many women."

How about the situation regarding women in occupied countries such as China, the Philippines, and Indonesia?

In this context, probably the most well-known example is the case of Dutch women. From February 1944 in Seraman Jawa, Dutch girls in their high-teens were forced to become comfort women by local Japanese military forces. This is the only case where the local military command was considered responsible by both the higher Japanese command and the postwar Dutch authorities. Upon investigation, the Japanese higher military command concluded that this had to be stopped immediately. The station was closed in April 1944. After the end of World War II, this case was brought to the Dutch military tribunal in 1947–48, which pronounced eleven guilty verdicts, including one death sentence. Accompanying records of the Kono statement include relevant court documents on this case.[66]

Some observers argue that Abe's cabinet decision in response to Tsujimoto's *Shitsumon Shuisho* ignores the Dutch case.[67] I argue that this is not the case. A careful checking may be needed in the wording of Abe's cabinet decision, but the Dutch case is too well known in Japan to be ignored. In fact, the June 14 *Washington Post* full-page advertisement specifically referred to the Dutch case, stating that "there were admittedly cases of breakdowns in discipline."

Regarding other cases, again, surprisingly, factual observation does not differ much between the two competing schools. In the occupied countries, there were clearly cases when women were raped and then taken by the military to serve officers and soldiers. Yoshimi precisely makes this point: "it is clear that coerced recruitment like slave hunting by officials and police took place in occupied areas such as China, Southeast Asia and Pacific Areas."[68] Hata also makes a similar analysis in relation to the situation in the Philippines.[69]

What makes Hata's argument different from Yoshimi's is that he maintains that these were rape cases basically unconnected to the comfort women system. In the Philippines there were 19 court-martial cases punishing the rapists before January 1943, and 80 cases where soldiers were punished in postwar tribunals. Hata argues that rape was impermissible and regrettable, but it was a crime against military orders, and this belongs to an entirely different category than the comfort women system.[70]

What is then the possible common picture on recruitment? We may list the following as the consensus that emerges from the two competing schools. First, enforced recruitment (*kyosei renko*) in principle did not take place in Korea, and even if it took place, it was an exception rather than the rule. Second, many Korean women were taken to the comfort stations by deception. Opinions vary concerning the proportion of women from Korea who arrived at comfort stations voluntarily or as the result of deception. I will examine this issue further in the next section. Third, in the occupied countries such as the Philippines, Indonesia, and China, there were cases where sexual service was coerced as the result of rape. Opinions vary over whether this rape should be considered a structural part of comfort stations. The Dutch case was a recognized case of where military discipline broke down with local military involvement. The question of rape in general is an issue which goes outside the parameter of this analysis.

Was the Comfort Station a Locus of Institutional Rape or Military Brothel?

This is the key question that fundamentally separates the two competing interpretations. Probably the Women's International War Crimes Tribunal on Japan's

Military Sexual Slavery in December 2000 provides the most voluminous testimonies covering major countries under the Japanese occupation. About 60 women who claimed to have been forced into sexual slavery testified. Testimonies were made by women from Korea (North and South), China, Taiwan, the Philippines, Malaysia, the Netherlands, Indonesia, and East Timor. All women who testified either through the taped video or in person denounced the comfort stations and described their own experience as nothing but rape.

The views of the institutional rape school are largely based on the testimony of those women who spoke up. The rape which they had to endure was a deliberate result of the system, and women were used as sexual slaves. Women were recruited by deception if not by physical coercion. Rapes in the occupied territory were the inevitable outcome of the comfort women system.

The advocates of the military brothel school see comfort stations differently, relying on historical memories other than the testimonies of the women at the Tribunal. First, what was the purpose of establishing comfort stations? Official documents of the period show that there were three objectives in establishing comfort stations: to prevent soldiers from raping local women, to prevent the spread of venereal diseases, and to prevent leaks of classified information. Yoshimi, based on his thorough analysis, confirmed the initial objectives of comfort stations.[71] Particularly the military leadership's concerns about the spread of venereal disease based on the experience of the Siberian intervention from 1918–22 are underlined as the primary cause of setting up comfort stations. The mass rape in Nanjing in 1937 is also emphasized as a driving force in the widespread establishment of comfort stations after 1938. The McDougal report cites these three factors as the reasons for establishing comfort stations.[72] The military was involved, but precisely for the purpose of preventing rape of other women outside of comfort stations.

Second, how were the comfort stations viewed by soldiers at the front? On March 28–30, 1992, the Kyoto Commission on War Victims in the Asia Pacific Region held open telephone interviews to hear the recollections of soldiers about comfort stations.[73] They received 132 telephone calls, and 83 of these gave intelligible answers. Out of 38 calls which described the atmosphere in the comfort stations, 29 gave a positive impression that the girls were lively and friendly, communications with them left very pleasant memories, and the girls they met received a sizable income from the money (yen cash or military check *gunpyo*) soldiers had to pay for having sexual intercourse. Nine stated that they felt very sorry for the girls who had to work under social pressure in a remote front region, or thought that it was morally wrong for the soldiers to spend time in such a place as comfort station. But none were aware that comfort women were physically coerced or deceived into working in the stations. Hiroo Onoda, aged 85, describes vividly his experience in China that comfort stations were nothing but brothels where an average soldier spent one-third of his income.[74]

Even in the Women's International War Crimes Tribunal on Japan's Military Sexual Slavery one of the two former soldiers who testified stated that "all women who worked in public brothels were under harsh conditions. Comfort women too.

They had no freedom because of their advance payment (which parents of poor families received by selling their daughters to the public brothels). Their activities were controlled by money."[75]

Third, one more widely reported account is the record of the detailed minutes of the results of American interrogations at a comfort station in Myitkyana, Burma, consisting of 20 Korean women and two Japanese brokers.[76] In general, this record gives the impression that the women came to Burma with full knowledge of their activities, received sizable incomes, and had a relatively lively life accompanying soldiers, some of whom seriously proposed marriage. "During World War II, owners of brothels from Japan and from Korea, which was a part of Japan then, went to the front in Asia where the Japanese military was stationed. These were sort of business trips abroad to make more money. From the point of view of the military, they positively accepted these groups and assisted the groups to perform their business in stations that the military had prepared. It was useful for the military to prevent rape and venereal disease."[77]

So they argue that depicting the comfort system as a center of systematic rape is a monstrous concoction by those who do not understand how Japanese military society worked under prewar conditions. Proponents of the military brothels school maintain that the fate many women suffered at the comfort station is truly painful and regrettable but concluding that Japan had a unique system of mass rape goes too far and that there was too much evidence to characterize this institution as equivalent to military brothels.

The Kono statement and its introductory document refrained from analyzing the basic nature of comfort stations. There is no analysis of the financial side of comfort station operations, including as how much soldiers paid, in what form, and what proportion of the money the comfort women received themselves. There is no comparative analysis of comfort stations and public brothels in Imperial Japan.

What the Kono statement did was confirm the three objectives for establishing comfort stations.[78] It drew the important conclusion that "they lived in misery at comfort stations under a coercive atmosphere." It did not go into a quantitative analysis of how much pain was inflicted on the comfort women. All three schools broadly agree that the comfort stations were led primarily by civilian owners but with military involvement. Kono took the position that the pains inflicted on comfort women were sufficient to assume the Japanese government's responsibility.

It seems possible to reach a reasonably common understanding of the basic nature of a comfort station on the following basis. First, comfort stations were established in order to avoid raping local women, to prevent the spread of venereal diseases, and to prevent leaks of classified information. Many soldiers commuted to comfort stations with the understanding that they were military brothels, i.e., paying money to receive sexual services within an accepted orderly system. Second, some women suffered extreme mental and physical pains in that system. Third, the Kono Statement recognized and acknowledged those pains, accepted the Japanese government's responsibility, and expressed apology and remorse.

How Many Comfort Women Were Recruited and from Which Countries?

The McDougal Report stated unambiguously that there were "over 200,000 sex slaves."[79] But even according to Yoshimi, such an unequivocal determination of the number of comfort women is not credible. There do not seem to be any reliable statistics. Yoshimi analyzes how these numbers were calculated, in some cases using Ikuhiko Hata's numbers. On this issue, both schools do not seem to be widely different. The rough number of Japanese soldiers stationed in Asia annually is calculated as 3 million. Then estimates are given for how many soldiers one woman was expected to serve per year. This ranges from 30, 50, or 100 per year. Another estimate is made on the issue of "how often women were replaced by new women?" It is not realistic that one woman continuously served throughout the stationing of one unit. Suppose that one unit stayed in China from 1938 till 1945. If the replacement ratio is 1.0, it means that a woman sent to the station in 1938 served for 8 years. If that ratio is 2.0, two women served each for four years. The replacement ratio was calculated as 1.0 (no change), 2.0 (one unit gets one full replacement), or 1.5.

Yoshimi quotes one of Hata's early writings where he gave one estimate based on the assumption that one woman served 50 soldiers per year with a replacement ratio of 1. This would make the number of comfort women 60,000. If the replacement rate were 1.5, the total number would become 90,000.

Yoshimi considers the replacement ratio as at a minimum 1.5, and with the highest ratio of one woman serving 100 soldiers the total number of comfort women becomes 45,000. If one woman served the lowest number of soldiers 30, the total number of women would become 150,000. Only with the replacement ratio of 2.0 in case one woman serves 30 soldiers is the figure of 200,000 comfort women reached.[80]

But Hata eventually changed his estimate. In 1999, he argued that 3 million as a base figure seemed to be too high and he preferred to calculate on a basis of 2.5 million. The number of soldiers served by one comfort women could be calculated as 150, and then with 1 to 1.5 as the replacement rate, the number of comfort women would be 16,000 to 25,000.[81]

When it comes to the country of origin of comfort women, this guesswork is even more confusing. No reliable statistics are preserved, either. Yoshimi quotes one statistics published by the Imperial General Headquarters on the number of soldiers with venereal disease and the women who most likely had been the origin. The statistics cover soldiers stationed abroad until 1940: Korean women 51.8%, Chinese women 36.0%, and Japanese women 12.2%. But he also quotes another figure of comfort women in and around Nanjing in 1942: Japanese 272, Chinese 261, Korean 48. Yoshimi refrains from giving overall speculative statistics on the origin of comfort women.[82]

Hata makes more definite assumptions. He started his analysis by using the traditionally accepted view that the ratio of Japanese to Koreans was 20%–30% to 70%–80%. Then, having gone through various documents giving concrete data, he eventually concluded that probably the number of Koreans was inflated and gave his estimate as Japanese 40%, locals 30%, Koreans 20%, and others 10%.[83]

Kono was careful not to have given any definite estimate. The introductory document to the statement concluded that "it is difficult to give the aggregate number of comfort women." As for countries of origin, the introductory document just limits itself to citing Japan, Korea, China, Taiwan, the Philippines, Indonesia, and the Netherlands.

CONCLUSION

Notwithstanding the three conflicting views that have appeared, it seems possible to reach a reasonably common understanding of the basic nature of comfort women stations as follows.

1. The comfort women stations were established in order to avoid raping local women, to prevent the spread of venereal diseases, and to prevent leaks of classified information. Many soldiers commuted to comfort stations with the understanding that these were military brothels;

2. With some exceptions of direct military operation, the majority of comfort stations were operated by civilian owners or private traders;

3. The military was, directly or indirectly, involved in the establishment and management of the comfort stations and transfer of comfort women;

4. Enforced recruitment (*kyosei renko*) as a general practice did not take place in Korea, and if it took place, it was an exception rather than the rule, but many Korean women were taken to the comfort stations by deception;

5. In the occupied countries such as the Philippines and China, there were cases where sexual service was coerced as the result of rape; the Dutch case was a recognized case of local military involvement;

6. As the result of all these situations mentioned above, there were some women who had to go through extreme mental and physical pain;

7. The Kono Statement recognized and acknowledged that the pain inflicted on comfort women, accepted government responsibility, and expressed apology and remorse. This position developed into the activities of the Asian Women's Fund. Some governments accepted this apology and cooperated with the Asian Women's Fund; while others refused to cooperate. The Fund terminated its activities in March 2007.

In order that this recognition will be shared by the international community, however, I argue that simply endorsing the Kono statement is not enough. Japan should make it understood that this recognition comes from the country as a whole, which feels the pains inflicted in the past on comfort women, that Japan should show this feeling not only by words but also by deeds; and that the newly emerging legal situation created by the Supreme Court verdict of April 27, 2007, can serve as a historic opportunity to convey Japan's moral responsibility on this issue.[84]

It remains to be seen how this issue is going to develop (or not develop) under Yasuo Fukuda's cabinet.

NOTES

1. The McDougal Report submitted to the United Nations states: "Between 1932 and the end of the Second World War, the Japanese Government and the Japanese Imperial Army forced over 200,000 women into sexual slavery in rape centres throughout Asia. These rape centres have often been referred to in objectionably euphemistic terms as 'comfort stations.'" At this opening paragraph of the appendix of the McDougal report, twice the word "rape center" is used. The term, "rape center," is often used by gender activists to argue that the system was nothing but an institution of continuous rape. But throughout this chapter, I avoid the term, "rape center," to avoid the misunderstanding, and I used the term, "institutional rape," instead. See the report online at the UN Commission on Human Rights Web site: http://www.hri.ca/fortherecord1998/documentation/commission/e-cn4-sub2-1998-13.htm [October 12, 2007] See also VAWW-NET Japan, *McDougal Report* (Tokyo: Gaisensha, 2000) p. 84.

2. On April 9, 1997, in a meeting of a parliamentary group, Abe questioned why this issue was not raised in the negotiations leading to the normalization of the relationship between Japan and South Korea in 1965, particularly if "coerced recruitment" really took place. He also stated that some of the statements made by former Korean comfort women might lack credibility (*Shukan Gendai,* April 14, 2007, pp. 25–28). In May 1997 he stated that "it is problematic that the Kono statement is still in force and that there are references on this issue kept in the [junior high] textbooks, when the foundation of that statement had already collapsed." *Sankei Shinbun,* October 4, 2006.

3. *Sankei Shinbun,* October 4, 2006.

4. *Yomiuri Shinbun,* October 6, 2006.

5. *Asahi Shinbun,* March 4, 2007.

6. The *New York Times,* March 2, 2007. The following opening paragraph, which did not take into account all the developments for more than a decade since the Kono statement made an overwhelming impact on all English written media: "Prime Minister Shinzo Abe denied Thursday that Japan's military had forced foreign women into sexual slavery during World War II, contradicting the Japanese government's longtime official position."

7. There were only six cosponsors for this resolution at the end of January, but this number increased to 77 by April 4. *Asahi Shinbun,* April 4, 2007.

8. *Asahi Shinbun,* March 14, 2007.

9. *Asahi Shinbun,* April 4, 2007.

10. The *New York Times,* April 28, 2007

11. *Washington Post,* June 14, 2007. Altogether 44 parliamentarians, including 29 Liberal Democratic Party (LDP) members, 13 Democratic Party of Japan (DPJ) members, and two independents, signed together with 19 opinion leaders from various professions.

12. *Asahi Shinbun,* July 31, 2007.

13. I also happened to represent the Japanese Government, as the Director General of European Affairs, to negotiate the reconciliation issue with the Dutch Government to prepare a meeting between Prime Ministers Willem Kok and Keizo Obuchi in February 2000. The prime ministers' meeting was conducted to pave the way to the Emperor's visit to the Netherlands, which took place in May the same year. In preparing the meetings with my Dutch counterpart, I learned about the Dutch comfort women issue and was profoundly shocked. Although I did not mention my specific impression on comfort women in my talks, it substantially reinforced my conviction that a clear message of apology should be pronounced by Prime Minister Obuchi to Dutch war victims, comfort women, and other internees.

This experience reinforced my position to support the Kono Statement. See Kazuhiko Togo, *Japan's Foreign Policy, 1945–2003: The Quest for a Proactive Policy* (Leiden: Brill, 2005), pp. 282–83.

14. Yoshimi Yoshiaki, *Jugun ianfu* (Tokyo: Iwanami shoten, 1995); Yoshimi Yoshiaki and Kawada Fumiko, *Jugun ianfu o meguru 30 no uso to shinjistu* (Tokyo: Otsuki shoten, 1997).

15. *Asahi Shinbun,* March 29, 2007.

16. *Asahi Shinbun,* March 28, 2007. A group of human rights advocates and lawyers have been attempting to enact a similar law since 1999. *Asahi Shinbun,* August 1, 1999.

17. *Asahi Shinbun,* April 7, 2007.

18. Before the McDougal Report, which was presented to the Commission of Human Rights on June 22, 1998, there was another report presented to the Commission of Human Rights on January 4, 1996 by Ms. Radhika Coomaraswamy on the comfort women issue (http://www.unhchr.ch/Huridocda/Huridoca.nsf/TestFrame/b6ad5f3990967 f3e802566d600575fcb?Opendocument; accessed October 12, 2007).

19. VAWW-NET Japan, *McDougal Report,* (Tokyo: Gaisensha, 2000), p. 84.

20. VAWW-NET Japan, *Q&A Josei Kokusai Senpan Hotei* (Tokyo, Akashi, 2002), p. 9. From 1991 onward, three cases from Korea, four from China, one from Taiwan, one from the Philippines and one from the Netherlands have been filed. (http://www1.jca.apc.org/ vaww-net-japan/slavery/courtcase.html; accessed April 20, 2007).

21. *Asahi Shinbun,* April 27, 2007.

22. Togo Kazuhiko, "Sengohosho hanketsu, wakai eno shintenki ga otozureta," *Asahi Shinbun,* May 17, 2007.

23. Hata Ikuhiko, *Ianfu to senjo no sei* (Tokyo: Shinchosha, 1999); "Maboroshi no jugun ianfu o netsuzo shita Kono danwa wa konaose," *Shokun* May, 2007, pp. 138–51.

24. Daishido Tsuneyasu, *Ianfu kyoseirenko wa nakatta* (Tokyo: Tentensha, 1999); "Abesori, Kono danwa no torikeshi ketsudan o!" *Seiron,* May 2007, pp. 105–37.

25. *Will,* May 2007, pp. 37–79.

26. Other opinion leaders who contributed to this issue included Yoshinori Kobayashi, Fuyuko Kamisaka, Birei Kim, and Hiroo Onoda.

27. *Sankei Shinbun,* February 10, 2005; "Abesori, Kono danwa no torikeshi ketsudan o," *Seiron,* May, 2007, pp. 128–37.

28. It was established under the name of "... *Young Parliamentarians.*" (Daishido, *Ianfu kyoseirenko,* p. 95).

29. On March 8 the Committee decided to ask the government only to research this matter, and not to request revisions to the Kono statement. *Asahi Shinbun,* March 8, 2007. On March 14, the Committee itself decided to postpone its research for the time being. *Mainichi Shinbun,* March 14, 2007.

30. For the time being, their activities are limited to hearings of experts' views (*Sankei Shinbun,* March 10, 2007).

31. Sakurai Yoshiko, "Nihon o otoshimetsuzukeru Kono Danwa toiu akurei,"*Will,* May 2007, pp. 37–38; Nishioka Susumu, "Subete wa Asahishinbun no netsuzokara hajimatta," *Will,* May, 2007, pp. 72–73.

32. Hata, *Ianfu to senjo no sei,* pp. 249–55.

33. *Sankei Shinbun,* February 26, 2007; Sakurai Yoshiko, *Shukan Bunshun,* May 8, 2007, pp. 144–45.

34. For the Kono statement and the accompanying documents, see Daishido, *Ianfu kyoseirenko,* pp. 249–55.

35. The Kono statement is found online at the Web site of the Ministry of Foreign Affairs of Japan: http://www.mofa.go.jp/policy/women/fund/state9308.html (accessed May 6, 2007).

36. For many years the Japanese government did not acknowledge the military involvement. Only on January 12, 1992, Chief Cabinet Secretary Koichi Kato acknowledged the military involvement and apologize for it. Daishido, *Ianfu kyoseirenko,* p. 28.

37. From the Kono statement, http://www.mofa.go.jp/policy/women/fund/state9308.html (accessed October 4, 2007).

38. Ibid.

39. Digital Museum, The Comfort Women Issue and the Asian Women's Fund. http://www.awf.or.jp/ (accessed April 21, 2007).

40. Some Korean intellectuals severely criticize the Korean obstinacy to reject any appreciation about Japanese good will. See Park Yuha, *Wakai no tameni* (Tokyo: Heibonsha, 2006), pp. 76–85.

41. Yoshiaki Yoshimi found this document at the Library of the Boei Kenkyujo in a confidential file pertaining to the communications between the military leadership in Tokyo and the expeditionary forces in China. *Asahi Shinbun,* January 11, 1992.

42. The document was entitled "Shina Jihen no keiken yorimitaru gunkishinsaku taisaku" and it was formulated by the Ministry of War. Yoshimi, *Jugun ianfu,* p. 36.

43. Sakurada Takeshi and Shikanai Nobutaka, *Ima akasu sengo hishi,* quoted in Yoshimi, *Jugun ianfu,* p. 37.

44. The June 14 *Washington Post* advertisement also carried a Korean newspaper report of August 31, 1939, in which local police, under Japanese jurisdiction, punished brokers who forced women to become comfort women.

45. Daishido, *Ianfu kyosei renko,* pp. 19–20, 26.

46. Hata, *Ianfu to senjo no sei,* pp. 80–81.

47. VAWW-NET Japan, Josei Kokusai Hotei, *Zenkiroku* (Tokyo, Ryokufu Shuppan, 2002), p. 64.

48. VAWW-NET Japan, *Zenkiroku,* p. 157.

49. Yoshimi, *Jugun ianfu,* pp. 124–27.

50. Hata, *Ianfu to senjo no sei,* pp. 189–91.

51. Daishido, *Ianfu kyosei renko,* pp. 1–17, 96.

52. Hata, *Ianfu to senjo no sei,* pp. 229–48.

53. Yoshimi and Kawada, *Jugun ianfu,* pp. 26–27.

54. Daishido, "Maboroshino jugun ianfu," pp. 106–7.

55. Yoshimi and Kawada, *Jugun ianfu,* p. 24.

56. Daishido, *Ianfu kyosei renko,* p. 58. Ishihara apparently further explained that if the Korean side insisted that if the Japanese side acknowledged coercion, then the Korean side would refrain from asking individual reparation. *Sankei Shinbun,* March 1, 2007.

57. Abiru's home page, http://abirur.iza.ne.jp/blog/entry/124549/ (accessed May 6, 2007).

58. The content of the interview was again reported in *Asahi Shinbun,* March 4, 2007.

59. *Shitsumon Shuisho* is a legally determined formula of questionnaire that any parliamentarian is allowed to submit to the government. The government is obligated to reply all the questions presented in this formula by cabinet decision.

60. *Yomiuri Shinbun,* March 17, 2007.

61. Hata, *Ianfu to senjo no sei,* pp. 382–86.

62. Yoshimi and Kawada, *Jugun ianfu,* pp. 17–18.

63. Yoshimi, *Jugun ianfu,* pp. 95–97, 102–4.

64. Larry Nicksch, *Memorandum,* Congressional Research Service, April 3, 2007, p. 11.

65. Hata, *Ianfu to senjo no sei,* p. 380.

66. This portion of the supporting document is published in Daishido, *Ianfu kyosei renko,* pp. 250–53.

67. Larry Niksch, in his report prepared for the Congressional Research Service, stated that the cabinet decision on March 16 "either ignore[s] or [is] a rejection of the findings of the Dutch War Crimes Tribunals' findings and verdicts." *Memorandum,* April 3, 2007, p. 22.

68. Yoshimi, *Jugun ianfu,* p. 24.

69. Hata, *Ianfu to senjo no sei,* pp. 192–208.

70. Ibid, p. 377.

71. Yoshimi, *Jugun ianfu,* pp. 13–56.

72. VAWW-NET Japan, *McDougal Report,* p. 89.

73. *Ianfu Joho Denwa, Sei to shinryaku* (Tokyo: Shakai Hyoronsha, 1993), pp. 263–76.

74. Onoda is a well known soldier of the Imperial Army who stayed in the mountains until 1974. *Will,* Special Edition, August 2007, pp. 148–55.

75. VAWW-NET Japan, *Zenkiroku,* p. 222.

76. Daishido, *Ianfu kyosei renko,* pp. 253–58.

77. Abe Akira, *Ianfumondai no karakuri* (Tokyo: Natsume shobo, 2005), pp. 20, 29. This book is recommended by Nobukatsu Fujioka on its book cover.

78. Daishido, *Ianfu kyosei renko,* p. 246.

79. VAWW-NET Japan, *McDougal Report,* p. 84.

80. Yoshimi, *Jugun ianfu,* pp. 78–80.

81. Hata, *Ianfu to senjo no sei,* p. 406.

82. Yoshimi, *Jugun ianfu,* pp. 81–84.

83. Hata, *Ianfu to senjo no sei,* p. 410.

84. Togo Kazuhiko, "Jugun ianfu ketsugi wa 'nihon gyokusai' no josho ka?" *Gekkan Gendai,* September 2007, pp. 48–55.

Part III —————————————————————————

Views from the Region

8

Japan's Neo-Nationalism and China's Response

Jin Linbo

In comparison with all its Asian neighbors, Japan was the first country in East Asia to embrace modern nationalism with great enthusiasm. "Being geographically isolated off the northeast coast of Asia and having developed, at an early date, a homogeneous people speaking a common language and worshipping indigenous gods, the Japanese soon developed a sense of group unity, and under strong external pressure, became the most nationalistic people in Asia."[1] From the Meiji Restoration until the end of World War II, Japanese nationalism not only deeply affected its internal and external affairs but also stimulated the awakening of national consciousness and the evolution of modern nationalism in China and other parts of East Asia.[2] However, Japanese nationalism, which began with a defensive nature at the beginning of its modern history, subsequently evolved into fanatical ultra-nationalism, imperialism, militarism, and even fascism from the late nineteenth century, leading to unlimited military aggression against neighboring countries and the crushing final defeat of the Japanese Empire in World War II. It was against this backdrop that Japanese nationalism, as both an ideology and a movement, lost not only its attractiveness to most Japanese but also became a taboo of sorts in Japanese mainstream discourse during the first three decades in the postwar period.

Change came in the early 1980s, when nationalist politician Yasuhiro Nakasone became prime minister. Strongly believing that Japan had reached a dramatic turning point in its postwar history, Nakasone expressed his intention to carry out a thorough "overhauling of postwar Japanese politics," calling on Japan to overcome the masochistic view of history nurtured by the International Military Tribunal for the Far East (Tokyo War Crimes Tribunal).[3] On August 15, 1985, Nakasone visited, in his official capacity, the controversial Yasukuni Shrine, which enshrines the war dead, including 14 Class-A war criminals. He was the first postwar prime minister who paid an official visit to the Yasukuni Shrine on August 15, the most sensitive date making the war's end. Nakasone's nationalistic views and stance were hailed and followed by a number of conservative politicians and right-wing groups at the time, and they brought about the first resurgence of new nationalism in postwar Japanese history. Although this revived new nationalism led by the country's right-wing political elite was quite striking, its substantial effects on Japan's overall national policies were relatively limited. Under the Cold War international environment, "top-down style" nationalism was echoed less by the Japanese society as a whole and it became neither part of mainstream public opinion nor a driving force for Japanese domestic and foreign policy.

In the late 1980s, Japan faced a brand-new political situation, and its position and role in the world became a hot topic, which drew broad attention and serious debate at home and abroad. On the one hand, the continuing economic boom and smooth social development had made the Japanese people feel confident about making the relationship with the United States more equal, and about playing a relatively independent role in the international stage. The well-known nationalist politician Shintaro Ishihara coauthored with a prominent business leader, the late Akio Morita (cofounder of the Sony Corporation), the controversial book *The Japan That Can Say No* in 1989. In it, they argued that the United States needed Japan as much as or more than Japan needed the United States and that Japan should act more independently and say "No" to the United States. The book, which sold over a million copies, symbolized Japanese pride and assertiveness as the world's second largest economic power at the time. But, on the other hand, dissatisfaction, complaints, and criticisms about Japan's inaction in the Gulf War in 1990–91 aroused a feeling of frustration, confusion, and embarrassment among the Japanese people. Although Japan paid $13 billion to support the war on Iraq, the most generous financial contribution of any country, this policy was derisively described as "checkbook diplomacy" at the time, and the failure to respond to U.S. and international demands for a "human contribution" provoked rebuke. The Gulf War had a grave impact on Japanese strategic thinking. After the war, the Japanese Diet passed an International Peace Cooperation Law (IPCL) in June 1992, allowing the dispatch of the Japanese Self-Defense Force (SDF) for UN-led peacekeeping operations (PKO). This was the first major change in Japan's security policy in the post–Cold War era, but this change raised serious concerns from its neighbors. China and South Korea had serious suspicions about Japan's political reasons for passing the IPCL. Japan, on the other hand, questions why its two immediate neighbors opposed its actions. As Tsuyoshi Hasegawa pointed out, the "opposition from its neighbors to its pursuit of great power status would revive history as a major issue, which, in turn, would rouse Japan's own nationalism."[4]

Since the mid-1990s, Japan has experienced a resurgence of neo-nationalism, as have China and South Korea. As in the previous decade, Japan's right-wing political elite led the way. But unlike in the 1980s, the new wave of nationalism has enjoyed a far more favorable environment within and outside of the country in which to flourish. With the end of the Cold War, the collapse of the Soviet Union, and the subsequent demise of left-wing forces in Japan, the political climate surrounding Japan has profoundly changed. In these circumstances, Japan's new nationalism has enlisted not only more enthusiastic support from an increased number of conservative politicians and nationalist groups, but also some degree of understanding and even grassroots acceptance. This was a quite new phenomenon, which indicates that most Japanese have not viewed the nationalist movement as dangerous. As more members of the World War II generation have passed away, there are fewer Japanese who remember the horrors of war. In other words, "most Japanese alive today never saw firsthand how popular nationalism can evolve into fascism and thus do not understand its perils."[5] This was a cause for alarm.

From the mid-1990s to the present, Japan's new nationalism has tended to manifest itself in various ways. These include visits to the controversial Yasukuni Shrine by top Japanese leaders, pursuit of a larger military role through a strengthening Japanese-U.S. alliance, adoption of *hinomaru* as the national flag and *kimigayo* as the national anthem, approval of a history textbook that downplays Japanese aggression in World War II, an increasing emphasis on patriotism education and amendment of the Fundamental Law of Education, the various movements for revising the "Peace Constitution," and the passage of the Constitution Referendum bill, among other developments. All these events and developments suggest that Japan has been in the midst of resurgent nationalism, and the nationalistic views and actions taken by the top Japanese leaders have already directly affected formulation of various national policies. The trend of Japan's neo-nationalism was further strengthened when the postwar-born nationalist leader Shinzo Abe was elected to the presidency of the ruling Liberal Democratic Party (LDP) and as prime minister in September 2006. Abe has long asserted that Japan should "[cast] away the postwar regime" by revising the Constitution and reforming the education system. In this context, it is no exaggeration to say that "neo-nationalism has become a major driving force behind Japan's foreign and domestic policy."[6]

Factors contributing to the revival of neo-nationalism can be found both inside and outside Japan. Domestically, Japan's willingness to become a political power in the international arena has given an endorsement to surging nationalistic sentiment. The broadly shared belief among Japanese people that Japan should become a "normal country" politically and militarily and enjoy a prestigious international stature commensurate with being the world's second largest economy and the most important financial contributor to the United Nations is growing stronger than ever in postwar Japanese history. Meanwhile, the collapse of the "bubble economy" and the resulting economic recession that lasted over a decade deeply affected many Japanese psychologically and nearly destroyed the hitherto accumulated overconfidence that stemmed from the long-continued Japanese economic boom prior to the 1990s.

The call for strong government leadership to embark on political and economic structural reforms was increasing, serving as a sort of stimulation for the spread of nationalism within Japan. In terms of outside factors, rising Chinese power and the possibility of a nuclear-armed North Korea seem to be Japan's main regional concerns. Continuation of rapid Chinese economic growth, accelerated military modernization, surging nationalism characterized by strong anti-Japan sentiment, persistent demand that Japan correct its view of recent history, and fierce opposition to Japan's bid for a permanent seat on the UN Security Council all have made Japanese feel insecure or even threatened, and, thus, have provided good grounds for nationalistic arguments that could be easily understood by the general public. Many Japanese now began to argue that Japan "should once more possess the military power to rival that of its neighbors."[7] In addition to the factor of rising China, North Korea's missile launches and pursuit of nuclear weapons have not only further strengthened and justified ongoing Japanese remilitarization but also have led some powerful politicians to publicly suggest the possibility of Japanese possession of nuclear weapons. Under these circumstances, how to deal with a situation where Japan reemerges as a "normal" military and political power inevitably became the pressing strategic issue for China, South Korea, and other countries to consider.

Profoundly affected by its own surging nationalism with enormous negative effects in a "reforming and opening" era, China, on the other hand, has been quite sensitive to a resurgence of Japanese neo-nationalism.[8] In fact, Japan, which played a decisive role in the awakening and evolution of modern nationalism in China, has ironically served as the primary target of Chinese nationalism for most of modern Chinese history. As a result, anti-Japan sentiment was deeply rooted in both prewar and postwar Chinese society. Normalization of diplomatic relations between the two countries in 1972 effectively changed the overall political atmosphere on both sides, but the rapprochement and the ensuing friendly exchanges between the two governments and two peoples fell short of ridding their bilateral relations of all past hatred and antagonism. It was against this background that even in its current response to Japanese neo-nationalism, China appeared to be quite emotional. As for the substantial content of China's response, two interconnected main themes have been always underlined: one is on "the issue of history" and the directly related issues such as Yasukuni and textbooks; the other is on "the issue of Taiwan" and the relevant security problems such as Japanese remilitarization and the Japanese-U.S. alliance. From the Chinese perspective, both the history and Taiwan issues have not only closely linked with the "political foundation of Sino-Japanese relations," but the Taiwan issue itself has also been the "core of China's national interests."[9] In other words, both the history and Taiwan issues bear great significance to China, and thus are not in principle subjects for compromise. Many Chinese tend to believe that both the political foundation of Sino-Japanese relations and China's most important national interest would be at stake if it failed to cope with the resurgence of Japanese nationalism with a tough stance and take effective measures not only at the present time but also in the years to come. It would be difficult to expect some dramatic change in this regard to take place in the near future.

NEO-NATIONALISM AND THE ISSUE OF HISTORY

In a sense, controversy over the issue of history seems unavoidable between Japan and its immediate neighbors, especially China. Both sides have attached great importance to this issue, and, thus, the constant controversy over it has become one outstanding feature of postwar Sino-Japanese relations. During the last 30-some years, Sino-Japanese relations have been frequently entangled and damaged by the issue of history, including the treatment of history in official Japanese textbooks, frequent attempts by high-ranking Japanese officials to whitewash wartime Japanese imperial army aggression and atrocities, and official visits to the Yasukuni Shrine by top Japanese leaders. On the part of China, affected by its political and ideological tradition of emphasizing morality as a general principle for overall national policies, history issues have long been given top priority in dealing with Sino-Japanese relations. In general, "taking history as a mirror and looking into the future" has been China's basic stance on the history issue, which puts a clear emphasis on both the past and the future. China's emphasis on the importance of history consists of following three interrelated dimensions: it argues that Japan should, first, "acknowledge and recognize the history of Japanese militaristic invasion against China" and express "profound introspection and apology to Chinese people"; second, "abide by the statement and promise to strictly restrain the right wings with concrete actions"; and third, "educate its people with correct perception of history."[10] Although the emphasis of the above-mentioned points has varied at different times, China's basic tone on the issue of history has never changed since 1972. In Japan, history and related issues have also become sensitive and significant since the early 1980s but for different reasons than in China. Japanese nationalists, eager to find a breakthrough to express publicly their revisionist view on Japanese history since the end of World War II, have launched the first new wave of postwar nationalism since the earlier one led by Prime Minister Nakasone, who was determined to make "a final accounting on the postwar Japanese political system." The textbook and Yasukuni controversies occurred under these circumstances, but both of them were doomed to face strong protests from China and other Asian countries.

THE TEXTBOOK CONTROVERSY

The first dispute over textbooks erupted in June 1982 when Japanese newspapers reported that in the textbook screening process, the previously used word "aggression" had been replaced by the word "entry" in describing the wartime Japanese military expansion in China, and some textbooks purposely downplayed Japan's responsibility for the Nanjing Massacre. Having long been cautiously observing Japanese political trends, China took this new movement as an ominous sign of a revival of Japanese nationalism and militarism, and it lodged strong protests through the media as well as through diplomatic channels. The South Korean government also made stern protests, and tensions further intensified. Under this unexpected pressure from China and South Korea, the Japanese government eventually issued a statement stating that the feelings and concerns of neighboring countries would be taken into consideration in future textbook screening processes. The Chinese government was not satisfied with this result because the statement did not make it clear that the past war was an aggressive one in nature, but it reluctantly accepted the measures taken by the Japanese government.

The first diplomatic fight over textbooks eventually died down without a complete resolution between the two governments. The incomplete solution to this issue foretold that this controversy would recur in the future, and it was repeated in 1986, 2001, and 2005. In 1986, "the National Congress to Protect Japan" published a high-school textbook that highlighted the revisionist view of history. When this textbook was about to pass the screening process, the Chinese government made stern protests through diplomatic channels, urging Japan to correct distortions of the historical record. Fearing a possible escalation of the tensions, the Japanese government acted swiftly in accordance with the principle established in 1982. The textbook was approved only after its publisher made many changes. In 2001, a history textbook for junior high schools from the *Atarashii Kyokasho o Tsukurukai* (the Association to Produce New History Textbooks—hereafter Tsukurukai), a group of conservative scholars, was published by Fusosha (part of the Fujisankei Communications Group, which also owns the conservative *Sankei Shinbun* newspaper). Tsukurukai's textbook was approved by the Ministry of Education after making certain corrections. The Chinese government strongly protested by stating that "despite some amendments, its reactionary and ridiculous nature can not be changed," and it urged the Japanese government "to be true in words and resolute in deeds and take effective measures at once to prevent any history book that denies and whitewashes the history of aggression from coming out."[11] But the Japanese government refused to make the changes demanded by China and the issue was left without a satisfactory solution. When the controversial textbook by the same publisher was again approved in 2005, the textbook issue again became a political problem for the two countries. In general, China's responses to both cases in 2001 and 2005 were similar to what had been done in the 1980s, but the results were different. Confronted by strong protests from China in both cases, the Japanese government refused to make the changes requested by China, and it explained in 2005 that views expressed in the new textbooks do not necessarily represent the views of the Japanese government.[12]

The Japanese government's attitude caused dissatisfaction and indignation within China that reached a higher level than on previous occasions and served as one of the key factors that triggered the mass anti-Japanese demonstrations in 2005. Although the actual adoption rate of the controversial new textbook by Japanese schools was very low, the dispute over textbooks remains unresolved, and constitutes one of the most difficult political problems between Japan and its neighbors. In recent years, the creation of two bilateral committees, between Japan and South Korea and between China and Japan, has raised hopes for deepening mutual understanding and for possibly creating a common textbook for schools in China, Japan, and South Korea in the future. However, it would be unrealistic to expect that the textbook issue can be completely resolved in the near future through the efforts of these committees.

THE YASUKUNI CONTROVERSY

Compared to the textbook issue, the controversy over Yasukuni visits by top Japanese leaders has not only caused extreme domestic political tensions in both China and Japan repeatedly since the mid-1980s, but has also caused much more serious damage than other issues to the postwar Sino-Japanese relationship. Even now when the Chinese and Japanese governments are trying hard to stabilize their bilateral relations, the Yasukuni issue remains one of the most sensitive issues that could once again dash the hope for further improvements in the relationship. China's basic view and position on Yasukuni visits consists of the following elements. First, as one of the key shrines of the Japanese Shinto religion, the Yasukuni Shrine served as "the spiritual prop of Japanese militarism for its aggression and expansion in prewar period,"[13] and it is in essence the symbol and embodiment of prewar Japanese imperialism and militarism even now. This stance indicates that even if the Class-A war criminals were removed from it, the nature of the Yasukuni Shrine cannot be changed, and official visits by top Japanese leaders to the shrine could still be politically problematic for Sino-Japanese relations. Second, the enshrinement of the Class-A war criminals who led the aggressive war that caused tremendous damage and suffering to China and other Asian countries added a further evil element to the shrine itself and made official Yasukuni visits even more intolerable. Third, since Yasukuni played an active role in stirring up militarism before and during World War II, postwar Japanese leaders ought to make a moral judgment and refrain from political activities that may be taken by Japan's neighbors as glorifying its militarist past. In other words, from the Chinese perspective the best way for Japan to show its sincerity of remorse and apology is for its top political leaders to avoid paying homage to the Yasukuni Shrine. In contrast to China's viewpoint, however, Japanese nationalists have regarded Yasukuni as the most sacred place for maintaining Japanese spiritual nationalism and have asked the country's top leaders, including the emperor, to pay homage to the shrine. A big gap clearly exists between China and Japanese nationalists, and this gap extends down to the grassroots level as well. For many ordinary Japanese citizens, the Yasukuni Shrine is, in a sense, just a place similar to many monuments in other countries for soldiers who died in war for their country, though it contains many problems such as the enshrinement of the Class-A war criminals and the separation of religion and politics prescribed in the Japanese Constitution. This widely shared view within Japan, which is far from China's position of taking Yasukuni as "spiritual prop of prewar Japanese militarism," has, in fact, made it even harder for many Japanese to understand China's vehement opposition to Yasukuni visits by Japanese leaders. It is unlikely that this gap could be narrowed in the near future through friendly exchanges between the two countries.

China's first diplomatic offensive against Yasukuni visits by Japanese leaders took place in 1985 when Prime Minister Nakasone visited the Yasukuni Shrine on August 15 of that year. On August 14, the day before his visit to the shrine, the spokesman of the Chinese Foreign Ministry warned that "if Japanese Prime Minister Nakasone and his cabinet members visited Yasukuni Shrine, the feelings of all people in the world especially Asian people including Chinese and Japanese who suffered most from the militarism, would be hurt," because "Hideki Tojo and other war criminals were enshrined at Yasukuni."[14] In fact, Nakasone's Yasukuni visit provoked not only strong criticism from within the Chinese government but also great resentment against Japan in Chinese society. Student demonstrations took place in Beijing and in other cities in China with slogans such as: "Objection to the revival of Japanese militarism," and "No to Japanese economic invasion."

In light of these massive protests, the Japanese government explained its position in November by saying that Nakasone's official visit to Yasukuni did not mean the justification of the Class-A war criminals and that the visit itself was not something that was institutionalized. This explanation implied that Nakasone would not visit the shrine again. In fact, he decided not to visit the shrine the following year. Although China was discontented with the Japanese attitude on this issue, Nakasone's decision not to visit Yasukuni again was a positive outcome, which set a precedent for future Japanese leaders to follow and also for China to deal with any similar cases in the future. In 1996, when Prime Minister Ryutaro Hashimoto visited Yasukuni, China easily stopped him from repeating the visit just by citing the precedent set by the Nakasone case.

However, this precedent was completely ignored when the stubborn conservative politician Junichiro Koizumi became the prime minister in 2001. During his tenure as prime minister from 2001 to 2006, Koizumi visited Yasukuni every year for a total of six visits including his last one on August 15, 2006. Koizumi's repeated visits made the Yasukuni issue a prime symbol of the bad blood between China and Japan. As a result, the Sino-Japanese relations deteriorated to the lowest level since the normalization of diplomatic ties between the two countries in 1972. Before and during his election campaign for prime minister in 2001, Koizumi declared that he would visit the Yasukuni Shrine on August 15 if he were elected prime minister. But after being elected as prime minister in April 2001, Koizumi found it not easy to keep his promise. Confronting enormous pressure from within and outside, Koizumi changed the date for his first visit to August 13, two days before the sensitive day of August 15. While noting the date change to avoid August 15, the Chinese government nevertheless expressed its "strong dissatisfaction and indignation" on the same day by saying that "the wrongful action taken by the Japanese leader has damaged the political basis of Sino-Japanese relations, hurt the feelings of the Chinese people and the people of the majority of victimized countries in Asia, and violated the series of solemn statements and commitments made by the Japanese government on the history issue," and urging "the Japanese side to practice what it preaches, and honor its statements and commitments made to the Chinese side in a truthful manner."[15]

On August 15, student demonstrations against the Yasukuni visit took place in Beijing. China's strong reactions somewhat exceeded Japanese expectations and Prime Minister Koizumi found it necessary to explain his position on Yasukuni directly to Chinese leaders. He made a one-day trip to China on October 8, 2001. Before his meeting with Chinese President Jiang Zemin in Beijing, Koizumi visited the Memorial Museum of the Chinese People's Anti-Japanese War in Lougouqiao (the Marco Polo Bridge) where the full-scale Sino-Japanese war broke out in 1937, and became only the second Japanese prime minister, after the socialist Prime Minister Tomiichi Murayama, to visit the museum. His visit was well received by the Chinese. Many Chinese expected that after visiting the Lougouqiao museum, Koizumi would make no new visits to Yasukuni, simply because the former is totally incompatible with the latter in nature. The relatively successful summit meeting between Jiang and Koizumi also supported this Chinese expectation. In the summit talks, Koizumi expressed Japan's regret for past history by saying that he saw the exhibits in the museum "with feelings of heartfelt apology and mourning," and thought "Japan must stand on the remorse for the past, learn a lesson from it and resolve that it must never again fight a war."[16] Koizumi also emphasized that Japan would attach great importance to advancing its relationship with China. President Jiang praised Koizumi's visit to the museum as "meaningful," and further stated that Sino-Japanese relations had experienced both good and bad times, and "when the relations were not good, it always had something to do with the textbook and Yasukuni issues."[17] Jiang therefore stressed the importance of Japan's addressing these issues properly.

After the successful meeting between Jiang and Koizumi, however, Chinese expectations soon turned into further disappointment and resentment when Koizumi repeated his Yasukuni visits in April 2002, January 2003, and January 2004. During this period Sino-Japanese relations fell into a state of psychological cold war, which further increased anti-Japanese sentiments among Chinese citizens and led to an explosion of violent demonstrations in many Chinese cities including Beijing and Shanghai in April 2005. The widespread massive demonstrations not only damaged the Japanese embassy building, consulate, and companies in China but also posed a threat to China's domestic stability.

The Chinese government soon recognized that it needed to improve its relations with Japan while maintaining political pressure on Japanese leader over the Yasukuni issue. Koizumi also faced mounting pressure from within Japan for government action to stabilize ties with China. Under these circumstances, President Hu Jintao and Prime Minister Koizumi met on the occasion of the Asian-African summit in Indonesia to find a way out. Hu made "five-point proposals" for improving the long-stymied China-Japan relations: (1) strictly abide by the three political documents (i.e., the Sino-Japanese Joint Statement signed in September 1972; the Sino-Japanese Treaty of Peace and Friendship signed in April 1978, and the Sino-Japanese Joint Declaration issued in November 1998); (2) take history as a mirror and look into the future; (3) correctly handle the Taiwan issue; (4) resolve differences properly through equal dialogue and consultations; (5) broaden the areas of exchange, cooperation, and mutual benefits.[18] Koizumi accepted Hu's proposals and stated that China's rapid economic development was an opportunity rather than a threat and he expressed his willingness to maintain friendly relations between China and Japan. One day before his meeting with Hu, Koizumi made a speech at the Asian-African summit meeting, in which he referred to Japan's past colonial rule and aggression in Asia and expressed "deep remorse and heartfelt apology," and it was well received by the Chinese side.

In their talks, the two leaders reaffirmed their shared recognition that developing friendly and cooperative Sino-Japanese relations was vital not only to the two countries but also to the region and the world.

The meeting between Hu and Koizumi helped avert further deterioration of China-Japan relations, but it did not find a solution to the Yasukuni problem *per se*. Several months after the meeting, Koizumi went to Yasukuni again in October, which forced China to give up its last hope for resolving the Yasukuni issue with Koizumi and pay more attention to the likely successor to Koizumi. In other words, the Chinese government no longer regarded Prime Minister Koizumi as its partner eliminating the "political obstacle" standing in the way of their bilateral relations. Thus Koizumi's last visit to Yasukuni on August 15, 2006, was from the Chinese perspective nothing but a desperate action taken by the outgoing Japanese leader who had expected that China would eventually give up its persistent opposition to his Yasukuni visits. The calmness with which the Chinese government reacted to Koizumi's last Yasukuni visit reflected China's readiness to embrace Japan's new leader regardless of political and ideological background and ideas.

When Shinzo Abe was elected as Koizumi's successor as the prime minister in September 2006, Abe's policy of ambiguity of "no confirmation, no denial" of a Yasukuni visit, his unexpected confirmation of the Murayama Statement of apology issued in 1995, and his new conceptualization of building a "mutually beneficial strategic relationship" between China and Japan marked a fresh start.[19] Although Abe was a principal advocate and supporter for former Prime Minister Koizumi's Yasukuni visits within Koizumi cabinet, he did not visit the shrine himself during his tenure as prime minister. Abe's initial statement and restrained attitude were received by China positively. After Abe's sudden resignation and Yasuo Fukuda's election as the new prime minister in September 2007, especially Fukuda's announcement that he would make no new visits to Yasukuni, has made the Yasukuni issue seem to be no longer a political obstacle for China-Japan relations, at least for the time being. But given the fast-changing political climate in Japan, it remains to be seen if the Fukuda cabinet will find a solution that would also be understood and accepted by China on the Yasukuni issue. In general, it seems indispensable for Japanese government to take a responsible attitude and effective measures in addressing the Yasukuni issue, while China should make some adjustment to the "history first" policy toward Japan, if the two countries are determined to resolve the Yasukuni issue and stabilize their bilateral ties as the long-term strategic partners in the decades to come.

JAPAN'S REEMERGENCE AS A "NORMAL" GLOBAL POWER

In some sense, the manifestation of Japanese neo-nationalism in history-related issues was just one symbolic dimension of the whole picture, if one takes Japan's reemergence as a "normal" political and military power in the international arena into consideration. Making Japan a normal political and military power has been a shared desire of Japanese nationalist politicians. As the second-largest economic power in the world, Japan's willingness to become a *Seiji no Kuni* (political country) in the international stage was first explicitly expressed by nationalist Prime Minister Nakasone, who tried hard to lay claim to Japan's own identity in the mid-1980s, and he argued that Japan should make itself into an "international state," which attached more importance to establishing Japan's own *Jishusei* (autonomy) among other nations.[20] Nakasone's ideas and arguments drew much attention from China as well as other countries. In fact, China's strong response to the textbook issue and Nakasone's Yasukuni visit at the time had much to do with Nakasone's political attitudes and his decision to abandon the principle of keeping the defense expenditure below 1% of GNP, which had caused great concern within China about Japan's remilitarization and the possible revival of militarism. But in general the idea of building a "political country" asserted by Nakasone at the time did not strike much of a chord among the general Japanese public.

In 1993, another conservative politician, Ichiro Ozawa, began to advocate a nationalist course for Japan. He published a book, *Blueprint for a New Japan,* that argued that Japan should become a "normal country," which could actively make an "international contribution" in security activities especially in the UN-led PKO activities that Japan had hitherto cautiously avoided due to constitutional constraints.[21] Within Japan, Ozawa's ideas found considerable support in the media and they also gradually gained understanding and support from ordinary citizens, although they were criticized by pacifists and leftists as a dangerous idea that could give rise to an expanded Japanese military (SDF) and lead to involvement in outside military conflicts and even large-scale wars, which had little to do with the defense of Japan.

In the international context, Ozawa's argument was regarded by China as a radical nationalist contention that would need to be carefully watched. China's apprehension was further intensified in the mid-1990s when Japan and the United States signed the Japan-U.S. Joint Declaration on Security in 1996 and revised the Guidelines for Defense Cooperation in 1997. China constantly urged the United States and Japan to clarify their objectives and the area of application under the new Guidelines, but the two governments maintained their "strategic ambiguity" thereafter. It seemed more than obvious for China that the reaffirmed U.S.-Japanese alliance not only gave a green light to future Japanese military buildups but also made resolution of the Taiwan issue and, hence, the realization of Chinese national unification even more difficult.

THE TAIWAN ISSUE

From the Chinese perspective, the United States and Japan are the two major powers that have both the intention and the capability to block Chinese unification. In other words, whether the Taiwan issue could be resolved peacefully depends more or less on American and Japanese attitudes. Many Chinese believe that Japan, perhaps even more than the United States, does not want to see a fully unified China, because Japan might want to use Taiwan to tie up China strategically. Japan's reluctance to explicitly exclude Taiwan from the scope of the new Guidelines further convinced the Chinese that Japan would be involved in a future conflict across the

Taiwan Straits. In fact, after the Chinese missile launching exercise over the Taiwan Straits in the middle of the 1990s, security thinking toward Taiwan became important to Japan. Some Japanese have openly voiced support for Taiwan's separation from China, viewing Taiwan as more strategically important for Japan than for the United States.[22] It was against such a backdrop that China has attached more importance to the issue of Taiwan when it came to Sino-Japanese and Sino-U.S. relations.

In June 1998, U.S. President Bill Clinton visited China and made his "Three Nos" (namely, No to Taiwan's independence; No to two Chinas or one China and one Taiwan; and No to Taiwanese membership in the United Nations and other international organizations that include only sovereign states) with regard to the U.S. basic position concerning the Taiwan issue. Clinton's statement was warmly welcomed by Chinese leaders. Given the active separatist movement in Taiwan and rising pro-Taiwan tendency within Japan, the Chinese government had much higher expectations that the Japanese government, with its better understanding about the Chinese position on Taiwan, could easily make a similar comment. In addition, Japan had followed a more cautious policy toward Taiwan in the previous decades compared to the United States.

In October of the same year, South Korean President Kim Dae-jung visited Japan and held a summit meeting with Prime Minister Keizo Obuchi. In the Joint Statement released after the meeting, Japan expressed its "remorse and apology" in written form to Korea. China viewed this as a sign that Japanese government was prepared to apologize in writing to China as well. China also expected that the first visit by a Chinese head of state to Japan would make great progress in resolving both the history and Taiwan issues.

However, Japan refused to respond positively to Chinese expectations before President Jiang Zemin's trip to Japan in November. The political climate surrounding Jiang's visit turned unfavorable . During his visit President Jiang made a comprehensive statement of Chinese principles and positions on both the Taiwan and history issues. Consequently, the summit meeting between President Jiang and Prime Minister Obuchi succeeded in adopting the Joint Declaration, the third principal document in Sino-Japanese relations.

Despite this positive development Chinese-Japanese relations soon began to deteriorate with Chinese concern over the negative effects of the Japanese-U.S. military cooperation under the new Guidelines emerging as the main issue. With regard to the new Guidelines, China took the following basic position: "Taiwan is an inalienable part of the territory of China." Therefore, "any action of including Taiwan into the scope of U.S.-Japan security cooperation, either directly or indirectly, will be strongly opposed and unacceptable to the Chinese government and people."[23] Based on this principal position, China persistently urged Japan to take concrete action.

In July 1999, Japanese Prime Minister Obuchi visited China, and noted that the U.S.-Japanese security cooperation system was completely for the purpose of defense and not targeted at any specific country or region. Obuchi's explanation seemed too weak to alleviate Chinese concerns. In February 2005, when the joint statement of the U.S.-Japan Security Consultative Committee explicitly stated that maintaining stability in the Taiwan Straits was one of their "common strategic objectives," China became convinced that it must take some action. The result was an anti-secession law, which the National People's Congress (NPC), China's legislature, formally approved in March 2005.

With regard to the issue of Taiwan, Japan-Taiwan relations, especially politicians' connections between Japan and Taiwan, have always been a major concern for China, besides the U.S.-Japan security cooperation. As Sino-Japanese relations worsened, relations between Japan and Taiwan began to improve. In April 2005, despite strong Chinese pressure against it, the Japanese government issued a visa to former "Taiwan president" Lee Teng-hui, ostensibly for the purpose of receiving medical treatment. Lee visited Japan on April 22–26, which marked a significant breakthrough in Japanese-Taiwanese relations. The Chinese government waged a rigorous struggle against Japan's decision, but it was not successful. Japanese-Taiwanese relations have become even closer after Lee's visit.

Japan's bold steps in its relations with Taiwan were strongly supported by Prime Minister Yoshiro Mori and other nationalist politicians at the time. Their pro-Taiwan posture was one example of these politicians acting to please Japan's neo-nationalists. Ever since the mid-1990s, many events strengthening Japanese neo-nationalism took place. For instance, after North Korea's Taepodong missile flew over Japan in August 1998, Japan started to develop a missile defense system with the United States, and launched its own information-gathering satellites. In 1999, the Japanese Diet passed the national flag and national anthem bill, which adopted the *hinomaru* as the national flag, and *kimigayo* as the national anthem. In 2000, Prime Minister Mori commented that Japan was a *Kami no Kuni* (divine country) which evoked an echo of wartime State Shintoism. And the Koizumi and Abe era saw the paying of homage at Yasukuni, the sending of troops to Iraq, bidding for a permanent seat on the UN Security Council, revising of the education law, and various attempts to revise the Constitution, all of which have drawn a great deal of attention from many countries. All these events have much to do with Japan's reemergence as a "normal" political and military power, simply because mainstream nationalists want Japan to have respect and political influence in world affairs.

CONCLUSION

The resurgence of neo-nationalism has become the most outstanding feature in Japanese political life since the early 1980s, profoundly affecting Japanese internal and external affairs. Generally speaking, Japan's quest for a new national identity through assertive nationalism is not a relapse to ultra-nationalism and an expression of aggressive militarism, simply because mainstream nationalists have expressed no support for military expansion and aggression. It is also unlikely that Japanese nationalism would lead to a major expansion of the Self-Defense Forces, not to mention the development of nuclear weapons in the near future. The revival of nationalism, however, has negatively affected Japan's relations with its neighbors, especially its relations with China and South Korea. It has also diminished Japan's leadership position as one of the most advanced democratic countries in East Asia. Japan's aggressive war against its neighbors ended over 60 years ago, but Japan still has some difficulty in squarely facing its past wrongdoings. As Kazuhiko Togo put it, it is fair to say that there has been a general feeling of remorse and apology among most Japanese, but at the same time there remained some undeniable feeling that not all that Japan did before the war was wrong, that many of the Japanese who died during the war sacrificed their lives for the country, and that their honor had to be preserved. The key question of what was wrong and what was right remains unanswered to this day.[24]

In this context, the Japanese government as well as the political leaders can and must take the inescapable moral responsibility and play a constructive role both at home and abroad. Japan's pursuit of being a political power on the international stage can be understood and welcomed by China and South Korea only after all the negative elements pertaining to Japan's neo-nationalism are cast away. For China, Japanese nationalism is something closely associated with the memory of the past militarism, and should be firmly opposed. Under the current circumstances, it is beyond imagination that Japanese nationalism could be understood or accepted by Chinese people in due course. Given the fact that nationalism with many negative elements has been also witnessed in China, the interactions between the two nationalisms would make the way to reconciliation in East Asia even harder and longer. In order to shorten the road to reconciliation the Chinese and Japanese governments need to make more efforts to keep their respective nationalism evolving in an open and healthy way.

NOTES

1. Delmer M. Brown, *Nationalism in Japan: An Introductory Historical Analysis* (Berkeley: University of California Press, 1955), pp. v–vi.

2. In the late nineteenth century, Chinese intellectuals and nationalists such as Liang Qichao and Sun Zhongshan (Sun Yat-sen) introduced the notion of nationalism and Japan's nationalist movements to China and made the most contribution to the early awakening of modern Chinese nationalism. Jin Linbo, "Chugokujin no Nihon kan," *Seiji Keizai Horitsu Kenkyu,* March 2002, p. 95.

3. Nakasone Yasuhiro, "Sengo no sokessan kara 21 seiki no Nihon e," *Gekkan Jiyu Minshu,* March 1984, pp. 28–29 and "Atarashii Nihon no shutaisei," *Gekkan Jiyu Minshu,* September 1985, pp. 35–36.

4. Tsuyoshi Hasegawa, "Japan's Strategic Thinking toward Asia in the First Half of the 1990s," *Japanese Strategic Thought toward Asia,* ed. Gilbert Rozman, Kazuhiko Togo, and Joseph P. Ferguson. (New York: Palgrave, 2007), pp. 59–60.

5. Eugene A. Matthews, "Japan's New Nationalism," *Foreign Affairs* 82, no. 6 (November/December 2003):80.

6. Chung-in Moon and Seung-won Suh, "Overcoming History: the Politics of Identity and Nationalism," *Global Asia* 2, no. 1 (2007):41.

7. Eugene A. Matthews, "Japan's New Nationalism," p. 81.

8. See Yuan Weishi, "Nationalism in a Transforming China," *Global Asia* 2, no. 1 (2007):21–27.

9. China's basic position on history and Taiwan issues can be found in Chinese Foreign Ministry's official Web site. See http://www.fmprc.gov.cn/eng/wjb/zzjg/yzs/gjlb/2721/2722/t15974.htm.

10. See the Chinese Ministry of Foreign Affairs' Web site: http://www.fmprc.gov.cn/eng/wjb/zzjg/yzs/gjlb/2721/2725/t16027.htm.

11. See Chinese Foreign Ministry, ed., *Zhongguo Waijiao 2002* (Beijing: World Affairs Press, 2002), pp. 42–43; Japanese Foreign Ministry, ed., *Diplomatic Bluebook 2002* (English Version), p. 58.

12. *Asahi Shinbun,* April 6 and 7, 2005.

13. Chinese Foreign Ministry, ed., *Zhongguo Waijiao 2002,* p. 44.

14. *Renmin Ribao,* August 15, 1985.

15. See the Chinese Ministry of Foreign Affairs' Web site: http://www.fmprc.gov.cn/eng/wjb/zzjg/yzs/gjlb/2721/2725/t16034.htm.

16. The Ministry of Foreign Affairs of Japan, http://www.mofa.go.jp/region/asia-paci/china/pmv0110/meet-2.html.

17. *Renmin Ribao,* October 9, 2001.

18. *Renmin Ribao,* April 24, 2005.

19. Gilbert Rozman, Kazuhiko Togo, and Joseph P. Ferguson, "Overview," in *Japanese Strategic Thought toward Asia,* ed. Gilbert Rozman, Kazuhiko Togo, and Joseph P. Ferguson (New York: Palgrave, 2007), p. 32.

20. Nakasone, "Sengo no sokessan," p. 30; and "Atarashii Nihon no shutaisei," pp. 35–36.

21. See Ozawa Ichiro, *Nihon Kaizo Keikaku* (Tokyo: Kodansha, 1993).

22. Ming Wan, "Japanese Strategic Thinking toward Taiwan," in *Japanese Strategic Thought toward Asia,* ed. Gilbert Rozman, Kazuhiko Togo, and Joseph P. Ferguson (New York: Palgrave, 2007), pp. 159–60.

23. Chinese Ministry of Foreign Affairs, http://www.fmprc.gov.cn/eng/wjb/zzjg/yzs/gjlb/2721/2722/t15974.htm.

24. Kazuhiko Togo, *Japan's Foreign Policy 1945–2003: The Quest for a Proactive Policy* (Leiden: Brill, 2005), p. 140.

9

Japan's Role in the Rise of Chinese Nationalism: History and Prospects

Zhu Jianrong

This chapter argues that Japan played a defining role in the formation of modern Chinese nationalism. The May Fourth Movement provoked by Japan's Twenty-One Demands was a major milestone in the growth of Chinese nationalism. The Japanese invasion of Manchuria in 1931 and the Sino-Japanese War that began in 1937 instilled a yearning for unification of China among ordinary Chinese. Although nationalist sentiments were suppressed under Mao Zedong and Deng Xiaoping, nationalism always has existed in the Chinese consciousness. This article also argues that under Jiang Zemin nationalism became a volatile movement, partly because of a reorientation of history education to emphasize Chinese nationalism— especially in its struggle against Japan—and partly because of an increasingly vocal middle class that emerged as a result of successful modernization. The eruption of anti-Japanese demonstrations provoked by Junichiro Koizumi's Yasukuni visits was not due to government manipulation, but was rather a genuine expression of Chinese public opinion. The Chinese government has attempted to defuse the crisis by downgrading the importance of the history issues. But whether or not the history issues can be toned down in the future will depend on the success of China's further economic growth.

ORIGINS OF MODERN CHINESE NATIONALISM

The concepts of nationalism and of nation-states were alien to two thousand years of Chinese history, until the middle of the nineteenth century. Based on the concept of the Middle Kingdom, the Chinese believed that the entire universe was controlled by the Chinese Emperor, and different political units and nationalities coexisted under a Sino-centric tributary system. Modern Chinese nationalism originated in the second half of the nineteenth century when the decline of the Qing dynasty due to the intrusion of Western powers introduced the concept of "nation-states" to China. The penetration of Western imperialism after the Opium War injected into the Chinese people an initial sense of nationalism tinged with xenophobia, which sporadically exploded into violent outbursts, like the Boxer Uprising, against foreign intruders. But modern Chinese nationalism emerged as a reaction to Japanese imperialism. It originated from the May Fourth Movement, and reached its zenith with the Japanese invasion of Manchuria and the Sino-Japanese War.

Needless to say, Western imperialist powers inflicted significant damage on China. When the British-French Allied forces occupied Peking in 1858, they devastated the Old Summer Palace, Yuanming Yuan, which was reputedly the most beautiful garden in the world. The Tsarist Russian army committed cruel massacres of Chinese in the northeast part of China many times at the end of the nineteenth century and in the beginning of the twentieth century. Western powers forced concessions, infringed upon Chinese sovereignty through extraterritoriality, and leased territories, ports, and railways. Nevertheless, one should stress that Japanese imperialist expansion and subsequent invasion of China were the defining factor giving birth to modern Chinese nationalism. Without dismissing the injuries that other Western powers inflicted on the Chinese, we need to underscore the plain historical fact that modern Chinese nationalism emerged above all in reaction to Japanese imperialism.[1]

In 1911, the Qing dynasty was overthrown, and the "Republic of China," (the first republic in Asia), was established. The overthrow of the Manchu dynasty and the establishment of the republic laid the foundations for a new national consciousness among the Chinese people. But the establishment of the Republic of China did not lead to Chinese national unification, as China was soon after thrown into the rule of warlords. While the Western powers were preoccupied with World War I, Japan imposed Twenty-One Demands on the Yuan Shih-kai government in 1915, and seized the rights and interests in Shandong Province held by Germany. Although China joined World War I on the side of the Allies, and appealed at the April 1919 Paris Peace Conference for nullification of Japan's Twenty-One Demands, the Versailles Treaty granted the Shandong Province to Japan. Outraged, university students launched a protest movement, the "May Fourth Movement," which demanded the return of Shandong to China. This movement marked the first event to awaken a sense of Chinese nationalism among the Chinese masses. During the 1920s, while the Chinese Nationalists organized the Northern Expedition in an attempt to unify China, mass anti-imperialist movements led by students and other groups spread all across China. Japan, more than other Western powers, was the primary target of these protests.

The Japanese invasion of Manchuria in 1931, and the creation of a Japanese puppet state, Manchukuo, further intensified Chinese nationalism. For the first time the Chinese public shared a sense of impending crisis, *Wangguo* (the "Doom of China"). Immediately after the start of the Sino-Japanese War in 1937, Chiang Kai-shek appealed to the whole nation using nationalist rhetoric, stating that "All Chinese people, no matter living in north or south, whether young and old, should be engaged in the life and death struggle against Japan."[2] It was only through the common experience of this eight-year anti-Japanese war that a sense of belonging to a Chinese nation, a common sense of identity that "we are all Chinese," was formed for the first time throughout China. The war against Japan was thus the most important defining moment for the burning aspiration of the unified Chinese nation-state, and the bitter memory of the war, experienced by all levels of Chinese society, formed the basis for Chinese national consciousness.

Before the Sino-Japanese War, the Communist Party of China (CCP) was on the verge of extinction in the civil war with Chiang Kai-shek's Nationalists, but after the Lu Gou Qiao Incident (Sian Incident) in 1936, the results of which forced Chiang Kai-shek to form a united front, the CCP gained strength, and its popular support and influence rose. The foundation from which the CCP came to dominate and unify the entire country only four years after the conclusion of the Sino-Japanese War was established during the war against Japan. Since then, from Mao Zedong to Jiang Zemin, the Communist Party justified its legitimacy in its heroic struggle against the Japanese in the Sino-Japanese War. In an attempt to legitimate its rule, the CCP reproduced and emphasized historical memory about the Japanese invasion and the struggle against Japan in the Sino-Japanese War.

When one examines the role of Japanese aggression in fostering Chinese national-ism, therefore, one must keep in mind two factors. First, Japanese imperialism and aggression decisively influenced the origins and formation of Chinese national con-sciousness, contributing to the Chinese national identity and integrating the Chinese people with the common mission of national unification. Second, the struggle against Japanese imperialism served and continues to serve as a potent instrument for the Communist Party to legitimize its rule.[3]

Until "anti-Japanese" demonstrations broke out in various parts of China in 2005, not only the Japanese but also many scholars and commentators almost exclusively focused on the instrumentality of "anti-Japanese" rhetoric and policies pursued by the Chinese government as leverage to exert political pressure on Japan. Many in Japan argued that these demonstrations were government instigated and manipu-lated. One should not forget, however, that Chinese national consciousness has always existed behind the government's policies and pronouncements and that the defining element of this national consciousness was the Chinese struggle against Japanese imperialism since World War I. The government can, and did at times, con-trol and manipulate this national consciousness, but ultimately this consciousness is far wider and deeper than government control. To mistake "anti-Japanese" demon-strations and sentiments merely as the result of government manipulation is to misunderstand the complex history of Chinese nationalism.

NATIONALISM UNDER JIANG ZEMIN

The nationalist elements of Mao Zedong's Japan policy were, generally speaking, restrained, although occasionally he exploited this issue to pursue specific policy objectives.[4] Deng Xiaoping also rarely used nationalist demands in his foreign policy for the following reasons.

First, the party and the government under Deng Xiaoping were preoccupied with the task of overcoming the negative legacies of the Cultural Revolution. Second, to promote four modernizations, Deng Xiaoping was more interested in restoring good relations with advanced industrial nations rather than criticizing former colonial powers. Furthermore, the Chinese people became familiar with the conditions of foreign countries under the "open door policy," initiated by Deng Xiaoping. After their contact with the outside world was completely cut off during the Cultural Revolution, they were shocked to discover that China was far behind other countries in development. Their frustrations and anger were directed at former government officials, particularly the "Gang of Four." Thus, there was little place for anti-Japanese feelings to become an issue at that time.[5]

This situation changed during the 1990s when Jiang Zemin took over. In Japan, President Jiang Zemin is generally known as the Chinese leader who purposely provoked nationalism among the Chinese masses and who also strengthened anti-Japanese themes in the education system. This characterization of Jiang Zemin is mistaken. Although China emphasized "patriotism education" from the beginning of the 1990s, it was not exactly a policy of stressing "anti-Japanese education."

According to research by a Chinese foreign student at Keio University in Japan,[6] the official Chinese textbook has consistently devoted two percent of its content to Japan-related subjects since the founding of the PRC. Even during the 1990s, the number of pages devoted to Japan did not increase. Moreover, after 1986, at least six different history textbooks exist. In 2001, the system of nationally authorized textbooks was abolished and a Japanese-style "textbook screening" system was introduced. It is interesting to note that many scholars promoting reform of the Chinese textbook system have studied in Japan since the 1980s.[7]

It is also a fact, however, that Chinese nationalism gained strength quickly and anti-Japan sentiment was intensified under the Jiang Zemin era.[8] In my view, several points should be made to explain the rise of nationalism under Jiang Zemin.

First, the Chinese Communist Party leaders came to realize that communist ideology alone was no longer sufficient to hold the country together after the Tiananmen Square Incident and the collapse of the Soviet Union and Eastern European communist regimes in 1989. Therefore, they decided to supplement the communist ideology with the "patriotic principle education," through which they tried to inculcate "love of our homeland blessed with the great civilization." In this education, the contents asking to take pride in "great ancient civilization" occupied more than any other subjects. For the modern period, the Chinese people's struggle against Japan is stressed, but more space is devoted to the struggle against Chiang Kai-shek than against the Japanese during the Sino-Japanese War. While the Chinese people were still isolated from the outside world, this kind of "patriotic education" tended to instill a blind antiforeign sentiment. An unintended consequence of "patriotism education" was that, combined with factors mentioned below, it gave rise to a grassroots nationalist movement, which had been successfully contained under the Mao Zedong and the Deng Xiaoping eras.

Second, the rise of nationalism was connected with economic growth during the 1990s, which created intermediate layers of population that may be aptly characterized as the "middle class." It is estimated that the number of this class extended from around 50 million people in the 1990s, to about 500 million people today.[9] This growing middle class asserted a consumers' rights and civil rights agenda, and, above all, demanded respect for China from other nations. Nationalism thus acquired a social basis.

The "Galaxy incident" in 1993, in which the U.S. Navy demanded a compulsory inspection of a Chinese cargo ship on the pretext that the ship was carrying chemical materials bound for Iran, provoked outrage amongst Chinese. In 1996, a book called *China Can Say No,* written by five young men, became an unexpected best seller. Nearly 90 percent of its content was anti-American.[10] This book is generally considered to symbolize the rise of nationalism that emerged from below despite the tight control of the publication. Further, in reaction to the U.S. missile attack on the Chinese Embassy in Belgrade, Serbia, in 1999, anti-American demonstrations sprang up at once all across China. All the windowpanes of the American Embassy in Beijing were broken and excited demonstrators broke into the U.S. Consulate in Chengdu, setting it on fire.

Thus, the target of this new wave of Chinese nationalism emerging in the 1990s was first the United States, not Japan. Anti-Japanese demonstrations had not occurred for ten years. It must be recognized, however, that the nationalistic feelings accumulated among the Chinese people had become an already powerful social movement.

The turning point of the Chinese nationalist movement came in 2001, when its target shifted from the United States to Japan. After 9/11, the United States and China improved their relations quickly under the common struggle against international terrorism. In contrast, after Japanese Prime Minister Junichiro Koizumi visited the Yasukuni Shrine repeatedly, where Class-A war criminals are enshrined, these visits became a contentious diplomatic issue between Japan and China, and the Chinese public began to express outrage against Japan. Protest against Japan rapidly spread among the emerging middle class through the Internet. Anti-Japanese sentiments spread like wildfire after 2002, as many public opinion surveys indicate.[11] Demonstrations protesting against Japan and demanding expulsion of the Japanese from China were held in various places. The anti-Japanese movement peaked in spring of 2005, when tens of thousands of people participated in demonstrations in Beijing, Shanghai, and other cities.

Third, it should be noted that the Chinese side should shoulder part of the responsibility. Although I do not believe that the Jiang Zemin administration intentionally provoked the demonstration, the nationalistic demonstrations that erupted were partly the result of an intensified effort by the Chinese government to instill anti-Japanese feelings through history education. The Chinese educational system for years emphasized Japan's invasion of China, but it made no effort in its textbooks to inform Chinese students that postwar Japan was democratic and pacifist. Chinese mass media always focused on the "history problem" of Japan, but it seldom presented an overall picture of Japanese society that included an accurate portrait of all walks of life of the Japanese people. In 1995, China commemorated on a grand scale the Communist Party's historical achievements at the 50th anniversary celebrations of "the antifascism war victory." During these celebrations, and in widely popular movies and television specials on the Sino-Japanese War, all Japanese presented were portrayed as villains and evil aggressors. Consequently, all this firmly established in the popular mind a negative image of Japan and the Japanese people.

The efforts to instill anti-Japanese sentiments through the educational system, the failure to discuss Japan's positive achievements, and the positive popular reception of this portrayal of the Japanese all reflected an inferiority complex buried deep in the psyche of the Chinese people from the leaders on the top down to the masses. Until the early part of the Jiang Zemin era, the Chinese economy was hopelessly behind those of other advanced capitalist countries, especially Japan. Chinese leaders lacked confidence about China's prospects for catching up with the advanced capitalist countries. To compensate for their lack of confidence in economic development, they sought to build up the greatness of China in history, and emphasized the glorious struggle of the Chinese people against Western imperialism, especially Japanese aggression.[12] Unlike the South Korean government, which issued a comment "expressing an extreme sense of regret" about Japanese Prime Minister Shinzo Abe's Yasukuni visit, the press officer of the Chinese Foreign Ministry issued a statement that did not specifically refer to the Yasukuni visit issue: "Both China and Japan have an agreement to promote healthy development of friendly cooperative relations by overcoming political obstacles that affect bilateral relations, and we believe that this agreement should be strictly observed."[13]

HU JINTAO'S POLICY TOWARD JAPAN

The collapse of the bubble economy and the subsequent economic recession that hit Japan and other Asian countries reversed this psychological trend. On the one hand, Japan lost its confidence in its ability to lead the Asian economy as the head of the "flying geese." On the other hand, China, which not only escaped from this economic reversal but also experienced double-digit economic growth, gained confidence. The previously felt inferiority complex was transformed into a sense of triumph, confidence, and superiority among the Chinese.

Koizumi's Yasukuni Shrine visits took place at this critical juncture of psychological change in both countries. On the one hand, Koizumi's shrine visits reversed the policy of restraint of the cabinet ministers that had lasted 20 years since the Nakasone government suspended Yasukuni visits, thereby serving as a red flag waved at resurgent Chinese nationalism. On the other hand, as Japan's confidence as one of the leaders of the world economies was shattered by the recession, Japanese nationalism emerged to compensate for this loss of confidence. Koizumi, who took advantage of this nationalist resurgence, could ill afford to accept the Chinese challenge to Japan's leadership of the Asian economy. Mindful of the nationalist forces that backed him, Koizumi handled the Chinese protests of his Yasukuni visits in the worst possible way. Unable to take into consideration that the Chinese protests were rooted in a broad spectrum of Chinese consciousness, Koizumi and the opinion leaders who supported his Yasukuni visits tended to treat the protests as manipulated by the government. In this manner, Koizumi's treatment of the Chinese protests exacerbated rather than ameliorated anti-Japanese sentiments among the Chinese populace.

Jiang Zemin belatedly recognized the danger of the rise in nationalism in both countries in the last three years of his term of office, and began to contain the anti-Japanese feelings and improve relations with Japan. When Prime Minister Zhu Rongji visited Japan in 2000, he expressed gratitude for Official Development Assistance (ODA) provided by Japan. In the same year, President Jiang Zemin also declared, when meeting with the Japanese delegation of the 5,000 Visit China team at the Great Hall of the People, that "Friendship with Japan is a long-term strategy of Chinese government." Therefore, if Koizumi had stopped visiting Yasukuni in the summer of 2001, Sino-Japanese relations would not have deteriorated. Despite these Chinese efforts, however, relations between the two countries did not significantly improve during Jiang Zemin's tenure.

Signals that the new administration of Hu Jintao might compromise on the history problem were sent again and again to Prime Minister Koizumi. At Hu Jintao's first summit meeting in St. Petersburg with Koizumi in May 2003 after becoming General Secretary of the Communist Party, he appealed to the Japanese prime minister "to deal with problems of bilateral relations from the higher strategic viewpoints and in the long-term perspective to develop long-term stable good-neighborly friendly relations," without specifically mentioning the Yasukuni issue. In August and September 2003, he sent Foreign Minister Li Zhaoxing and Chairman of the Congress of People's Deputies Wu Bangguo, who occupied the number two position in the Communist Party hierarchy, to Japan to meet Koizumi in order to break the diplomatic stalemate. Furthermore, at the Sino-Japanese Prime Ministers' Conference at Bali, Indonesia, in October, Chinese Prime Minister Wen Jiabao intentionally avoided mentioning the Yasukuni issue. Despite this consideration, Koizumi made it clear in the plane when returning to Tokyo his intention to visit Yasukuni at least once a year and added that this resolve was understood by Prime Minister Wen Jiabao. Koizumi's statement led to criticism of Wen Jiabao from within the Chinese Communist leadership, and provoked an intensification of anti-Japanese sentiment among the masses.[14] But Koizumi totally ignored these signals from the Chinese side.

When Shinzo Abe became Japanese prime minister after Koizumi's resignation, the leaders of both countries tried hard to mend fences by reaching a compromise on the Yasukuni issue. When Prime Minister Wen Jiabao visited Japan in April 2007, his statements were conciliatory and gave the Japanese people a good impression. For example, he highly praised the peaceful path that Japan had followed in the postwar period, Japan's generous economic assistance to China, and the apologies that the Japanese government had made about their aggressions to China.[15] This speech was televised in China as well, an indication that the Chinese government had consciously begun working on calming the anger of the Chinese people. Abe was silent about whether or not he had visited or whether or not he intended to visit the Yasukuni Shrine. But when it became known that he had dedicated flowers to the shrine in April, China reacted to this news with restraint. It appears that the Hu Jintao Administration wished to remove the history problem from the center of relations between both countries, placing more emphasis on "future-oriented relations" rather than "looking back in history."

When one views the rise of Chinese nationalism, it is useful to compare the Chinese case with the experiences of Japan in the 1960s and South Korea in the 1980s. Japan and South Korea experienced an upsurge in nationalism before the 1964 Tokyo Olympic Games and the 1988 Seoul Olympic Games. The common feature of Japan and South Korea then and China now is rapid economic growth and the attendant emergence of a middle class. In this sense, the rise of nationalism in contemporary China is arguably a social phenomenon of this rising middle class during a period of rapid economic growth.[16]

The argument that further continuation of Communist Party rule is contingent upon successful implementation of anti-Japanese propaganda is no longer valid. If the Communist Party succeeds in developing the economy further, it will not need the strong support of nationalism to legitimize its rule. Conversely, if development goes wrong, the Communist Party may fall back on provoking nationalist feelings to buttress its rule.

DIRECTION OF CHINESE NATIONALISM

As China's economy is increasingly integrated into the international economy, China's confidence has grown. Chinese leaders as well as intellectuals and businessmen are beginning to express their views about the problems they face more frankly than before. They also recognize the need for international cooperation, especially the need to improve Sino-Japanese relations. The conciliatory gesture that Prime Minister Wen Jiabao showed during his Japan visit is therefore not merely a temporary tactic but also an expression of the new foreign posture of the Chinese leadership.

It should be recognized, however, that at the level of the Chinese people, acquiring this kind of confidence may still take a while. If the 2008 Olympic Games in Beijing and the 2010 Shanghai Expo are held successfully, and if domestic social and political contradictions are somewhat eased, the Chinese people will acquire confidence in the future of the country. Xenophobic nationalism will accordingly likely recede. But if the economy and the society lapse into confusion, xenophobic nationalism will again raise its head. Even if China develops into a mature economic power, it does not mean that future conflict is not likely to occur. Such conflict, however, will not be the same kind of xenophobic nationalism that has occurred in China before. The problem that China faces now is how to respond to the new factors such as the diversification of society and information technology progress. In this challenge the task is not only to suppress the "wrong" and "inward-oriented" feelings of the people and overcome the outdated form of nationalism, but also how to gain the international recognition of China's place as one of the world powers.

Such a rosy picture is far from being certain at the current state of China's development. In order to attain historical reconciliation and to build new national consciousness, the important task is to study the various efforts and experiences that many countries went through during their painful economic development, listen earnestly to opinions from outside of China, and actively engage in a dialogue with scholars, policy-makers, businessmen, journalists, and other leaders of foreign countries.

NOTES

1. South Korean Scholar Choi Zang-jip states that nationalism in Korea and China developed in reaction to Japan's expansion to Korea and China. He argues that the Japanese should understand that nationalism in Korea and China was essentially defensive nationalism. *Asahi Shinbun,* November 9, 2006.

2. Quoted in Lu Shan, *Zhonghua Tongjian: Yingxiang Lishi de 100 Pian Mingzuo,* vol. 1 (Guangxi Minzu Chubanshe, 1966), p. 189.

3. For the relationship between the Sino-Japanese War and the Chinese Communist Party, see John K. Fairbank and Albert Feuerwerker, eds., *The Cambridge History of China,* vol. 13, *Republican China 1912–1949* (Cambridge: Cambridge University Press, 1982); Nozawa Yutaka and Tanaka Masatoshi, eds., *Koza: Chugoku kin-gendaishi,* vol. 6, *Konichi senso* (Tokyo: Tokyo daigaku shuppankai, 1978); Himeda Mitsuyoshi, ed., *Chugoku 20 seikishi* (Tokyo: Tokyo daigaku shuppankai, 1993).

4. For Nationalism under Mao Zedong, see Michael B. Yahuda, *China's Role in World Affairs* (London: Croom Helm, 1978); Harry Harding, "China's Changing Roles in the Contemporary World," in *China's Foreign Relations in the 1980s,* ed. Harry Harding (New Heaven and London: Yale University Press, 1984); Peter Van Ness, *Revolution and Chinese Foreign Policy: Peking's Support for Wars of National Liberation* (Berkeley and Los Angeles: University of California Press, 1970).

5. See chapter 3, Zhu Jianrong, "Ko Takumin no Chugoku: uchigawa kara mita 'Posto Toshohei' jidai" (Tokyo: Chuko shinsho, 1994).

6. Wang Xueping, "Chugoku no kyokasho kara miru bundan shita nihon zo to nicchukankei," Wang Xueping, *Toa,* no. 4 (2006): 72–81.

7. See Zhu Jianrong, *Hu Jintao: Tainichi senryaku no honne* (Tokyo: Kadokawa shoten, 2006), chapter 2, sect. 2, "Chugoku no 'hannichi kyoiku' ni taisuru sai kensho."

8. For recent nationalism in China, see Peter Hays Gries, *China's New Nationalism: Pride, Politics, and Diplomacy* (Berkeley and Los Angeles: University of California Press, 2004).

9. According to the statistics for 2005, 250 million people are in the category of "the intermediate layers of population" with the annual household (three-member family) income above the equivalent of 3 million Japanese yen. An additional 250 million—one-child generation and newly employed young people, who follow the similar life pattern, behavior, and

consciousness—can fall in this category, although their income does not reach that level. I estimate, therefore, that 500 million people can be classified as "the middle class."

10. *Zhongguo Keyi Shuo Bu* (Beijing: Zhongguo Gongshang Chubanshe, 1996). According to C. X. George Wei and Xiayuan Liu, *"China Can Say No* can be considered as the second anti-Western wave." C. X. George Wei and Xiaoyuan Liu, *Exploring Nationalisms of China: Themes and Conflicts (Contributions to the Study of World History)* (Westport CT: Greenwood Press, 2002), p. 28.

11. According to the opinion survey conducted by the Institute of Japan of the China Social Science Academy in September-October 2004 (3300 from all over China were polled), those who answered, "I feel no friendly feelings at all toward Japan," and "I do not have much friendly feelings toward Japan," increased to 53.6% compared with 43.3 % in the previous survey conducted in September, 2002. Jian Lifent, "Di2ci Zhongri Yulun Diaocha," *Riben Xuekan,* no. 6 (2006): 3–6.

12. Zhu Jianrong, *Hu Jintao,* pp. 86–91. In chapter 1 of this book I analyzed the Japanese perceptions of the Jiang Zemin government, and pointed out three differences between Jiang Zemin's and Hu Jintau's policy toward Japan.

13. *Renmin Ribau,* May 9, 2007.

14. See Chapter 1 of Zhu Jianrong, *Hu Jinatao*; and Shimizu Miwa, *Chugoku ga 'hannichi' o suteruhi* (Tokyo: Kodansha purasu arufa shinsho, 2006).

15. *Renmin Ribau,* April 13, 2007.

16. See Chapter 10, Section 2, Zhu Jianrong, "Higashi Ajia moderu ga shisasuru mono," *Chugoku no keizaikozo kaikaku,* ed. Nihon Keizai Kenkyu Senta and Quinhua Daigaku Kokujo Kenkyu Senta (Tokyo: Nikkei shuppan, 2006).

10

Historical Memory and the Resurgence of Nationalism: A Korean Perspective

Cheol Hee Park

Historical memory remains a subject of political and diplomatic contention in East Asia. Unlike in Europe, where historical reconciliation made progress, historical memory works as a stumbling block to building a cooperative community in East Asia. Nationalism in Northeast Asian countries—Japan, South Korea, and China—is resurging, which widens the perception gap among nations in the region. In Europe, shared visions for regional integration cast a guiding light for moving ahead on the history issues. However, unlike the European situation, East Asian countries have long experienced dual fragmentation that made cooperative ties among East Asian countries difficult for a long time. On the one hand, Asian countries have long been fragmented by Cold War logic. Ideological conflict prevailed during the Cold War period among China, Japan, and South Korea. Absent a common enemy, East Asian countries showed antipathy toward one another. On the other hand, East Asian countries, many of which experienced civil war, have been internally divided in the historical process of state-building. The Korean peninsula was divided into South and North Korea, while China was split into the People's Republic of China and the Republic of China (Taiwan). Internally divided nations concentrated their energy on reintegrating their divided nations instead of constructing a regional structure for peace and coprosperity.

Most of all, during the Cold War era, security concerns overshadowed historical controversies in the region. Under the Cold War context, nationalist sentiment was subdued between South Korea and Japan in order to facilitate security and economic cooperation between the two countries. Alignment despite antagonism was the rule rather than the exception.[1] This does not mean that anti-Japanese sentiment in South Korea faded away during the Cold War period. It simply means that the governing elite expedited cooperative ties before they pushed forward a nationalist sentiment. In other words, strategic concerns overwhelmed emotional residues.

The end of the Cold War brought in new strategic settings in Northeast Asia. It opened a new window of opportunity that had been unavailable in the past. The so-called "communist bloc" against which free nations were united was gone. Instead analysts began focusing on the rise of a single country, China. The challenge of a rising China dominated the discourse on East Asia.[2] South Korea developed normal diplomatic ties with Russia and China in 1990 and 1992, respectively. This changed diplomatic contours in the region, which elevated North Korea's sense of isolation. Above all, nationalism, long suppressed due to security concerns, emerged on the surface. Historical controversy comprised an important facet of visible tensions among East Asian countries.[3]

In this chapter, as part of an intellectual adventure to understand East Asian nationalism, I would like to examine the shifting nature of South Korean nationalism in its historical and structural contexts. The genesis, development, and resurgence of South Korean nationalism will be outlined first. Then I will discuss how and why historical memory comes into play between South Korea and Japan. In this section, I will delineate how the logic of political contention has changed over time. In addition, I am going to present a Korean interpretation of the Japanese move related to historical controversy. The final part of this chapter will suggest the strategic implications of Japanese action and inaction in the post–Cold War context.

I make three general arguments with regard to the nature of South Korean nationalism and its connection to historical memory linked to Japan.

First, I argue that anti-Japanese sentiment and anticommunism has constituted a core of South Korean nationalism.[4] Korean nationalism in modern times was formed out of a struggle for independence from colonial rule. After liberation from Japanese rule, South Korean identity was framed by efforts to keep the country from communist infiltration. In that sense, Korean nationalism, which was principally driven by external forces, has come to take on a defensive nature. Defending the South Korean identity from external threats comprised the core element of South Korean nationalism. However, in the course of subsequent political and economic developments, nationalism in South Korea acquired a twisted nature. In order to make economic gains, South Korean leaders attenuated anti-Japanese sentiment. With the attainment of political democracy coupled with economic growth, South Koreans gained an elevated sense of self-confidence. Resilient democracy with growing international economic competitiveness awarded a sense of victory over North Korea. This brought about new-fashioned nationalism, which is neither defensive nor diffident.[5] Korean minds began groping for a new identity on the basis of overcoming Cold War–style confrontation and subservient attitudes toward Japan.

Second, Korean nationalism has been redefined in the post–Cold War setting. Anticommunism was weakened over time after the end of the Cold War. A desire to achieve national reintegration constituted an integral part of resurging nationalism in South Korea. North Korea is viewed as a country to coexist peacefully with in the first place and then to be embraced for reconciliation instead of being a country to be cornered or to be contained. On the other hand, unlike the popular conception that anti-Japanese sentiment is on the rise, nationalism in South Korea linked to Japan turned out to be more reactive than proactive.[6] Submerged but not forgotten memories are stirred whenever Japanese action or inaction provokes dormant anti-Japanese sentiment. Korean-Japanese conflict regarding historical controversy after the mid-1990s illustrates this point, which will be elaborated below.

Third, it is my contention that historical controversy does not serve Japan's strategic interests. Controversy between South Korea and Japan over historical issues concerns not only South Korean and American strategists but also strategically aware Japanese policy-makers, because Japanese right-wing voices contain contradictory elements in their proposals for dealing with East Asian regional affairs. Japanese action and inaction may serve domestic political interests in Japan, but the Japan-centric view presented by Japanese right wingers may raise internal contradictions that Japan should address in one way or another. Putting the historical memory issue in a larger geo-strategic setting will clarify the implication of the history-related controversy between South Korea and Japan.

KOREAN NATIONALISM IN HISTORICAL AND STRUCTURAL CONTEXT

The Genesis of Modern Korean Nationalism

Reflecting Korea's tragic modern history, Korean nationalism has long been defined by externally driven factors. Japanese colonialism gave rise to modern Korean nationalism. Resisting Japanese colonialism constituted the very core of Korean nationalism in modern times.[7] Even after liberation from Japanese colonial rule, historical memory related to Japanese rule exerted an overwhelming influence on the mind-sets of Koreans. Another critical experience that molded Korean minds was the Korean War. Though it was a war between peoples of the same ethnic origin, the war left a strong imprint on the course of the South Korean nation.[8] Since the war, anticommunism became a political slogan in South Korea for integrating Korean people. Hence, nationalism in South Korea cannot be discussed without referring to the Korean War. It is not coincidental that, during the 1950s when Syngman Rhee ruled Korea, anticommunism and anti-Japan sentiment constituted a core of Korean national identity in South Korea.[9]

It is not surprising that, in modern times, Korean nationalism sprang from a dire need to defend the Korean national identity from external threats. Korean nationalism related to anti-Japanese sentiment is closely intertwined with the independence movement from colonial rule. Efforts to defend the Korean identity from Japanese encroachment constituted a core of its elements. In addition, anticommunism stemmed from a need to guard the Korean identity against the tide of communist expansion in Asia. South Korea tried to defend its identity from the communist threat.

As a consequence, Korean nationalism, from the very beginning, came to acquire a defensive tone. In other words, Korean nationalism originated in response to external threats to the Korean identity. This defensive nature of Korean nationalism in its initial stage is quite different from Japanese-style nationalism, which had a strong offensive element despite its defensive rhetoric in modern times.[10]

The Development of Twisted Nationalism during the Cold War Period

Although the Cold War logic expedited cooperation between Korea and Japan, President Rhee refused to compromise with Japan.[11] After Park Chung-hee assumed power, Korea stepped back on the anti-Japanese front from a realistic need for boosting its economy.[12] At least at the elite level, ambiguity was the norm as far as anti-Japan feeling was concerned. Rivalry with North Korea was a linchpin that connected Korea and Japan strategically. At the background of this cooperative move lay the South Korean elite's awareness that South Korea lagged behind North Korea. Catching up with and surpassing North Korean economic development drove the South Korean elite to closely tie with Japan.[13] For the Korean leaders, a desire to learn from Japan's high-growth economy prompted a cooperative stance with Japan. They compromised the anti-Japanese element of Korean nationalism to expedite their anticommunist goals. It is no coincidence that South Korea linked its troop dispatch to Vietnam to gain access to the United States as an ally as well as to acquire financial benefits for economic growth.[14]

It should be noted, however, that South Korea's halfway compromise with Japan was feasible under specific conditions. First, the Park Chung-hee government was an authoritarian regime, which could make relatively autonomous decisions without political intervention from the general public. The Korean public, especially intellectuals and students, opposed the normalization treaty with Japan, fearing Japanese domination and infiltration. Also historical memory was a living memory, in particular, to the older generation that experienced colonialism personally. However, Park Chung-hee ignored public opinion and pushed for normalizing relations with Japan. Second, the United States urged Japan and Korea to cooperate in order to serve its needs in the Cold War struggle against the Soviet Union and communist China.[15] The United States was the linchpin actively associating Japan and South Korea. Third, Japanese self-restraint should also be appreciated. During the Cold War period, Japan abstained from pursuing a militarist policy, instead satisfying itself with becoming an economic giant based on mercantile realism.[16] This combination of a trading state economic strategy under the protection of the U.S. nuclear umbrella gave comforting signs to Japan's neighbors. Also because of a strong left-wing opposition, the Japan Socialist Party, the Japanese Liberal Democratic Party (LDP) governments abstained from provoking Japan's Asian neighbors.

South Korean nationalism during the Cold War period was twisted in that the preferences of the ruling elite did not necessarily match those of the South Korean public. Though the national elites of the two countries developed extensive cooperative ties with each other, the Korean public was not fully prepared to accept a new Japanese presence on Korean soil. This gap widened because the Korean public did not acquire the right to travel overseas until 1987. The South Korean masses knew of Japan only from their school education and the mass media, which was highly critical of the Park regime. Still, during this period, most Koreans held a dual image of Japan. On the one hand, Japan was regarded emotionally as a national enemy that had colonized the nation for 38 years and denied Korean's their national identity. On the other hand, they viewed Japan as an example of rising economic power on a global scale. The Park Chung-hee regime could take the initiative to gain access to Japan, because Japan was a key economic role model even while remaining an irreconcilable enemy emotionally.[17] Though there were sporadic anti-Japanese demonstrations, Japanese presence in Korea was perceived more in economic than political terms. Historical memory still lingered, but it did not necessarily hamper strategic cooperation.

The End of the Cold War and the Resurgence of Nationalism

The end of the Cold War changed the political and diplomatic dynamic related to historical memory in three ways.

First of all, after the end of the Cold War, South Korea opened diplomatic ties with the Soviet Union and China in 1990 and 1992, respectively.[18] On the one hand, normalizing diplomatic relations with China and the Soviet Union eased tensions with these long-standing allies of North Korea. This meant that South Korea gained diplomatic access to North Korea's backyard. On the other hand, diplomatic ties with China opened a new window of opportunity in the historical memory controversies. During the Cold War period, South Korea had no choice but to reluctantly compromise with Japan after rounds of political turmoil regarding historical controversy with Japan. The political wall between South Korea and China made South Korea a lonely, and separate, dissident to Japan. After South Korea gained access to China, however, China and South Korea became natural allies, not just in security terms but also in political terms, against Japan, if historical memory comes into a political play. Since then, the playing field of historical memory came to be literally regional, not bilateral.

Second, after the Berlin wall collapsed, the Koreans also longed to dismantle the Cold War structure on the Korean peninsula. On December 13, 1991, South and North Korea signed a South-North Basic Agreement that signaled a course for coexistence. In 1992, both Koreas, South and North, became formal member states of the United Nations. The military strain, however, remained unchanged despite these events. Furthermore, the first North Korean nuclear crisis in 1992 and 1994 provided a momentum for change in threat perception. At that time, the United States almost executed a preemptive strike against North Korea without seriously consulting South Korea.[19] After this event, South Koreans began to feel that the Koreans themselves should decide the fate of Korea.[20] After North Korea suffered a huge natural disaster caused by flooding in 1995, sympathy toward North Korean people rose. Nationalism, formerly bound by anticommunism, shifted toward national reconciliation. This move was possible because South Koreans gained confidence over the North Korean regime in terms of military and economic capabilities. After 1987, South Korea achieved democratization of the regime, which in turn gave the South Korean people a comforting relief in a competition for political legitimacy against North Korea. Also, in terms of economic performance, the South Koreans felt that the rivalry with North Korea no longer made sense, giving an absolute advantage to South Korea. This elevated sense of confidence opened a new horizon to embrace North Korea with the engagement strategy. Also, with this elevated sense of confidence, Korean feelings of inferiority and of being victimized by Japan have attenuated over time. The South Koreans have come to perceive Japan as one of their strongest neighbors, not as a leader or a model. As an extension of this, anti-Japanese feeling declined.[21]

Third, in the domestic political arena, new political dynamics evolved. Progressive voices on the Korean soil had long been oppressed under the successive authoritarian regimes under Syngman Rhee, Park Chung-hee, and Chun Doo-hwan. However, the end of the Cold War at a global and regional level made it possible for South Koreans to raise progressive voices. The unshackled progressives in South Korea put new political agendas on the table. Staging anti-American protests, questioning the collaborators from the authoritarian and colonial past, promoting inter-Korean reconciliation and cooperation talks are examples of the new agendas pushed by the progressives. Civic groups in the progressive camp took a rather mild posture toward North Korea, advocating the engagement policy initiated by the Kim Dae-jung regime. However, these progressive civic groups were not sympathetic to the historical issues related to Japanese colonial rule. As a result, progressive civic organizations took a tough stance toward Japan, inheriting the traditional anti-Japan position. Not all South Koreans resonated to this move. These groups also did not constantly raise these issues to the political forefront. Whenever a Japan-related historical controversy was raised, however, the presence of progressive civic groups became intensely visible. It should be noted that their advocacy of ethnic nationalism is not wildly popular among ordinary Koreans. But it is often the case that anti-Japanese campaigns did not last long. Also the anti-Japanese voices were overwhelmed by increasing personal contacts between the two countries.[22]

REAWAKENED HISTORICAL MEMORY AFTER THE MID-1990s

From a Proactive Initiative to a Reactive Response

One should be reminded that the Korean stance toward Japan eventually shifted from a proactive initiative to a reactive response. It is undeniable that, until the early 1990s, South Korea often made proactive initiatives to Japan, requesting apology, regret, or monetary compensation regarding historical controversy.

The logic of raising historical memory issues changed drastically from the mid-1990s. First of all, South Korea rarely initiated anti-Japanese claims on its own initiative. South Korea responded to the Japanese claims only when the Japanese side took a renewed position on the traditional history agenda. More often than not, Japanese actions came out of domestic political conflicts. The comfort women issue turned wildly controversial in Japanese political circles after the Kiichi Miyazawa, Morihiro Hosokawa, and Tomiichi Murayama cabinets took strong initiatives—first, recognizing the existence of the comfort women issue and, then, partially compensating them.[23] The history textbook issue came up as an extension of the comfort women issue. When the Society for Composing New History Textbook, or *Atarashii Kyoka-sho o Tsukurukai* (Tsukurukai), published a new textbook and applied for its approval to the Japanese Ministry of Education, the textbook controversy became rekindled. The Yasukuni Shrine visits by Prime Minister Junichiro Koizumi are not what neighboring countries urged at all. It was a political step by Koizumi to fulfill an ill-advised campaign promise during the 2000 LDP presidential election. All those issues that provoked intense responses from the Korean public were Japanese-initiated, not Korean-initiated, moves.

Second, even though anti-Japanese demonstrations in South Korea are visually presented in the media and voices of anger are heard when historical controversy emerges, they do not proliferate to the general masses. Nor do they last long. Anti-Japanese protests are made in designated places like in front of the Japanese Embassy in Seoul without larger voluntarily participating masses.[24] In areas distant from the Japanese Embassy, one can hardly find anti-Japanese moves. In particular, anti-Japanese agendas are not primary issues of student demonstrations on campus at all. In addition, there may be a week-long demonstrations and media coverage on the issue, but one can hardly identify long-standing media coverage on the issue, either. In other words, anti-Japanese movements are temporary and limited.

Third, despite claims that anti-Japanese sentiments are politically exploited, the effects of the political use of anti-Japanese feeling are dubious or at least tenuous. When historical controversy comes up as a political and diplomatic issue, Korean presidents are almost obliged to react intensely to the issue. For example, when Korea entered into territorial conflict regarding Dokdo, or Takeshima, in February 2005, the president took a strong stance against Japan, which he described as a "diplomatic war with Japan." Coming just before local elections in mid-April 2005, it is unsurprising that political use of history issues would seem advantageous to the ruling party. However, the ruling party was completely defeated in the April local elections.[25] More often than not, despite twists and turns regarding historical memory controversies, it was always the ruling party in Korea that lost local elections. This suggests that political use of anti-Japanese sentiment is no longer an effective tool of political maneuvering. If the ruling regime in Korea planned on taking full political advantage of the history issue, this political move did not necessarily achieve its aims. Often political use of the issue is ineffective or the political use of the historical controversy with Japan produces only a minimal increase in political popularity. When Koizumi visited the Yasukuni Shrine in 2001, Korean President Roh Moo-Hyun harshly criticized the move. This principled criticism may have briefly boosted his popularity, but his longtime low popularity was determined by factors other than by his policy toward Japan.[26] In other words, political manipulation of anti-Japanese sentiment in Korea is often claimed, but its practical political efficacy and outright effects are minimal. Hence, domestic political use of anti-Japanese feelings in South Korea should not be misinterpreted or overestimated.

Interpreting Japanese Actions and Rationale: A Japan-Centric Idea

The Japanese intellectuals who had long been wary of putting history issues on the political marketplace began throwing out new agendas in the mid-1990s. It began as a response to the Japanese Socialist Party's left-wing initiative to reflect critically on Japan's past history. Right-wing intellectuals actively raised their voices on issues such as the comfort women, criticized what they called repentant diplomacy, and assailed the "self-torturing" historical interpretation. Though these agendas developed out of domestic Japanese political debates, they immediately affected relations with neighboring countries, including South Korea.

What provoked the South Koreans most was Prime Minister Koizumi's visit to the Yasukuni Shrine. Koizumi, in the middle of the LDP presidential election, promised to visit the Yasukuni Shrine every year.[27] His promise was kept during his tenure, but this was done without considering its diplomatic consequences.[28] The Yasukuni Shrine is a place where 14 Class-A war criminals responsible for the past war are enshrined.[29] Also the Yushukan, a *de facto* war memorial museum operated by the shrine, is a symbolic political construct where the past war is justified as if it were solely a war of self-defense and a war for liberating the Asian people from Western aggression. Therefore, visiting the Yasukuni Shrine is a significant political act symbolizing defense of the past war. Though Koizumi claimed that he did not go there to pay respect to the Class-A war criminals,[30] his excuse was incomprehensible and unconvincing because separating ordinary soldiers from the Class-A war criminals who are enshrined at the same place was practically impossible. Therefore, Koizumi's actions made it appear as if he tacitly approved of wartime atrocities and wrongdoings. Despite repeated advice and criticisms from South Korea and China, Koizumi never stopped his Yasukuni Shrine visits, unlike former Prime Minister Nakasone. In order to attenuate the political impact of the Yasukuni Shrine visits, Koizumi almost repeated the Murayama Declaration when he attended the Asia-Africa Summit meeting in Jakarta, Indonesia, on April 22, 2005. However, on the same day, 93 Japanese politicians paid a visit to the Yasukuni Shrine in Tokyo on his behalf. From the Korean perspective, there were ample reasons to ask which actions reflect the true signal to Japan's neighbors.

The Dokdo/Takeshima dispute was another example of conflicting interpretation of historical memory. When the Shimane prefectural assembly in Japan passed a resolution that made February 22 "Takeshima Day" and celebrated on March 16, 2005 the 100th anniversary of annexing Takeshima, the South Korean government regarded it as a politically contrived provocation at the local prefectural level to reverse the status quo. Though the South Korean government gave advance warning that this would provoke public criticism in Korean that the government would be unable to control, the Japanese government turned a deaf ear with the excuse that in a democracy like Japan the actions of a local government could not be controlled. This was interpreted in South Korea as a convenient excuse to implicitly defend the actions of the Shimane prefectural assembly.[31] Incensed by the Japanese government's inaction, Korean President Roh Moo-hyun announced a new Japan policy doctrine on March 17, 2005, and declared a "diplomatic war" with Japan. For Korea, the year 1905 had special meaning. It was the year that Japan annexed Dokdo, but 1905 was also the year when Japan reduced Korea to the status of a virtual protectorate of Japan, thus taking away its sovereignty and initiating the first step toward its colonization. Proclaiming the 100th anniversary of the annexation of Takeshima sounded as if the Japanese were trying to justify their colonial rule of Korea that virtually began in 1905, although Japan's formal annexation of Korea did not occur until 1910. When Shimane prefecture took this political action, it carelessly and insensitively provoked submerged Korean sentiment related to tragic historical memory.[32]

The textbook issue is another example of negatively responding to Korean requests. It is reasonably expected that the two nations cannot have the same *historical interpretations.* It is possible, however, to share common *historical facts.* In the past, Japanese scholars did not hesitate to acknowledge wrongdoings in the prewar period even without Korean pressure. From the mid-1990s, however, right-wing Japanese intellectuals took a strong initiative to erase unpleasant historical facts from history textbooks. This prompted Korean and Chinese protests of the Japanese government's approval of such textbooks, which whitewash Japan's past transgressions.

The comfort women issue is another example where Japanese actions provoked Korean intellectuals and the news media. Victimized comfort women, or wartime sex slaves, began confessing their own shameful personal history since the early 1990s. Though Prime Minister Murayama and subsequent Japanese cabinets took the initiative and sent messages of apology to the comfort women and partially compensated them through the Asian Women's Fund, right-wing intellectuals criticized this policy. For them, it is a national shame and disgrace even to acknowledge that the Japanese government was responsible for the system of comfort women. They began focusing on whether there was any coercion in the process of recruiting the comfort women and whether this coercion was officially organized by the Japanese military. However, whether they were minimally enforced or maximally coerced, or whether it was officially organized by the Japanese military, there is no change in the truth that the Japanese military operated the comfort women facilities, which is a violation of human rights. Prime Minister Abe's remarks on March 1, 2007, that there was no empirical proof that comfort women were forcefully recruited have not yet been verified. Those claims are also morally reprehensible. Japanese politicians' support of Abe's remarks provoked a reaction from the unexpected quarters. It outraged American politicians, and helped the U.S. House of Representatives to pass a nonbinding resolution on July 30, 2007 demanding that the Japanese government apologize to the comfort women.

All these issues originate from right-wing views that contain politically dangerous elements of advocating prewar Japanese actions and the prewar political system.

Their claims are primarily centered on resurrecting the pride and glory of the Japanese nation and its people while closing their eyes to the guilt of past wrongdoings. The Japanese postwar political system is founded on two critical reflections on past history. The first is a judgment that prewar militarism was illegitimate and wrong and caused harm to ordinary Japanese as well as to neighboring countries. Unlike the prewar system, the postwar political system is a democracy where the Japanese people have real power. The second pillar of the postwar system is that the Class-A war criminals were responsible for the past war. In this interpretation, ordinary Japanese were also victims rather than wrongdoers. Therefore, right-wing arguments that advocate for the Class-A war criminals, dismiss the comfort women issue, and justify prewar territorial annexations can be interpreted as justifying the prewar system and denying Japan's wartime responsibility.

This does not mean that Japan has to continue to apologize and repent to its neighbors. Negating repeated apologies to neighbors is one thing, and advocating prewar conducts is quite another. Advocating the wartime misdeeds and disclaiming the responsibility of the war criminals, as the right-wing intellectuals do, can send the wrong message that Japanese elites long nostalgically for prewar glory. As opposed to these right-wing views, Japan can be proud of its postwar performances and achievements such as building an advanced economy under a democratic political system, while contributing to global peace and prosperity through humanitarian aid.

CONTROVERSIES OVER HISTORICAL MEMORY AND CONTRADICTIONS IN JAPANESE HANDLING OF THIS ISSUE

The irony of the Japanese right-wing movement is that, by trying to politically manipulate historical memory, their actions and rationale reveal internal and international contradictions. All too often, Japanese policies backed by the right wing negatively affect Japanese strategic interests. Claims of Japanese right-wing intellectuals to resurrect a glorious past may be acceptable only to those who are sympathetic to their claims. However, locating historical memory in a larger historical and geo-strategic context enables us to redirect attention to the internal contradictions of their claims.

Do Korea and China Belong in the Same Cart?

By bringing history issues to the political front, Japanese right-wing activists ended up putting Korea and China, two Northeast Asian neighbors, in the same diplomatic cart. As long as Japan actively raises history issues, South Korea, though unwillingly and reluctantly, drifts away from Japan, because Korea as a victimized nation sympathizes with Chinese claims. During the Cold War period, Korea had no choice but to remain on the side of Japan who aligned with the United States, while harboring resentment of Japan's past colonial rule. However, with the normalization of diplomatic relations between South Korea and China, South Korea can now ally diplomatically with China in confronting Japan, as far as historical memory is reawakened.

This should not be construed as a deliberate political strategy by South Korea to shift away from Japan and toward China as a strategic partner. The Korea-China linkage on historical memory issues is of Japan's own making.

Japan claims that it wants to strengthen diplomatic ties with democratic countries coupled with market economies and the rule of law. South Korea is one of those countries in the region that has attained political democracy and economic development, and which seeks to further integrate into a global market economy. Despite this Japanese contention, however, historical controversies unwittingly put democratic South Korea and authoritarian China together. Japan pushes South Korea toward the side of China because of self-centered interpretations of historical memory. If Japan adheres to the principle of establishing friendly ties with democratic countries, Japan should embrace South Korea more actively. If not, Japanese words and deeds may be contradictory.

Can Japan Turn Its Back on Asia While Questioning American Postwar Design?

Japan has long pursued a balanced approach of establishing friendly ties with Asian countries while maintaining close ties with the United States. Together with UN-centered diplomacy, these policies represented three core principles of Japanese diplomacy.

Historical controversy acts against these principles in a profound way. When history issues emerge on the surface, conflict with Asian neighbors is unavoidable. Koizumi's diplomacy is a good example. Although he strengthened and amplified diplomatic and security ties with the United States, his Asian diplomacy was a disaster. The absence of the Asian strategy marked the latter half of the Koizumi period.[33]

However, it can be much more disastrous if Japan pursues the core agenda of the right-wing intellectuals. Advocating the Class-A war criminals, negating the legitimacy of the International Military Tribunal for the Far East, rejecting Japan's responsibility for the comfort women, and emphasizing the enforced nature of the Japanese Constitution can be a formidable challenge to the good will of the American occupation policy. Pursuing right-wing claims to the extreme would make American policy-makers embarrassed in a sense that their claims ultimately blame the United States while defending prewar Japanese acts.

If Japan engages in a diplomatic conflict with its Asian neighbors while simultaneously risking a clash with the United States, it may end up pursuing an isolationist course. This policy line contracts with the long-preserved core principles of the Japanese diplomacy.

Are Korea and China Just Crybabies?

When Abe questioned whether there existed coercion when mobilizing comfort women, he also questioned the essence of the Kono statement in 1993 under the Miyazawa cabinet. Acknowledging that his view contradicted the Kono statement, later, on March 26, 2007, Abe made it clear that his cabinet also followed the spirit of the Kono statement. However, use of force at the recruitment stage is not the only problem in the comfort women issue. Bringing comfort women onto a battle-field is itself a human rights violation, even judged with the standards of that time. In addition, as far as comfort women issues are concerned, China and South Korea are not the only victimized countries. Women from the Philippines and the Nether-lands were also forcibly mobilized. Hence, targeting Korea and China as the only complainers is a misplaced criticism.

When the Yasukuni Shrine visits became a contentious issue between Japan and its neighbors South Korea and China, South Korea and China raised their voices against Prime Minister Koizumi's Yasukuni shrine visit. Koizumi often claimed that China and South Korea were the only countries that annoyed Japan with history issues. However, it should never be underestimated that there were mounting voices of criti-cism even within Japan. The Japanese public was widely divided over this issue.[34] Intellectuals, both liberal and conservative, raised fundamental questions as to whether Yasukuni Shrine visits by government officials could ever be justifiable.[35] The claim that Korea and China are the only gripers on this issue ignores a large body of Japanese opinions that question the justification of Yasukuni visits by officials. If these voices of opposition were influential enough to counter the right-wing claims, Korea and China would have little reason to cast doubts on Japanese intentions. In other words, how to handle historical memory ultimately depends on the soundness of Japanese democracy.

NOTES

1. Victor Cha, *Alignment despite Antagonism* (Stanford: Stanford University Press, 1999).

2. Avery Goldstein, *Rising to the Challenge* (Stanford: Stanford University Press, 2005).

3. Thomas Berger, "Power and Purpose in Pacific East Asia: A Constructivist Interpreta-tion," in *International Relations Theory and the Asia-Pacific*, ed. John Ikenberry and Michael Mastanduno (New York: Columbia University Press, 2003).

4. Chong Sik Lee, *Japan and Korea: the Political Dimension* (Stanford: Stanford University Press, 1985).

5. A *Chosun Ilbo* article characterized this kind of new-fashioned nationalism as ROK nationalism contrasted against Korean ethnic nationalism. *Chosun Ilbo,* September 3, 2007. As for the Korean ethnic nationalism, refer to Gi Wook Shin, *Ethnic Nationalism in Korea* (Stanford: Stanford University Press, 2006).

6. Cheol Hee Park, "Shifting Korean Identity, Altering Agenda Setting, and Korea-Japan Relations in the Post-Cold War Period," An article in Korean presented at the international conference organized by the Korean Association of Contemporary Japanese Studies on June 15, 2007, in Jeju, South Korea.

7. Lee Chong Sik, *Hankook Minjokjueui eui Chongchihak* (Seoul: Hanbat Publisher, 1982).

8. Bruce Cumings, *The Origins of the Korean War,* 2 vols. (Princeton: Princeton University Press, 1982).

9. Syngman Rhee formally argued that anticommunist and anti-Japanese policies were two core principles that the South Korean government pursued.

10. A good example is a discourse on the Greater East Asian Coprosperity Sphere. Though it sounds as if Japan tried to defend Asian countries from Western imperialism, it contained a strong element of annexing weak Asian states in times of colonialism. In that sense, Japanese nationalism in prewar times was offensive. See Carol Gluck, *Japan's Modern Myths* (Stanford: Stanford University Press, 1985).

11. Chong Won Lee, *Higasiajia reisen to Kanbeinichi kankei* (Tokyo: University of Tokyo Press, 1998).

12. Diplomatic normalization with Japan in 1965 symbolized this move. As for a study on Korea-Japan diplomatic normalization, see Won Deok Lee, *Hanil Gwagusa Chori eui wonjom* (Seoul: Seoul National University Press, 1996).

13. Winning over communism, *seung gong,* was a political catchphrase during the Park era.

14. Cheol Hee Park, "The Development of Korea's Regional Strategy in Northeast Asia," in *Cooperation Experiences in Europe and Asia,* ed. Hoon Jaung and Yuichi Morii (Tokyo: DESK [Deutschland und Europa Studien in Komaba], University of Tokyo, 2004).

15. Koo Youngnok, ed., *Mikook kwa Dongbuka* (Seoul: Seoul National University Press, 1984).

16. Eric Heginbotham and Richard Samuels, "Mercantile Realism and Japanese Foreign Policy," *International Security* 22, no. 4 (Spring 1998): 171–203.

17. Rapid economic development of Japan after the Korean War and Japanese entry to OECD may have changed Korean perceptions of Japan. The hosting of the Tokyo Olympics in 1964 also elevated the image of Japan as an economic success that is fully accepted by many countries.

18. Concluding friendly ties with those two nations was possible because of the active pursuit of the so-called Northern Policy under the Roh Tae Woo administration.

19. Don Oberdorfer, *The Two Koreas* (New York: Addison-Wesley, 1997), pp. 171–203.

20. The voices for an autonomous decision provided momentum for the rise of an anti-Americanism that was qualitatively different from that of previous years. Unlike anti-Americanism linked to its support of the South Korean authoritarian regime, from this moment on, progressive intellectuals in South Korea viewed American unilateralism as a potential threat to peace on the Korean peninsula.

21. The Kim Dae-jung–Obuchi Joint Declaration in 1998 was possible with the background of this newly evolving confidence in the quality of Korea's systems and achievements.

22. As of 2006, 4,690,000 people crossed the border to visit the two countries. Altogether 2.37 million Koreans visited Japan and 2.32 million Japanese visited Korea in 2006.

23. The Kono Statement on August 4, 1993, Hosokawa's speech in August 1994, and the Murayama Statement on August 15, 1995.

24. There are regular "Wednesday Demonstrations" by comfort women groups and their political allies, but they are almost regularized events rather than instant responses to Japanese moves.

25. In the by-election held on April 15, 2005, the Grand National Party won 5 seats and an independent obtained 1 seat, while the ruling Open Uri Party failed to secure even a single seat.

26. When the Dokdo incident drew the attention of the Korean public, the approval rating for President Roh went up to 39.4 percent, which was highest in two years, as of March 29, 2005, but his popularity plummeted again to 24.1 on August 30, 2005.

27. It is reported that Koizumi made this promise in order to gain the support of the Society for Bereaved Families, which had long supported the Hashimoto faction. *Asahi Shinbun,* April 19, 2001.

28. Koizumi visited the Yasukuni Shrine on August 13, 2001, April 21, 2002, January 14, 2003, January 1, 2004, October 17, 2005, and August 15, 2006.

29. As for the controversy regarding the Yasukuni Shrine visits, see Takahashi Tetsuya, *Yasukuni Mondai* (Tokyo: Chikuma Shinsho, 2005).

30. Koizumi claimed that his Yasukuni Shrine visits were not intended to pay respect to the Class-A war criminals. *Yomiuri Shinbun,* March 4, 2006.

31. At best the Japanese government acted to restrain the move only at the final moment.

32. Ironically the Shimane prefecture's move produced the unintended consequences of contradicting the Japanese government's official position by suggesting that Japan annexed the island only from the year 1905. The Japanese official government position is that the island is legally and historically Japanese territory. If Japan annexed the island in 1905 as Shimane prefecture declared, it is tantamount to admission that the island belonged to Korea before that date. In this sense, the Shimane prefecture's move was not politically correct even from the Japanese standpoint, in terms of maintaining a consistent and coherent argument that the islands had always been Japanese.

33. Cheol Hee Park, "Japanese Strategic Thinking toward Korea," in *Japanese Strategic Thought toward Asia,* ed. Gilbert Rozman et al. (New York: Palgrave, 2007), pp. 183–200.

34. In an opinion survey done by *Asahi Shinbun* between October 17 and 18, 2005, 42 percent of the respondents positively evaluated Koizumi's Yasukuni Shrine visit, while 41 percent opposed the move. This survey shows that the Japanese public was evenly divided on this issue.

35. Wakamiya Yoshibumi and Watanabe Tsuneo, *Yasukuni to Koizumi shusho* (Tokyo: Asahi Shinbunsha, 2006).

Part IV ————————————————————————————

Two Bystanders

11

The United States and Reconciliation in East Asia

David Straub

The growing rivalry between a more "normal" Japan and a rising China could pose a threat to East Asian regional and even global peace and security in coming decades. Because differences between the two countries over history are not only a symptom but also a cause of their great-power competition, historical reconciliation between them needs to be addressed not only as a humanitarian but also as a security issue.

The United States' role is significant in both respects. Given the great and increasing importance of East Asia in global affairs, the peace, stability, and prosperity of the region is a vital security interest of the United States. As the outside power with the most influence on Japan and China, and as one of the two superpowers "present at the creation" of many of the current historical disputes in East Asia, the United States also bears some moral responsibility for the state of Sino-Japanese relations.

There remain historical differences among many nations in East Asia, but this chapter will focus on the differences between Japan, on the one hand, and China and Korea, on the other, stemming primarily from Japan's imperialist behavior in the twentieth century. Given the size of the economies, populations, and militaries of Japan and China, their weight in the region is outsized and their rivalry runs the greatest risk of destabilizing the region. Korea is also included because the Korean Peninsula is a secondary but still major source of long-term risk in the region, divided as it is between two heavily armed states still technically in a state of war. Moreover, even though Japan invaded and occupied a number of Asian countries during its imperialist phase, public opinion polls show that feelings about Japan are by far the most negative in China and Korea.[1]

Many observers long expected that historically based anti-Japan feelings would began to disappear among Chinese and Koreans as a younger generation that did not experience colonial rule or war came of age. That did not happen. In fact, some experts believe that the emotions of the younger generation in China and Korea are more intense than those of their elders. The civic education that the younger generation received included a component focusing critically on Japanese colonial and wartime behavior, unleavened by the complexities of actual life experience.

With a view to aid in charting ways in which the United States could make a larger contribution to the related goals of promoting historical reconciliation and enhancing security in East Asia, this chapter examines the U.S. role in historical disputes in East Asia since World War II, discuss American attitudes, and critically analyze U.S. policy. It concludes with some suggestions for U.S. policy regarding the handling of historical disputes.

HISTORICAL PRIMACY OF STRATEGIC INTERESTS

During World War II, the United States devoted relatively great attention to an analysis of Japanese history and politics with the intention of ensuring that Japan would never again pose a threat to the United States and its interests or constitute a future source of instability in the region. The American occupation was carefully planned over an extended period; American occupation personnel were trained in the Japanese language and culture; and American executive and Congressional leaders were committed to an extended occupation regime and determined to achieve its aims. In the immediate postwar years, the United States dealt directly and indirectly with historical issues through the U.S.-led Allied occupation of Japan.

Even in the early years of the occupation, however, U.S. authorities did not pursue historical justice primarily for its own sake. The overarching aim was to influence Japan not to be a threat to American security and other vital interests. U.S. authorities also took into account various realities as they saw them, correctly or not. Thus, the United States preserved the Imperial institution in Japan for the sake of stability and never seriously examined publicly the Emperor's involvement in and responsibility for historical issues. In addition, U.S. authorities did not try many notorious civilian and military figures; they even decided not to pursue justice against members of the infamous Unit 731, in exchange for "intelligence" from them about their nightmarish biological warfare experiments on living human beings.

Within only a few years after the end of World War II, the relative success of the occupation of Japan and the beginning of the Cold War prompted a major shift in American focus. Americans became far less concerned about a possible future Japanese threat to American interests and much more concerned about the communist "bloc." Soviet expansion in Eastern Europe, the establishment of "Red China" by the Communist Party of China in October 1949, and the outbreak of the Korean War in June 1950 were viewed with alarm by the United States. Americans began to regard former enemies Japan and Germany as potential allies in the struggle against the global communist menace. The United States encouraged Japan gradually to play a larger supporting role to the United States in East Asian regional security.

The San Francisco Peace Treaty between the U.S.-led allied powers and Japan, signed in September 1951, marked the formal end not only of the Pacific War but also of the U.S. occupation. It was supposed to settle a number of historical issues, including territorial matters, overseas Japanese assets, and compensation for prisoners of war. However, the treaty did not address or anticipate a number of matters that have since become the source of major controversies between Japan, on the one hand, and China and Korea, on the other. These include Japan's history textbooks, the relationship between the Yasukuni Shrine and the Japanese government, compensation for the so-called comfort women, and the status of the Liancourt Rocks, known in Japan as Takeshima and in Korea as Dokdo. Article 21 of the San Francisco treaty, however, did make provision for Japanese talks later with China and Korea to provide *de facto* compensation to those countries.

Although Japan, in committing to the San Francisco Treaty, pledged in Article 11 specifically to accept the results of the International Military Tribunal for the Far East, before the decade of the 1950s was over the Japanese Diet and other governmental institutions had taken steps to rehabilitate those convicted or implicated in the Tribunal. It appears that U.S. authorities did not seriously challenge such actions due to concern about damaging relations with a friendly Japan that had become increasingly significant strategically as the Cold War deepened.

As the Vietnam War became increasingly intense, it was important to the United States that its two major allies in the region, the Republic of Korea (ROK; South Korea) and Japan, should have normal relations. In 1965, at U.S. urging, South Korea and Japan did normalize relations, in a treaty that was supposed to settle historical and territorial issues between them. The agreement was extremely controversial at the time, especially in Korea, where many nationalists and left-wing forces regarded it as inadequate and unfair. The opponents also objected to U.S. pressure to conclude the agreement.

After the Sino-Soviet split, the United States and China began to consider a rapprochement to counter the Soviet Union. Under the Nixon administration, the United States undertook a serious effort in this regard, and on July 15, 1971, President Nixon announced U.S. contacts with the People's Republic of China leadership and the fact that he had been invited to visit Beijing. In the late 1980s and early 1990s, the collapse of the Soviet Union and its satellite states in Eastern Europe, China's rapid emergence as a major U.S. bilateral trading partner and its rise as an influential power in East Asia, and the bursting of the Japanese economic bubble, led the United States under President Bill Clinton to seek increased cooperation with China. Many Japanese, who had complained of the United States' "Japan bashing" over trade issues as their economy boomed, now expressed concern that the United States was engaged in "Japan passing."

With the bursting of the economic bubble around 1990, Japan entered a so-called lost decade of economic stagnation, political turmoil, and introspection about Japanese identity. It emerged from the decade with moderate economic growth restored and dominated politically by a resurgent Liberal Democratic Party (LDP). By then the LDP was led by a younger, postwar generation, who questioned why they should have to continue to make penance for the sins of their grandparents. The LDP was no longer significantly checked by the traditional left, which had collapsed with the end of the Cold War.

While the Japanese economy had benefited substantially from a huge increase in trade with a growing China, the Japanese establishment became increasingly anxious about the implications of the rise of China for Japan's status and security in the region and the world. China's military might was growing rapidly along with its economic progress, including the development of long-range missiles to match its existing nuclear weapons stockpile. (Japan foreswore nuclear weapons after World War II.) China, unlike Japan, was a permanent member of the UN Security Council, and China's diplomatic influence in the region and globally was steadily increasing, including relative to Japan. The Japanese establishment's concern coincided with the view of some in the United States that, with the fall of the USSR, China was the only potential rival to U.S. power in coming decades. That led to a renewed emphasis among some circles in the United States on U.S.-Japanese security cooperation to hedge against the rise of China.

In short, in the post–World War II era the U.S. government did not ignore historical issues involving Japan but treated them as distinctly secondary in importance to perceived strategic interests. To the extent historical issues were addressed by the United States, they were dealt with primarily because of their implications for security interests.

AMERICAN ATTITUDES

During the past two decades, a number of historical issues have roiled Japan's relations with China and Korea. These include Japan's history textbooks, the Yasukuni Shrine, the "comfort women," and the Takeshima/Dokdo and Senkaku Islands/Diaoyutai territorial disputes.

U.S. officials followed these issues with concern but rarely spoke publicly about them.[2] When they did, it was almost always simply to express the United States' general interest in the maintenance of good relations between the major states in the region and the U.S. desire that the issues be resolved amicably among the concerned parties.[3] There are a number of reasons that explain this attitude on the part of the United States, in addition to the overarching strategic interests already addressed.

First, in war, Americans tend to be better winners than losers. In the case of the stalemate with North Korea, the defeat in Vietnam, and the inconclusive nature of the first Gulf War, the United States has, respectively, still not established relations with North Korea five decades after the war, established normal relations with Vietnam but only after the passage of two full decades, and invaded Iraq a second time and occupied the country. In contrast, the American occupation of Japan, coming after an extremely brutal and racist war on both sides, was relatively well intended and well conducted. The American government and people were also greatly relieved and gratified that the Japanese people accepted and cooperated with the occupation. With the rise of what was perceived as a worldwide communist threat only a few years later, the American image of Japan changed quickly from horribly negative to quite positive.

Second, there was also some reflection after World War II on the part of Americans about whether U.S. policy had contributed to Japanese aggression or at least had not done all that it might have to prevent it. Some Americans questioned the fairness of the International Military Tribunal for the Far East (Tokyo War Crimes Tribunal), and many Americans remained troubled by such wartime American actions as the firebombing of Tokyo and the atomic bombings of Hiroshima and Nagasaki. These were not insignificant debates about trivial issues. To cite just one example, General Eisenhower wrote to his brother in 1945 that "I voiced to him [Secretary of War Henry L. Stimson] my grave misgivings, first on the basis of my belief that Japan was already defeated and that dropping the [atomic] bomb was completely unnecessary, and secondly because I thought that our country should avoid shocking world opinion by the use of a weapon whose employment was, I thought, no longer mandatory as a measure to save American lives."[4]

Third, legally, the San Francisco Treaty was supposed to take care of compensation issues involving Japan. The United States government has remained consistent in its respect for the treaty, including this provision, even in the face of criticism from directly affected American citizens and interest groups. The United States has a general interest in the sanctity of treaties and also fears that not supporting the treaty could set a precedent that would expose the United States to many foreign claims and suits. The precedents of policy and law, including court decisions, built up over more than six decades, would pose a formidable obstacle to an effort to have the United States play a larger and more direct role in resolving historical issues in East Asia.

Fourth, given its own behavior in the Pacific War and more generally historically, U.S. government intervention on behalf of a particular party in historical disputes with Japan would expose the United States to charges that it lacked the moral standing to involve itself. As a senior U.S. government official commented sarcastically to the author in 2005: "Yes, the U.S. should mediate between China and Japan, and then China could mediate between Texas and Mexico" (over American settlers' forcibly taking the Texas territory from Mexico in 1836). Japanese angered by American criticism of their country's behavior could cite many examples of American misconduct. Regarding comfort women, the Japanese government established brothels in Japan immediately after World War II for the use of U.S. occupation personnel; these were similar to the "comfort stations" that Japan had established abroad for its own forces during the war. U.S. personnel widely used these facilities, with the knowledge and tacit acceptance of U.S. authorities, a situation that changed only after the rate of venereal disease among U.S. personnel reached astronomical levels. The United States also had its own colonial history, including the takeover of the Native Hawaiian government by American citizens at the end of the nineteenth century. Most Koreans are well aware that in 1905 the United States reached a secret understanding with Japan (the Taft-Katsura Agreement) acquiescing in Japan's colonization of Korea in exchange for Japan's recognition of American interests in the Philippines. As for textbooks, it was only in recent decades that American history textbooks began to address frankly and fully the victimization of Native Americans and of African slaves in the United States.

Finally, and of great importance, U.S. officials have been concerned that even mere mediation, not to mention advocacy, in such historical disputes would probably make matters worse. Inevitably one side would regard the United States as favoring the other, and the likelihood of achieving a resolution might become more remote. Even if a dispute were eventually formally resolved, significant domestic elements in one country or the other, or both, might feel that their side had been shortchanged. They would likely seek to reopen the issue while blaming the United States for an "unfair" agreement.

One notable recent exception to the United States' hands-off approach was the high-level official U.S. criticism in the first half of 2007 of Japanese Prime Minister Shinzo Abe's statements about the comfort women issue. Such criticism came not only from the U.S. State Department spokesperson, but also from the U.S. ambassador to Tokyo, Thomas Schieffer, who publicly equated the treatment accorded the "comfort women" with "rape."[5] This was all the more remarkable in that Schieffer is an intimate of President Bush, and President George W. Bush is an outspoken supporter of the U.S.-Japan alliance.

The exception, however, is more apparent than real. To most Americans today, the comfort women issue is less a historical than a gender issue. There has been a major evolution in Americans' views about gender relations in recent decades; sexual behavior and issues that they would have ignored or regarded as regrettable but inevitable due to "human nature" only a couple of decades are now widely condemned. Perhaps Prime Minister Abe, having contemplated the record of seeming U.S. official indifference to historical issues involving Japan, was surprised at the U.S. government's reaction to his apparent retreat from the Kono Statement of 1993 on the comfort women. (The Kono Statement represented the Japanese government's most forthcoming position on the matter.)

By the time Abe visited Washington, DC for the first time as prime minister, in May 2007, he and President Bush had apparently had their staff members work out how the two leaders would deal publicly with the comfort women issue. Thus, at their joint press conference, after Abe had stated his position, President Bush responded that he "accepted" Abe's "apology." In actuality, as many experts noted, Abe neither gave a clear apology in Washington nor was Bush in a position to accept an apology, not having been a "comfort woman" himself and not representing the comfort women. But Bush's response, while inappropriately phrased, was consistent with the position taken by previous U.S. presidents on such historical issues involving Japan. Basically, most U.S. officials genuinely hope for the amicable resolution of historical disputes, for reasons both humanitarian and strategic, but are not prepared publicly to press their Japanese ally.

The subsequent passage by the U.S. House of Representatives of a nonbinding resolution (the "Honda resolution" or House Resolution 121) criticizing Japan's handling of the comfort women issue does not mean that American politicians have a different attitude from U.S. executive branch officials on such issues. Such a resolution had been introduced in the House for a number of years but had never passed. It was Abe's remarks in the Japanese Diet about the issue in early 2007 that troubled some American lawmakers and gave unusual impetus to the resolution. Even so, it appeared that Abe's more carefully worded statements during his visit to Washington and vigorous lobbying by the Japanese government had turned the tide. But a full-page advertisement in *The Washington Post* on June 14 by right-wing Japanese politicians and opinion leaders criticizing the resolution offended most of official Washington, and as a result the resolution passed the full House on July 30 with no member expressing opposition (even though some were actually adamantly opposed).[6]

Most members of Congress appeared to feel that the public statements and writings of Prime Minister Abe and the right-wing Japanese politicians and opinion leaders had left them no real option of opposing what most Americans regarded as a vote on gender rights. But they seemed also to feel very awkward about criticizing Japan, a country that is one of the world's major powers and a close ally of the United States. Predictably, in the aftermath of the vote, few in Washington said anything further about the comfort women issue. Japan's response was only to express regret about the resolution's passage and to cite the Kono Statement, this time without elaboration, as fully reflecting its position. On September 5, the U.S. House of Representatives passed another resolution on Japan, this one praising Japan's "values" and its security cooperation with the United States, apparently to ease the sting of the earlier resolution.[7] It thus appeared unlikely that the U.S. Congress would pass another resolution on the comfort women issue in the future.

All of this is not to say that U.S. officials over the decades have not been concerned about historical disputes involving Japan. They have been, primarily for the strategic reasons described. At times, many have also been concerned personally, because American officials, like most knowledgeable American citizens, tend not to sympathize with Japanese conservatives' positions on several of the disputes.

In the case, for example, of then-Prime Minister Koizumi's controversial visits to the Yasukuni Shrine, the United States government refrained from all official criticism and stuck to its standard position of expressing hope that good relations would be maintained and that the parties to the controversy would resolve the matter amicably. Many U.S. officials, however, became increasingly concerned about the rise in tensions in the region, as the Chinese and South Korean governments suspended top-level dialogue with Japan for many months and even years.

Privately, many U.S. officials at all levels, on a personal basis and without specific authority, told Japanese counterparts that the Yasukuni issue risked damaging not only Japan's relations with China and Korea but also with the United States. These officials pointed out that the version of the history of the Pacific War that Americans had learned (and still learn) in school was radically different from the "revisionist" version laid out in the museum attached to the Yasukuni Shrine and espoused by some right-wing Japanese politicians. They cautioned that, the longer and more heated the controversy over Yasukuni became, the more would Americans take note of the issue and the more would they disagree with Japan and sympathize with Chinese and Korean feelings.

Given the number and the intensity of such personal messages passed to Japanese officials and influential citizens, Prime Minister Koizumi almost certainly understood that his position with American friends on the issue had become increasingly delicate. It was in this context that he publicly stated in August 2006, "Even if President Bush advised me not to go [to Yasukuni] I would still go—although President Bush wouldn't say something so childish."[8]

It appeared that Prime Minister Koizumi was warning President Bush, whom he perhaps expected to raise the issue, that doing so would not help and would only make matters worse, not only between Japan and its neighbors China and Korea, but also between Japan and the United States. He appeared to be saying to President Bush, "Please understand that I must continue to visit Yasukuni; I'm banking not only on Japan's importance to the United States but also on our personal relationship that you will not raise this difficult issue with me."

Prime Minister Koizumi continued to visit the Yasukuni Shrine throughout his term in office, but his successor's decision to take a more low-profile approach to Yasukuni may have stemmed not only from a desire for improved relations with China and Korea but also from an understanding of U.S. concerns that had been quietly expressed.

Another example of official American concern about historical issues, although between the United States and Japan rather than involving China and Korea, was the internal debate among officials of the American embassy in Tokyo in the period leading up to the 50th anniversary of the atomic bombing of Hiroshima on August 6, 1945. The American ambassador, Walter F. Mondale, was personally interested in a more complete historical reconciliation between the United States and Japan, and, as a former vice president of the United States, could take decisions on his own discretion that otherwise might have required approval from Washington. Thus, in a first for an American ambassador, he decided in 1995 to attend the annual Tokyo municipal commemoration of the American firebombing of Tokyo that occurred on March 10, 1945. The event was not directed against the United States, and Ambassador Mondale's attendance received little coverage in the Japanese and American media. But Mondale expressed concern to the author, then an officer at the embassy, about a number of critical letters he subsequently received from American veterans of World War II.

Later in the same year, with then-President Bill Clinton scheduled to travel to Japan to participate in the annual Asia-Pacific Economic Cooperation summit in Osaka, officials of the American embassy in Tokyo debated among themselves whether to recommend that President Clinton take the opportunity also to visit the atomic bombing memorial in Hiroshima to pay respects to those who died there in 1945. Ambassador Mondale listened carefully over several months to the various arguments. Advocates argued that a visit was morally the right thing to do and that it would strengthen bilateral relations. Opponents did not take issue with such intentions but expressed concern that many American citizens, especially World War II veterans, would criticize the President. They said the actual result would be to reopen old wounds and hurt bilateral relations. As evidence, they pointed to the controversy that had erupted just in the previous year, when the Smithsonian Institution in Washington, DC, planned to stage an exhibition of the aircraft that had dropped the atomic bomb on Hiroshima, only to be condemned by U.S. veterans' groups arguing that the exhibition script focused on the human casualties and shortchanged the military necessity of dropping the bomb. In any event, President Clinton cancelled his participation in the 1995 APEC meeting due to a crisis over the passage of the nation's budget. He did visit Japan the following year but did not travel to Hiroshima.

CURRENT U.S. POLICY

Because, for American policy makers, strategic considerations have consistently trumped issues of equity in historic disputes involving Japan since World War II, a brief look at current U.S. policy toward East Asia is warranted. Strategically, the administration of President George W. Bush initially was strongly inclined against China and toward Japan. Some members of the U.S. foreign policy establishment, especially Republicans, tended to regard the PRC as possibly becoming "the next Soviet Union." The resulting emphasis on strengthening the alliance with Japan was highlighted in the publication in 2000 of a bipartisan study of U.S. policy commonly called the "Armitage Report," after Richard L. Armitage, the study cochairperson who later served as deputy secretary of state in during George W. Bush's first term. It was in this report that the goal was put forward of Japan becoming an ally of the United States on the order of Great Britain.[9]

In the first few months of President Bush's first term, his administration's approach toward China was distinctly hostile. Then-Secretary of Defense Donald H. Rumsfeld, for example, opposed almost all military exchanges with the PRC. It was the terrorist attacks of 9/11 that prompted President Bush to take a different, more positive approach, as he came to regard China as potentially a major ally in the "global war on terror." Moreover, as the United States laid the groundwork for a preemptive attack on Iraq, the administration sought to minimize the chance that China would play an obstructionist role at the United Nations or even cast a UN Security Council veto.

Nevertheless, the impetus toward enhancing the U.S. alliance with Japan was undiminished. This was due in part to the fact that President Bush and Prime Minister Koizumi enjoyed a remarkable personal chemistry. (Koizumi's last visit to the United States as prime minister even involved President Bush's flying him to Tennessee on Air Force One to visit the home of Koizumi's musical hero, Elvis Presley.) Senior political appointees at both the state and defense departments were also deeply committed to having Japan play a larger security role.

While the Bush administration has continued to work with some success to improve relations with China, it has proceeded with earlier plans to hedge, at least, against China's rise. In addition to the enhanced alliance with Japan, the United States has strengthened military ties with Australia, and has encouraged a nascent trilateral alliance involving the United States, Japan, and Australia. The United States has sought to improve relations with other countries on China's periphery, especially India.

The Bush administration also sharply criticized China for increases in its defense spending and for not being more transparent about its defense budget and activities. Senior U.S. officials, including the vice president and the secretary of defense, publicly chided China, asking what threat it faced to warrant such an approach.[10] With the United States seeking improved relations with many states ringing China and with U.S. defense spending alone almost equal to the total defense spending of the rest of the world's countries *combined*, the Chinese were clearly angered by the American criticism.[11]

LOOKING AHEAD

While pragmatic Bush administration officials, such as then-Deputy Secretary of State Robert Zoellick, put forward the more positive notion of China as an international "stakeholder," there needs to be a review and reconsideration of U.S. strategic policy in East Asia. The Bush administration's approach of hedging against China could, if not every carefully calibrated, make matters worse by provoking a Chinese overreaction.

It is this context that makes the current historical disputes between Japan and China and Korea even more important. The long-standing U.S. desire for Japan to play an increasing role in regional security affairs threatens to backfire on U.S. interests as long as Japan's closest and most powerful neighbors fear that its failure to "understand" the past may cause it eventually to repeat the past.

Further complicating matters is that many members of the Japanese foreign policy establishment genuinely appear to believe that the main problem is that the Chinese and South Korean governments have cynically used Japanese historical issues to boost their domestic support. They do not appreciate the depth of feeling about the historical disputes in China and Korea, not only on the part of the citizenry but also of most leaders.

On the other hand, many Chinese and Koreans do not appreciate just how different the Japan of today is from that of 70 years ago. They view Japanese words and deeds through the lens of collective—in some cases, manufactured—memories, and tend to focus on anything that seems to affirm their suspicions about Japan while ignoring evidence to the contrary. There has, for example, been much concern expressed publicly in China and Korea in recent years about Japanese "militarization." It is doubtful that more than a few percent of the citizens of the PRC and the ROK know that, in fact, Japanese defense spending has been reduced five consecutive years through 2006.[12]

With the next U.S. presidential election occurring in November 2008, consideration of U.S. policy toward East Asia, including the U.S. approach toward historical issues involving Japan, is timely. Presidential candidates and their advisers are looking at the issues afresh to establish their campaign platforms, and the winning candidate, whether Republican or Democrat, will initiate many policy reviews at the beginning of his or her term. In all probability, however, whoever becomes the next U.S. president will not substantially change the U.S. approach toward Japanese-related historical issues, for the reasons discussed above. The situation could change slightly if the Japanese government takes more provocative positions, as happened when Prime Minister Abe backtracked on the comfort women issue.

The situation is not necessarily bleak. A strategic concern for good relations among Japan, the PRC, and the ROK will probably prompt all three countries to seek to prevent a profound worsening of relations. For example, Premier Wen Jiabao's diplomatically worded speech to the Japanese Diet in April 2007 appeared to have been the result of a revised policy calculus among the Chinese leadership after anti-Japanese demonstrations in Chinese cities became violent.[13] Similarly, Japanese Prime Minister Abe adopted a more circumspect approach toward China and the ROK in the wake of the controversy surrounding his predecessor's visits to the Yasu-kuni Shrine, and Abe's successor, Yasuo Fukuda, publicly indicated he intended to be even more sensitive to the historical concerns of Japan's neighbors. Strong and wise leaders will recognize that letting the most extreme elements in each country set the agenda on such matters is not in the interest of any of the concerned countries.

Several related factors, however, make it unlikely that historical issues will simply disappear of their own accord. They include the increasingly open nature of politics and society in all three countries, rising levels of wealth and education, and the communications revolution, especially access to the Internet. Thus, a billion and a half people in the region will soon be a part of the dialogue about, and the process of addressing, historical issues. But it also means that they will travel to and live and work in the neighboring countries much more than in the past. They will be better educated and much better informed. Whether, on balance, these factors will serve to resolve the issues or to inflame them, remains to be seen. People tend to seek out and absorb information consistent with their existing beliefs. Wise government leadership in all concerned countries, including the United States, will probably yet be of decisive importance.

SUGGESTIONS FOR U.S. POLICY

U.S. support for historical reconciliation should and must be just a part of a much larger U.S. policy of helping integrate a rising China fully into East Asian and world affairs. That will take a more farsighted foreign policy toward the region and especially China than the United States has proved capable of so far. Putting the focus on the future and the opportunities available if the countries and the peoples of the region work together will not only make for a better life for all but will also help to create a context in which historical reconciliation will become easier to achieve.

Given Japan's anxiety about the rise of China, the United States must also offer Japan constant and credible reassurance of its support. In strengthening the U.S.-Japan alliance, both the United States and Japan should "speak softly and carry a big stick." That is sometimes the opposite of what they are doing now. The U.S.

approach must also include a better effort to understand South Korean concerns and address the challenges posed by North Korea. The United States should intensify efforts to transform the current Six-Party Talks into a standing Northeast Asian regional leadership forum. While keeping a strong military presence in the Asia-Pacific region, the United States should lower the profile of its military forces there and devote considerably more attention and resources to diplomacy.

As for specific historical issues, for the most part the U.S. government will not—and should not—become directly involved, for the reasons discussed above. The U.S. government should, of course, continue to stress publicly and privately its vital interest in good relations among all the countries of the region. U.S. officials should also continue to offer advice privately to counterparts from the concerned countries when nationalist dynamics become excessive. Rather than frontally addressing most historical disputes, the United States should seek to address the roots and the context of the issues.

U.S. universities and NGOs could make a contribution to increased understanding that the U.S. government *qua* government cannot. The U.S. government should offer increased financial and other support to universities and nongovernmental organizations pursuing serious scholarship and promoting international understanding. Ideally, such scholarship should be focused on historical research conducted on a collegial basis by leading academics and experts from all concerned countries, designed, primarily, to narrow the range of differences about factual issues. People-to-people exchanges should concentrate on the younger generation, in programs designed to give them the experience of actually living, working, and playing together for an extended period of time.

Finally, the primary long-term focus should be on teaching young people in all countries to think critically about history and politics, including those of their own country. Recognizing our common humanity, including our common failings, is fundamental to facilitating the discussion and resolution of the historical differences among us. The result will be wiser and more informed citizens and leaders.

NOTES

1. A BBC public opinion survey conducted in late 2005 found that, among the people of eight Asian countries, South Koreans and Chinese had by far the most critical views of Japan, with 54% of South Koreans and 71% of Chinese responding that Japan's influence in the world was "mainly negative." See http://www.globescan.com/news_archives/bbc06-3.

2. Following is a typical exchange between a journalist and the State Department spokesperson involving the spokesperson's refusal to comment at all. JOURNALIST: Do you have any comments on the...diplomatic dispute between Korea and Japan now on the island of Tokdo [*sic*], in Japanese name, Takeshima? SPOKESPERSON: No. JOURNALIST: This make really great tension between two countries. SPOKESPERSON: No, I don't. I have nothing to say on that one. From the U.S. Department of State Daily Press Briefing, March 15, 2005. http://www.state.gov/r/pa/prs/dpb/2005/43486.htm.

3. Following is an example of such an exchange between a journalist and the State Department spokesperson. JOURNALIST:...Koizumi visited Japanese [Yasukuni] shrine again, and

Chinese and South Korean angry…So are you concerned? SPOKESPERSON:…we would hope that countries in the region could work together to resolve their concerns over history in an amicable way and through dialogue.…we all share an interest in good relations among the countries of the region and…would hope that in light of that that they could work through any concerns that they might have through dialogue, through negotiation, through respectful dialogue. From the U.S. Department of State Daily Press Briefing, October 17, 2005. http://www.state.gov/r/pa/prs/dpb/2005/55210.htm.

4. Dwight D. Eisenhower, *Mandate for Change, 1953–1956: The White House Years* (Garden City: Doubleday, 1963), pp. 312–13.

5. "'Comfort Women' Military Rape Victims: Schieffer," *The Japan Times,* March 18, 2007. http://search.japantimes.co.jp/cgi-bin/nn20070318a2.html.

6. *Sense of House that Japan Should Apologize for Its Imperial Armed Force's Coercion of Young Women into Sexual Slavery* HR Res. 121, 110th Congr., 1st sess. (July 30, 2007): H 8870. http://thomas.loc.gov/cgi-bin/query/F?r110:1:./temp/~r110Dp8q8h:e0:.

7. *Recognizing the Strong Security Alliance between Japan and the United States.* HR Res. 508, 110th Congr. 1st sess. (September 5, 2007): H10091. http://thomas.loc.gov/cgi-bin/query/D?r110:20:./temp/~r110Tur33t::.

8. Brian Walsh, "Between the Shrine and a Hard Place," *Time,* August 16, 2006. (http://www.time.com/time/world/article/0,8599,1227612,00.html).

9. "The United States and Japan: Advancing Toward a Mature Partnership" (also known as The Armitage Report or The Nye-Armitage Report) (Washington, DC: Institute for National Strategic Studies, National Defense University, October 11, 2000).

10. "Rumsfeld Warns on China Military," CNN.com, June 4, 2005. http://www.cnn.com/2005/WORLD/asiapcf/06/04/rumsfeld.asia.ap/.

11. Based on estimates of the Stockholm International Peace Research Institute, U.S. defense expenditures in 2006 were about 45 percent of the world total. http://first.sipri.org/non_first/milex.php.

12. Through the year 2006, according to the Stockholm International Peace Research Institute. http://yearbook2007.sipri.org/chap8.

13. The full text of Wen's speech is at http://chineseinvancouver.blogspot.com/2007/04/full-text-of-wen-jiabaos-speech-to.html.

12

Russia and Historical Memories in East Asia

Tsuyoshi Hasegawa

In recent conflicts over historical memories between Japan and its neighbors, Russia has not figured prominently. Russia has been a silent bystander on Japanese Prime Minister Junichiro Koizumi's Yasukuni Shrine visits, the textbook controversy, and comfort women issues that have caused passionate debates between the Japanese and their neighbors in Korea and China. It is important to stress, however, that Russia, too, has a great deal to do with the battle of historical memories. In fact, the tortuous postwar relations between Japan and Russia have evolved around historical memories about what the Japanese call the "Northern Territories" issue. What is unique about Russia's place in historical memories is not that Russia has little to do with them. Rather, it is that the battle of historical memories between the Japanese and the Russians has been waged in a different context than the one that has been fought between Japan and its Asian neighbors. Neither the Koreans, nor the Chinese, nor the Japanese have shown any interest in including the Russian dimension in the debate of historical memories.

There is another important aspect that distinguishes the conflict over the historical memories between Russia and Japan from the one between Japan and its East Asian neighbors. As far as the memories of World War II are concerned, the Japanese feel that they were the victims of unjust aggression by the Soviet Union in a similar way that the Chinese and Koreans feel that they were victims of Japan's aggression and colonialism. The victim-victimizer relations are reversed in Russo-Japanese relations, in contrast to Sino-Japanese and Korean-Japanese relations.

This chapter is an attempt to broaden the scope of the debate on historical memories to include Russia. By so doing, we may be able to compare the uniqueness of Japanese imperialism that encroached into Korea and China in competition with Russian imperial ambitions. By including Russia, we may be able to elevate the debate to a higher level by placing it in the context of imperialist expansion in East Asia. The Japanese argument that Japan's imperialist aggression in Korea and China can be justified in the light of the standards that existed at the time has a certain merit, but placing Japan's aggression in the context of comparative imperialism will help highlight the uniqueness of Japanese imperialism, thereby underscoring the legitimate grievances that the Chinese and the Koreans have specifically directed against the Japanese. Second, and more importantly, by transferring the sense of victimization the Japanese hold against the Soviet Union to the sufferings the Chinese and the Koreans experienced by Japan's own actions, the Japanese may be able to reach a new understanding of the accusations that the Chinese and the Koreans have leveled against Japan's aggressions and colonialism.

TERRITORIAL DISPUTE

Russia and Japan have not been able to accomplish historic reconciliation by concluding a peace treaty. This is because they have not been able to resolve the territorial dispute involving what the Japanese call the "Northern Territories" and what Russians call the "southern Kuril islands," three islands (Etorofu, Kunashiri, Shikotan) and the Habomai group of small islets in the southern part of the Kuril Chain. Historical claims are at the center of this dispute.

The Shimoda Treaty in 1855 between Russia and Japan demarcated the border between Uruppu and Etorofu. Russia thus acknowledged the currently disputed islands as Japanese territory. In 1875, both countries concluded the St. Petersburg Treaty, by which Russia and Japan exchanged Sakhalin and the rest of the Kurils. Thus, the entire island of Sakhalin became Russia's territory, while the entire Kurils became Japan's possession. In 1905, at the end of the Russo-Japanese War, Russia and Japan concluded the Portsmouth Treaty, by which Russia ceded south Sakhalin to Japan. Sakhalin became divided into Russian north, and Japanese south. During the Russian Civil War after the Russian Revolution, Japan sent troops to Siberia and the Russian Far East, and occupied northern Sakhalin. The Japanese eventually withdrew troops from the Soviet territory, and concluded a treaty in 1925 with the Soviet Union to restore diplomatic relations, but no territorial changes took place. Thus, until the Soviet Union entered the war against Japan on August 9, 1945, the Japanese held south Sakhalin (which it acquired after the Russo-Japanese War) and the entire Kurils, which it had legitimately obtained by two peacefully concluded treaties.[1]

In April 1941, Japan and the Soviet Union concluded a Neutrality Pact, which obligated one party to stay neutral in a war in which the other party was involved. When the Pacific War began with Japan's attack on Pearl Harbor in December 1941, the United States solicited Soviet participation in the war against Japan. Citing the Soviet commitment to the Neutrality Pact as well as the Soviet preoccupation with the war against Germany, Stalin refused to accept President Franklin D. Roosevelt's plea to join the war against Japan at that time. But the tide of war changed in 1943, and Stalin hinted at the possibility of joining the war against Japan after the German defeat. Finally, in February 1945, Roosevelt and Stalin (joined by Churchill) concluded a secret Yalta Protocol by which Stalin committed to joining the war against Japan three months after the German defeat in exchange for securing concessions over railways and ports in Manchuria, the return of south Sakhalin, and "handing over" of the Kurils to the Soviet Union.[2]

The Soviet Union entered the war against Japan on August 9 in violation of the Neutrality Pact. Only after the Japanese government accepted surrender on August 14 did Stalin order the ill-prepared Kuril operation. By skillfully combining diplomatic maneuvers with military operations, Stalin managed to occupy the entire Kurils, including the southern part of the Kurils (Etorofu, Kunashiri, Shikotan and Habomai) that had never been Russia's territory.[3]

After Japan's defeat and six years' occupation by the Allied powers, Japan gained independence by concluding the San Francisco Peace Treaty in 1951. By accepting this treaty, Japan renounced all claims, rights, and privileges over the Kurils. But the Soviet Union did not sign the San Francisco Peace Treaty, thereby losing the chance to legitimize the possession of the Kurils that Japan had renounced. Furthermore, the treaty did not precisely define the boundaries of "the Kurils."[4]

In 1955–56 Japan and the Soviet Union engaged in negotiations for the conclusion of a peace treaty, but, unable to resolve the territorial dispute, they only managed to restore diplomatic relations by signing and ratifying the Joint Declaration, by which the Soviet government pledged to return the two smaller islands, Shikotan and the Habomai group, after concluding a peace treaty. This territorial provision was unilaterally abrogated by Khrushchev in 1960, when Japan renewed the Security Treaty with the United States.[5]

From then on the Japanese government and the Soviet/Russian governments have been engaged in endless debate over the disputed territories. Japan claims that the disputed territories were part of Japan's inherent territory that it legitimately gained through the peaceful treaties with the Russian government. As for the San Francisco Peace Treaty, the Japanese government has engaged in a legal contortion by claiming that the "Kurils" over which Japan renounced its claims refers only to the northern half of the Kurils, distinct from the southern part of the Kurils. For this reason, the Japanese government ceased to use the term, "*Minami Chishima*," and invented the term, "the Northern Territories."[6] The Japanese government has consistently taken the position that the return of all "the Northern Territories" is the precondition for concluding a peace treaty.[7]

The Russian/Soviet governments have countered the Japanese demand for retrocession of the disputed islands by arguing (1) that the Russians first discovered, colonized, and took possession of the disputed territories; (2) that the treaties of 1855 and 1875 were forced upon the Russian government under duress; (3) that the Yalta Agreement legitimated the Soviet (hence, Russian) claims over the Kurils; and (4) that Japan had already renounced its claims over the disputed islands by signing the San Francisco Peace Treaty. The intransigent positions on both sides have prevented the Soviet Union/Russia and Japan from concluding a peace treaty and achieving historic rapprochement to this day.[8]

A brief history of the territorial dispute between Russia and Japan makes it clear that the center of contention was their divergent historical interpretations and historical memories. The territorial dispute is not merely a dispute over the contested islands. Behind this dispute looms a dispute over historical memory in a larger context, about which I will discuss in more detail later in this chapter.

China's position on the Russo/Soviet-Japanese territorial dispute has gone through a drastic transformation in accordance with geopolitical change in East Asian international relations. At the height of the Sino-Soviet dispute, in which China considered Soviet hegemonism its most dangerous threat, China supported Japan's position over the Soviet-Japanese territorial dispute. Mao Zedong declared in 1964 that the Kurils should be returned to Japan, while Zhou Enlai twice stated in 1972 and 1973 that China would support Japan's demands for the return of the disputed islands. In 1976 the vice-president of the People's Congress Standing Committee even went as far as to state to the Japanese delegation from Hokkaido: "Unless you fight, the Soviet Union will not be satisfied with obtaining the four islands as its territory, and it will lay its hands on Hokkaido, too."[9]

As Beijing and Moscow began rapprochement in the early 1980s, China spoke less frequently about the Soviet-Japanese territorial dispute. It stopped characterizing the disputed territory "under Soviet occupation since the Second World War." After Sino-Soviet rapprochement was achieved at the time of Gorbachev's visit to Beijing in 1989, China's position on the territorial dispute became neutral. In March 1991, the Chinese government issued a statement: "The northern territories represent a problem between Japan and the Soviet Union. We hope that this matter will be settled by negotiations between the two states."[10]

South Korea's position on the "Northern Territories" dispute is not clear. It seems that the South Korean government took no position on this dispute during the Cold War. On the one hand, the Soviet Union was an avowed enemy that supported North Korea in the Korean War, but on the other, Japan was the former colonial power, which the Koreans had little reason to support. In fact, after South Korea and the Soviet Union restored diplomatic relations in 1989, the South Korean government tacitly approved the operation of South Korean fishing vessels along the disputed territories in agreement with the Soviet fishing authorities. The South Koreans, thus, implied recognition of the Soviet sovereignty over the disputed islands, although the Soviet government discontinued this practice for fear that it would complicate its relations with Japan.

In the new geopolitical reality after the Cold War, the position of either China or South Korea on the Russo-Japanese territorial dispute is not clear. But it is important to note that the Russo/Soviet-Japanese territorial dispute, which had been separated during the Cold War from the territorial disputes between China and Japan and between South Korea and Japan, has become merged into one territorial issue in the broader context of the World War II settlement. China and Japan have a territorial dispute over the Senkaku/Diaoyutai islands, which are also claimed by Taiwan. In 1978, when Japan and China concluded a treaty of peace and friendship, both countries agreed to leave the sovereignty over of the islands unresolved. But with the rising tide of nationalism in China, there has emerged a grassroots demand to claim the islands.

Japan also has a territorial dispute with South Korea over the Takeshima/Dokdo islands. The islands are now under Korean control, but the Japanese claim its sovereignty over the islands. In 2005 Shimane prefecture passed a resolution claiming Japan's possession of the islands, fanning the Korean nationalist movement for the sole possession of the islands.

Although neither the Chinese nor the Koreans have thus far connected their territorial claim over the disputed islands with the "Northern Territories" question, the Japanese can no longer isolate the "Northern Territories" question from other territorial disputes. Japan's claims to historical legitimacy for each of these islands are encountering virulent nationalistic sentiments in China, South Korea, and Russia. To the extent that these territorial issues resulted from World War II settlement, and, further, that none of these three countries with the territorial dispute with Japan was a party to the San Francisco Peace Treaty, there exists a possibility that they might forge a united front against Japan over the territorial dispute in a larger context of Japan's responsibility for the war. Japan's territorial disputes with its neighboring countries will inevitably be placed in a larger context of reconfigurations of power relations in Northeast Asia. Japan's isolation in the recent Six-Party Talks with regard to the North Korean nuclear issue might lead to the formation of the loose coalition among Russia, China, and South Korea. There is a distinct possibility that such a coalition will be strengthened by their concerted position on the territorial dispute against Japan, especially if Japan's right wing pushes the argument justifying Japan's involvement in World War II.

JAPAN'S GRIEVANCES AGAINST THE SOVIET UNION

To the Japanese "the Northern Territories Dispute" was not merely a territorial dispute. Japan's intransigent demand for the return of all four islands as a precondition for concluding a peace treaty is a symbolic expression to redress historical justice for the sum total of wrongs that the Soviet Union committed against the Japanese in the concluding weeks of the Pacific War. The Soviet Union attacked the Japanese forces in Manchuria and Korea by surprise, in violation of the Neutrality Pact that was still in force, and precisely at the moment when the Japanese government was requesting Moscow's mediation to terminate the war. The Soviet troops quickly penetrated into Manchuria, Korea, and southern Sakhalin (Karafuto), committing atrocities against Japanese civilians and pillaging their properties. There were approximately 2.7 million Japanese in the Soviet occupied territories at the end of the war. Approximately 150,000 disappeared, and more than 640,000 Japanese, both government officials and the military personnel, were captured by the Soviets, and sent to the forced labor camps that were scattered throughout the Soviet Union.

More than 60,000 Japanese POWs died in the camps, and the last POWs did not return to Japan until 1956. Stalin ordered the Kuril campaign only after the Japanese government accepted unconditional surrender on August 14 and occupied the entire Kurils, including the southern Kurils that had never been a part of the Russian/Soviet territory. More than 420,000 Japanese were driven out of Sakhalin and the Kurils, of whom 27,000 were from the Kurils.

As Kazuhiko Togo argues in Chapter 3, despite a small, vociferous voice of the right wing that justifies Japan's past colonialism and aggression, the majority of Japanese accept that Japan committed the transgressions of colonialism against Korea and a war of aggression against China and southeast Asia. In contrast, the over-whelming majority of the Japanese consider the Soviet actions in the waning weeks of the Pacific War "dastardly," "illegal," and "treacherous," and characterize them as a "*kajiba dorobo*," a thief who steals at the site of fire from those who are victimized by fire. Public opinion surveys have consistently registered the Soviet Union and Russia, even after the collapse of the Soviet Union, as the number one disliked country among the Japanese.[11]

How have the Japanese navigated the treacherous moral channels between their culpability in the past transgressions of colonialism in Korea and aggressions in China and Southeast Asia and their justifiable grievances against the Soviet actions in the closing weeks of the Pacific War? The answer is simple: the Japanese do not treat the Soviet-Japanese War as a part of the Pacific War. There were two completely separate events. While most Japanese accept that they were the perpetrators of colonialism in Korea and the war of aggression in China and Southeast Asia, they believe that they were the victims of Soviet aggression and unjust conduct. The Cold War that began soon after the end of the war before Japan restored diplomatic relations with the Soviet Union, reinforced Japan's sentiments against the "crimes" committed by the Soviet Union. The Soviet war against Japan, together with the American atomic bombings on Hiroshima and Nagasaki, injected into the Japanese a sense of victimization, greatly contributing to their failure to face their own culpability in the war Japan waged in Asia.

There is another peculiarity about Japanese historical memory about Russo/Soviet-Japanese relations: its memory begins only after August 9, 1945, when the Soviet troops crossed the Manchurian border, and it never extends back before that date. But Russians' historical memory goes farther back. They remember the humiliation of the defeat in the Russo-Japanese War, which injected what Jonathan Haslam calls the "Portsmouth complex."[12] During the peace negotiations to end the Russo-Japanese War, Russia's chief negotiator, Sergei Witte, told his Japanese counterpart, Jutaro Komura, not to be vengeful for demanding territorial concessions, citing the example of Alsace-Lorraine after the Franco-Prussian War. Komura did not heed this plea, insisting on the concession of South Sakhalin.[13] Not only the defeat of the war but also the territorial concessions instilled a sense of humiliation among the Russians. This eventually led to Stalin's famous victory statement: "We, old generation, have waited for forty years to remove this humiliation."[14]

During the Russian civil war, Japan engaged in the "Siberian intervention," dispatching troops to Siberia, the Soviet Far East, and Northern Sakhalin. Japan's ostensible purpose was to help the Czech legion that revolted against the Bolshevik regime, but from the very beginning, its foremost objective was its territorial aggrandizement. But its goal was frustrated by the United States as much as by the Soviet resistance. Atrocities were committed by both sides. If the Japanese remember the massacre of 300 Japanese civilians by the Soviet partisans in Nikolaevsk in 1920, Japanese troops also committed equally brutal atrocities against the Russians in Vladivostok and the village of Ivanovka. The legend of Sergei Lazo, the partisan leader, who was burned to death in the boiler of a locomotive, has been immortalized in Soviet textbooks.[15] The Historical Museum in Vladivostok displays a photograph of the Japanese soldiers proudly displaying several severed heads of Russian victims in the massacre in Vladivostok.

Japan's invasion of Manchuria in 1931 opened a new page in Soviet-Japanese relations, as Japan's expansionism posed a real threat to Soviet security. The Soviets attempted to diffuse this threat through various methods, including appeasement and collective security, but in the end they had to rely on their military strength to prevent Japanese aggression. The Soviet government built the Pacific Fleet, double-tracked the Siberian Railway, fortified the border, created the Far Eastern Military District, and reinforced troops and equipment in the Far East. When border conflicts occurred in Lake Khasan in 1938 and in Nomonhan in 1939, the Soviet army defeated the Japanese forces. The Japanese threat was not a figment of the imagination of the suspicious Soviet dictator. It was real, as there existed a powerful faction within the military that favored the invasion of the Soviet Union as Japan's first priority. If Japan did not attack the Soviet Union, as it invaded Manchuria in 1931, it was due to Soviet military strength. The development of Stalin's totalitarian regime in the 1930s had its own internal logic, but Japan's threat to the Soviet security played one part in it.[16]

When Soviet Foreign Minister Eduard Shevardnadze visited Japan in December 1988, he appealed for mutual understanding of the historical past, saying that both sides should feel the pains caused to one side by the other. Most of Japanese took this statement as a significant admission that the Soviet Union had caused pains on Japan by its actions in the Soviet-Japanese war in the concluding weeks of the Pacific War. But only a few extended Shevardnadze's statement to its own history and pondered upon how much pain the Japanese had caused the Russians and the Soviets.

The Japanese have legitimate grievances against the Soviet actions in the Soviet-Japanese War from August 9 through September 5, 1945. But these grievances must be placed in three additional historical contexts. First, the Japanese should recognize that the Soviet Union joined the war against Japan as an ally of the United States, China, and other allied powers. Although Stalin entered the war to achieve his geostrategic goals, and although Truman and some of his advisers became concerned with Soviet expansionism in the Far East, the United States solicited and encouraged Soviet entry into the war, at least, until February 1945. Some, like Army Chief of Staff George C. Marshall and Secretary of War Henry L. Stimson, considered Soviet entry into the war a favorable factor in forcing Japan's surrender. Chiang Kai-shek clearly welcomed Soviet participation in the war. The Japanese government had an option to end the war before the Soviets launched a surprise attack, but it unrealistically pursued the policy to seek Moscow's mediation to terminate the war, thereby falling into Stalin's trap. That was a colossal diplomatic failure, for which the Japanese themselves are to be blamed. Certainly the Soviet entry into the war against Japan was a clear violation of the Neutrality Pact. But no other nation except Japan blamed the Soviet Union for this violation. Besides, the Neutrality Pact was a transparent marriage of convenience, and the Japanese themselves contemplated breaking it if the opportunity presented itself. Thus, the Soviet-Japanese war must be placed in the context of the overall history of World War II, and the Soviet entry into the war must be understood in the broader context of international relations at that time.[17]

Second, the Soviet-Japanese War should be understood in the longer historical context of Russo/Soviet-Japanese relations. The Japanese have legitimate claims over the "Northern Islands," but at the same time, they should remember that the Russians also suffered the humiliation of ceding to Japan southern Sakhalin, a part of its inherent territory in the same way that the southern Kurils are a part of Japan's inherent territory, after it suffered defeat in the Russo-Japanese War. The brutality with which the Soviet troops treated the Japanese civilians was inexcusable, but at the same time the Japanese should also remember that Japan's Siberian expedition in 1918–22 also involved numerous atrocities committed against Soviet civilians by Japanese soldiers.

The last point is most relevant to this volume: Japanese historical memory of the Soviet-Japanese war must be viewed in the broader context of the historical memory of the Pacific War. The relationship between victims and perpetrators is reversed in the Soviet-Japanese War, on the one hand, and Japan's colonial rule over Korea and the Sino-Japanese War, on the other. When Japanese feel the pain that was inflicted on their fellow citizens by the Red Army soldiers, they must also be able to feel the similar pains that Japanese soldiers inflicted upon the Chinese. If the Soviet treatment of 640,000 Japanese prisoners in Soviet labor camps was an inexcusable act, then the Japanese should be able to feel the pains of the Chinese and the Koreans, dragooned to forced labor in Japanese industries and mines, and recruited as comfort women in service of the Japanese soldiers. Japan's legitimate grievances must therefore be accompanied by its own repentance for the past transgressions.

JAPANESE IMPERIALISM AND RUSSIAN/SOVIET IMPERIALISM

Manchuria and China

Since the late nineteenth century Russia and Japan were the most important, predatory imperialist rivals in East Asia, eager to expand their influence at the expense of China and Korea. In 1858 and 1860, Russia concluded two treaties with the weakened Qing dynasty, and obtained an enormous area of land north of the Amur and east of the Ussuri. From then on, Russia and modernized Japan crossed swords to expand their respective influence in Manchuria. The strategic Liaodong Peninsula with the commercial port of Dairen/Dalian and the naval base of Port

Arthur (Lüshun) changed hands, first to Japan after the Sino-Japanese War in 1894–95, which Japan was forced to give up by the Russian-led Triple Intervention, only to see the Russians retake it in 1898. But after the victory of the Russo-Japanese War, the Japanese regained the peninsula until the end of World War II. To protect Japanese interests, the Kwantung Army was established.[18]

Two railways that constituted the arteries in Manchuria were vital to the control of the region. As a Tokyo magazine observed, "The means of extending one's territory without the use of troops...is railway policy."[19] After the Sino-Japanese War, the Russians secured the right and the control of the Chinese Eastern Railway that traversed Manchuria, connecting the Trans-Siberian Railway directly to Vladivostok. The Russians built the Southern Manchurian Railway connecting the Chinese Eastern Railway down to Port Arthur in the Liaodong Peninsula. Following the victory of the Russo-Japanese War, the Japanese gained two-thirds of the Southern Manchurian Railway, which they protected with the Kwantung Army.

After the Russo-Japanese War, Japan and Russia established their respective spheres of influence by concluding three conventions. These conventions were designed to defy the Open Door policy by preventing the intrusion of other powers into Manchuria. Northern Manchuria was placed under the Russian sphere of influence and the southern part under Japan's control. Outer Mongolia proclaimed independence after the Qing dynasty fell, but soon the Russian government incorporated it under its sphere of influence.[20]

The outbreak of World War I left Japan free to pursue its interests in Asia. After declaring war against Germany, Japan quickly moved forces to Shandong, which had been leased to Germany, and presented the Twenty-One Demands to China in 1915, attempting to expand its influence not only in Manchuria but also in northern China. Britain and the United States lodged lukewarm protest against Japan's Twenty-One Demands, but to keep Japan in alliance against Germany accepted Japan's expansion. Trying to preserve its interests in Manchuria and Outer Mongolia, Russia did not protest, and in 1916, concluded an alliance with Japan. The Chinese joined the war on the side of Allies, and appealed to the Allies at the Paris Peace Conference to repeal the Twenty-One Demands, and restore Shandong. But the Allies ignored China's plea, granting Shandong to Japan in the Versailles Treaty. The Chinese strongly reacted to Japan's expansion, initiating the May Fourth Movement in 1919. It is worth remembering that Japan's expansionism played a major role in the birth of the modern Chinese nationalist movement.[21]

Japan's Intervention in Siberia and the Far East during the Russian Civil War did not alter the territorial arrangements over Manchuria. Japan participated in the Washington conference and concluded the Nine Power Treaty, which respected China's independence and territorial integrity, and the Four Power Treaty, which respected the mutual interests of powers in the Far East.[22] The Soviet Union was excluded from the Washington system. Although the Soviet government renounced the unequal treaties concluded by the Tsarist government, it gradually regained their privileges that had been established in pre-Revolutionary times. The Soviet Union made Outer Mongolia its first satellite country, and kept the ownership of the

Chinese Eastern Railway. When the Manchurian Warlord Jang Zuolin attempted to seize the railway, the Soviets used their superior military force to protect it.[23]

Japan invaded Manchuria in 1931, which was followed by the establishment of Manchukuo. Nominally headed by the Manchurian Emperor, Puyi, Manchukuo was Japan's puppet government, with the Kwantung Army controlling every facet of the government. For instance, the commander-in-chief of the Kwantung Army, who was simultaneously Japanese ambassador to Manchukuo, "had at his disposal both the force and the authority to insist on having his own way in almost everything."[24] The Japanese invasion of Manchuria and its control over all Manchuria posed a serious security threat to the Soviet Union. The Soviet government sold the coveted Chinese Eastern Railway to the Japanese. But this appeasement did not assure Soviet security, which could be guaranteed only by the reinforcement of the military strength in the Soviet Far East. The Soviets scored a resounding victory over the Japanese army at Lake Khasan and in Nomonhan, thus deterring Japan's further attack on the Soviet Union. The outbreak of the second Sino-Japanese War in 1937 helped to divert the direction of Japanese aggression into China rather than to the Soviet Union. And when the Japanese attacked Pearl Harbor, the Soviet Union was finally spared from Japanese aggression.[25]

The Yalta Secret Agreement that Stalin concluded with Roosevelt and Churchill in February 1945 included the Soviets' preeminent rights over the Chinese Eastern Railway (CER), Southern Manchurian Railway, Dairen, and Port Arthur. During the Sino-Soviet negotiations for accepting the Yalta Agreement, the Chinese side resisted accepting these provisions as violations of China's sovereignty, but as the Soviets attacked the Japanese forces in Manchuria without a treaty with China, they had to accept them.

After the Chinese Revolution, Mao and Stalin clashed over these provisions, but Mao had to compromise on the condition that the railways and ports would be returned in due course. The CER was returned to China in 1952 and Dairen and Port Arthur in 1955.

Korea

Russia's and Japan's interests first clashed over Korea. Russia considered Korea, with its ice-free ports, a gateway to the Pacific. But to Japan, Korea represented a dagger pointed to Japan's belly.[26] It was Japan that forced an unequal treaty on Korea to pry open the hermit kingdom in 1876, as western imperialist powers had opened Japan. After this Russia and Japan jockeyed for influence in Korean dynastic politics. After Japan succeeded in ending China's nominal suzerainty over Korea, after the victory of the Sino-Japanese War in 1894–95, Japan gained dominance in Korean internal affairs. Japanese agents assassinated Empress Myeongseong, who was interested in inviting Russia to counter Japan's influence. But soon Russia succeeded in regaining its influence. Having abducted King Gojong to the Russian legation, the Russians secured timber concessions, appointed a Russian as the economic adviser for the Korean government, and established the Russo-Korean Bank. Japan was interested in resolving the differences by offering a deal by which Russia would agree to Japan's paramount concerns in Korea in return for Japan's recognition of Russia's primary interests in Manchuria. Nevertheless, Russian policy was increasingly dominated by Aleksandr Bezobrazov, an irresponsible adventurer who was engaged in unscrupulous timber concessions in the Tumen and Yalu river valleys. Tsar Nicholas II overruled Sergei Witte's wise counsel to seek peaceful resolution of differences with Japan, and favored an adventurous, intransigent position. Having acquired a major ally by the conclusion of the Anglo-Japanese Alliance, and unable to resolve the differences over Korea in the protracted negotiations, Japan launched an attack on Russia in 1904. Korea was the direct cause for the Russo-Japanese War of 1904–5.[27]

The Japanese defeated the Russians in the Russo-Japanese War. Russia was forced to recognize Japan's paramount political, military, and economic interest in Korea. Japan's exclusive interest in Korea was also recognized by the United States in the Taft-Katsura Agreement in 1905, by which Japan recognized U.S. paramount interest in the Philippines in return. Korea became Japan's protectorate in 1905. Japan's intrusion of all spheres of Korean politics, economy, and security, however, provoked Korean resistance. Japan's foreign minister Jutaro Komura recommended to the cabinet in 1909: since "Korean officials and people have not yet been brought into a completely satisfactory relationship with us," Japan must take actions in such a way so that "it cannot be resisted from within or from without."[28] After signing the second Russo-Japanese convention in 1910, and exploiting the assassination of Hirobumi Ito, Japan's former prime minister and Resident-General of Korea, in Harbin Station by a Korean patriot, An Jung-guen, Japan proceeded to annex Korea in 1910. The proud hermit kingdom lost its independence, and was reduced to a colony of the Japanese Empire.[29]

Japan established repressive military rule over Korea under the Governor-General. It undertook modernization by establishing a central bureaucracy, a modern police force, a system of railways and roads, the postal system, public health measures, and a universal educational system. But all these measures were designed to assimilate Korea into Japanese imperial rule under the Japanese Emperor. Through the educational system the Japanese imposed Emperor Worship on the Koreans, and forced the Koreans to worship in Shinto shrines and assume Japanese names. The Koreans were drafted into the Imperial Army, dragooned to forced labor, and recruited as "comfort women" to houses of prostitution in service for Japanese soldiers.

The Japanese imperial rule inevitably provoked Korean nationalism. In 1919, a nationwide demonstration, known as the March 1 (Samil) movement took place. Korean patriots formed secret organizations, and read the "Proclamation of Independence." Korean independent movements were brutally suppressed. The Koreans took inspiration from two sources for their independence movement, first, from Christian missionaries, and second, from Marxism from the Soviet Union. In fact, after the Japanese annexation of Korea, many Koreans fled to the Soviet Union, where future Korean communists to become North Korean leaders were trained by the Soviets. Nevertheless, as the Japanese threat became serious, the suspicious Soviet government deported more than 170,000 Koreans in the Soviet Far East to Central Asia in 1937, engaging in the first Soviet ethnic cleansing that was to be repeated in the Caucasus and the Crimea later during the war.

Although the Cairo Declaration in 1943, signed by Roosevelt, Churchill, and Chiang Kai-shek, pledged Korea's independence after the war, the Yalta secret agreement concluded between Roosevelt and Stalin did not include any provisions for Korea. Roosevelt felt that Korea was not ready for independence, and proposed a trusteeship. Stalin agreed to a trusteeship, but an agreement on Korea was never reached among the Allied powers.

When the Soviets entered the war on August 9, 1945, the Soviet troops moved into northern Korea. In response, the United States hastily drew a line at the 38th parallel to divide the country into the Soviet occupied north and the American occupied south. Denied full-fledged independence under a unified Korea after 35 years of the colonial rule under Japan, the Koreans were to see their country divided into the Communist-ruled North Korea (DPRK—Democratic Peoples' Republic of Korea) under Kim Il-sung and South Korea (ROK—Republic of Korea) ruled by authoritarian Syngman Rhee. In 1950, the North Korean invasion of the south touched off the Korean War.

Sino-Soviet Conflict

The relations between the Chinese Communist Party (CCP) and the Soviet Union have a checkered past. Immediately after its formation, the CCP was instructed to join the Guomindang in 1923 by the Comintern, but this policy that they had reluctantly accepted led to their wholesale massacre at Chiang Kai-shek's coup in 1927. Only remoteness from Moscow helped Mao Zedong to craft an indigenous revolutionary path based on the peasants. Stalin did not think China's communist revolution was realistic, calling the Chinese Communists "margarine Communists." When the CCP was making the last offensive against the Nationalists, Moscow counseled to halt their offensive at the Yantze. Mao's negotiations with Stalin after the successful Chinese Revolution were rancorous as they differed on the territorial issue. After having resisted Kim Il-sung's plea to invade South Korea, Stalin finally approved the invasion on the condition that Kim obtained Mao's approval. Although China's goal was to complete its national unification by incorporating Taiwan, Mao decided to support Kim's invasion of the south. Thus, the Korean War began. Facing the annihilation of the North Korean communists in the war, Stalin asked the Chinese to intervene. When Chinese volunteers crossed the Yalu, and saved the North Korean comrades from being overrun by the Americans and the South Koreans, the promised Soviet air cover never materialized. The Soviets extended military aid to China, but on a loan for China to repay.

From then on the Sino-Soviet split widened. As China plunged into the Great Leap Forward, all Soviet engineers assisting with China's nuclear development were withdrawn. China began labeling the Soviet Union as a revisionist power, too eager to compromise with the imperialist powers, and began portraying itself as the champion of anticolonial movements. The ideological conflict became elevated to a military conflict. In 1969, China and Russia fought a border war. As far as China was concerned, the Soviet Union became the number one security threat, and the Soviets contemplated a nuclear preemptive attack on China. With the normalization of relations with the United States and with Japan, China became a semi-security partner of the United States and Japan against "Soviet hegemonism." It was not until Gorbachev's visit to Beijing in 1989 that the Sino-Soviet conflict, which lasted three-quarters of a century, finally came to an end.

Russo-Japanese Imperialist Rivalry and Historical Memories

What does the Russo-Japanese imperialist rivalry mean in terms of the contemporary debate over historical memories between Japan and its neighbors? First of all, it means that Japan and Russia, even later the Soviet Union, were predatory imperialist power that sought expansion of interests and territory at the expense of China and Korea. Although the Soviet Union played an important role in defeating Japan in the Pacific War, it was by no means a liberating force that brought independence either to China or to Korea. The Soviet government was more anxious to secure the railways and the ports promised by the Yalta Agreement, and preferred to deal with the Nationalist government in China. The Soviet occupation in the northern half of Korea led to the division of Korea, and eventually led to the tragic Korean War. The Chinese and the South Koreans thus have many grievances against the Russians. There is a good reason, therefore, for neither China nor South Korea to bring Russia into the debate over historical memories.

Japanese conservatives make the argument that Japanese imperialism was nothing different from the conduct of other imperialist powers. They maintain that Japanese imperialist expansion into China and Korea was justified, if judged by the standards that existed in the age of imperialism. Japan's victory of the Russo-Japanese War signaled the first victory of non-European power against European imperialism, inspiring national liberation movements in Asia and Africa.[30] The Greater East Asian Co-Prosperity Sphere was the creation of Japan's economic bloc similar to the British Commonwealth, necessitated for the survival in the aftermath of the economic depression that began in 1929. These arguments are specious, however. China and Korea bore the brunt of Japanese aggression and colonialism more than from any other imperialist powers. As Beaseley states: "It is impossible to read the record of Japanese actions without recognizing that in the last resort Japan commanded."[31] Despite its aggressive intent, the Russians did not invade Manchuria and create a puppet government. They did not colonize Korea. Modernization that was achieved in puppet Manchukuo and colonized Korea cannot justify the very fact of aggression and colonialism just as any "civilized mission" cannot justify imperialism elsewhere.

As one of the important characters of Western imperialism was racism, Japanese imperialism was also marked by its own racism. Japanese expansion was ostensibly supposed to free Asia from the Western imperialist powers and establish partnership with these oppressed peoples in the areas into which Japan expanded. But this partnership was by no means equal: the Japanese were to command, and imposed *kokutai,* manifested in Japan's "imperial way."[32] Racial superiority was an overriding psychological motivation that governed Japanese conduct from the top policy-makers down to the soldiers on the ground. Racism imparted an especially brutal character in Japanese imperialism, unique even among imperialist powers. These include the Nanjing massacre in 1937 and the gruesome biological experiments conducted on the Chinese by Unit 731, which referred to the human subjects as "*maruta*" (logs), and the massacre of the Korean residents in the aftermath of the Great Kanto Earthquake in 1923.[33]

CONCLUSION

If the Russian factor is incorporated into the current debate over historical memories, we might enrich our understanding of the contentious issues fought between Japan and its neighbors and help to contribute to the eventual reconciliation.

Comparison between Russian imperialism and Japanese imperialism in China and Korea helps us to understand the uniqueness of Japanese aggression and colonialism. Historical grievances can be legitimately raised by people in former colonial and semi-colonial powers that suffered exploitation, oppression, destruction of indigenous cultures, as well as territorial losses, at the hands of imperialist powers. Like the Indians' grievances against the British, the Vietnamese grievances against the French, and the Philippines' grievances against the Americans, the Chinese and the Koreans, whose most prominent colonial power happened to be Japan, more than any other imperialist power, have legitimate grievances against Japan's transgressions in the past.

All imperialist powers—Japan, Russia, Britain, France, and the United States—wronged China, and Japan, Russia, and the United States also wronged Korea. But of all these imperialist powers, the brutality with which the Japanese carried out their imperialist expansion and rule was unique. Although Japanese imperial expansion in Asia was carried out with the ostensible goal to expel Western imperialist powers from Asia, the Japanese treatment of other Asian peoples was imbued with their own kind of racism. Japan's revisionist history that justifies Japanese aggression and colonialism, ignoring this racism, should be repudiated. Such a past can hardly be associated with the tradition of "beautiful Japan."

Japan's legitimate grievances about Soviet transgressions in the waning weeks of the Pacific War should not be isolated from the larger picture of the turbulent history of East Asia that culminated in World War II in Asia. It must be remembered that, although Soviet participation in the war against Japan was motivated by its geopolitical gains, the Soviet entry into the war (rather than the atomic bombings on Hiroshima and Nagasaki) was the single most important factor that finally forced the Japanese leaders to accept surrender. It is therefore a serious mistake for the Japanese to think that their grievances against Soviet actions in the Soviet-Japanese War can be automatically supported by the United States, China, and the former Allies against Japan. The end of the Cold War means that neither the United States nor China automatically supports Japan's claims against Russia, since the need to counter the Soviet threat is gone. Above all, Japan's claims over the "Northern Territories" against Russia can no longer be separated from other territorial disputes that Japan still has with its neighbors: the Senkaku/Diaoyutai islands with China and the Takeshima/Dokdo islands with South Korea. In fact, the right-wing nationalists' assertion that Japan's involvement in the war in Asia and the Pacific was a justifiable act of self-defense has the potential of pushing all Japan's neighbors to form a coalition against Japan, and further forcing the United States to abandon the neutral stand and side with China and South Korea on specific issues.

Finally, a sense of the national humiliation and pain that the Japanese suffered at the hands of the Soviets during the brief Soviet-Japanese War should be transferred to help the Japanese comprehend the similar humiliation and pain that the Chinese and the Koreans felt at Japan's aggression and colonialism. As Shevardnadze said in 1988, feeling the pain that a country caused in the past to others is a necessary first step toward reconciliation.

Nationalism, based on pride of national honor and tradition, cannot be incompatible with understanding and respect of others. Despite divergent interpretations of the past, the Asia-Pacific region is now experiencing a totally new opportunity that has not existed since the end of the nineteenth century. In the past, this region was characterized by fundamental conflicts between major powers. But such rivalry does not exist now. There has appeared an opportunity for the first time that major powers can established a new international order based on cooperation. Some aspects of international cooperation have been discernible, but divergent historical memories and the virulent debate on them have been impeding the process toward the establishment of such an international system.

Toward the reconciliation of the Asian nations and toward the establishment of such a system, it is essential that we incorporate the Russian factor in the debate on historical memories.

NOTES

1. See Chapters 1, 2, Tsuyoshi Hasegawa, *The Northern Territories Dispute and Russo-Japanese Relations,* vol. 1, *Between War and Peace, 1697–1985,* and chapter 14, vol. 2, *Neither War Nor Peace, 1985–1998* (Berkeley: International and Area Studies, University of California Berkeley, 1998).

2. See Chapter 1, Tsuyoshi Hasegawa, *Racing the Enemy: Stalin, Truman and the Surrender of Japan* (Cambridge, MA.: The Belknap Press of Harvard University Press, 2005).

3. Ibid.See chapter 7.

4. See Chapter 3, Hasegawa, *Northern Territories Dispute,* vol. 1.

5. Ibid. Chapter 4.

6. Before the Pacific War, Chishima was equivalent with the Kurils. Thus the argument that the Kurils refers only to the islands north of Uruppu is to say that the southern Kurils are not the Kurils. To justify this tortuous argument, the Japanese government eliminated all reference to Chishima from the official maps after 1956. Even the title of the prewar map, originally entitled "Mimani Chishima," in the National Geogrraphic Agency [*Kokudo chiriin*]

was changed to *"Hoppo ryodo,"* as if this new name had existed before the war. Hasegawa, *Northern Territories Dispute,* vol. 2, pp. 518–19.

7. Ibid. For more details, see chapter 14, vol. 2.

8. Ibid.

9. Joachim Glaubitz, *Between Tokyo and Moscow: The History of an Uneasy Relationship, 1972 to the 1990s* (Honolulu: University of Hawaii Press, 1995), pp. 136–42.

10. Ibid., p. 142.

11. Tsuyoshi Hasegawa, "Japanese Perceptions of the Soviet Union and Russia in the Postwar Period," in *Japan and Russia: The Tortunous Path to Normalization, 1949–1999,* ed. Gilbert Rozman, (New York: St. Martin's Press, 2000), pp. 273–312.

12. Jonathan Haslam, *The Soviet Union and the Threat from the East, 1933–41* (Pittsburgh: University of Pittsburgh Press, 1992), p. 1.

13. Wada Haruki, *Hoppo ryodo mondai: rekishi to mirai* (Tokyo: Asahi Shinbunsha, 1999), pp. 120–22.

14. Hasegawa, *Racing the Enemy,* p. 187.

15. See Hara Teruyuki, *Shiberia shuppei: kakumei to kansho, 1917–1922* (Tokyo: Chiku-mai shobo, 1989).

16. For the importance of the Japanese threat in Soviet foreign policy, see Haslam, *The Soviet Union and the Threat from the East,* chapter 2; Hasegawa, *Northern Territories,* vol. 1.

17. For this see Hasegawa, *Racing the Enemy.*

18. For Japanese imperial expansions, see W.G. Beasley, *Japanese Imperialism, 1894–1945* (Oxford: Clarendon Press, 1987); Peter Duus, *The Abucus and the Sword: The Japanese Pen-etration of Korea, 1895–1910* (Berkeley and Los Angeles: University of California Press, 1995), pp. 1–25. For Russian expansion into Asia, see G. Patrick March, *Eastern Destiny: Russia in Asia and the North Pacific* (Westport, Connecticut: Preager, 1996).

19. Quoted in Beasley, *Japanese Imperialism,* p. 74.

20. Beaseley, *Japanese Imperialism,* pp. 90–108. Also see Yoshimura Michio, *Nihon to Roshia,* rev. ed. (Tokyo: Nihon Keizai Hyoronsha, 1991), chapters 2 and 3.

21. Beaseley, *Japanese Imperialism,* pp. 108–15; Yoshimura, *Nihon to Roshia,* chapter 4.

22. See Akira Iriye, *The Origins of the Second World War in Asia and the Pacific* (London: Longman, 1987); Beaseley, *Japanese Imperialism,* chapter 11.

23 March, *Eastern Destiny,* chapters 20 and 21; Boris Slavinsky, *Chugoku kakumei to soren: Konichisen made no butaiura, 1917–1937* (Tokyo: Kyodo tsushinsha, 2002), chapters 1, 2, and 3.

24. Beaseley, *Japanese Imperialism,* p. 196.

25. Hasegawa, *Northern Territories,* vol. 1, chapter 2; Slavinsky, *Chugoku kakumei to soren,* chapters 4, 5, and 6.

26. For Japanese expansion into Korea before the annexation, see Duus, *The Abacus and the Sword.*

27. Beaseley, *Japanese Imperialism,* chapters 4, 5, and 6; March, *Eastern Destiny,* chapters 16, 17, 18; Duus, *The Abucus and the Sword,* chapters 1, 2, 3, 4, and 5. For the Russo-Japanese War, see John W. Steinberg, Bruce W. Menning, David Schimmelpenninck van der Oye, David Wolff, and Shinji Yokote, *The Russo-Japanese War in Global Perspective: World War Zero* (Leiden: Brill, 2005); Yokote Shinji, *Nichiro sensoshi* (Tokyo: Chuko shinsho, 2005).

28. Quoted in Beaseley, *Japanese Imperialism,* p. 89.

29. Beaseley, *Japanese Imperialism,* pp. 86–90; Duus, *The Abacus and the Sword,* chapter 6.

30. For the revisionist interpretation of the Russo-Japanese War, see Hirama Yoichi, *Nichiro senso ga kaeta sekaishi* (Tokyo: Fuyo shobo, 2005).

31. Beaseley, *Japanese Imperialism,* p. 256.

32. Ibid., p. 204.

33. For Japanese racism during the Pacific War, see John W. Dower, *War without Mercy: Race & Power in the Pacific War,* Part II (New York: Pantheon Books, 1986). For Japanese racism against the Koreans, see Duus, *The Abucus and the Sword,* chapter 11.

Conclusion

Tsuyoshi Hasegawa and Kazuhiko Togo

East Asia is blessed with unprecedented opportunities. Its economy is one of the most vibrant in the world. Imperialism and the ideological competition that characterized the conflict in this region since the end of the nineteenth century and during the Cold War have receded to the past, and the region now has great opportunities to forge an international system based on common security concerns and economic cooperation. Nevertheless, the rise of nationalism that has replaced ideology as the unifying force in each country is rekindling the memories of the past and hindering the formation of such an international system. East Asia is looking backward, when it should be looking forward.

Japan's Prime Minister Junichiro Koizumi's repeated visits to the Yasukuni Shrine, the Shimane prefecture's resolution to commemorate Japan's sovereignty over the contentious Takeshima/Dokdo Islands, the Japanese government's approval of a textbook reputed to "whitewash" Japan's past, and Prime Minister Shinzo Abe's reported denial of the government's involvement in recruiting comfort women have all triggered protests not only from the governments of China and South Korea, but also from the citizens of Japan's two neighbors. These protests have, in turn, generated anger among the right-wing politicians and opinion leaders in Japan. It appeared for a moment that the conflict over historical memories was spiraling into a major political crisis.

In the fall of 2007, however, we have witnessed important political changes in East Asia. In Japan, the Liberal Democratic Party suffered a catastrophic defeat in the

Upper House election in July, and in September, Prime Minister Abe abruptly announced his resignation. Yasuo Fukuda was chosen to succeed Abe as the prime minister. The succession from Abe to Fukuda brought about a clear change in the political atmosphere in Tokyo. Such issues as Yasukuni or comfort women, which provoked conflict with Japan's neighbors under Koizumi and Abe, are hardly heard in the fall of 2007. Fukuda was elected as prime minister primarily in order to tackle the difficult issue of the pension fund and to regain the credibility of the political system. But he also faces difficult foreign policy issues. Already in October 2007, Japan was forced to withdraw its naval ships from the Indian Ocean to support the coalition forces in Afghanistan. Given Fukuda's past record that emphasized Japan's friendly relations with its Asian neighbors, and further considering the internal and external agenda of higher priority, it is unlikely that history issues will be raised again under him in a provocative manner.

In China, the Chinese Communist Party reshuffled the leadership at the 17th Central Committee meeting in October 2007. Although Jiang Zemin still maintains his influence, Hu Jintao's leadership position seems to have been strengthened with the appointments of two new members to the Politburo to lead China after Hu Jin-tao's reign. The main focus of Hu's report was "scientific development," and he argued that the new leadership must squarely confront several structural problems in the Chinese economy, such as overheated investment and the income gap. The new Chinese leadership, given its huge internal problem and some tension within it between the pro-Hu group and pro-Jiang group apparently unresolved, will most likely not want to stir the political balance by raising the historical memory issue. The new leadership would have little to gain by fueling the emotions of public opin-ion, because it could easily be retargeted to the government itself, and, therefore, it is unlikely that China will initiate, unless provoked, any action to complicate its relations with Japan over historical issues.

In Korea, in the December election, Lee Myung-bak from the Grand National Party won a crushing victory against Chung Dong-young and put an end to the two terms of liberal leadership under Kim Dae-jung and Roh Moo-hyun. Although Lee shares a basic inclination toward the ultimate unification of North and South Korea, his pro-American foreign policy is expected to bring about more stability in South Korea's external relations. The new South Korean leadership under Lee Myung-bak, given the formidable task of siding more with the Americans while not alienating public sentiment to narrow the distance with North Korea, would find little reason to alienate Japan on historical issues, unless provoked by the Japanese side.

These changes may indicate that the tension that has existed for the past five years may lead to a period of lull. We must not, however, confuse this temporary lull for the ultimate resolution of the conflict over historical memories. What is needed now is to take advantage of this temporary respite, to take active and assertive measures to defuse the divergent historical memories in order to forge a new international system based on cooperation, bound by common economic and secu-rity interests, that will be able to withstand the differences of historical memories.

The authors who contributed to this volume do not speak in one voice on specific issues. There are disagreements on how to interpret Abe's statement on comfort women, on how best to resolve the Yasukuni visit issue, on whether Japan's apologies for the past transgressions are inadequate (compared to the Germans' repentance), on how the United States should be involved in the contentious issues of historical memory, and on whether or not optimism is warranted in looking for resolutions to the conflict on historical memories. Nevertheless, the authors are in unanimous agreement on a number of points.

We unanimously recognize the seriousness of the contentions on historical memories that are preventing three major East Asian countries from moving forward to create a system of cooperation. We all agree that the three East Asian powers must find ways to defuse the conflict on historical memories, if not to resolve it completely. It does not serve anyone's national interests to provoke tension over historical memories.

To borrow Thomas Berger's methodological approach to historical memory, each nation has a different historical experience, different political and national needs to maintain historical memory, and different cultural idioms by which to interpret history. Therefore, it is difficult and even impossible to achieve uniform historical interpretations acceptable to all nations and all peoples in these nations. But the authors agree on the need to maintain the dialogue through which people in different nations attempt to understand how other nations and other people interpret history differently. Recognizing differences and the roots of these differences is an important step, as Hiroshi Mitani and Mikyoung Kim argue, to narrowing the gap and toward writing regional histories that transcend national boundaries.

As Cheol Hee Park, Zhu Jianrong, and Kazuhiko Togo demonstrate, the rise of nationalism in China, South Korea, and Japan is the result of complex social, economic, political, and psychological changes that are taking place within each country, and these forces are often beyond the control of the government. It is therefore not enough for the governments to reach agreements as to how to handle the issues of historical memory or for the Japanese government to issue statements of apology, although such agreements and apologies would clearly help to ease the paths to reconciliation. Sustained efforts by scholars, politicians, opinion leaders, media, and business people through multiple avenues must be explored and intensified in order to come to a better mutual understanding. Already some attempts have been made, as Hiroshi Mitani points out, and positive results have been gained.

Historical disputes cannot be overcome in a zero-sum game. As Kazuhiko Togo argues, since the defeat of World War II, polarized views on modern Japanese history have existed. The first view, which became popular immediately after the war and has been held by the left-wing intellectuals, treats the history of modern Japan as an unmitigated series of aggressions abroad and oppression of the masses at home. In their view, the peoples in China and Korea as well as the Japanese masses were the victims of the Japanese ruling class. In contrast, there has been an opposing view that holds that the Japanese should feel proud of its past successful modernization and survival as a great power in the face of the constant threat of Western imperialism.

The most extreme faction of this view is represented by right-wing revisionists that justify, and even glorify, Japan's invasions of China, the colonialism in Taiwan, Korea, and Manchuria, and the Pacific War as Japan's justifiable reactions to the threat of Western imperialism.

The authors of this volume are unanimous in rejecting the views of the right that justifies and glorifies Japan's past transgressions in China and Korea as necessitated by the historical circumstances. Historical reconciliation is not possible without Japan's coming to terms with their past aggressions and colonialism that inflicted tremendous damage on the peoples of their neighboring countries. The right-wing revisionist view will further antagonize the governments and the citizens of China and South Korea against Japan, isolate Japan from its neighbors, push South Korea unwittingly to form a closer alliance with China, and create conflict with the United States.

Nevertheless, coalition by the Japanese left and Chinese and Korean nationalism will not necessarily lead to reconciliation, either, because this will not satisfy the need felt by many Japanese to take a sense of pride in the positive achievements that Japan has accomplished in its modern history. The solution will be provided only by the Japanese realist school, which, cognizant of the roots of nationalism in China and Korea that stemmed from Japanese expansion into China and colonialism in Korea, does not treat its own past as a total negative legacy. The realist school argues that it is all the more important to overcome the negative legacies of the past more forthrightly and squarely in order for Japan to assert its leadership in the international arena. In this volume, authors such as Kazuhiko Togo, Akihiko Tanaka, and Hiroshi Mitani represent this school. Their views have the acceptance of the scholars from the region such as Jin Linbo, Zhu Jianrong, Cheol Hee Park, and Mikyoung Kim.

It is important to note, however, that this middle-of-the road realist school has to take a more assertive role in policy-making in Japan, influencing the Japanese government and public opinion. With Abe's resignation and Fukuda's taking the leadership, there is a good opportunity for Japan to now move in a positive direction. Whether or not "things will get worse before they get better," as Gilbert Rozman predicts, depends partially on their role.

As Jin Linbo and Cheol Hee Park point out, the recent crisis involving historical memory was provoked by Japanese actions. As both argue, nationalism in both China and South Korea is reactive to Japanese actions. Therefore, it is incumbent upon Japan to restrain the right-wing provocations and assert strong leadership to diffuse the crisis.

As nationalism in China and South Korea is a natural reaction to the confidence they gain from their economic achievements and a result of profound political, social, and psychological change, nationalism in Japan also is a reaction to the psychological need among the Japanese to assess with pride the virtue, vision, and leadership that led Japan to modernity unique among the Asian nations. The Japanese right therefore has some grounds that have resonance among many Japanese. Nevertheless, in order for Japan to take more assertive leadership that is respected by others, there are two absolute prerequisites.

First, Japan's nationalism must be of the kind that is capable and willing to understand the pain of others. If the Japanese feel proud of the efforts of their forefathers to rid themselves of the unequal treaties imposed by Western imperialist powers, and if they feel the pains of their fathers and forefathers, victimized by the incendiary bombings, the atomic bombings, and Soviet invasion of Manchuria, Korea, South Sakhalin, and the Kurils, then it is possible, and even necessary, for the Japanese to feel the pain that their fathers and forefathers caused other peoples in Asia.

Second, the reevaluation of values must be directed inward. Those traditional values—humility, care, self-sacrifice, hard-work, courage, creativity, and initiative—that made Japan's modernization possible but that have been lost or diminished in contemporary Japan can be restored without chauvinistic exhortations directed against its neighbors. The right is justified in calling for Japan's spiritual rejuvenation by restoring public virtue in contemporary Japan where egocentric values predominate. Their voice, if directed at correcting the excessive results of modernization, can be constructive.

While we believe that the initiative to pave a path to reconciliation must be taken by the Japanese, this initiative must also be reciprocated by the Chinese and the Koreans. As Togo maintains, apology is a one-way act that is initiated by the perpetrators' side, but reconciliation is a two-way act. The Chinese and the Koreans must be prepared to accept Japan's apology and give thoughts to their own nationalism so that it does not turn into an emotional chauvinism. The Chinese word *suan*—settling accounts—has also another meaning, "let pass" and "move on." The past must be squarely faced, but we should not be haunted by it. The reflection of the past must give us the chance for mutual understanding and the courage to "move on."

It is also important to remember that the conflict over historical memory does not remain a tempest in a teapot among East Asian neighbors. Sooner or later the conflict is bound to influence U.S.-Japanese relations as well, since, under the veneer of the U.S.-Japanese alliance, there looms widely differing perceptions about each other. After all, the United States fought a bitter war against Japan in the Pacific War. As David Straub argues, the Unites States has placed security interests above everything else, relegating historical issues to the background. That does not mean, however, that the U.S. government and the American public do not share the basic historical interpretations held by Chinese and Korean nationalists against Japanese aggressions and colonialism. Differing interpretations of the American bombings on Hiroshima and Nagasaki and Japan's attack on Pearl Harbor have the potential to create a crisis of alliance. It should be noted that the main target of attack by at least one faction of the right-wing revisionists, as the clear message of the exhibit at Yushukan attached to the Yasukuni Shrine suggests, is aimed at the United States.

Finally, the issue of historical memory should be viewed more broadly by including Russo-Japanese relations. As Tsuyoshi Hasegawa argues, the Northern Territories dispute between Japan and Russia can no longer be separated from Japan's territorial disputes with China and South Korea. Furthermore, by comparing the Japanese expansion into its neighboring countries with the Russian expansion, we can better understand the nature of Japanese aggressions and colonialism that provoke nationalism in China and Korea. Also, the pain that the Soviets inflicted on the Japanese in the last four weeks of the Pacific War, Hasegawa argues, should help the Japanese to comprehend the pains they themselves inflicted on the Chinese and the Koreans.

The authors of this volume sincerely hope that this book will help contribute to the eventual reconciliation of East Asian nations. The East Asian people and governments have much to gain by reconciliation, and much to lose by letting themselves be haunted by the past.

Index

Abe, Shintaro, 127

Abe, Shinzo: apology for Japanese aggression/colonization (1995), 71; China, approach to, 217; China, visit to (2006), 70; comfort women issue, 49, 65, 143, 152, 153, 199–200; as conservative nationalist, 139; decline of popularity, 55; and Dutch comfort women case, 154; emergence of; on Japanese War responsibility, 72; on Kono statement, 143–44, 200–201; Korean abduction issue, 50, 53; Korean perspective on, 198; legacy, 56; on Muruyama statement, 174; and nationalism, 63, 167; policy of "no confirmation, no denial," 174; resignation as prime minister, 143–44, 238; textbook agenda of, 53; and Tsukurukai, 87; U.S. criticism of, 212; Yasukuni Shrine issue, 33, 51, 73, 120, 186–87

Albania, 45

Allied powers: and Korea, 231; in Post–World War II Germany, 23; war crimes by, 27; war goals, 27

American Occupation of Japan, 59; and Emperor's role, 208; and goal of Japanese stability, 208; Japanese attitudes toward, 27, 59; Japanese brothels during, 211; and Japanese historical narrative, 27; and Japanese history issue, 60, 61, 208; neutralization of Japanese threat, 208; retention of Showa Emperor, 27, 60; and Unit 731, 208; use of existing government institutions, 60

An Jung-guen, 230

Anglo-Japanese Alliance, 230

anime, 110–11

anticommunism: in Asia, 30, 44; in Japan, 44; in South Korea, 2, 192–93, 195

APEC summit meeting (2002), 136

Apology, vs. regret, 103

Arab-Israeli dispute, 19

Armenian diaspora, 34

Armitage Report, 215

ASEAN+3, 52; meeting in Bali, 136; meeting in Singapore, 53, 55

Asia: communist expansion in, 193; current Japanese policy toward, 63; dealing with history issues, 36; Japan, U.S. joint interests in, 60; Japanese culpability for war in, 147; Japanese

expansion in, 221; Japanese perception
of, 98; and nationalism, current, 1, 2;
Northeast Asia, 94–95, 109; recession of
1990s, 1; regional cooperation, obstacles
to, 1; regional institutions, 17; role of
historical narrative in, 42; and territorial
disputes, 2
East Asian Summit, 52, 55
East China Sea, 33
Eastern Europe, 2, 33
East Timor, 50
Eisenhower, Dwight D., 211
Estonia, 34
Eto, Shinkichi, 76
Etorofu island, 221
European Union, 24, 25, 34
Europe's historical memory, 26–27

Falun Gong sect, 113
February 28 Incident (1947), 95
First Gulf War, 210
Four Power Treaty, 228
France, 18, 26–27, 35
Frühstück, Sabine, 9
Fujinami, Kosei, 127
Fujio, Masayuki, 130
Fujioka, Nobukatsu, 69, 147
Fujiwara, Kiichi, 95
Fukuda, Takeo, 62
Fukuda, Yasuo: and Chinese/Korean
concerns, 217; comfort women issue, 65,
157; and East Asian Community, 55;
Japanese forced labor issue, 68; and
Japanese War responsibility, 72;
orientation toward Asia, 63; support for
China, 56; visit to China, 53; and
Yasukuni Shrine, 74, 120, 139, 174
Fukuzawa, Yukichi, 98
Fundamental Law of Education (2007),
113, 167

Galaxy Incident, 184
"Gang of Four," 183
Geertz, Clifford, 21
General Headquarters (GHQ), 121
Germany: attitude toward its history, 18,
24; compensation by, 23–24; deaths

caused by, World War II, 23; and
Jewish community, 23, 24; as model
penitent, 17–18; moral responsibility
for war, 26–27; official history narrative,
24; pressures to apologize, 24; relations
with France, 35; relations with Poland,
35; and the United States, 23;
victimization, sense of, 34; war crimes
tribunals in, 23; and Western
Europe, 23
globalization, 31–32
Gojong, King, 229
Goldman, Nahun, 25
Gorbachev, Mikhail, 223, 232
Gorer, Geoffrey, 21
Gotoda, Masaharu, 128
Greater East Asian Co-Prosperity Sphere,
232
Great Kanto Earthquake, 233

Habomai island group, 221
Haider, Jörg, 25
Hamamoto, Ryoichi, 4–5
Han Yongu, 109
Hasegawa, Tsuyoshi, 2, 11–12, 54, 166,
241–42
Hashimoto, Ryutaro, 62, 102, 131, 132–
33, 134, 172
Haslam, Jonathan, 225
Hata, Ikuhiko, 64, 131, 147, 151, 153–54,
157
Hatoyama, Ichiro, 29
Hayashi, Fusao, 71
Heisei generation, 54
"Hideyoshi's Aggression and Chosun's
Counterattacks," 97
Hiranuma, Kiichiro, 123
Hirohito, Emperor. See Showa Emperor
Hiroshima, 29, 96, 211
Hirota, Koki, 122
"Historical Memories and Resurgence of
Nationalism in East Asia: Paths to
Reconciliation" (conference), 3
historical memory, 63, 72; Chinese
perspective, 9; vs. cooperative East Asian
community, 190, 238–39; cultural
position, modified, 6; diffusion of

projects with China, Korea, 89–90; as honor-ridden society, 54; within international structure, 63; and Iraq, 166; Joint Communiqué with North Korea (2002), 47–48; joint textbook with South Korea, 88–89; Korean culture boom in, 75; Manch, invasion of (1931), 2; missile defense system development, 177; neglect of historical reconciliation, 47; "Northern Territories" issue, 220; and North Korea's nuclear weapon test, 51; past as just responses, 54; patriotism in, 54; post-Imperial identity, 28–29; post–World War II adaptation, 60; principles of diplomacy, 200; racism vs. other Asians, 233; reaction to modernization, 112; reaction to Western imperialism, 112; "realist" imperative, 54; as realist state, 43–44, 56; recession of 1990s, 1; regional identity of, 94; responsibility for pre-1945 atrocities, 31, 54; right-wing agenda, 200; right-wing vs. left-wing division, 53; security relationship with United States, 28; separation of religion/state, 73, 121, 124, 129, 139, 172; and Shandong Province, 181; "Siberian intervention," 225–26; Taiwan issue, 176; territorial disputes with China, 33, 234; territorial disputes with Korea, 33, 234; territorial disputes with Russia, 33, 234; as threat to Soviet security, 226; traditional values, 240; transition from prewar to postwar period, 61–62; Twenty-One Demands, 181; uniqueness of aggression/colonialism, 233; and United States vs. communism, 30; and UN Security Council, 52, 168; as U.S. ally, 44, 215; values assertiveness worldview, 51; and Versailles Treaty, 181; as victim of atomic bombings, 96; as victim of Russian atrocities, 224–25; as victim of Soviet aggression, 220; war crimes by, 31

Japan as "normal country," 9, 47, 167, 174–75

Japanese apologies: for aggression/colonialism, 70, 71, 173; comfort women, 102–3, 148; Japanese atrocities in China, 70; Japanese opinion on, 102; to Kim Dae-jung, 71; Kono statement, 148; Korean annexation, 70; by LDP leaders, 62; Muruyama statement, 131; Nanjing massacre, 66; and national pride, 32; by Prime Minister Toshiki Kaifu, 32; and Sino-Japanese relations, 36; soldiers' apologies for atrocities, 70; synthesis, 7; and textbooks controversy, 69

Japanese apologizers, 62–66, 70–71, 74, 76. See also Japanese political left

Japanese army veterans association (*Kaikosha*), 66

Japanese Association of Bereaved Families of the War Dead. *See* Nippon Izokukai

Japanese atrocities: American occupation authorities' narrative of, 27; in China, 70; Chinese criticism of, 130; Class-A war criminals responsibility for, 61; and East Asian liberalization, 31; efforts to whitewash, 169; Japanese political left view of, 29; Koizumi's actions concerning, 197; memory of, in Northeast Asia, 111–12; Nanjing massacre, 65; in Northeast Asian memory, 111–12; reemergence of issue, 31; remorse for vs. need for pride, 7, 76; vs. Soviets, 226, 227; unapologetic Japanese stance on, 17; victims groups vs., 31

Japanese colonialism: acknowledgement of responsibility, 131; and Korean nationalism, 192; legacy in South Korea, 109; as source of Japanese shame, 110; as source of Korean shame, 111; South Korean attitudes toward, 195

Japanese conservatives: and Imperial enterprise, 29; and official historical narrative, 30; opposition to war regime, 29; post–Cold War, 46; and reentry into Northeast Asia, 44; resistance to apologies, 32; and United States, 30; and Yasukuni Shrine, 130. *See also* Japanese nationalists, Japanese revisionism

127–28; visits to Yasukuni Shrine, 24, 31–32, 120, 124, 129, 166, 171–72

Nanjing massacre, 97–98, 155; Chinese claims, 65; deniers of, 65–66; as historical memory issue, 63; at IMTFE, 65; Japanese "apologizers" and, 65; in Japanese textbooks, 103, 169; Japanese veterans association on, 66; "nationalists'" opinion, 66; racism in, 233; textbooks controversy, 66

Nanjing Massacre Museum, 65

National Congress to Protect Japan (*Nihon o Mamoru Kokumin Kaigi*), 130, 170

nationalism: vs. communist ideology, 2; conflicts arising from, 2; vs. Confucian world view, 43; as defining issue, 49; and East Asian internationalism, 237; and new international order, 234; post–Cold War, 2; and rapid economic growth, 187; replacement for ideology, 237; resurgence in East Asia, 1, 2, 190; and social change, 2. *See also nationalism by individual country name*

nationalist history, pros and cons of, 87

National Shinto, dismantling of, 121

NATO (North Atlantic Treaty Organization), 24, 30

Nazi aggression, in Eastern Europe, 24

Nazi atrocities, 17–18, 22

Neighboring Country Clause, 96–97, 98

The Netherlands, 148

Neue Wache, 33

New Zealand, 52

Nicholas II, Tsar, 230

Nicksch, Larry, 153

Nihonjinron literature, 53

Nine Power Treaty, 228

Nippon Izokukai, 124, 131, 134

Nishibe, Susumu, 69

Nishio, Kanji, 69, 87

Nishioka, Tsutomu, 147

Nixon, Richard, 45, 209

Northern Expedition, 181

"Northern Territories" issue, 220–24, 234

North Korea: abduction vs. comfort women issues, 48–49; first nuclear crisis, 194; and Japanese history problem/issue,

47, 48; Japanese vilification of, 51; military-industrial expansion, 44; as nuclear-armed power, 168; nuclear weapon crisis, 43, 51–52, 177; relations with Japan, 47, 61; relations with South Korea, 194, 238; sense of isolation, 191; sociopolitical isolation, 95; and U.S.-China relations, 52

nuclear weapon crisis, 43, 51–52

Obuchi, Keizo, 32–33, 36–37, 62, 71, 133–34, 149, 176

Official Development Assistance (ODA), 45, 186

Oguma, Eiji, 86

Ohira, Masayoshi, 62

Okawa, Shumei, 123

Okinawa, Japanese textbooks controversy, 104

Onoda, Hiroo, 155

Onuma, Yasuyuki, 74

Open Door Policy, 228

Opium War, 1, 181

Ostpolitik, 24

Outer Mongolia. *See* Mongolia

Ozawa, Ichiro, 175

Pacific War: deities from, in Yasukuni Shrine, 121; historical memory of, 227; as history issue, 27, 100, 214; and reconciliation, 4; responsibility for, 101; San Francisco Peace Treaty, 209; as source of Japanese shame, 111; vs. Soviet-Japanese War, 12, 225; Soviet participation, 222; U.S. behavior in, 211. *See also* World War II

Palace Gyeongbokgung, 88–89

Paris Peace Conference, 181

Park Cheol Hee, 9–10, 239, 240

Park Chung-hee, 30, 44, 109, 193, 195

Park Yuha, 75

"Patriotism Clause," 113

Peace and Friendship Exchange Program, 68

Pearl Harbor, 222, 229

Peng Zhen, 126

Peoples Republic of China (PRC). *See* China

war crimes: charges vs. Japan, 27; tribunals, in Germany, 23

Watanabi, Shoichi, 66, 75, 147

Watanabi, Tsuneo, 4–5

Wen Jiabao, 9, 75, 136, 137, 186–87, 217

Witte, Sergei, 225, 230

Women's International War Crimes Tribunal on Japan's Military Sexual Slavery, 63–64, 145, 150, 154–56

World Jewish Congress, 25

World War I, 34, 90, 121, 181, 228

World War II. *See also* Pacific War: and atomic bombings, 233; Japanese as victims, 28–29; Japanese responsibility for, 28–29; Japan's unconditional surrender, 43; judgments against Japan, 61; mortality, 23; reparations paid by Japan, 28; as source of Japanese shame, 110; Soviet aggression, 220; Soviet-Japanese War in context of, 227

World War II and Japanese defeat, 28, 59, 61–62; and Japanese values, 59; nature of, 59; popular reaction, 59, 60; reasons for, 59, 60; role of atomic bombings, 233; and Soviet entry, 233; territorial losses, 59

Wu Bangguo, 186

Yagi, Hidetsugu, 69, 147

Yalta Agreement, 223, 229, 232

Yalta Protocol, 223

Yalta secret agreement, 231

Yamazaki, Taku, 135

Yanagi, Muneyoshi, 88–89

Yang Daqing, 90

Yang Zhenya, 127

Yasukuni Shrine, issue: in 2001 LDP presidential election, 134–35; and American sympathies, 21; call for renationalization of, 124; and China/Japan relations, 131, 132; Chinese criticism of Prime Minister Nakasone's visit, 125–26; and Chinese interference in Japanese domestic affairs, 130; Chinese protests, 126; Class-A war criminals in, 72, 73, 122, 123, 129, 139; Class-B/C war criminals in, 122; conflict over in domestic politics, 129; conservative nationalists and, 127, 130, 171; enshrinement of war dead, 122; formalizing official visits to, 124; history, 120; issue of "re-nationalization," 122; "nationalizing" proposal, 73–74; nation-building symbol, 120–21; non-Shintoist critics, 138; and ordinary Japanese, 171; and paying respect for war dead, 120; as private religious corporation, 138; proposed moratorium on issue, 73; public secular vs. private religious institution, 121, 124; Religious Corporation Law, 121; restricted to government soldiers, 121; revisionists and, 138; role of Ministry of Health and Welfare, 122; and separation of religion/state, 73; and Shinto belief, 72; as shrine for ordinary people, 120; and Sino-Japanese relations, 171; and Sino-Japanese relations, 171; suspension of Yasuhiro Nakasone's visits, 127; after Yasuhiro Nakasone, 131

Yasukuni Shrine, visits: Chinese/Japanese interpretations of, 134–35; Chinese objection to, 32, 72, 106, 180; Chinese vs. Japanese context, 132–33; contention of constitutive rules in, 129; as controversial symbolic act, 119; deities from 1930s, 1940s, 121; and East Asian nationalism, 2; effect on Japanese nationalists, 62; by Ryutaro Hashimoto, 132–33; by international guests, 138; interpretations, 136; as "justification of aggression," 138; by Junichiro Koizumi, 8, 33, 50, 62, 73, 87, 119–20, 134–38, 172–74, 184, 185–86, 196, 214, 237; Korean objection to, 197; by Takeo Miki, 124; by Kiichi Miyazawa, 125, 131; by Yasuhiro Nakasone, 24, 32, 46, 124–30, 132, 138, 166, 171–72, 175; by Masayoshi Ohira, 130; by prime ministers, 125; and relations with neighbors, 119–20; by Showa Emperor, 74, 123–124, 125, 138; and Sino-Japanese relations, 72; by Zenko Suzuki, 130; as symbolic acts, 128–29

Yasukuni war museum (Yushukan), 73
Yokota, Kisaburo, 74
Yomiuri Shinbun, 72
Yoon Tae Rim, 107
Yoshida, Shigeru, 29
Yoshida Doctrine, 60
Yoshimi, Yoshiaki, 63–64, 145, 149, 154, 157
Yoshino, Sakuzo, 88–89

Yugoslavia, 22
Yushukan. *See* Yasukuni war museum

Zhang Shu, 129
Zhou Enlai, 45, 223
Zhu Jianrong, 9, 239, 240
Zhu Ronji, 135–36, 186
Zoellick, Robert, 216

About the Editors and Contributors

THE EDITORS

Tsuyoshi Hasegawa is a Professor in the Department of History and the codirector of the Center for Cold War Studies at the University of California at Santa Barbara. He has written *The Northern Territories Dispute and Russo-Japanese Relations*, 2 vols. (1998), which received Ohira Masayoshi Memorial Prize in 1999; *Racing the Enemy: Stalin, Truman, and the Surrender of Japan* (2005), which received the Robert Ferrell Book Prize, and *Anto: Sutarin, Toruman to Nihon kofuku* (2006), which received the Yomiuri-Yoshino Sakuzo Price in 2006 and the Shiba Ryotaro Prize in 2007.

Kazuhiko Togo is currently a Visiting Professor at Temple University Japan Campus. He joined the Foreign Ministry of Japan in 1968, and worked extensively on Soviet/Russian affairs. He served as Ambassador of Japan to the Netherlands and retired in 2002. He has a wide range of teaching experience at universities in Moscow, Tokyo, Leiden, Princeton, Tansui (Taiwan), Santa Barbara, and Seoul. His recent publications include *Japan's Foreign Policy 1945–2003: The Quest for a Proactive Policy* and *The Inside Story of the Negotiations on the Northern Territory: Five Lost Windows of Opportunity* (in Japanese).

THE CONTRIBUTORS

Thomas U. Berger is an Associate Professor, Department of International Relations at Boston University. He is the author of *Cultures of Antimilitarism: National Security in Germany and Japan* and coeditor of *Japan in International Politics: Beyond the Reactive State* (2007). His articles and essays have appeared in numerous edited volumes and journals, including *International Security, Review of International Studies, German Politics,* and *World Affairs Quarterly.*

Jin Linbo is a Research Professor of the China Institute of International Studies in Beijing. He received his M.A. and Ph.D. in Political Science from Nagoya University, Japan. From 1995 to 1997 he was a Visiting Scholar at Reischauer Institute of Japanese Studies, Harvard University and, from 2001 to 2002, a Japan Society for the Promotion of Science Invited Scholar at the Graduate School of Law, Kyoto University. His research focuses on politics and foreign policy of modern Japan and international relations in East Asia. He has published many articles in Chinese and Japanese on Sino-Japanese relations and East Asian security issues.

Mikyoung Kim is an Assistant Professor at the Hiroshima Peace Institute and Hiroshima City University. Before assuming the current position, she was a Fulbright Visiting Professor at Portland State University. She holds a Ph.D. in Sociology and M.A.s in International Relations, Sociology, and Women's Studies from the U.S. and Korea. She has many articles published with referred academic journals and is currently editing a book on collective memory in Northeast Asia. In addition, she is also writing two books: one on North Korean refugees' human rights issues in China and Korea, and another on the peace movement and women's labor activism in Japan and Korea.

Hiroshi Mitani is a Professor at the University of Tokyo, Komaba. His major field is the nineteenth century history of Japan and East Asia. He is interested in writing both political-social history and international history with a strong concern for methodology. His major works include *Escape from Impasse: the Decision to Open Japan* (2003 in Japanese, 2006 in English), *Meiji Regeneration and Nationalism* (1997, in Japanese) and *Thoughts on the Meiji Regeneration* (2006, in Japanese). He also edited *Public Sphere in East Asia* (2004, in Japanese) and *Contentious Issues in Sino-Japanese relations* (2006, with Liu Jie and Yang Daqing, both in Japanese and Chinese, forthcoming in English). Mitani is now engaged in the publication of East Asian regional history in cooperation with various specialists in China, South Korea, and the United States.

Cheol Hee Park is currently an Associate Professor at the Graduate School of International Studies at Seoul National University, Korea. After he received his B.A. and M.A. from Seoul National University, he earned his Ph.D. at Columbia University. His major field of study is Japanese politics and diplomacy. His dissertation was on electoral strategies in urban Japan after the electoral reform, which was published in Japanese with the title of *Daigishi no tsukurarekata* (*How a Japanese Dietman Is Made*). He has written many articles on Japanese politics, Korean-Japanese relations and international relations in East Asia at major newspapers, including *Chosun Ilbo, Joongang Ilbo, Yomiuri Shinbun,* and *Asahi Shinbun.* In recognition of his academic achievement and contribution to improving Korean-Japanese relations, he was awarded the First Nakasone Yasuhiro Award in June 2005.

Gilbert Rozman is the Musgrave Professor of Sociology at Princeton University, where he has taught since 1970. Recent books include: *Northeast Asia's Stunted Regionalism* (2004); *Korea at the Center: The Dynamics of Regionalism in Northeast Asia* (coedited with Charles Armstrong, Samuel Kim and Stephen Kotkin, 2006); *Russian Strategic Thought toward Asia* and *Japanese Strategic Thought toward Asia* (both coedited with Kazuhiko Togo and Joseph Ferguson, 2006, 2007); *Strategic Thinking about the Korean Nuclear Crisis: Four Parties Caught between North Korea and the United States* (2007); and *South Korean Strategic Thinking toward Asia* (coedited with In-Taek Hyun and Shin-wha Lee, 2008).

David Straub is currently a Pantech Research Fellow at the Walter H. Shorenstein Asia-Pacific Research Center at Stanford University. In 2006 he retired as a senior foreign service officer after a 30-year career in the Department of State focused on Northeast Asia affairs, including as the department's director of Japanese and Korean affairs. He has also taught at the Johns Hopkins School of Advanced International Studies and the Graduate School of International Studies of Seoul National University. Straub has published a number of articles in scholarly journals on U.S. foreign policy in Northeast Asia.

Akihiko Tanaka is a Professor of International Politics at the Interfaculty Initiative in Information Studies and the Institute of Oriental Culture, University of Tokyo. His specialties include theories of international politics, contemporary international relations in East Asia, and issues in Japanese-U.S. relations. He has written numerous books and articles in Japanese and English, including *The New Middle Ages: The World System in the 21st Century.*

Zhu Jianrong is a Professor at Toyo Gakuen University in Japan. Born and educated in China, he now teaches in Japan. During the past decade, he has established himself as an internationally recognized expert in East Asian international relations and modern Chinese history. The author of 27 books on Chinese contemporary political situations for Japanese readers, he has also worked on the resolution of political and economic barriers to open discourse among Asian countries and the United States.